The Politics of Cultural Development

T0330651

There is a growing recognition of the role that culture can play in sustainable development strategies. This development has generally been welcomed, but also raises a number of questions: What are the implications in policy and practice? Who are the most influential voices in promoting a global agenda for culture and development, and to what extent has the creation of new international policy instruments reflected a consensus? More fundamentally, what is meant by "culture" in these discussions and who has the power to give particular definitions political and legal authority?

The Politics of Cultural Development seeks to provide a theoretically and historically informed response to such questions, illustrated by reference to case studies (including the European Union, the Caribbean and China). Particular attention is paid to the formation of the UNESCO *Convention on the Protection and the Promotion of the Diversity of Cultural Expressions*, a landmark instrument in debates about culture and development. The book goes on to explore some of the practical implications that this international treaty is beginning to have for the ways that culture is (and is not) being integrated into contemporary development policy and practice.

This book will be useful for students, academics and policymakers in the fields of international development, international relations, international political economy, cultural policy and cultural theory.

Ben Garner is a Senior Lecturer at the University of Portsmouth, UK, where he also leads the undergraduate programme in International Development Studies.

Routledge Studies in Culture and Sustainable Development

Series editors: Katriina Soini
University of Jyväskylä, Finland, and Natural Resources Institute, Finland and Joost Dessein, Institute for Agricultural and Fisheries Research (ILVO) and Ghent University, Belgium

Culture as an aspect of sustainability is a relatively new phenomenon but is beginning to attract attention among scholars and policy makers. This series opens up a forum for debate about the role of culture in sustainable development, treating culture and sustainability as a meta-narrative that will bring together diverse disciplines. Key questions explored in this series will include: how should culture be applied in sustainability policies; what should be sustained in culture; what should culture sustain; and what is the relationship of culture to other dimensions of sustainability?

Books in the series will have a variety of geographical foci and reflect different disciplinary approaches (for example, geography, sociology, sustainability science, environmental and political sciences, anthropology, history, archaeology and planning). The series will be addressed in particular to postgraduate students and researchers from a wide cross-section of disciplines.

Culture and Sustainability in European Cities
Imagining Europolis
Edited by Svetlana Hristova, Milena Dragićević Šešić, and Nancy Duxbury

Theory and Practice in Heritage and Sustainability
Between past and future
Edited by Elizabeth Auclair and Graham Fairclough

Cultural Sustainability and Regional Development
Theories and practices of territorialisation
Edited by Joost Dessein, Elena Battaglini and Lummina Horlings

The Politics of Cultural Development
Trade, cultural policy and the UNESCO Convention on Cultural Diversity
Ben Garner

The Politics of Cultural Development

Trade, cultural policy and the UNESCO Convention on Cultural Diversity

Ben Garner

Routledge
Taylor & Francis Group

LONDON AND NEW YORK

First published 2016 by Routledge

2 Park Square, Milton Park, Abingdon, Oxfordshire OX14 4RN
711 Third Avenue, New York, NY 10017

Routledge is an imprint of the Taylor & Francis Group, an informa business

First issued in paperback 2017

British Library Cataloguing-in-Publication Data
A catalogue record for this book is available from the British Library

Library of Congress Cataloging-in-Publication Data
Names: Garner, Ben, author.
Title: The politics of cultural development : trade, cultural policy and the
UNESCO Convention on Cultural Diversity / Ben Garner.
Description: Abingdon, Oxon ; New York, NY : Routledge, 2016. |
Series: Routledge studies in culture and sustainable development
Identifiers: LCCN 2015046210| ISBN 9781138947818 (hb) |
ISBN 9781315669854 (ebook)
Subjects: LCSH: Convention on the Protection and Promotion of the
Diversity of Cultural Expressions (2005 October 20) | Multiculturalism–
Law and legislation. | Culture and law–Economic aspects. | Freedom of
expression. | International law and human rights.
Classification: LCC K487.C8 G37 2016 | DDC 338.9–dc23
LC record available at http://lccn.loc.gov/2015046210

ISBN: 978-1-138-94781-8 (hbk)
ISBN: 978-0-8153-5592-2 (pbk)

Typeset in Goudy
by Wearset Ltd, Boldon, Tyne and Wear

Contents

PART II

Abbreviations

ACDHR	Amazigh Commission for Development and Human Rights
ACP	African, Caribbean and Pacific Group of States
ANC	African National Congress
AFN	Assembly of First Nations
ASEAN	Association of South-East Asian Nations
CaMINO	Caribbean Music Industry Networking Organisation
CAN	Caribbean Audiovisual Network
CARICOM	Caribbean Community
CARIFORUM	Caribbean Forum of African, Caribbean and Pacific States
CCD	Coalition for Cultural Diversity
CCIBN	Caribbean Creative Industries Business Network
CCIN	Caribbean Cultural Industries Network
CCL	Caribbean Copyright Link
CCTV	China Central Television
CEDA	Caribbean Export Development Agency
CFG	China Film Group
CIE	Caribbean Creative Industries Exchange
CMO	Collective Management Organisation
Convention	UNESCO Convention for the Protection and Promotion of the Diversity of Cultural Expressions (adopted 2005)
COSCAP	Barbados Copyright Society of Composers, Authors and Publishers, Inc.
CRNM	Caribbean Regional Negotiating Machinery
CSME	Caribbean Single Market and Economy
DFAIT	Canadian Department of Foreign Affairs and International Trade
EDF	European Development Fund
EMFTA	Euro-Mediterranean Free Trade Area
EPA	Economic Partnership Agreement
EU	European Union

FERA	*Fédération Européene des Réalisiteurs de l'Audiovisuel*
Florence Agreement	UNESCO Agreement on the Importation of Educational, Scientific and Cultural Materials (adopted 1950)
FTA	Free Trade Agreement
G77	Group of 77
GACD	UNESCO Global Alliance for Cultural Diversity
GATS	General Agreement on Trade in Services
GATT	General Agreement on Tariffs and Trade
GPRC	Government of the People's Republic of China
IADB	Inter-American Development Bank
ICH	Intangible cultural heritage
ICH Convention	UNESCO Convention for the Safeguarding of the Intangible Cultural Heritage (adopted 2003)
ICT	Information and communication technologies
IFCCD	International Federation of Coalitions for Cultural Diversity
IFCD	UNESCO International Fund for Cultural Diversity
IGO	Intergovernmental organization
ILC	International Liason Committee of the Coalition for Cultural Diversity
ILO	International Labor Organization
IMF	International Monetary Fund
INCD	International Network for Cultural Diversity
INCP	International Network on Cultural Policy
IP Declaration	UN Declarations on the Rights of Indigenous Peoples (adopted 2007)
IPDC	UNESCO International Program for the Development of Communication
JAMPRO	Jamaica Promotions Corporation
JBC	Jamaican Broadcasting Commission
JCTU	Jamaica Confederation of Trade Unions
MAI	Multilateral Agreement on Investment
MEFTA	US-Middle East Free Trade Agreement
Mexico Declaration	Mexico City Declaration on Cultural Policies (adopted 1982)
MONDIACULT	The World Conference on Cultural Policies (Mexico City, 1982)
MPAA	Motion Picture Association of America
NAFTA	North American Free Trade Agreement (signed 1992)
Nairobi Declaration	UNESCO Recommendation on the Participation by the People at Large in Cultural Life and Their Contribution to it (adopted 1976)
NCF	National Cultural Foundation of Barbados
NGO	Non-governmental organization

NIEO	New International Economic Order
NTFCI	Barbados National Task Force on Cultural Industries
NWICO	New World Information and Communication Order
NWU	Jamaica National Workers' Union
OECD	Organisation for Economic Co-operation and Development
OIF	Organisation International de la Francophonie
OTN	Caribbean Office of Trade Negotiations
PDAM	Amazigh Democratic Party
Protocol	Protocol on Cultural Cooperation (part of the ECONOMIC PARTNERSHIP AGREEMENT between the CARIFORUM States, of the one part, and the European Community and its Member States, of the other part) (signed 2008)
RCCI	China Research Centre for Cultural Industries
RTFCI	Caribbean Regional Task Force on Cultural Industries
SAGIT	Cultural Industries Sectoral Advisory Group on International Trade
SAPPRFT	State Administration of Press, Publication, Radio, Film and Television
SDGs	Sustainable Development Goals
Stockholm conference	Intergovernmental Conference on Cultural Policies for Development (Stockholm, 1998)
SWAPO	South-West Africa People's Organization
TTFC	Trinidad & Tobago Film Company
TTIP	Transatlantic Trade and Investment Partnership
TRIPS Agreement	Agreement on Trade-Related Aspects of Intellectual Property Rights
TWF	Television Without Frontiers Directive
UK	United Kingdom
UN	United Nations
UNCTAD	United Nations Conference on Trade and Development
UNESCO	United Nations Educational Scientific and Cultural Organization
Universal Declaration	UNESCO Universal Declaration on Cultural Diversity (adopted 2001)
US	United States of America
UWI	University of West Indies
WCCD	UN-UNESCO World Commission on Culture and Development
WIPO	World Intellectual Property Organization
WTO	World Trade Organization

Acknowledgements

Research for this book was carried out at the University of Manchester, with the financial support of the UK's Economic and Social Research Council.

I would like to thank all those that supported me along the path which I began in Manchester, and in particular Tony Bennett, Paul Kelemen, Mike Savage and Nick Thoburn.

Above all, thanks to my family for their love and support. This book is dedicated to them.

1 Introduction

A Magna Carta for international cultural policy?

Questions concerning the role of culture in sustainable development have risen on the international agenda since the turn of the millennium. They were given urgency in the late 1990s amidst a growing sense of anxiety regarding the accelerating pace of transformations going under the name of "globalisation", particularly following the inauguration of the World Trade Organisation (WTO) in 1995. A number of campaigns calling for greater political and juridical recognition of culture in trade and development came to focus in this period on the United Nations Educational, Scientific and Cultural Organisation (UNESCO), the specialised agency of the United Nations (UN) that is delegated with addressing cultural matters. This campaign was initiated by stakeholders from Europe and Canada following a series of high-profile trade disputes with the US, but it soon snowballed into a broad international coalition of states and civil society organisations. Some of this momentum was carried forward into a campaign calling for the inclusion of specific targets and indicators for culture in the creation of the post-2015 Sustainable Development Goals (SDGs), which set out the UN's global development agenda until 2030. The inclusion of references to culture in the SDGs has been welcomed by the campaign as a significant step forward in the sustainable development agenda, although it fell short of what they had hoped for (ultimately, culture was explicitly acknowledged in only four of the 169 targets) (*The Future We Want Includes Culture*, 2015; United Nations, 2015).

This book is an attempt to take stock of the recent rise of culture on the international development agenda, placing it in historical context and investigating some of its effects – and lack of effects – in policy and practice. The most notable breakthrough has been the adoption of two new instruments at UNESCO, which have become central reference points in the international debate and which are the focus of the analysis in this book: 2001 saw the adoption of the Universal Declaration on Cultural Diversity (UNESCO, 2001; hereinafter the "Universal Declaration"), and this was followed in 2005 by the adoption of a binding international treaty, the Convention on the Protection and Promotion of the Diversity of Cultural Expressions (UNESCO, 2005;

hereinafter "the Convention"). Although not without controversy and criticism, as we will see below, the Convention has come to be recognised as a keystone in contemporary international cultural policy, and marked the first multilateral legal instrument to include concrete provisions for the link between culture and development (Vlassis, 2015). In the words of UNESCO, reflecting on the tenth anniversary of the Convention in 2015, the Convention had "ushered in a new international framework for the governance and management of culture" (UNESCO, 2015). The level of political support behind the Convention is also impressive, measured by the fact that it was adopted by a majority of 148 states to two, followed by a rapid process of ratification around the world that secured its entry into force in 18 months – an unusually quick time for an international treaty.[1]

With the passage of the Convention, a series of longstanding controversies concerning the role of culture in development – how to define and defend it, how to give recognition to it and to regulate it, how to create mechanisms for its protection and promotion – appears to have found an authoritative solution with widespread political support:

> The speed at which this Convention was adopted is considered an extraordinary achievement and signals the urgency and commitment for action from governments around the world.... As a binding international legal instrument, the 2005 Convention has been heralded as the Magna Carta of International Cultural Policy reaffirming the right of governments to maintain, adopt and implement cultural policies and measures they deem necessary to protect and promote the diversity of cultural expressions and to ensure the free flow of ideas and works.
>
> (UNESCO, 2010: 1)

Some of the provisions contained in the Convention that are specifically related to development include the commitment that parties "endeavour to integrate culture in their development policies at all levels for the creation of conditions conducive to sustainable development" (Article 13), alongside a number of provisions aimed at promoting international cultural cooperation: notably the requirement that developed countries grant preferential market access to developing countries for their cultural exports (Article 16) and the establishment of a donor fund (International Fund for Cultural Diversity) aimed at supporting the formation of cultural enterprises in developing countries (Article 18). Echoing the Convention on Biological Diversity adopted at the Rio Earth Summit in 1992, the Universal Declaration and Convention together set out a collection of rights and obligations through which state parties have agreed to manage cultural diversity as an essential resource: "the cultural wealth of the world" which is "as necessary for humankind as biodiversity is for nature". The Universal Declaration is prefaced in this spirit by the hope that it can become "an outstanding tool for development, capable of humanizing globalization" (UNESCO, 2001).

However, there is some debate over the practical effectiveness of the new instruments on cultural diversity. On one hand, some analysts have highlighted the breakthrough that has been made by the Convention in addressing a long-standing absence of cultural concerns in global governance. For Beat Graber (2006: 564), for example, it "fill[s] a lacuna in public international law regarding cultural values"; for Bernier and Ruiz Fabri it has taken "a major step towards the emergence of an international cultural law" (cited in Richieri Hanania and Ruiz Fabri, 2014: 3). The adoption of the Convention was meanwhile received by its key sponsors in Canada and Europe as providing "the basis of a new pillar of world governance in cultural matters [and] a consensus that the international community has never before reached on a variety of guiding principles and concepts related to cultural diversity" (European Commission, 2006).

At first sight, however, such high sounding claims appear out of proportion for a set of instruments adopted at UNESCO. This is after all an organ of international administration which became sidelined by international society in the 1980s, coming to resemble something of a cross between a white elephant and a black sheep in the United Nations family. The kind of jibes that are reported to have come from delegates in the 1980s referring to UNESCO as the organisation at which "U Never Eat Sleep or Cogitate" (Gulick, 1982) have proven difficult to shake off. The emergence of such a broad political consensus behind an international cultural instrument has been all the more remarkable given that barely three decades ago the North and South had been at loggerheads at UNESCO over the controversies that centred on the demands for a New World Information and Communication Order (NWICO). The NWICO agenda was driven by the Non-Aligned Movement of Third World countries who called upon UNESCO to transform from an agency accused of perpetuating forms of one-way "cultural modernisation" on behalf of the more powerful states into one that would assist in the ongoing project of "cultural decolonisation". Such demands drew accusations from the Western bloc (notably from the US, UK, Canada, Japan, the Netherlands, Switzerland and West Germany) that the organisation was being mismanaged and "politicised" into a platform for a Third World agenda to place restrictions on the free operation of international media enterprises, cultural industries and news agencies. These controversies proved divisive enough to cause the US and UK to withdraw their memberships from UNESCO in 1984 and 1985 respectively, taking one third of the organisation's budget with them and effectively consigning UNESCO, along with the NWICO agenda, to the dustbin of history.

With the adoption of the Convention 20 years later, however, UNESCO has been brought back to the centre of a serious debate about global governance. This time it has been the US which has retreated with a bloody nose, inflicted as much by the rest of the North (including the UK, which rejoined UNESCO in 1997) as by the South who joined forces to secure the adoption of the Convention by an overwhelming majority. A diplomatic offensive by the US delegation to try to weaken support for the Convention, after rejoining UNESCO in 2003, only served to alienate potential allies and highlight its distance from the new consensus as it was ultimately only joined by Israel in voting against its adoption – prompting commentators in *Foreign Policy* to reflect on a "disastrous" campaign by the US (Crossette, 2006).

Despite the ways in which UNESCO and the instruments' supporters have framed the Convention as an expression of a politically and legally significant international consensus, a number of other analysts have drawn attention to the weaknesses of its provisions and the instrument's relatively low standing in international law. Craufurd Smith (2007: 53–54), for example, has described the Convention as "a document that evades controversy, which establishes general objectives and frames them in purely exhortatory terms. As a political manifesto, with little legal substance, it is hardly an advance on the international declarations on cultural diversity which preceded it".

The vague wording found throughout the Convention may have helped it to sustain sufficient political support and build in some flexibility in its implementation, but it has also created confusion about its objectives. There is no doubt that it stands on shaky conceptual grounds. The text asserts, for example, that "cultural goods, services and activities" have a "dual nature": they carry more than a commercial value, because they are also "vehicles of identities, values and meanings" that "embody or convey cultural expressions, irrespective of the commercial value they may have" (UNESCO, 2005: 2–5). What exactly this means is given no real explanation in the text, and yet it provides the basis for the Convention's only substantive right: that since cultural activities, goods and services are not only objects of trade but also vehicles of identities, values and meanings, they should not be treated in policy solely as objects of commercial exchange nor subjected to the same pressure of trade liberalisation as other sectors. For this reason, state parties to the Convention are granted the sovereign right to "maintain, adopt and implement policies and measures that they deem appropriate for the protection and promotion of the diversity of cultural expressions on their territory" (UNESCO, 2005: 3).

This is problematic because Article 4 of the Convention provides eight definitions around which the instrument is built, and these ultimately go around in circles. These definitions are: 1) cultural diversity; 2) cultural content; 3) cultural expressions; 4) cultural activities goods and services; 5) cultural industries; 6) cultural policies and measures; 7) protection; and 8) interculturality. The problem here is quickly demonstrated with just a glimpse at the substance of some of these definitions: the key term, *cultural expressions*, is defined as "those expressions that result from the creativity of individuals, groups and societies, and that have cultural content", while *cultural content* is defined as "the symbolic meaning, artistic dimension and cultural values that originate from or express cultural identities". However, *cultural identities*, and *culture*, are left without any definition in the text, raising fears that this leaves the instrument with something of a black hole at its centre. Such concerns were aired at one of the early UNESCO Expert Group Meetings, which aimed to establish a framework of basic operational definitions and methodological guidelines from which to begin the process of implementing the Convention's provisions. Its final report emphasised that "[g]iven the nature and the language of the 2005 Convention, an understandable concern about definitions and terms such as diversity, cultural expressions, cultural diversity or cultural goods, services and activities, emerged" (UNESCO, 2007: 4). How to render operational the notion of *cultural activities* posed the biggest difficulty of all since it was noted that "they often overlap with *cultural practices*" and that "it was unclear to which extent expressions that are not marketed or commodified fell under the 2005 Convention" (UNESCO, 2007: 4).

Many would argue that the framers of the Convention have had a near impossible task here, because their problem partly reflects the fact that culture – for Raymond Williams "one of the two or three most complicated words in the English language" (Williams, 1983) – has a number of different, and constantly shifting, referents in everyday usages, intellectual disciplines and systems of thought. If we were to take as a preliminary guide Williams's (1983) identification of the three broad meanings that culture accumulated in modernity – 1) as a description of "a general process of intellectual, spiritual and aesthetic development"; 2) as a way of demarking "a particular way of life, whether of a people, a period, a group, or humanity in general"; and 3) as "the independent and abstract noun which describes the works and practices of intellectual and especially artistic activity" ("music, literature, painting and sculpture, theatre and film", but which today tends to encompass a growing number of forms from "high" to "low" culture) – then it would appear that culture in the Convention could refer to any, or all three, of these. The formula that was agreed upon in Article 2 of the Convention largely leaves it up to governments to decide: "nothing in this Convention shall be construed to limit the sovereign authority of a Party to define such terms and concepts as 'culture', 'cultural diversity', and 'indigenous or national culture' in a manner it considers appropriate to the characteristics of its particular society" (UNESCO, 2005).

Despite this apparently broad remit, the purpose of the Convention has in fact been quite specific: namely, to establish a framework for the production and circulation of cultural goods and services, and in particular the audiovisual sector, that does not follow the conventional logic of international trade agreements (which, the sponsors of the Convention claim, fail to recognise the special characteristics of cultural goods and services). In this respect, at least, the Convention's subject has been relatively uncontroversial, addressed to phenomena such as "printed matter, literature, music, visual arts, cinema, photography, radio, television, games and sporting goods" (this is a conventional definition of cultural goods and services that has been used, for example, in UNESCO studies of cultural trade flows) (Disdier *et al.*, 2009). Singh (2011: 107) has argued that the Convention is therefore something of a "Janus faced" instrument, since its context and preamble evoke broad notions of "cultural diversity" on the one hand, while on the other its specific provisions and implementation are geared toward regulating narrow conceptions of "cultural industries". This feature of the Convention is, in fact, key to understanding its adoption and political success, since it has provided the basis for a broad international political consensus between groups with previously divergent interests (developed and developing countries, as well as industry and civil society groups) around the role of the cultural industries in development as carriers of simultaneously cultural and commercial value.

This focus of the Convention is in many ways a reflection of the way that the economic and political significance of the "cultural and creative industries" has risen dramatically in the context of a "new" global economy of information, communications and intellectual property.[2] Worldwide, imports of cultural goods increased by 347% between 1980 and 1998 (from US$47.8 billion to 213.7 billion), compared with 189% for all commodities over the same period (Disdier *et al.*, 2009: 576). With the ongoing rise of digital content and technologies, the political and commercial stakes surrounding the regulation of the cultural sector have therefore become extremely high, bringing about a shift in cultural policy and its practical concerns. According to David Throsby, for example, one of the many consultants and policy experts involved during the creation of the Convention at UNESCO: "the rise of the so-called creative economy and the growth of the cultural industries has shifted the policy emphasis towards the economic potential of the arts and culture sector" (Throsby, 2010: x).

This new policy emphasis has combined, however, with the contemporary context of international trade liberalisation, which has raised anxieties over the ability of states to implement policies of preferential protection and stimulation for their domestic cultural sectors. From the late 1990s, a number of governments therefore came to seek refuge at UNESCO, where there is some degree of autonomy from the kinds of pressures felt in fora such as the WTO (where its critics lament that culture generally appears as "nothing more than a rhetorical statement ... possibly expressing an anthropological ideal [but] out of place amidst the terminological rigour of negotiations in which American lawyers play a key role" (Regourd, cited in Bernier, 2004: 68)). The kinds of cultural policy measures that have been the primary focus of attention in the discussions around the Convention have therefore been those measures of support to domestic producers of cultural goods and services that have been challenged in recent rounds of trade negotiations: mechanisms such as domestic quotas, subsidies, preferential treatment, competition policy, government procurement, systems of content review, and so on.[3]

In short, it is by reinforcing the right of states to maintain, adopt and implement such measures that the Convention seeks to protect and promote cultural diversity, which is understood here as the plurality of the cultural goods and services produced by the world's different *ways of life* (which are effectively equated, somewhat problematically, with *nation states*). In this sense, cultural goods and services are seen to bridge the second and third definitions of culture identified by Williams above (as commercial expressions of particular ways of life), and by creating mechanisms aimed at proliferating their production in different contexts the aim is to augment "the cultural wealth of the world" and to contribute to the universal cause of human development (in the first of Williams's senses, as a general process of human development).

However, with no stable core definitions the Convention appears to give governments an extremely broad scope to assert their sovereignty under the pretext of protecting the right to policies which may be questionable under international trade and human rights legislation (this was the central objection made by the US in opposing the Convention, as we will see later). The assertion of cultural sovereignty has been used by states in the past to justify practices such as the suppression of internal religious or ethnic minorities, to uphold racist and patriarchal institutions and customs, or to place restrictions on the flow of information and reporting. Arguments invoking cultural sensitivities in trade disputes in areas such as the limitation of practice by foreign attorneys (Japan), the defence of agricultural subsidies (France), the support of the steel industry (US), or in opposing foreign investment in the insurance sector (Saudi Arabia), also demonstrate how the term culture can be deployed to attempt to counter pressures for liberalisation in any number of areas (indeed as Suranovic and Winthrop (2005) had already noted in 2005, such cases have become more frequent since the 1990s). The extent to which the kind of roles and qualities now being claimed for culture in policy can in fact be adequately recognised within the existing provisions of the WTO has also been a matter of some controversy, prompting debate regarding the rationale behind the Convention in the first place and the problem of interpretation between different legal frameworks.[4] These were all concerns that were regularly expressed during the Convention's drafting and have resurfaced following its first formal deployment in a dispute at the WTO in 2009, when the Chinese government referred to its sovereign right to impose restrictions on the import of audiovisual and published material, a claim which opponents accused of being a guise for censorship and illegal protectionism (a case that we will consider in detail later).

The focus of this book

Throughout the post-war period until the end of the Cold War, questions of culture and cultural diversity were generally given a low priority in development. Where culture did feature as a consideration for policymakers, it tended to be as an obstacle to be removed or reformed on the path to modernisation. The entry into force of the Convention, along with the emergence of a number of more culturally aware policies amongst major donors, international agencies, and national governments (what Nederveen Pieterse (2001) has referred to as the "cultural turn" in development theory and practice), have therefore generally been welcomed as a progressive development – even if there is still reason, as we have seen, to remain sceptical about the practical effectiveness of instruments such as the UNESCO Convention.

These developments, however, also raise a number of questions that we are now in a position to begin to investigate. What have been some of the implications of contributions such as the UNESCO Convention for policy and practice in the period since its adoption? Who have been the most influential promoters and stakeholders of this new politics of cultural development, and to what extent does the Convention really reflect a new "international consensus" around the role of culture in international development? More fundamentally, what exactly is meant by "culture" – a notoriously slippery and contested concept – when it is invoked in contemporary development policies and international treaties? Who is able to give particular definitions of culture such authority, and what kinds of political, economic or other opportunities are opened up – or indeed closed down – in the process?

This book aims to provide a critical theoretically and historically informed response to such questions, with reference to a number of international case studies. The UNESCO Convention, the centrepiece achievement of the cultural turn in development, is used as a focal point for the study but the work of other international agencies are also considered, as well as the policies of regional and national governments. The book is consciously interdisciplinary, seeking to address the simultaneously cultural, political and economic themes that are raised by contemporary attempts to integrate culture into international development policy and practice – attempts which themselves involve a blurring of some of the traditional boundaries between hitherto relatively distinct policy domains of culture and political economy.

In taking this approach, this book is distinct from the major works that have responded to the UNESCO Convention in a number of ways. There has been very little sustained historically or theoretically informed examination of the Convention outside of the field of international trade law, and little work that takes questions of culture and development – as opposed to culture and trade – as a central concern. I argue in Chapter 2 that the commentary that has surrounded the new framework for culture and development has too often viewed it uncritically as the fruit of a progressive international alliance against a domineering US/Hollywood-led process of neoliberal globalisation, or otherwise approached the Convention within the context of a series of largely technical questions regarding its legal application and its impact within the global regulation of the trade in audiovisual goods and services. This is partly a reflection of the Convention's provenance as an instrument aimed primarily at issues, such as the global regulation of trade in the audiovisual sector, that have been of relatively little concern outside of the developed world and specialist debates in international trade policy an law.

However, we might also ask how it is that culture came to be written into an instrument in this way with such widespread support from governments and civil society and how it has come to be ascribed such a prominent role in the contemporary work of policy makers, trade negotiators, lawyers and development institutions. It is puzzling that, just as a concern for culture has been in the ascendant through the contemporary cultural turn in development, there has also been a sense of unease in intellectual and anthropological debate about the term culture and its applications in policy, prompted by works such as Edward Said's *Orientalism* (Said, 1978) and the rise of interpretive and discourse-analytical methodologies (for example, Balibar, 1991; Kuper, 1999; Eriksen, 2001; Mamdani, 2002; Bayart, 2005). Following the work undertaken by

Bennett (1998), Yúdice (2003) and Hale (2005) there has also been a productive series of enquiries into the ways that the domain of culture is entangled with contemporary neoliberal and post-neoliberal strategies of government, along with a fresh readiness to engage politically with the field of cultural policy. This book also therefore attempts to reflect on the theoretical and analytical contributions of such work in light of contemporary and emerging practices of cultural development and international cultural policy.

The book is also an attempt to offer a different picture of the Convention than that which is beginning to emerge from the official Periodic Reports that parties have submitted to UNESCO since 2012. These reports have been prompted by the obligation, in Article 9 of the Convention, that parties should share information and best practices by, in particular, submitting a report to UNESCO every four years on "measures taken to protect and promote the diversity of cultural expressions within their territory and at the international level" (UNESCO, 2005). At the time of writing, a total of 76 such reports had been submitted to UNESCO between 2012 and 2015.[5] Richieri Hanania and Ruiz Fabri (2014: 4) have noted that the obligation on information sharing has therefore generated one of the clearest examples of the Convention's implementation around the world so far, producing dozens of reports and allowing UNESCO to build up a detailed picture of the state of implementation that can help identify trends and weaknesses, areas requiring intervention and needing primary attention, as well as good examples of measures and policies that can be replicated in other countries.

However, records such as these also limited in a number of ways. First of all, they are based on government reports which only provide official accounts of the issues under question, and taking such reports at face value offers a picture that is thin on critical historical and theoretical context. What is more immediately striking, however, when examining these Periodic Reports, is the international imbalance in their production: the 2014 analytical summary produced by the Secretariat reported that, despite receiving 71 reports by October 2014, this was only 61% of the total number of reports that should have been received from parties in the period since 2012 (UNESCO, 2014: 4–5). Most of the reports received had been from European countries, which meant that the 39% of countries that did not fulfil their reporting obligations largely came from the less developed regions: Latin America and the Caribbean (only 52% of the reports that were expected from that region were submitted, with the majority of the Caribbean countries not submitting), Asia-Pacific (which submitted 55% of the expected reports) and Africa (32%) (UNESCO, 2014: 4).

This imbalance between the developed and developing regions is down to a range of factors. Amongst developing countries there has been limited financial capacity, limited technical know-how and insufficient political will (UNESCO, 2014). Meanwhile the Secretariat itself has been hampered by substantial budget cuts at UNESCO in recent years, meaning that only one programme staff member at the UNESCO headquarters is fully dedicated to periodic reporting, and there have been limited funds available to implement the required training at country level. In addition, the time and resources that can be dedicated to support periodic reporting on the Convention within UNESCO's national level field offices is generally extremely limited. Therefore, although the periodic reporting is beginning to create a picture of the Convention's implementation around the world, this is a picture that is limited and biased in its scope, whilst being reflective of the differences in resources, priorities and political commitment that exist between developed and developing regions.

Overview

In taking up the questions and blind spots that have been considered above, this book is split into two main parts. Part I covers in greater detail the theoretical and political controversies that have surrounded the adoption of the Convention, and the debates about the connections between trade, culture and development more broadly. Part II then turns to explore in greater detail the nature and effects of the contemporary cultural turn in development through a series of analyses and case studies.

Part I of the book is split into two chapters. Chapter 2 covers in greater detail the key debates that have surrounded the Convention's formation and adoption, looking in particular at the controversies over the relationship between trade and culture as they came to take on a heightened significance in the 1990s. It also considers how we might situate the new international framework of cultural policy within wider debates in cultural theory, looking in particular at the work of Bennett and Yúdice regarding the relationship between culture and governmentality. Yúdice (2003) has advanced the thesis that the ways that culture has come to feature in political and economic life today suggest that we have entered "a new epistemic conjuncture", arguing that neoliberal globalisation has brought about a transformation in the conceptualisation and role of culture into a "resource" – for capital accumulation and economic development, for urban regeneration and employment, and also as a warrant for political recognition – and that UNESCO has been central in effecting this shift internationally. In Yúdice's account, the reciprocal permeation of the *cultural* with *economic* and *political* management that we see today has rendered problematic the kind of critiques of "commodification" or "instrumentality" that have typically provided the thrust of critical theory. These theoretical discussions are then used to draw out in greater depth some of the key questions that are at stake in examining the new international framework of cultural policy.

Chapter 3 looks more closely at the work that took place at UNESCO prior to the formation of the cultural diversity campaign in the late 1990s. It focuses in particular on the period of the World Decade for Cultural Development (1988–1997), which paved the way for the consensus that would subsequently emerge at UNESCO and provided much of the intellectual groundwork for the cultural diversity instruments that were adopted in the 2000s. A huge amount of work was done over the 1980s and 1990s not only intellectually in the field of cultural development but, equally importantly, through the reforms that the organisation underwent in response to the political turbulence it encountered the 1980s. As Babbili (1990) had noted in 1990, the defeat of UNESCO and NWICO in the 1980s was indeed a testament to the North's bid to reassert its authority over the process of development in the South in the 1980s, but I also argue here that it was an opportunity for the reinvention of UNESCO over the 1990s in a way that ultimately created the possibility for the international alliance that would attempt to turn the tables on Washington in the 2000s.

Part II of the book is split into three chapters. The themes developed in the previous chapters regarding the emergence of an international consensus around trade, culture and development at UNESCO are carried forward in Chapter 4, which turns to analyse the precise points of the new consensus and how exactly it constitutes a "check" on the reign of the US/WTO in international cultural regulation and global governance. Examining some of the measures that have started to come out of the provisions of the Convention, I challenge a number of accounts that see in the new framework of cultural policy an attempt to resuscitate the spirit of NWICO to counter the tenets of neoliberal globalisation. Not only is the new framework far distanced from the politics of the 1970s and 1980s but it is also more closely aligned within the core principles of neoliberal reform than has generally been assumed. This is illustrated in particular by considering the process of contemporary cultural policy reform in China, which in 2009 became the first test case for the new cultural diversity instruments when they were deployed by China in a high-profile dispute with the US at the WTO. This case has revealed both the weaknesses and the strengths of the new instruments, but more importantly it has served to demonstrate the extent to which cultural policy has come to turn on some of the characteristic themes of market reform: decentralisation, privatisation, enterprise formation and competitive insertion into the global market are all defining motifs of the new cultural policy in China and form a key part of the government's attempt to rise as an economic and cultural power in the twenty-first century.

Chapter 5 considers the new consensus around cultural diversity at UNESCO alongside the relative *lack* of consensus that has been struck on alternative international cultural instruments that have been proposed over the same period. In particular it contrasts the rapid fruition of the Convention with the difficulties and slow progress that have been experienced with instruments such as the UNESCO Convention on the Safeguarding of Intangible Cultural Heritage (adopted 2003) or the UN Declaration on the Rights of Indigenous Peoples (adopted 2007). I also consider the emergence over the 1990s of a distinctive legal vocabulary of representations and claims turning on the "rights" of diverse cultures and ways of life that have made these instruments possible: international concerns over biodiversity and the sustainable management of "intangible" and "traditional" heritages, knowledges and practices in the context of neoliberal globalisation and the "new" economy of intellectual property have provided opportunities across a variety of struggles to articulate claims to recognition through the universalisation of the discourses of human rights and an expanded ("anthropological") concept of culture. Where culture is concerned, this development has changed the dynamics of international treaty making, posing both opportunities and problems for the expansion of capitalist protocols and the consolidation of international and national hierarchies. In comparing these different instruments and the fortunes of the different campaigns that have been behind them, I attempt to bring into sharper relief some of the limits to the "universalism" that has been claimed for the Convention, arguing in particular that the effect of the new framework of cultural development has been to marginalise claims to cultural recognition that turn on demands such as the "right to land, tenure and place" or those that cannot be translated into internationally valuable, alienable and marketable expressions. In developing the argument in this chapter I also examine records from the process of the Convention's drafting between 2003 and 2005 in order to identify some of the lines of tension between the North and South that have been papered over by the language of consensus.

Chapter 6 then turns to a case study of the framework's first major example of implementation in a trade agreement: the Economic Partnership Agreement (EPA) that was concluded in late 2008 between the European Union and the Caribbean regional trade grouping known as CARIFORUM. Alongside sweeping measures aimed at liberalising trade between the two regions this agreement included a set of provisions on cultural cooperation that were widely hailed as a novel "blueprint" for the implementation of the development components of the UNESCO Convention. These provisions on cultural development have been presented within the Caribbean as an opportunity to assist in restructuring the region's political economy faced with the loss of EU trade preferences and the daunting task of adjustment and reform that is now required for a new phase of integration into the global economy. I examine the way in which the EPA negotiations have been related to a number of attempts to reconceptualise the cultural field in the Caribbean as the value of culture as a resource for export development has been elevated as a primary concern in the region's search for a new and sustainable development strategy. This allows us to begin to take stock of the new culture and development strategy as it has been evident – and *not* been evident – in the Caribbean over the last decade, and helps to draw out some of its implications within the broader debates concerning culture's transformation into a resource in the contemporary era.

One of the arguments advanced over the course of this work is that the Convention, while clearly limited in its practical influence, has signalled the emergence of a politically significant consensus around the contemporary role of cultural policy in the global economy. This consensus has effectively been struck upon the principle of the "cultural exception": that goods and services that are deemed to have cultural characteristics are deserving of special treatment in the context of trade liberalisation and international development. One of the problems with this formula, however, is that how such a distinction between "the cultural" and the "merely economic" is determined is a deeply contentious one, particularly once it becomes a factor in deciding how particular sectors and populations should be treated in international trade regulation and negotiations. Such decisions have the potential to impact significantly on competing claims over areas such as the right to land, tenure and place, as well as subsidies and other forms of protection from international competition, and can be used to determine entitlements to development assistance and international market access. I argue that the new framework leaves little room for those that do not fit into authoritative models of cultural diversity in which cultural rights and recognition are largely conflated with the right of the state to promote enterprise, production and trade in forms of activity that it deems to be worthy of recognition on cultural grounds. This may be a welcome development to those that are well positioned to benefit from the contemporary concern to enter the cultural and creative global economy. But it has also tended to weaken the position of others whose claims to cultural recognition are inseparable from demands which have little or no national or international protagonism in this framework – and who have largely borne the brunt of neoliberal reforms and development strategies. It has also not made much impact regarding the campaign to include culture within the post-2015 sustainable development framework – something which is addressed in the book's conclusion.

In carrying out this work I have drawn on a number of different sources, including in particular archives, reports and policy documents from organisations such as UNESCO, the World Bank, UNCTAD and the WTO, as well as national governments. The research is also based on time spent gathering information at hearings within UNESCO and the European Parliament on the implementation of the Convention and contact with government ministries, civil society and industry organisations that have been involved in one way or another in campaigns for the Convention's adoption, ratification and implementation. For the purposes of analysing the new framework of cultural policy I have found it useful to follow the guidance of Dominguez (1992) and Yúdice (2003): rather than trying to arrive at a definitive answer to what culture "is" (or "should be"), it is more productive to attempt to understand what culture means today when it is invoked to describe, analyse, argue, justify, and theorise by focusing on *what is being accomplished* socially, politically and discursively – and on the ways its present usages are derived and differentiated from those in the past. In this vein, one of the key themes explored here is the nature of the contemporary relationship between the policy domains of *culture* and *economy*: too often the processes that define these domains as arenas of governmental attention and intervention in the first place are taken as given, rather than problems for investigation in themselves. If we begin by acknowledging that the boundaries and overlaps between these categories are not given but related to historically mutable – and contested – rationalities and technologies of government, then their problematisation involves more than simply an inquiry into a set of conceptual or epistemological questions but can also offer greater analytical purchase on the basis of the new international consensus at UNESCO and begin to open some of its effects up to closer analytical scrutiny.

To develop some of the above themes, it is also worth noting that whilst culture has been a constant part of UNESCO's mandate since its foundation at the end of the Second World War, the ways in which it has been conceived and the roles that it has been expected to play have varied over time. To begin to put the Convention's contemporary significance into perspective, the remainder of this chapter therefore briefly introduces some of the different ways in which culture has featured in the organisation's work and in some of the key debates that have surrounded it over the postwar period. This will establish a few important landmarks and points of reference that will be returned to in the discussions over the following chapters.

Culture at UNESCO: a historical overview

Work at UNESCO is carried out under a number of "sectoral programmes" in the fields of education, the natural and human/social sciences, culture, communication and information, as well as a number of intersectoral and interdisciplinary programmes.[6] UNESCO's work in the sector of culture is what most people know the organisation for, particularly through its work in World Heritage (UNESCO now lists over 1,000 sites on its World Heritage List, which are visited by millions of people around the world each year) although its programmes related to the protection and promotion of cultural diversity for socioeconomic development are in fact far greater than those related to heritage (Singh, 2011: 83–108).

Although UNESCO is the specialised agency with competence for culture within the UN system, we should stress from the beginning that the organisation does not assume the role of setting the cultural policies of states. While it has a degree of moral authority and intellectual clout that is perhaps unrivalled within the UN system, the practical reach of this authority is limited in a number of ways. UNESCO is not a funding or development organisation such as the World Bank and it is also very much a member-state driven organisation – one which, furthermore, has very limited capabilities and resources to fund programmes and activities (the organisation's budgetary resources amount to only a billion dollars biennially, less than the budget for a large research university in the US) (Singh, 2011: 8–28; 100). Since the NWICO controversies of the 1980s, it has also passed through some difficult periods of reform and had to weather a series of budgetary crises, all of which have taken a toll on its activities (cutting back on staff and programmes, reducing the number of field offices through which it consults with national authorities, and so on). The latest crisis came in 2011, when the US again withdrew all financial contributions to UNESCO in protest at the admission of Palestine as a full member, accounting for 22% of the organisation's entire budget. This prompted the Director General to announce the temporary suspension of the entirety of UNESCO's undertakings for the remainder of the year (and also resulted in the US losing their voting rights within the organisation in 2013).

Rather than assuming the responsibilities of a global ministry of culture, UNESCO's role is therefore largely limited to providing "leadership" and "guidance": aiming to foster international agreement, exchange and cooperation;

convening national representatives and experts; and attempting to build capacity and foster initiative towards the achievement of the various rights, obligations and guidelines that are contained in its body of work. It is also important to note here that, while UNESCO may be a leader on culture within the UN family, its work in this field often overlaps with other agencies of global governance and international development. The WTO is a case in point, since it oversees and enforces global rules governing the trade in cultural products, which raises questions about the relative competence of UNESCO and the WTO and the degree of overlap in the global governance of trade and culture.

In other words, there is often a mismatch between the organisation's ambitious mandate and the way that its programmes and instruments are implemented in practice. This is evident in the case of the Convention on cultural diversity which, despite being a binding international treaty, contains no meaningful dispute settlement mechanisms and largely leaves the scope and nature of its implementation down to governments. This is consistent with the way that the key discussions that take place within the organisation tend to frame culture in national terms – even as the organisation has tried in recent years to distance itself from the privilege that it has traditionally accorded to the state (for example, by inviting contributions from civil society). Tomlinson (2002: 70–75) has pointed out that the nation is the mold into which narratives of cultural identity tend to be squeezed at UNESCO, generally leaving little room for those who are not recognised within officially sanctioned narratives of national culture.

To illustrate this point very briefly here we might note, for example, that France, which has been one of the key supporters of the Convention at UNESCO and a global champion of cultural diversity, does not officially recognise the existence of minorities on its territory.[7] Similar themes have been evident in Turkey, where the Convention could only be presented to parliament for ratification on the condition that a series of Reservations were introduced that would contain the instrument's potential impact on matters related to the status of Kurdish and Armenian minorities. This has meant limiting the application of provisions in the Convention that pertain to the status and rights of minorities and Indigenous peoples, since these provisions were judged to be incompatible with the Turkish Constitution. Commenting on this development, Turkey's UNESCO representative at the time of the Convention's adoption in 2005 has noted that these are not the important issues anyway, since the Convention is conceived as primarily a question of reinforcing the state's ability to strengthen its national cultural industries against its competitors, and in particular to "rein back Anglo-Saxon influence in the globalisation process" (Hazar, cited in Cetingulec, 2015). At the time of writing, the Convention is still awaiting ratification in Turkey, due in particular to sensitivities over such questions regarding the status of ethnic and religious minorities.

In light of the broad observations that have been made above about culture at UNESCO, it is important to briefly mention a few points regarding the way that I have approached this study. First of all, UNESCO's work over the following chapters is approached as a site for the contestation and formulation of general principles rather than as definitive policy prescriptions. Rather than taking related programmes and instruments at UNESCO at face value as legal/policy documents, I have been more concerned to examine the processes of political contestation and debate that have gone into defining their normative content and authority, and to look for the effects of such programmes and instruments as they are implemented – or not – in particular local contexts and according to specific policy problems.

I have also considered UNESCO's work alongside the work of other international organisations, situating the Convention in particular in the context of broader efforts at international and national levels addressed to the contemporary definition and mobilisation of culture within policy. Finally, although we have seen above that UNESCO is not the only agency whose work addresses culture at the international level, it nevertheless remains the foremost international organisation in this field, and as such its work offers a valuable record of the concerns that have informed and driven the international debates around the role of culture in sustainable development. To prepare grounds for examining these debates in more detail over the following chapters, the remainder of this chapter will establish some of the key points in debates about culture at UNESCO since its foundation at the end of WWII. This will be split very schematically into three broad periods: modernisation (1945–1960), decolonisation (1960–1984) and globalisation (1984–).

Modernisation, 1945–1960

In the organisation's early work, culture is largely referred to as performing a mission of "civilising", "educating" and "uplifting". It carried few of the extra roles that have become ascribed to it today as a resource for trade and development, for the expression of different *ways of life*, for the realisation of democratic pluralism and human rights, and so on. This was consistent with the organisation's initial role in the task of postwar reconstruction, and also of course reflected the paternalistic and colonial biases of representatives from the 20 nations that founded the organisation at the end of WWII. The organisation's Constitution, drawn up in 1945, still resonates with the experiences of the war, opening with the words of the American poet Archibald MacLeish: "Since wars begin in the minds of men, it is in the minds of men that the defences of peace must be constructed" (UNESCO, 1945). This set out the blueprint for a particular kind of Bildung in its work: in short, an attempt to cultivate, at the international level, an enlightened, cosmopolitan humanism fit for the postwar liberal order. The signatories to the Constitution noted that a peace "based exclusively upon the political and economic arrangements of governments" – of the kind being created through the UN Charter/Security Council and Bretton Woods institutions – required complementary activity in the fields of education, science and culture. UNESCO would be the specialised agency of the UN responsible for encouraging the liberal peace to take root in something deeper than political and economic reconstruction, by cultivating what it described as "the intellectual and moral solidarity of mankind" (UNESCO, 1945).

The intellectual and practical autonomy of the *cultural* from those disciplines and institutions concerned with the *economic* and the *political* was thus cast in an institutional division of labour in which UNESCO took on the lofty role of the *tête pensante* of the UN, evolving from the precedents and materials left by the International Institute for Intellectual Cooperation (begun in 1926 but dis-membered during the war), and positioning itself as the centre of an epistemic community of professionals, intellectuals, scholars, scientists, librarians and other "learned societies". As such, the policy domain of culture was given a noble birth but in practice was largely left at the bottom of the priorities and hierarchies of international administration. This is illustrated by the fact that while cultural matters would be deliberated at UNESCO's headquarters in Paris, matters related to the global regulation of economics and politics were kept on a much shorter leash in the new imperial centres Washington and New York (in the form of the UN headquarters, Security Council, World Bank and IMF).

As it was written into its early work, culture was largely equated with the kind of repositories of knowledge and materials of learning which could provide the key to peace and understanding and the nourishing, uplifting stimuli neces-sary for building a liberal world order in "the minds of men" (a formula since changed to "and women"). Article 1 of the Constitution spells out its objectives to

> maintain, increase and diffuse knowledge by assuring the conservation and protection of the world's inheritance of books, works of art and monuments of history and science [and to] encourage cooperation among the nations in all branches of intellectual activity, including the international exchange of persons active in the fields of education, science and culture and the exchange of publications, objects of artistic and scientific interest and other materials of information.
>
> (UNESCO, 1945)

In this spirit the organisation's early programmes largely focused on establish-ing international cooperation in areas such as the preservation and circulation of works of art, monuments and heritage (mostly those deemed to be of "iconic" status, and mostly located in the Western hemisphere – a bias that would be challenged by other countries over the following decades). There was also an emphasis on the supervision of education and the "re-education" of the so-called "ex-enemy peoples" (for example, through the revision of history textbooks in post-war Germany and Japan) as well as the attempt to discredit scientific racism in the 1950 Statement on Race.

One of UNESCO's first major instruments was therefore the 1950 Agree-ment on the Importation of Educational, Scientific and Cultural Materials, or "Florence Agreement" (UNESCO, 1950), which was conceived along the lines of the 1947 General Agreement on Tariffs and Trade (GATT). This set out "to foster international agreements as may be necessary to promote the free flow of ideas by word and image", for example, in the agreement that states undertake not to apply customs duties or other charges on the importation of books, publications and educational, scientific and cultural materials (UNESCO, 1950). The role of culture in policy in this period was largely equated with the role that the fine arts and literature could play in providing individuals with the kind of "healthy personality" and "balanced maturity" that was deemed necessary for proper participation in civic life – and without which, it was claimed, "a cultural civilization cannot persist" (UNESCO, 1952).

Although divisions at UNESCO soon became apparent between the founding nations with the onset of the Cold War (see Graham, 2006), the most dramatic controversies played out between the First and Third Worlds as the process of decolonisation gathered pace over the 1960s and 1970s. UNESCO's work in the South during this period of modernisation largely took the form of technology transfer and the promotion of a one-way flow of both hardware (printing presses, broadcasting transmitters, etc.) and content (radio, news, television programming and so on) (Arizpe, 2004). This generally occurred within the Cold War framework of development and modernisation theory, which tended to look upon culture as a secondary consideration in the drive for economic growth, employment, capital-intensive technology and productivity, or which otherwise looked upon cultural differences as expressions of inhibiting institutions and values in need of reform for the successful implementation of programmes of modernisation and the fostering of a culture of enterprise (Esteva, 2005; Escobar, 1995). Within this framework, the key indicators of cultural development were generally seen to be urbanisation, literacy, mass media exposure and participation in public life. This broad model of cultural modernisation was reflected in UNESCO programmes such as those aimed at ensuring that every country had at least ten copies of a daily newspaper, five radio receivers, two television sets and two cinema seats per thousand inhabitants (Carlsson, 2003: 6).

The term diversity featured twice in the Constitution but only as part of the establishment of some procedural matters between the founding nations (rather than forming any overall objective, value or guiding principle): 1) as part of a domestic jurisdiction reservation clause, a standard diplomatic formula guaranteeing that no participating governments would be ceding sovereignty ("With a view to preserving the independence, integrity and fruitful diversity of the cultures and educational systems of the States Members of the Organization, the Organization is prohibited from intervening in matters which are essentially within their domestic jurisdiction"); and 2) regarding the need to achieve a balanced distribution in electing Members to the Executive Board ("the General Conference shall have regard to the *diversity* of cultures and a balanced geographical distribution") (UNESCO, 1945, emphasis added). Similarly, diversity barely features in early measures such as the Florence Agreement, mentioned once in the first lines of its preamble: "the widest possible dissemination of the diverse forms of self-expression used by civilizations are vitally important both for intellectual progress and international understanding, and consequently for the maintenance of world peace" (UNESCO, 1950, emphasis added).

In this context there was little room for those that did not fit into the framework of exchange between what were deemed to be civilisations – a term largely reserved for the Western industrial societies. No consensus could be reached within the organisation on the question of human variation outside of this framework, with scientists at the organisation caught up in the recurring debates of the period regarding the primacy of "socio-environmental" or "genetic" explanations. Indeed, the Statement on Race of 1950 was revised a year later to reaffirm a biological definition of race and to note the differences between "non-literate" and "more civilized" people on intelligence tests. This would remain a sore point over the following decades, rarely separable from parallel controversies over segregation, colonialism and Cold War *realpolitik* (Brattain, 2007).

Decolonisation, 1960–1984

The colonial and paternal biases evident in UNESCO's early work began to change over the following decades. The main impetus for this came with the waves of decolonisation and the shift in the composition of the organisation's membership with the entry of the newly independent nations in the 1960s and 1970s, who soon became a numerical majority. Such majority presence can translate into real political weight at UNESCO (where procedures follow a nominally democratic voting process between member states), unlike other bodies in the UN family such as the Security Council, World Bank or IMF, whose agendas are more readily influenced by the powerful states (through mechanisms such as permanent seats, weighted voting systems, controls over the use of budgets and the appointment of top-level personnel, and so on). By the 1980s, the 20 founding participants of 1945 had grown to 160, and UNESCO was seen to have been the site of a "Third World takeover" as it became a platform for the demands of the Non-Aligned Movement, advanced through collective fronts such as the Group of 77 (G77) (Smith, 1980; Tomlinson, 2002).[8]

The agenda of cultural "modernisation" that was characteristic of the postwar period therefore came to be challenged by an agenda for cultural "decolonisation" as UNESCO was called upon by its new members to become an agency that would assist Third World countries towards the independent development of national information and communication systems (Carlsson, 2003). The controversies and widespread accusations of UNESCO's "politicisation" during this time – often associated with the tenure of the Senegalese Director-General Amadou-Mahtar M'Bow (from 1974 to 1987) and emanating in particular from the more powerful nations and news agencies (see Gulick, 1982; Wells, 1987; Preston *et al.*, 1989) – are indicative of the ways in which UNESCO was turned into a key battleground regarding international cultural regulation in this period. It is important to be clear here that while this conflict involved the claims of a number of progressive national liberation movements, these tended to be expressed through a cadre of representatives who, while seeking to carve out spaces of autonomy from neocolonial ambition and interference, were also in the process of constructing domestic structures of domination that often proved to be equally severe (Hardt and Negri (2000: 132–134) captured this well in their description of the "poisoned gift of national liberation").

The work of the International Commission for the Study of Communication Problems (or "MacBride Commission"), published as the "The MacBride Report" (MacBride *et al.*, 1980), became a key reference point in these international controversies. Although this report was adopted by the UNESCO General Conference of 1980, most of its recommendations proved too politically divisive to come to fruition. Its call for a "New World Information and Communication Order" (NWICO) paralleled the demands being pursued by the G77 at the United Nations Conference on Trade and Development (UNCTAD) for a "New International Economic Order" (NIEO). In more radical moments, those driving the NWICO agenda forward at UNESCO dared to assert the right of [national] cultural autonomy in the face of "cultural imperialism" and neocolonial control over the flow and content of communications, information, news, and so on.[9] Such a diagnosis reflected anxieties over the influence of a handful of overwhelmingly dominant players in international media and communications: from the work of the "big 4" international news agencies (Reuters, UPI, AP, AFP) to the activities of transnational advertisers, the control of satellite and communications infrastructure, distribution networks, the export of TV/radio programmes, films, newspapers and Disney comic books, amongst other things.

The Third World calls for NWICO in the late 1970s/early 1980s, along with the authoritative backing that they received in the MacBride Report, ultimately resulted in the withdrawal of US membership under the Reagan administration in 1984, followed by the UK (in 1985) and Singapore (in 1986). There were also threats to do the same from Canada, Japan, the Netherlands, Switzerland and West Germany. Their accusation was that UNESCO was being "politicised", "mismanaged" and used to place restrictions on the free flow of information. This was backed up by a concerted smear campaign by a number of media interests and partly reflected concerns, in particular those of the US, to protect assets and market access by promoting deregulation and privatisation in the international arena as the neoliberal mantra took hold (Wells, 1987; Preston *et al.*, 1989). Colleen Roach, reflecting on her time working for the US at UNESCO, stated the crux of the problem in explaining US hostility to NWICO: "The imperative for US transnational telecommunications business interests is concretely reflected in the 'deregulatory fever' and the move toward the privatization of the public sector" (Roach, 1987).

This emergence of a challenge to international cultural regulation at UNESCO in the post-independence period has been associated with a parallel "expansion" in the concept of culture, reflecting the claims of representatives from the newly independent nations in addressing some of the biases that had characterised UNESCO's work in the past. UNESCO's own review of the evolution of the concept of culture in its work describes these changes over the 1970s in the following terms: "the concept of culture was expanded to encompass that of 'identity' itself", and this is explained by a growing resistance to "the homogenising effects of uniform technology" on one hand, and "the ideological imperialism of the powerful states in an emerging Cold War context" on the other (UNESCO, 2004: 3). Some of the symptoms of this change can be drawn out here by considering two landmark measures that were taken at UNESCO in the late 1970s and early 1980s: the 1976 Recommendation on the Participation by the People at Large in Cultural Life and Their Contribution to it (UNESCO, 1976) and the 1982 Mexico City Declaration on Cultural Policies (UNESCO, 1982).

The first of these came out of the fiery nineteenth General Conference in Nairobi in 1976, at which a number of delegates from the Western bloc walked out on several occasions in protest at a number of claims that international cultural regulation reflected and reinforced a neocolonial bias. The 1976 Nairobi Recommendation was UNESCO's first significant statement regarding what was now being referred to as the need to "democratize the means and instruments of cultural activity" and "broaden access to culture by endowing it with its true meaning" (UNESCO, 1976). This called for the need to articulate a space of [national] cultural autonomy from neocolonial interference and the designs of orthodox development models. We thus read in one passage of the Nairobi 1976 recommendation that:

> [C]ulture is not merely an accumulation of works and knowledge which an elite produces, collects and conserves in order to place it within reach of all; or that a people rich in its past and its heritage offers to others as a model which their own history has failed to provide for them; that culture is not limited to access to works of art and humanities, but is at one and the same time the acquisition of knowledge, the demand for a way of life and the need to communicate.
>
> (UNESCO, 1976)

Six years later, at the World Conference on Cultural Policies ("MONDIA-CULT") held in Mexico City in 1982, these points were reiterated in the "Mexico Declaration", again with some controversy (for UNESCO's arch-critics, such as the Reaganite Heritage Foundation,[10] MONDIACULT was confirmation that UNESCO had been transformed into "a very large amphitheatre for international political propaganda" (Gulick, 1982)). The 1982 Mexico Declaration was notable for including the first authoritative statement that "in its widest sense, culture may now be said to be the whole complex of distinctive spiritual, material, intellectual and emotional features that characterize a society or social group" (UNESCO, 1982). The Mexico Declaration went on to state that giving international recognition to this broader concept of culture, widened from the elitist, ethnocentric and geographical biases that characterised its use in the modernisation period, was a key aspect in the struggle to address systemic international inequalities in the control, flow and content of cultural representation, as well as the continuing economic and political dominance of the North over the South – and was therefore a key aspect of wider attempts by the South to establish a New World Information and Communication Order (UNESCO, 1982: point 36) and New International Economic Order (point 50).

Globalisation, 1984–

The calls for NWICO and an agenda of decolonisation proved too divisive, however, and soon came to be replaced with an alternative, "depoliticised" agenda which I refer to here as "globalisation". This was paralleled by major reforms to UNESCO itself and, more broadly, the rise to hegemony of neoliberal globalisation with the end of the Cold War. With the withdrawals of the US, UK and Singapore from UNESCO and the subsequent transformations in the Third World that unfolded through the debt crisis and the collapse of the Soviet Union, the NWICO agenda faded into history and UNESCO entered a period of crisis. According to critics such as Herbert Schiller, the sidelining of UNESCO in the 1980s was the opening act in a new age of global corporate domination:

> In sum, the call for [NWICO] to increase the number of voices in the global discourse has been set aside. Instead of the hoped-for openness, there is a corporate regimen [and] the now commanding vision: "world-class products being sold by uniform advertising campaigns on commercial television around the world.
>
> (Schiller, 1989: 145)

However, accounts such as Schiller's present a misleading account of the political dynamics that emerged from the ruins of the 1980s (as I will argue in more detail in Chapters 3 and 4). This is not only because instruments such as the Convention have presented a challenge to this "regimen" by seeking, at least on the face of it, to replace uniformity with diversity, but more importantly because such accounts underestimate the consensus that was ultimately forged between the North and South over the 1980s and 1990s concerning the core principles of cultural regulation: the multiplication and differentiation of the enterprise form and the strategy of competitive insertion into the global marketplace have become touchstones of cultural policy around the world and are now informing the creation of mechanisms that are aimed precisely at building the capacity of local cultural producers while promoting a more multi-directional process of international cooperation and exchange. Moreover, the kind of accounts of cultural imperialism and the culture industries on which such accounts have traditionally rested have become increasingly untenable on theoretical grounds (a theme which is developed in particular in Chapter 2).

Nevertheless, after the NWICO controversies in the 1980s it is undoubtedly the case that we see important changes in culture's conceptualisation at UNESCO. This is prompted by the new set of problems that are posed by the combination of technological change, the end of the Cold War and the reinvention of development as a process of integration into the global market through economic liberalisation – a set of processes that come to be referred to over the 1990s as globalisation. According to UNESCO, the acceleration of globalisation has brought a

> radical change not only in the economic and technological order, but also in the mentalities and the ways of conceiving the world [and so requires a] redefinition of the type of actions and strategies to be established in order to preserve and promote cultural diversity, in particular at a time when new global markets are being formed and the statute of cultural goods compared to that of ordinary goods is being debated.
>
> (UNESCO, 2004: 4)

In this account by UNESCO, the importance of cultural diversity is seen to have gained a heightened poignancy in the face of the twin threats of cultural homogenisation and the rise of ethnic conflict and religious fundamentalism. The recognition of humanity's diversity is now seen to be an ethical and practical imperative across a number of areas of the new "global governance": it is inseparable from respect for human dignity, the realisation of pluralist democracy and social cohesion, and international peace and security; furthermore, its value as "a source of exchange, innovation and creativity" in the context of the development of a knowledge based economy is recognised as being an integral part of both economic and cultural development, and it is in this sense that cultural diversity is formulated in the new instruments as a resource "as necessary for humankind as biodiversity is for nature" (UNESCO, 2001: 2; UNESCO, 2005).

This recognition is seen to have given UNESCO a new international relevance in advocating for the recognition and affirmation of the crucial role of cultural diversity in national and international sustainable development strategies (UNESCO, 2004: 20), and indeed "for the future benefit of humanity" (UNESCO, 2001: Article 1). With the emergence of the new instruments on cultural diversity in the 2000s, UNESCO has put cultural diversity at the centre of its mission. UNESCO today summarises its work in the field of culture, and the body of instruments that it has adopted over the postwar period more broadly, as "assisting Member States in the protection and promotion of cultural diversity through the adoption of measures encompassing heritage protection, rehabilitation and safeguarding, and the development and implementation of cultural policies and sustainable cultural industries" (UNESCO, 2011: 5). This has brought UNESCO into closer relationship with the other international development institutions and has blurred some of the distinctions between UNESCO's competences in the field of culture with the work of organisations delegated with trade (such as the WTO), economic development (the World Bank, UNCTAD) or intellectual property (the World Intellectual Property Organisation).

Both the Universal Declaration on Cultural Diversity (UNESCO, 2001) and UNESCO's own review of its work over the postwar period (UNESCO, 2004) describe this mission in the era of globalisation as continuing the progressive democratisation of the concept of culture over the 1960s, 1970s and 1980s, and carried on through the 1990s at UNESCO by the efforts of the World Decade for Cultural Development (1988–1997), which sought to mainstream an appreciation of culture as the "last frontier of development" in international development policy in order to overcome the economistic biases of orthodox development models. Similarly Obuljen (2006), in a brief review of the different ways that culture and cultural diversity had featured in the debates over the wording of the Convention, notes that the adoption of the final text had built on some of the key contributions of NWICO and the World Decade for Cultural Development periods in order to enshrine a truly universal concept of cultural diversity in a way that had overcome some of the conceptual differences and controversies of the past. In this account the adoption of the Convention had "prove[n] that it was possible to take into account all these different aspects [and that] it was time to leave 'conceptual' dilemmas aside" (Obuljen, 2006: 23). The formulation of the principle of the "dual nature" of cultural goods and services provides a key point in this conceptual evolution. This principle gains its first formal international recognition in the Universal Declaration on Cultural Diversity, where it is proclaimed that cultural goods and services should be awarded special status as objects of regulation since they are bearers of not only commercial value but also "vectors of identity, values and meaning" (UNESCO, 2001: Article 8).

The recognition of such principles at an international level has been presented in this way as the outcome of an increasingly inclusive trajectory, one which transcends past divisions and controversies over the international regulation of culture. As the UNESCO Director General Kōichirō Matsuura wrote in his foreword to the Universal Declaration on Cultural Diversity:

> the debate between those countries which would like to defend cultural goods and services and those which would hope to promote cultural rights has thus been surpassed, with the two approaches brought together by the Declaration, which has highlighted the causal link uniting two complementary attitudes.
>
> (UNESCO, 2001)

This is echoed in UNESCO's own review of its history, which traces the gradual evolution of an increasingly inclusive concept of culture in its work culminating in the contemporary emphasis on cultural diversity (UNESCO, 2004). Over the course of this work, I will attempt to problematise such narratives about the evolution of an increasingly inclusive concept of culture.

Notes

1 The dynamics of the 148 to two vote on the Convention at UNESCO are neatly summarised by Moghadam and Elveren (2008: 743): "Voting against the Convention were the United States and Israel. Australia abstained because of Article 20 pertaining to the relationship between the Convention and other treaties, while Liberia, Nicaragua, and Honduras abstained because of intense lobbying by the US". Australia, one of the four abstentions, has since altered its position (ratifying the Convention in September 2009).

2 The terms cultural and creative industries are well established today but are used differently in different contexts and have generated much debate around their definition (see, for example, Flew and Cunningham, 2010; Garnham, 2005). Conceptual controversies aside, in practice they tend to be used interchangeably today by policymakers to refer to those industries involved in the creation of cultural goods and services (Throsby, 2008). The term "creative industries" is sometimes used more broadly than "cultural industries" to encompass industries such as advertising, software design or fashion that have come to be associated with the generation of intellectual property and the policy agendas of the "creative economy" and "information society". The prototype for this policy agenda is often seen to derive from the strategy devised by the UK's Department for Culture, Media and Sport from 1997.

3 Examples of such support measures include the *Canadian Radio-Television and Telecommunications Commission's* quotas reserving air-time for Canadian televisual and musical productions; France's long-standing systems of quotas on film screenings and mechanisms of domestic subsidisation through taxation on box-office receipts; Europe's *Television Without Frontiers* and *Audiovisual Media Services* Directives, through which broadcasters are required to reserve a majority proportion of their transmission time for European works, and many others. For more detailed discussions of such measures, see Beat Graber *et al.* (2004) or Voon (2007: 18–23).

4 The investigation of such questions as they relate to the Convention has been underway in the literature for some time now. (See, for example, Beat Graber *et al.*, 2004; Carmody, 1999; Head and Mayer, 2009; Nenova, 2008; Voon, 2007; Wouters and de Meester, 2008).

5 The Periodic Reports are available at https://en.unesco.org/creativity/monitoring-reporting/periodic-reports.

6 For a detailed overview of each of these programmes, as well as a more general history of the organisation itself, see Singh (2011).

7 This was made clear when the French government submitted a declaration under Article 27 of the International Covenant on Civil and Political Rights (1966), which was aimed at strengthening the rights of national cultural minorities: the French declaration implied that, since the French Constitution prohibits all distinctions between citizens based on grounds of origin, race or religion, no minorities exist in France and therefore Article 27 is not applicable under French law. The French Constitutional Court has further declared that the Charter on Regional Minority Languages (1992) and the Framework Convention on National Minorities (1995) of the Council of Europe are incompatible with the French Constitution on the basis of the same argument (Donders, 2008: 24).

8 The Group of 77 (G77) is a coalition of developing countries organised for more effective cooperation and collective negotiation on international matters within United Nations fora; see www.g77.org. The Non-Aligned Movement formed in 1961 and gathered increasing support over the following years from Third World governments as a forum for articulating claims to national sovereignty, territorial integrity, the condemnation of racism and colonialism, and calling for world peace against competing First and Second World ambitions in the Cold War context; see www.nam.gov.za.

9 The demands of NWICO at UNESCO, although never turned into a coherent programme, involved issues such as "the adoption of national communication policies", "defining a new concept of news not based on sensationalism", "multiplying exchange agreements among the countries of the Third World", "consolidating and developing the infrastructures of information", "promoting national agencies and the Non-Aligned News Agencies ['POOL']", "creation of regional information systems", "creation of centres for the training of journalists in the developing countries", etc. (Carlsson, 2003: 13; MacBride *et al.*, 1980). Sustained discussions of the NWICO debates and controversies can be found in a special issue of *Media, Culture and Society* (12 July 1990).
10 *The Heritage Foundation* is an influential Washington DC-based think-tank and one of the key sources of Reagan and Bush I/II-era domestic and foreign policy.

Bibliography

Arizpe, L. 2004. "The Intellectual History of Culture and Development Institutions". In Rao, V. and M. Walton (eds). *Culture and Public Action*. World Bank/Stanford: Stanford University Press.

Babbili, A.S. 1990. "Understanding International Discourse: Political Realism and the Non-Aligned Nations". *Media, Culture and Society*. 12(3).

Balibar, E. 1991. "Is there a Neo-Racism?" In Balibar, E. and I. Wallerstein. 1991. *Race, Nation, Class*. London: Verso.

Bayart, J.F. 2005. *The Illusion of Cultural Identity*. London: Hurst & Company.

Beat Graber, C., M. Girsberger and M. Nenova (eds) 2004. *Free Trade Versus Cultural Diversity: WTO Negotiations in the Field of Audiovisual Services*. Zurich: Schulthess.

Beat Graber, C. 2006. "The New UNESCO Convention on Cultural Diversity: A Counterbalance to the WTO?" *Journal of International Economic Law*. 9(3): 553–574.

Bennett, T. 1998. *Culture: A Reformer's Science*. London: Sage.

Bernier, I. 2004. "A UNESCO Convention on Cultural Diversity". In Beat Graber, C., M. Girsberger and M. Nenova (eds). *Free Trade Versus Cultural Diversity: WTO Negotiations in the Field of Audiovisual Services*. Zurich: Schulthess.

Brattain, M. 2007. "Race, Racism, and Antiracism: UNESCO and the Politics of Presenting Science to the Postwar Public". *The American Historical Review*. 112(5).

Carlsson, U. 2003. "The Rise and Fall of NWIO – and then?" Paper presented at the EURICOM Colloquium, Venice 5–7 May 2003.

Carmody, C. 1999. "When 'cultural identity was not at issue': Thinking about Canada – certain measures concerning periodicals". *Law and Policy in International Business*. 30(2).

Cetingulec, T. 2015. "Does Turkey care about cultural diversity?" *Al Monitor*, 17/08/2015. Available online at: www.al-monitor.com/pulse/originals/2015/07/turkey-unesco-is-not-ratifying-cultural-diversity-convention.html; accessed 18/08/2015.

Craufurd Smith, R. 2007. "The UNESCO Convention on the Protection and Promotion of Cultural Expressions: Building a New World Information and Communication Order?" *International Journal of Communication*. 2007(1): 24–55.

Crossette, B. 2006. "Urgent: Damage Control". *Foreign Policy*. July/August 2006.

Disdier, A., S. Tai, L. Fontagne and T. Mayer. 2009. "Bilateral Trade of Cultural Goods". *Review of World Economics*. October 2009: *Online First*. Available online at: www.springerlink.com/content/033j37v11815v677/; accessed 30/10/2009.

Dominguez, V.R. 1992. "Invoking culture: The messy side of cultural politics". *South Atlantic Quarterly*. 91(1).

Donders, Y. 2008. "The History of the UNESCO Convention on the Protection and Promotion of the Diversity of Cultural Expressions". In Schneider, H. and P. van den Bossche (eds). *Protection of Cultural Diversity from a European and International Perspective*. Oxford: Intersentia.

Escobar, A. 1995. *Encountering Development: The Making and Unmaking of the Third World*. New Jersey: Princeton University Press.

Esteva, G. 2005. "Development". In Sachs, W. (ed.). 2005. *The Development Dictionary: A Guide to Knowledge as Power*. London and New York: Zed Books.

Eriksen, T.H. 2001. "Between Universalism and Relativism: A critique of the UNESCO concepts of culture". In Cowan, J., M. Dembour and R. Wilson (eds). *Culture and Rights: Anthropological Perspectives*. Cambridge: Cambridge University Press.

European Commission. 2006. FAQ: UNESCO Convention on Cultural Diversity – a new instrument of international governance. Available online at: http://eu-un.europa.eu/articles/en/article_6630_en.htm; accessed 02/07/2015.

Flew, T. and S. Cunningham. 2010. "Creative industries after the first decade of debate". *The Information Society: An International Journal*. 26(2).

Garnham, N. 2005. "From cultural to creative industries: An analysis of the implications of the 'creative industries' approach to arts and media policy making in the United Kingdom". *International Journal of Cultural Policy*. 11(1).

Graham, S.E. 2006. "The (Real)politiks of Culture: U.S. Cultural Diplomacy in UNESCO, 1946–1954". *Diplomatic History*. 30(2).

Gulick, T.G. 1982. *UNESCO: Where Culture Becomes Propaganda*. Washington: Heritage Foundation.

Hale, C.R. 2005. "Neoliberal multiculturalism: The remaking of cultural rights and racial dominance in Central America". *Political and Legal Anthropological Review*. 28(1): 10–28.

Hardt, M. and A. Negri. 2000. *Empire*. London: Harvard University Press.

Head, K. and T. Mayer. 2009. "Restrictions on trade in audiovisual services: Whom are we protecting from what?" *VoxEU.org*, 19/03/2009.

Kuper, A. 1999. *Culture: The Anthropologist's Account*. London: Harvard University Press.

MacBride, S. and The International Commission for the Study of Communication Problems. 1980. *Many Voices, One World: Toward a New More Just and More Efficient World Information and Communication Order*. Paris: UNESCO.

Mamdani, M. 2002. "Good Muslim, Bad Muslim: A Political Perspective on Culture and Terrorism". *American Anthropologist*. 104(3): 766–775.

Moghadam, V.E. and D. Elveren. 2008. "The making of an international Convention: Culture and free trade in a global era". *Review of International Studies*. 34(4): 735–753.

Nederveen Pieterse, J. 2001. *Development Theory: Deconstructions/Reconstructions*. London: Sage.

Nenova, M. 2008. "Trade and Culture: Making the WTO Legal Framework Conducive to Cultural Considerations". *Manchester Journal of International Economic Law*. 5(3).

Obuljen, N. 2006. "From Our Creative Diversity to the Convention on Cultural Diversity: Introduction to the debate". In Obuljen, N. and J. Smiers (eds). *UNESCO's Convention on the Protection and Promotion of the Diversity of Cultural Expressions: Making it Work*. Zagreb: Institute for International Relations.

Preston, W., E. Herman and H. Schiller. 1989. *Hope and Folly: The United States and UNESCO, 1945–1985*. Minneapolis: University of Minnesota Press.

Richieri Hanania, L. and H. Ruiz Fabri. 2014. "The effectiveness of the UNESCO Convention on the Protection and Promotion of the Diversity of Cultural Expressions". In Richieri Hanania, L. (ed.). 2014. *Cultural Diversity in International Law: The Effectiveness of the UNESCO Convention on the Protection and Promotion of the Diversity of Cultural Expressions*. Oxon: Routledge.

Roach, C. 1987. "The US Position on the New World Information and Communication Order". *Journal of Communication*. 37(4).

Said, E. 1978. *Orientalism*. New York: Pantheon.

Schiller, H.I. 1989. *CULTURE, INC.: The Corporate Takeover of Public Expression*. Oxford: Oxford University Press.

Singh, J.P. 2011. *United Nations Educational, Scientific and Cultural Organisation: Creating norms for a complex world*. London and New York: Routledge.

Smith, A. 1980. *The Geopolitics of Information: How Western Culture Dominates the World*. Oxford: Oxford University Press.

Suranovic, S. and R. Winthrop. 2005. "Cultural Effects of Trade Liberalisation". Available online at: http://home.gwu.edu/~smsuran/Suranovic-Winthrop.PDF; accessed 15/05/2008.

The Future We Want Includes Culture. 2015. Communique: Culture in the SDG Outcome Document: Progress made, but important steps remain ahead. Available online at: http://culture2015goal.net/; accessed 18/10/2015.

Throsby, D. 2008. "From culture to creative industries: The specific characteristics of the creative industries". Paper presented at *Troisième Journées d'Economie de la Culture: Nouvelles Frontières de l'Economie de la Culture*, Musée du quai Branly, Paris, 2–3 October 2008. Available online at: http://jec.culture.fr/Throsby.doc; accessed 13/07/2015.

Throsby, D. 2010. *The Economics of Cultural Policy*. Cambridge: Cambridge University Press.

Tomlinson, J. 2002. *Cultural Imperialism*. London: Continuum.

UN. 2014. *Resolution on Culture and Sustainable Development*. A/RES/68/223. United Nations General Assembly, 12 February 2014. Available online at: www.un.org/en/ga/68/resolutions.shtml; accessed 05/08/2015.

UN. 2015. *Transforming our world: the 2030 Agenda for Sustainable Development*. United Nations. Available online at: https://sustainabledevelopment.un.org/post2015/transformingourworld/publication; accessed 02/10/2015.

UNESCO. 1945. *Constitution of the United Nations Educational, Scientific and Cultural Organization*. Paris: UNESCO. Available online at: http://portal.UNESCO.org/en/ev.php-URL_ID=15244&URL_DO=DO_TOPIC&URL_SECTION=201.html; accessed 09/07/2007.

UNESCO. 1950. *Agreement on the Importation of Educational, Scientific and Cultural Materials*. Paris: UNESCO. Available online at: http://unesdoc.UNESCO.org/images/0011/001145/114589e.pdf#page=138; accessed 12/01/2008.

UNESCO. 1952. *The Visual Arts in General Education*. UNESCO/CUA/36. Paris: UNESCO. Available online at: http://unesdoc.UNESCO.org/images/0012/001271/127197eb.pdf; accessed 12/01/2008.

UNESCO. 1976. *Recommendation on Participation by the People at Large in Cultural Life and Their Contribution to it*. Paris: UNESCO. Available online at: www.UNESCO.org/culture/laws/nairobi/html_eng/page1.shtml; accessed 09/07/2007.

UNESCO. 1982. *Mexico City Declaration on Cultural Policies*. Paris: UNESCO. Available online at: http://portal.UNESCO.org/culture/en/ev.php-URL_ID=12762&URL_DO=DO_TOPIC&URL_SECTION=201.html; accessed 09/07/2007.

UNESCO. 2001. *Universal Declaration on Cultural Diversity*. Paris: UNESCO. Available online at: http://unesdoc.UNESCO.org/images/0012/001271/127160m.pdf; accessed 09/07/2007.

UNESCO. 2004. *UNESCO and the Issue of Cultural Diversity: Review and Strategy, 1946–2004*. Paris: UNESCO.

UNESCO. 2005. *Convention on the Protection and Promotion of the Diversity of Cultural Expressions*. CLT-2005/CONVENTION DIVERSITE-CULT REV. Paris: UNESCO. Available online at: www.unesco.org/culture/en/diversity/convention; accessed 14/03/2007.

UNESCO. 2007. *Report of the expert meeting on the statistical measurement of the diversity of cultural expressions*. CE/07/1.IGC/INF.4. Paris: UNESCO. Available online at: www. UNESCO.org/culture/culturaldiversity/december07/igc1_rapport_montreal_en.pdf; accessed 12/01/2008.

UNESCO. 2010. *International Fund for Cultural Diversity*. Paris: UNESCO. Available online at: www.unesco.org/culture/culturaldiversity/IFCD_ExplanatoryNote_EN.pdf; accessed 05/09/2010.

UNESCO. 2011. *Register of Best Safeguarding Practices, 2011*. Paris: UNESCO. Available online at: www.unesco.org/culture/ich/doc/src/17332-EN.pdf; accessed 02/07/2015.

UNESCO. 2014. *Item 7a of the provisional agenda: Quadrennial periodic reporting: new reports and analytical summary*. CE/14/8.IGC/7a. Paris: UNESCO. Available online at: http://en.unesco.org/creativity/sites/creativity/files/8IGC_7a_analysis_periodic_ reports_EN.pdf; accessed 12/08/2015.

UNESCO. 2015. "Countries mark 10th anniversary of UNESCO Convention on Diversity of Cultural Expressions". UNESCO Press, 09/06/2015. Available online at: www. unesco.org/new/en/media-services/single-view/news/countries_mark_10th_anniversary_of_unesco_convention_on_diversity_of_cultural_expressions/#.VdH9GXvCZ5w; accessed 10/06/2015.

Vlassis, A. 2015. "Culture in the post-2015 development agenda: the anatomy of an international mobilisation". *Third World Quarterly*. 36(9).

Voon, T. 2007. *Cultural Products and the World Trade Organization*. Cambridge: Cambridge University Press.

Wells, C. 1987. *The UN, UNESCO and the Politics of Knowledge*. London: Macmillan.

Williams, R. 1983. *Keywords: A Vocabulary of Culture and Society*. London: Fontana.

Wouters, J. and B. de Meester. 2008. "The UNESCO Convention on Cultural Diversity and WTO Law: A Case Study in Fragmentation of International Law". *Journal of World Trade*. 42(1): 205–240.

Yúdice, G. 2003. *The Expediency of Culture: Uses of Culture in the Global Era*. London: Duke University Press.

Part I

2 Trade and culture

Introduction

To understand the framework of cultural development that has emerged over the last decade, and in particular the UNESCO Convention on the Protection and the Promotion of the Diversity of Cultural Expressions (hereinafter "the Convention"), it is necessary to place it within the context of a series of debates concerning culture's place within international trade. Examining some of the key themes in this debate helps to contextualise the Convention's significance as a response to a series of high-stake international political and commercial conflicts regarding the appropriate regulatory balance between trade liberalisation and cultural policy.

The first section of this chapter therefore outlines the contours of this so-called "trade and culture debate" and its international political and commercial stakes. It then goes on to argue that the debate has tended to be limited by a focus on a set of largely technical and legal questions regarding the appropriate status of cultural goods and services within the frameworks of international trade negotiation and administration. In this way, the focus of the discussion and analysis that has surrounded the Convention has tended to leave unproblematised a number of more awkward conceptual and normative questions. It has also tended to relegate questions related to development, as transatlantic and North American concerns about trade have been centre stage.

The second half of the chapter then draws on a series of contributions from social and cultural theory in order to prepare the grounds for a more searching and critical approach to the new framework of cultural development. Particular attention is paid to the Foucault-inspired work on cultural policy, notably Tony Bennett's and George Yúdice's attempts to go beyond the accounts of commodification and instrumentalisation that had been developed earlier in the twentieth century by the Frankfurt School of critical theory. In particular I examine Yúdice's (2003) argument that the recent period of neoliberal globalisation has brought about the transformation of culture into a "resource" for trade and development. I end with some critical reflections on the value of such an account as a framework for analysing the implications of more recent developments in the field of international development and cultural policy. The following chapter then takes up the theme of culture and development in greater detail.

Trade and culture

Understanding the significance of the UNESCO Convention on cultural diversity, and the nature of its contribution to debates about cultural and sustainable development, first requires considering a long-running debate about "trade and culture". This debate has precedents earlier in the twentieth century but intensified in the late 1990s and was the key driver in the Convention's drafting and adoption. Although the adoption of the Convention in 2005 drew something of a line under the debate, it only offered a partial solution and the debate very much remains alive today (as seen most recently in ongoing negotiations between the US and EU over a Transatlantic Trade and Investment Partnership (TTIP)).

The debate has been well rehearsed in the literature[1] and so will be given a relatively brief overview here in order to prepare grounds for critical discussion. It revolves around the following kinds of questions:

> To what extent should free trade principles apply to different sorts of "artistic" and "linguistic" products and services? Are certain so-called cultural goods and services more tradeable than others and therefore more susceptible to global dissemination? If so, should they be treated differently? To what extent should international trade policies defer to the cultural policies of national governments, even if those policies include the protection, or subsidisation, of cultural goods and services in the interests of the preservation of cultural identity and cultural heritage?
>
> (Footer and Beat Graber, 2000: 1)

Two broad "pro-culture" and "pro-trade" positions have tended to divide opinion on these questions. These will be explored briefly below.

"Pro-culture" and "pro-trade"

The campaign for the drafting and adoption of the Convention was spearheaded by the governments of France and Canada, working together with stakeholders in the cultural industry sector but eventually extending to a broad coalition of states and civil society organisations from developed and developing countries. The rationale for the creation of the Convention was largely built on the "pro-culture" argument – articulated by a range of actors including trade negotiators, industry stakeholders and specialists in international trade law – that unchecked liberalisation in the cultural sector threatens the cultural policy capacity of states, with negative implications for cultural diversity at both national and international levels. In a context of international market liberalisation and rapid technological change, it is claimed that international conglomerates and oligopolies in the audiovisual and publishing sectors that have been nurtured in larger and wealthier domestic markets are able to consolidate market power on an ever greater scale. This is seen to threaten the commercial viability of local production and therefore reduce the diversity that is offered to audiences at global and national levels. At the same time, the pressures of contemporary trade negotiations and regulations are seen to threaten the capacity of states to provide measures of support to domestic producers through mechanisms such as domestic quotas, subsidies, preferential treatment, competition policy, government procurement or systems of content review.[2]

More fundamentally, it is often claimed on this pro-culture side in the debate that the vision of "pure market ideology" that sees in everything a commodity to be traded and subject to "the ordinary laws of commerce" is based on a crucial misunderstanding: that "unlike wheat or coal, cultural products are also intimately bound with matters of social identity and consciousness" (Scott, 2002). In this vein France and Canada in particular came to take the position from the late 1980s that cultural goods and services should be subject to the principle of "l'exception culturelle"/"cultural exception" (or sometimes "cultural exemption") for the purpose of international trade negotiation and administration.[3]

For these reasons, UNESCO – with its specialised competence in the field of culture – was seen by pro-culture campaigners to be a fitting organisation to house an instrument that could provide some form of counterweight to the momentum of trade liberalisation by reasserting the value of national cultural policy measures and the legitimacy of the principle of the special status of cultural goods and services. In the process, the language of "cultural exception" used by France and Canada in the context of disputes over trade has been widened to a broader concern for "cultural diversity" and its role within sustainable development. UNESCO welcomed this opportunity to become a focal point for the pro-culture campaign, with the Director-General opening the first session of the Conference of Parties to the Convention by noting that: "It is not by chance that UNESCO was entrusted with the task of drawing up the Convention. The point is to ensure sounder management of the cultural, and not just the economic, aspects of cultural activities, goods and services" (Matsuura, 2007: 2). During this First Conference of Parties to the Convention, Jean Musitelli (one of the key figures involved in the drafting of the instrument, and a key member of the French delegation at UNESCO) further elaborated on the purpose of the instrument to create a new balance between trade and culture:

> The object and objective of the text reside in the idea that works of the mind should not be subjected to the ordinary laws of commerce. This means they are recognized as having a specific nature; culture and cultures express the souls of peoples, and cannot be reduced to products that are bought and sold. The Convention establishes, for the first time and with force, that cultural products have a double nature: economic, because naturally creators have to be remunerated, but also a nature that cannot be reduced to market value and which has to do with meaning and symbolism. The Convention

is trying precisely to establish a legal framework that takes into account the dual characteristics of cultural products.

(Musitelli, in interview 14 June 2007)

On the other side of the debate, those occupying the "pro-trade" position – most prominently US trade representatives and more orthodox economic liberals – have argued first that free trade is merely a mechanism by which consumers select the most successful and efficient producers, while also disseminating technology and raising incomes around the world in a way which ultimately allows domestic forms of cultural production to flourish. This position has also gained intellectual weight from those who argue that the notion of "protecting" culture is to deny its fundamentally fluid and hybrid character in a way which paves the way for essentialising and authoritarian political agendas (see, for example, the accounts of Rushdie, 1999; Appiah, 2006).

Indeed, by positioning itself as the guardian of the free flow of commerce and of culture, the US has combined both the first and second of these arguments in setting out its opposition to the Convention. The US has stressed that, for the purpose of trade negotiation and regulation, the cultural sector should *not* be subject to exceptional rules and that the WTO – not UNESCO – is the most appropriate forum for dealing with what should be regarded a matter of trade, not culture (for the US's official statements regarding the Convention, see Oliver, 2005; Martin, 2005; US State Department, 2005). As Dan Gioia, then US Chairman of the National Endowment for the Arts, put it in explaining the US's objection to the Convention in 2005, "cultural diversity is best served by recognising that culture changes": by granting states the right to implement protectionist policy, it is argued that the text fails to establish a properly open process of mutual cultural exchange while potentially allowing governments to "restrict the free flow of ideas and information" or to "justify government censorship – both political and cultural" (Gioia, 2005). More fundamentally, it is argued that the text fails to recognise that "culture is migratory, it's dynamic, it transcends national boundaries" – indeed, such a conceptualisation is described as being "fundamental to America's vision of itself and our vision of how culture operates in a free world" (Gioia, 2005). These points were emphasised in the opening remarks of the US delegation's statement to UNESCO which explained its lonely "no" vote over the Convention:

> The United States is the most open country in the world to the diversity of the world's cultures, people, and products. It is not only a part of our heritage but the essence of our national identity. It is therefore with regret that we stand in opposition today to this Convention because of those who have indicated a clear intent to use this convention to control – not facilitate – the flow of goods, services, and ideas.... [The text] lends itself too easily to being used as a tool to undermine UNESCO's Constitutional obligation to promote "the free flow of ideas by word and image".
>
> (Oliver, 2005)

The "pro-culture" and "pro-trade" positions that have been staked out over the UNESCO Convention are reflective of a growth in the stakes around the liberalisation of trade in cultural products towards the end of the twentieth century, but the debate has precedents that go further back than this. The worldwide dominance of Hollywood that had become apparent by the end of the First World War, coupled with the political sensitivity of film as a medium of mass communication within the industrial states, focused the international debate from an early stage on the film industry, with a number of countries arguing for the necessity of protective measures to nurture their own industries and preserve space for autonomy in national policy. Following WWII such claims found their most significant recognition in Article IV (Special Provisions Related to Cinematograph Films) of the General Agreement on Tariffs and Trade (GATT).

Such concessions to national regulation, however, also preserved a degree of frustration on the part of advocates for greater international liberalisation, most notably those in the US, and as the pressures to break down this compromise on trade liberalisation have gained in intensity in the neoliberal context, so has the debate over trade and culture. In the recent rounds of multilateral trade negotiations this has been evident at least since the Tokyo Round (1973–1979), when the US filed complaints about 21 countries' subsidies to their cinema and television industries (Footer and Beat Graber, 2000). By the time of the Uruguay Round (1986–1993), which gave birth to the WTO and raised the prospect of extending liberalisation to cultural services under the negotiations for the General Agreement on Trade in Services (GATS), such disagreements had sharpened and become one of the most significant sources of tension in the negotiations.

A range of perspectives over the treatment of culture were expressed in the negotiations over GATS, with a number of countries making a variety of proposals for a form of special treatment for the cultural services sector based on its role within national culture (Beat Graber *et al.*, 2004; Voon, 2007: 24–25). The starkest differences of opinion, however, were between the EU (and in particular France), and the US. The main issue was the EU's 51% programming quota for domestic television content that had come out of the European Council's Television Without Frontiers (TWF) Directive, just as the Uruguay negotiations were drawing to an end (Singh, 2008). US negotiators were seeking improved market access in this sector, while France's mobilisation of the principle of *l'exception culturelle* as part of the European negotiating position played an important part in Europe ultimately refusing to make any commitments. This episode reflected the way in which the transatlantic cultural trade war has taken on an increasingly regional quality as Europe has begun to articulate coherent positions on cultural policy in its external relations.[4] Similar controversies have resurfaced more recently in the context of US and EU negotiations over the TTIP, which are ongoing at the time of writing (see Bartsch, 2014; European Commission, 2014; Committee on Culture and Education, 2015).

Those that have attempted to find a third way in this trade and culture debate have pointed out that the "pro-culture" and "pro-trade" perspectives need not be mutually exclusive, and have explored the possibility of developing alternative mechanisms, or improving existing trade regulations, in a way that could result in a more effective regulatory solution (see, for example, Nenova (2010) for an overview of such arguments). One of the factors that has tended to harden the respective pro-trade/pro-culture stances in the debate, however, has been the sizeable political, economic and commercial stakes that have been in play, as the cultural and creative industries have become identified as a strategically important sector in many countries since the 1990s. Sensitivities over the commercial and cultural influence of the exports of political rivals have also been heightened against a backdrop of growing trade deficits in film and television production, as seen, for example, between the US and the EU (where the EU deficit reached US$6 billion in 1998) or the US and China (particularly following China's accession to the WTO in 2001; see Chapter 4). Meanwhile there has been a keen recognition among negotiators on both sides of the debate concerning the importance of holding as strong a position as possible for the areas of expansion in the "new" economy of information and communications, intellectual property, and digital products and services.

It is unsurprising therefore that the accusations that the Convention's lofty references to cultural diversity are a form of "disguised protectionism" on behalf of its key sponsors are largely backed up by a close analysis of its substantive provisions (as Beat Graber (2008) has shown for example) – even if the weakness of the Convention in relation to existing international legal commitments appears to limit the ability of states to use the treaty's provisions in this way in order to circumvent prior WTO commitments. While it is important to be wary of the way that the pro-culture position in the debate has been caricatured by pro-traders as one of backward-looking, reactionary protectionism, there is also some truth in the arguments of analysts such as Des Beauvais (2014), who has noted that the cultural exception as it is invoked today in the French context is increasingly addressed to the defence of subsidies to well established firms and actors in the cultural sector (often at the expense of emerging French talent).

Of course the US has also had a strong interest in the debate as it pursues an "open door" trade policy that seeks to establish and maintain advantages for its powerful cultural exporters. Since the 1990s, these have become the jewel in America's trade crown, becoming an increasingly important source of international trade surpluses and, by 1996, surpassing traditional manufacturing industries to become the US's largest export industry (Bruner, 2008; Disdier *et al.*, 2009: 576). The US's position on the UNESCO Convention was therefore worked out in close cooperation with lobby groups such as the Motion Picture Association of America (MPAA), whose members include the "Big Six" of major Hollywood studios and whose former leader Jack Valenti had, by the mid-1990s, earned a reputation as the most formidable trade lobbyist in the US (Bruner, 2008: 356).

The US interest in the global regulatory regime for the trade in cultural products largely explains the diplomatic energy that it put into opposing the Convention. Such an instrument came into conflict not only with the US's claim (ideological or otherwise) to keep the international trading system intact and to uphold the free flow of trade and information, but also its sizeable commercial interests. Bonnie J.K. Richardson, who has been both Vice President for Trade and Federal Affairs with the MPAA and chief US negotiator for the services market access negotiations during the Uruguay Round, typifies this confluence of interests in the US's stance on such international trade issues. Thus, in setting out the MPAA's plea to keep the issue of culture within the context of the WTO, she points out that "Culture and trade are mutually reinforcing.... A cultural instrument that removes culture from trade rules does not solve problems – it invites anarchy" (Richardson, 2004: 115–119). The US subsequently sought to stoke opposition to the instrument in the run-up to the vote – an effort which backfired (Donders, 2008).

With the US effectively finding itself isolated against the 148 states that voted for the adoption of the Convention, it is generally accepted that the passage of the Convention at UNESCO marked something of a victory for the pro-culture advocates, taking the "first step to filling the existing lacuna for cultural values and interests in international law" (Beat Graber, 2008: 157). In their study of the negotiation and voting processes that led to the adoption of the Convention at UNESCO, Moghadam and Elveren (2008: 744) have reflected that, although the resulting instrument was not as strong as its supporters had hoped for, "[w]hat should be noted is the member-states' strong adherence to the idea of cultural diversity and preservation, and the inability of the US to influence the normative debate".

The stalling of the Doha "Development" Round of multilateral negotiations at the WTO since 2001 has created another sub-plot in these conflicts over trade and culture. With the multilateral liberalisation agenda in limbo, the US has turned to a new generation of bilateral free trade agreements (FTAs) through which it has sought to strike deals in areas that have largely been off-limits at the WTO. One of the priorities for US negotiators in these bilateral negotiations has also been to step up its search for new market opportunities in strategic areas such as those in the digital economy and information and communication technologies, sectors in which it has come to have a particularly keen interest (Bernier, 2003; Mukherjee *et al.*, 2007; Vlassis and Richieri Hanania, 2014). This has formed part of a strategy in which the US has attempted to counter the attempts by the main supporters of the UNESCO Convention to have the cultural sector excluded in totality or in part from trade negotiations. The US has used such bilateral agreements to lay down markers and precedents concerning the regulation of audiovisual services, and in particular the digital network of content delivery, in a way which seeks to immunise them from cultural exception arguments in future negotiations (Bernier, 2003; Vlassis and Richieri Hanania, 2014).

These further developments have given the trade and culture debate a complex tactical character, as sectoral alliances and trade-offs have been sought in bilateral deals as part of the jostling for position and legal precedent that characterises contemporary international trade negotiations. This is significant because the authority of the UNESCO Convention in the context of trade disputes and negotiations very much depends on how widely its principles are recognised and ratified, as well as the political will of parties to take its provisions regarding the special nature of cultural products into account when negotiating new agreements (Vlassis and Richieri Hanania, 2014). For these reasons, the trade and culture debate has been conducted on an increasingly international scale as a matter of trade diplomacy and alliance-building among industry and civil society stakeholders, as Canada and the EU (and in particular France) have campaigned around the world for the Convention's adoption and ratification whilst seeking to enshrine principles of the special "dual" nature of cultural products in their own bilateral trade negotiations and agreements.

Finally, it is also important to note some of the complementarities of interest that exist between certain countries and market coalitions on the question of trade and culture. This has been evident, for example, with the relationship that has been struck between the US entertainment and Japanese electronics industries since the 1980s. Following Sony's acquisitions of Hollywood institutions Columbia Pictures Entertainment, Inc. (in 1989) and Metro-Goldwyn-Mayer (in 2005), Japan has also come to hold a considerable stake and influence in the work of the MPAA. It has also become a major international player in its own right in content production (now accounting for more than 60% of animation sales worldwide), notably in Asia, where Japanese rivalries with the US are less salient than rivalries with countries such as South Korea or China (Fiegenbaum, 2007). For these reasons, tensions between Japan and the US over the Convention have been much less evident than between the US and other countries/regions such as Canada or France/the EU. Japan worked alongside the US during the drafting negotiations in an attempt to weaken the Convention's standing in international law (Fiegenbaum, 2007; Moghadam and Elveren, 2008).

Caveats to the trade and culture debate

Having noted some of the main points of contention in the trade and culture debate, it is necessary to note a number of caveats. First of all, the emphasis on the uniquely cultural and linguistic aspects of cultural products has tended to be overplayed by the pro-culture supporters, since what has tended to be at stake in the policy measures that are being defended by those countries asserting the unique nature of cultural products has not in fact been the ability to generate national *content* as such but rather to implement origin-specific measures and to support national *production*. According to the cultural support measures that have been the focus of the debates in France and Canada, for example, whether a cultural product is deemed French or Canadian in content depends less on the nature of its sign systems (stories, images, sounds, and so on) and more on the nationality of those who financed and managed it (Voon, 2007: 58–59). Given the increasingly international nature of production, this creates situations where films shot in French, with French directors, actors and technicians, have been ineligible for French support because the production company was controlled by a foreign firm (as in the case of *Un Long Dimanche* for example, which was produced by Warner Brothers). Similarly, Hollywood-style films shot in English and casting American actors (such as *The Fifth Element*) have had no trouble in getting state backing as long as they are produced by a French company (Voon, 2007: 58–59).

A second point relates to the way that transatlantic political and commercial rivalries have tended to drive the debate, and the way that respective diplomats and delegations at UNESCO have articulated their cases for and against the Convention in narratives aligned with UNESCO's constitutional mandate to promote international harmony through the free flow and exchange of ideas and images. An effect of this is that the debate has often been waged on both sides through "exceptionalist" narratives as there has been a bid to establish ethical and legal leadership over the management of a "universal" process of cultural intercourse and exchange. Taking note of this helps to expose some of the contradictions in the arguments of the different sides. For all the attempts that we have seen above by the US to make a claim to its own form of exceptionalism on questions of cultural regulation and diversity (what Yúdice (2003) has referred to as the US's "we are the world" complex), it has also been noted that the US is itself highly protectionist. Not only do its cultural imports represent no more than 2% of its total consumption (Moghadam and Elveren, 2008: 744, fn 30) but, historically, it has adopted a highly protectionist stance on culture and the key questions of intellectual property and cultural production (and continues to do so) (Tian, 2009: 131–137; Forsyth, 2004).

By the same token, the lead taken by France and Canada at UNESCO, and the prioritisation of questions related to their particular trade concerns, has meant that questions related to the role of culture in development have tended to be brought into the discussion as a secondary consideration. Singh (2011: 98–107) has argued that, despite the claims about the universal support behind the cultural diversity agenda at UNESCO, the creation of the Convention has in fact been a highly politicised initiative that is reflective of the concerns of its chief backers from the developed world. In the process, he points out, the Convention has tended to eclipse some of the broader intellectual and policy debates about culture and development that had been taking place over the previous decade. One of the aims of this book is therefore to examine in greater detail how this happened and to draw out some of its implications.

Taking note of this bias in the Convention, however, does not mean that voices from outside the transatlantic debate have been absent altogether. Indeed, the Convention would not have been able to come to fruition at UNESCO without generating widespread international momentum and political support. There has been an increasingly assertive group of emerging countries seeking space in which to further their interests in the cultural sector (such as China, Brazil, South Africa, Egypt, India and Nigeria), and a number of these have been active supporters of the Convention. Many of the smaller developing countries, with less at stake in the trade and culture debate, have also come to identify the cultural sector as an important area for development, particularly those that are seeking to exploit potential in tourism and in lucrative diaspora markets, as well as those that are looking for ways to diversify their export base. This has been the case in the Caribbean, for example, where the cultural and creative industries have been proposed as a new engine of growth, one which can offer more sustainable development options than traditional exports because the sector draws on the creativity of local artists and entrepreneurs, generating higher levels of local value-added (Nurse, 2012).

A number of developing countries have therefore seen in the Convention an opportunity to strike an alliance with the Franco-Canadian campaign on the question of the special treatment of culture in trade, securing innovative provisions in the Convention on international development cooperation. Most notably, Article 16 holds out the possibility of preferential market access from developed countries to developing countries in the cultural sector, while Article 18 establishes an International Fund for Cultural Diversity which developing countries can draw on in order to develop their cultural sector. However, the benefits of such provisions in practice, and their significance in the context of longer term debates about culture and development, remain to be seen. These are also therefore themes that are taken up in the following chapters.

A final point, and one which has often been lost in the discussions surrounding the Convention, is that the substantive issues at stake have *not* in fact concerned an opposition between "culture" on the one hand and processes of "marketisation", industrialisation and commercialisation on the other. Nor have they concerned a conflict over policies aimed at preserving the sanctity of the traditional domains of "high" culture or the arts (opera, ballet, classical music, the fine arts, and so on) from the encroachment of "low" or popular culture and the influence of the culture industries. The US, like other countries, openly subsidises its national arts institutions and the right of other countries to do so has not been under question (even if such subsidies and their legitimacy have come under general pressure in national contexts of reform and fiscal retrenchment) (Bruner, 2008). Rather, it is important to stress that the debate has been concerned with the *simultaneously* cultural and economic status of cultural goods and services as objects of international commercial exchange, and the most appropriate market rules for fostering diversity in their production and trade. As the government of Québec, which has been one of the most active sponsors of the Convention, noted for example, "It is not a matter of denying that cultural goods and services are objects of trade, but rather of recognizing that they cannot be subject to the standard rules of trade" (Gouvernement du Québec, 2006). In this sense it is also important to stress that the Convention not only offers governments scope for protection and prohibition (a central objection of the US, as we have seen) but also for promotion and production (aimed, for example, at reinforcing the validity of domestic support measures, and opening new possibilities for international cooperation, co-production, investment and market access). We will return to some of these points below, and in Part II of the book we will look at some of the effects of this new framework of cultural regulation and development as they are starting to become apparent through the Convention's implementation.

Limitations of the trade and culture debate

We can now begin to sketch out some of the limits within which the trade and culture debate has been conducted, and some of its blind spots. The bulk of scholarly attention has come from the field of international law, tending to focus on a set of largely technical questions regarding the effective interpretation and implementation of the Convention's provisions, particularly as this relates to the high stake debates surrounding international trade negotiations and administration.[5] The deadlock over audiovisual services liberalisation has provided the focus for this analysis, with the literature responding to this problem growing considerably since the 2000s and occupying much of the academic discussion that has responded to the Convention's drafting and entry into force. However, this focus has meant that a number of more awkward conceptual, political, theoretical and historical questions raised by the Convention have tended to have a secondary or residual importance in the analysis.

There have, nevertheless, been a number of attempts to confront some of the more conceptual issues raised within the debates that have surrounded the Convention's adoption and entry into force. This includes a series of attempts to integrate culture into the conceptual and practical concerns of economics and economic policy, for example by those stressing the contemporary value of the cultural sector as a resource for trade and development, and by those taking up the tasks of quantifying and measuring the various contributions of culture to economic development. Contributing to this has been the work done within the discipline of cultural economics, which has drawn on work in other fields such as the sociology of arts and culture management in order to develop a branch of economics adapted to the specific features of the cultural sector.[6] Some useful work has been done in such fields, particularly as it has helped to inform policy. It has fed, for example, into the creation of UNESCO's Culture for Development Indicators Toolbox, which was developed between 2009 and 2013 within the framework of the implementation of the Convention, and with the financial support of the Spanish Agency for International Development Cooperation, to provide evidence-based indicators to policymakers in low and middle income countries who are increasingly tasked with strengthening statistics and monitoring systems related to culture and sustainable development.[7]

As with the legal analyses that we considered above, however, work undertaken in fields such as cultural economics tend to neglect the ways in which "culture" comes to be defined and delimited as a particular sector or domain of intervention and regulatory concern in the first place. This neglect is much more than simply an intellectual or conceptual problem. In the case of the debate over trade and culture it is worth stopping to reflect on how it is that certain sectors have come to be proposed as legitimate areas for exceptional treatment within the context of trade negotiation and regulation. Taken to a logical conclusion, once categories such as "creativity" or "values, identities and meanings" are asserted as criteria for such exceptional treatment and policy intervention, every possible economic sector or domain of human activity could potentially be implicated. This is why it was stressed by a host of groups involved in the Convention's drafting process – from legal experts, intergovernmental and developmental organisations such as the WTO, WIPO and UNCTAD, to representatives of states both opposed and in support of the Convention – that there needs to be a pragmatic use of the concept of culture in order to "keep a lid" on a potentially unlimited number of disputes and to prevent the system of international trade from unravelling completely (Shin-yi, 2009: 661–662).

This is not so straightforward, however, because how such boundaries between "the cultural" and the "non-cultural" (or "merely economic") are determined is a deeply contentious issue, particularly once it becomes a factor in determining how certain sectors should be treated in international trade regulation and negotiations. In this context, such boundaries have the potential to impact significantly on competing claims to material distribution, employment, subsidies and other forms of protection, or to determine entitlements to development assistance and international market access. There has been a keen debate, involving a range of lawyers, policymakers and stakeholders, regarding whether digital and online games, for example, should be classified as cultural: in the context of EU law the answer to this question has implications for whether state aid to the sector is legitimate; in the realm of international law and trade negotiations it may determine, among other things, whether digital games must be classified in a subsector of GATS where governments have accepted commitments to liberalise trade (Beat Graber, 2009).

This is only the thin edge of the wedge however. Although the Convention itself largely shied away from providing narrow and exact definitions (see Chapter 1), the audiovisual, music and publications sectors have been prioritised to such an extent in the creation of the Convention and the debates over its implementation (based on the claim that they are the international transmitters *par excellence* of "values, identities and meanings") that these debates have tended to reflect the concerns and priorities of a relatively small group of countries with particular stakes in these sectors. Contrary to similar disputes over the implications of trade liberalisation for issues such as food security, international inequality, the environment or human rights, for example, the dispute over trade and culture has not run so clearly along the developing–developed country divide, but instead has been largely a preoccupation between the industrialised countries (De Witte, 2001). From the early stages of the Franco-Canadian campaign for cultural diversity and the start of the drafting process at UNESCO, one of the problems in creating a binding international treaty has been how to generate enough political support amongst the majority of countries at UNESCO that had previously looked upon the disputes over the cultural exception at the WTO as "little more than transatlantic rivalry" and "a war of images among the well-to-do" (Musitelli, 2006: 2; UNESCO, 2003: Appendix 4; UNESCO, 2004).

In raising this point we should also note that this bias in the way that the trade and culture debate has been framed does not necessarily mean that the Convention cannot be used to advance claims in categories and sectors other than those that have been prioritised by the more powerful countries in the debate. In Bolivia for example, where the new constitution (2009) of the country's first Indigenous government since the Spanish conquest has recognised the coca leaf as a symbol of "cultural heritage, a natural and renewable resource of biodiversity in Bolivia and a factor of social cohesion", President Evo Morales supported the Convention and cited its provisions at the United Nations to make a case for recognising the legitimacy of the cultivation and use of the leaf amongst the Indigenous Andean and mestizo populations of Bolivia as well as those across Peru, Ecuador, Colombia, and northern Argentina and Chile (Morales, 2009). Despite its continued categorisation as a Schedule 1 narcotic under the UN Single Convention on Narcotic Drugs, and the criminalisation of its cultivation and trade by the US and Europe, the Convention has provided some recourse for articulating its legitimacy as a source of cultural identity and as a valuable resource for commercial exploitation and export (in what is one of the poorest countries in the region), with plans underway in Bolivia for its industrialisation and branding into a range of potentially lucrative commodities such as shampoos, creams, altitude sickness pills, tea bags, food flavourings, liqueurs and soft drinks. In 2013, Morales also secured recognition from the UN of the legitimacy of the use of coca for traditional practices within Bolivia's borders, against the opposition of 15 countries led by the US and UK (*Merco-Press*, 2013).

However, such uses of the Convention are likely to remain relatively isolated cases and ultimately are not backed up with the kind of internationally authoritative norms or political support that is needed for them to have significant impact. Coombe (2005) has made the point that while more powerful states and interests in Europe have been able to overcome opposition to the US in a bid to gain recognition at the WTO for legal concepts recognising particular "cultural" qualities within certain agricultural products (such as wine and cheese), less powerful states and interests have generally struggled to have similar forms of recognition extended to other agricultural products on the basis that they are expressions of a distinctive way of life (such as rice, tea, sugar, coffee, potatoes, as well as pharmaceutical and other products derived from agricultural inputs).

In this context, countries and populations reliant upon agricultural production and exports have increasingly drawn attention to the fact that intellectual property laws protect Europe's privileged forms of agriculture but few if any of their own particular crops and products. As a result, they have actively sought the extension of such laws against firm opposition from developed countries such as the US, Canada, Australia, Japan and the EU (the EU has maintained that such protections should be reserved only for particular products – such as, unsurprisingly, those that are produced exclusively in particular regions of Europe) (Coombe, 2005: 46). The Mexican government's bid, which was an exception to this, to have protection extended to tequila was successful only because it fell within the category of alcoholic beverages that have already been recognised, while local distinctions amongst agave plants were relatively easily elaborated in cultural terms (Coombe, 2005: 46). To refer again to the example of the coca growers' bids in Bolivia to legalise the cultivation and exploitation of the coca leaf, it is reported that diplomats view as "extremely remote" the possibility of a global consensus on changing the international blacklist of substances, while the response of EU officials to Morales's cultural arguments has been to complain, in a dismissive and patronising tone, that "[t]he debate over coca has not been very rational" (cited in *Reuters*, 2006). As we will explore in Chapter 5, other instruments aimed at providing more effective legal resources for such campaigns (such as the UN Declaration on the Rights of Indigenous Peoples), have received comparatively little of the kind of political investment and support from the more powerful states that would be necessary to elevate a set of "cultural" provisions to the level where, like those of the cultural diversity Convention, they are discussed and evaluated for their potential impact on proceedings at the WTO.

A broader objection to the focus of the commentary that has surrounded the Convention can be raised by considering the criticisms made by anthropologists such as Albro (2005). He notes that as the conflicts and debates over trade and culture framed the primary concerns of the Convention, there emerged no stable subject or referent for diversity outside the legislative and policy arenas of market regulation. This has meant that, despite its apparently open-ended language, the Convention in fact left little opportunity for the articulation of identities that do not fit into a notion of cultural diversity borne from a particular set of regulatory and commercial concerns with the cultural industries. Thus Albro notes in particular that longer standing debates at UNESCO over culture's place in international frameworks of rights and recognition have, with the passage of the Convention, become blurred with debates over the appropriate regulatory regime for the cultural marketplace:

> [D]ebates over the diversity Convention were not so much about the relationship of culture to the marketplace, or the relevance of culture outside the marketplace, as about what the rules of the cultural marketplace should be.... The diversity of voices that might advance claims turning on the recognition of cultural differences within or between states, or outside any obvious market calculus altogether, are largely marginalized.
>
> (Albro, 2005: 252)

In light of such observations, it is perhaps surprising that many of the more critical accounts to be found in the literature on trade and culture have assumed that the Convention's recognition of the "extra-economic" value of cultural goods, services or activities represents a challenge to contemporary forms of "instrumentality" or "commodification" in cultural policy. Such accounts are misleading not only in their interpretation of the Convention but also in their tendency to fall back on an unproblematised concept of culture that sets it apart in its essence from the realm of commerce and administration. We can draw this point out by considering accounts of cultural policy in the UK, which has been an incubator for the discourses of the knowledge economy and the cultural and creative industries that have now become so prominent internationally. A number of critiques have been directed at the kinds of approaches that have been taken towards culture and the arts since the late 1970s and early 1980s and, more recently, by the Department of Culture, Media and Sport (for examples of such critiques see Galloway and Dunlop, 2007; Gray, 2007). In their critique of contemporary British cultural policy Galloway and Dunlop (2007: 28–29) argue, for example, that to place cultural activities within the framework of the knowledge economy and the creative industries is "to lose sight of the distinctive public good contribution of culture" and to "subsume it [culture] within an economic agenda to which it is ill-suited". They therefore call for alternative frameworks of cultural regulation in order to steer away from what they see as a colonisation of culture by an instrumental and commercial rationality. The Convention is invoked in this scenario as offering a direct challenge to the kind of instrumental discourses of the creative industries promoted by the UK. As Dunlop and Galloway go on to argue for example:

> The UK's "knowledge economy" approach contrasts strongly with the definitions of cultural goods and services and of cultural industries proposed by UNESCO [in the Convention]. These combine the concepts of creativity and intellectual property with a strong emphasis on the importance of symbolic meaning, which means that they (cultural goods) "embody or convey cultural expressions, irrespective of the commercial value they may have".
>
> (Galloway and Dunlop, 2007: 28)

A number of neo-Marxist and other critics have argued in a similar vein that the contemporary worldwide extension of frameworks of private property to the public or common domain of intellectual and immaterial production amounts to a "fetter" on human development. This is argued to be a consequence of the process by which intellectual property today "commodifies and instrumentalises the cultural outputs with which it is concerned" and "facilitates a form of cultural domination by private interests" (see, for example, Macmillan, 2008: 169–173; Hardt, 2009; Albert, 2000). In such accounts, the contemporary momentum of privatisation and commodification, and agreements pertaining to intellectual property (notably, TRIPS), require that progressive criticism and activism focus on resisting this contemporary enclosure of common life.[8] For Macmillan, the Convention has therefore emerged as a similar point of reference to that used by Galloway and Dunlop above: by asserting the extra-economic value of culture in trade and development and enshrining the importance of "access to power" and "the right to participate in the cultural life of the community", it has offered an antidote – however weak its standing in international law – to the contemporary extension of intellectual property and the ongoing privatisation of public life (Macmillan, 2008: 173).

The problem with such accounts, however, is a tendency to fall back on unproblematised notions of culture's prior autonomy from administration and commodification. Again, this is more than simply a conceptual and epistemological question since it has implications precisely in terms of how critical analysis situates culture in contemporary capitalism. Of course, we might note that to invoke culture's "distinctive public good contribution" in the way that Galloway and Dunlop do above is to make a nonsense of their charge of instrumentality because such arguments imply that culture has equally instrumental functions (intellectual and democratic contestation and vitality, civic formation and uplift, creative diversity and productivity, and so on). As Bennett (1998) and others have argued, and as we will examine in more detail below, it can be disingenuous for critique to rely on a separation of culture and administration in this way, since a recognition of culture's imbrication with government and its constitution as a field of regulatory action and reform is precisely the condition for effective analysis and political intervention. More fundamentally, it is a mistake to see the Convention as articulating an alternative framework of development to that which has been offered by neoliberal globalisation and its related prescriptions of marketisation and intellectual property: as we will also examine in more detail over the course of the following chapters, the Convention is set more squarely within the discursive and ideological parameters of neoliberal development than has generally been asserted by its supporters and assumed in analysis.

In summary, the accounts of the contemporary debates concerning trade and culture that we have considered here have tended to preclude an investigation into some of the epistemological underpinnings and normative implications of the framework that has been proposed by the Convention. Indeed we might argue they have clouded the ways in which recent attempts to elevate the importance of "values, identities and meanings" are implicated in the strategies of contemporary "cultural" capitalism. There are, however, a number of other accounts that are useful to consider which, while not addressing the Convention or the debate over trade and culture directly, can be used to establish some broader theoretical background and to develop in more depth some of the questions that are at stake in approaching the new framework of cultural policy and cultural development.

Culture and administration

It has become a commonplace that recent decades have been characterised by an intensified politicisation of identity and difference: socially and politically oriented theories have made use of terms such as "identity politics" and the "politics of recognition" (Bauman, 2004; Taylor, 1992), or even spoken in terms of a paradigm shift in the terms of political contestation, from "redistribution to recognition" (Fraser, 1997; Fraser and Honneth, 2003). As a range of formerly marginalised groups have had some success in mobilising and gaining improved political recognition, we have also seen the development of a number of policies of multiculturalism and models of cultural citizenship in different national contexts, as well as a growing international authority behind notions of "cultural rights" (Cowan *et al.*, 2001). The work of figures such as Will Kymlicka (Kymlicka, 1995; 2013) or Charles Taylor (Taylor, 1992) on reconciling group and cultural rights with liberal political theory have provided important intellectual reference points in this period – with parallel efforts at organisations such as the UN and UNESCO to elevate the place of culture in the frameworks of trade liberalisation, development, democratisation and human rights.

Discussions concerning the ascendancy of cultural and identity politics often draw upon the concept of culture as a "way of life" that has been established through the intellectual traditions of structuralism and social anthropology – as in the classic examples set by Edward Burnett Tylor or Franz Boas (discussed, for example, in Bennett (1998: 87–88); also see Chapter 1). In such ways culture has come to be used as a shorthand to demark distinct systems or structures of beliefs, practices, signification and meaning that have an autonomous logic or coherence of their own. This has been an important motif in campaigns for the recognition of the claims of a range of social groups in the contemporary period: as we saw in Chapter 1, for example, it was a key theme within the calls for a New World Information and Communication Order (NWICO) at UNESCO in the 1970s and 1980s, with the Mexico Declaration of MONDIACULT notably proclaiming that "in its widest sense, culture may now be said to be the whole complex of distinctive spiritual, material, intellectual and emotional features that characterize a society or social group" (UNESCO, 1982). Such deployments of culture in theory and practice have undoubtedly had progressive effects – not least in challenging some of the implications of the more explicitly value-laden (eurocentric/bourgeois/elitist/patriarchal) conceptions of culture. However, there are a number of important points that need to be drawn out in making such observations.

The politics of cultural claims

Seyla Benhabib's *The Claims of Culture* (Benhabib, 2002) develops one line of criticism of contemporary identity politics, referring explicitly to the work of Kymlicka and Taylor as part of her identification of the reductionist sociology of culture which she argues underlies much contemporary work in legal and political philosophy and analysis, and which we see in practice today across a wide spectrum of politics and policy, academia, law, civil society and the media.[9] Benhabib argues that what tends to characterise this culturalist discourse is a mixture of the anthropological view of the democratic equality of all cultural forms or expression and a Romantic, Herderian emphasis on each form's irreducible uniqueness or essence. Whether from conservative or progressive agendas, there is a tendency to assume that groups "have" some kind of culture with distinctive qualities, traits or expressions of their genius or identity and which anchors individuals in webs of meaning, ideas and values – with a correlative set of assertions that political communities are to be strengthened and realised by preserving and propagating such cultures and cultural differences.

However, Benhabib argues that this is not only an essentialising view – and one which usually rests on the flawed assumption that clear boundaries can be drawn around particular cultures or ways of life – but also one which privileges an external perspective of coherence, more often than not one which reinforces the status of particular elites, ethnicities, classes or genders that position themselves as guardians of particular regions, nations or communities.[10] Chetan Bhatt (2006: 104) has argued along similar lines, pointing out that the result of this political concern for cultural recognition tends to be a reinforcement of the positions and values of designated leaders of culturally defined groups – who are also invariably the least progressive, undemocratic and stern representatives of whichever group is under the policy gaze.

In such ways, it is argued that the discourses of cultural identity and recognition can have the consequence (often unintended) of legitimating existing forms of subordination by bolstering the positions of dominant national/regional/local bureaucracies, regions, classes, ethnicities or genders (to Benhabib's critique here we could also add the role that invocations of cultural difference have played in legitimising forms of "ethnodevelopment" and racial segregation – as they did under South African apartheid for example). The target of critiques such as Benhabib's is therefore more than just the faulty epistemological premises of the contemporary discourses of cultural identity – it is also their "grave normative and political consequences for how we think injustices among groups should be redressed and how we think human diversity and pluralism should be furthered" (Benhabib, 2002: 60).

It may be that Benhabib's critique here neglects the potential for what Gayatri Spivak termed "strategic essentialism" – in other words, the way that collective identities such as culture or ethnicity may be used as a front behind which subaltern groups are able to temporarily advance more effective claims for rights, political inclusion, access to territory and resources, and so on (also see Young, 2002: 82–91). A related point is that, in contexts where colonial and contemporary strategies of indirect rule or governing through designated "communities" have engendered models of citizenship and socio-economic entitlement based on ethnic, religious or cultural categories, it can be misplaced to put so much emphasis on the kind of critique which Benhabib seeks to advance. As Mamdani (2001) notes, for example, in his discussion of postcolonial citizenship in East Africa, given the ways in which colonial authority sought to politicise ethnicity as a mode of entitlement it should come as no surprise that a land-poor peasant sees the struggle for land as also a struggle for ethnic belonging. Without attention to the administrative and legal contexts in which cultural and ethnic identities and categories are deployed – and contested – the effect of the critique of the concept of culture can itself often turn into a depoliticising and decontextualising approach to contemporary struggles and conflicts, in which a fetishised analytical-methodological focus on (the deconstruction of) cultural identity merely reproduces a privileged gaze and too readily dismisses culture's increasing protagonism as a call to political action (also see, for example, Chakrabarty (1998); Barsh (1999) or Coombe (2003)). Indeed

Žižek (1997; 2013) has argued that such a focus tends to naturalise and dehistoricise contemporary narratives of cultural superiority, in which a conveniently "decentred", enlightened and tolerant liberal identity is defined against the "essentialist" and "fundamentalist" identities of those who find themselves on the outsides of hegemonic narratives of global diversity, integration and inclusion.

In light of the above points raised by critics such as Benhabib, Spivak or Žižek there are a series of points that we might raise for one potential line of scrutiny of the recent instruments that have been adopted at UNESCO: to what extent might they in fact give new and renewed sources of legitimacy to exclusionary and neo-imperial forms of culturalist discourse, and to what extent do they give extra force to the kinds of cultural tectonics and topologies (real or imagined, or both) that have come to appear so threatening to world security today – whether deployed by, just to refer to the typical high profile examples, prominent foreign policy makers and analysts (as we have experienced in the post-Cold War analyses of Samuel Huntingdon, Francis Fukuyama, Robert Kagan, Robert Cooper, and so on), cultural racisms targeted at the non-liberal Other (as with the recent international concerns regarding Islam) or religious or ethnic hatred (groups such as the Taliban, Boko Haram, Hindutva), and so on? For critics such as Eriksen (2001) or Appiah (2006) for example, UNESCO is guilty in this respect, because it tends to support a concept of cultural diversity that fails to recognise culture's dynamism and fluidity and therefore opens the way for cultural content to be manipulated and controlled by those in positions of power and authority.[11]

In fact, UNESCO's recent position in these regards has become more ambiguous than critics such as Eriksen or Appiah suggest. First, we should recall that the Convention's primary concern is, in fact, how to situate cultural goods and services within market regulation, rather than with the protection of particular customs, social practices or ways of life. This is a point that is missed in such criticisms of the Convention, many of which begin with a face-value reading of the text and the claims of its supporters. In this respect at least, analysts working within the framework of the trade and culture debate are correct when they point out that, precisely by focusing the instrument on questions of the protection and promotion of tangible cultural expressions within the framework of market regulation, the framers of the text have limited the danger that it could be used to justify the cultural practices of certain social groups as violations of international human rights standards (Beat Graber, 2008: 144–145).

Second, we should note that the organisation's work over the last decade has been marked by efforts to reject the kinds of bounded, static models of culture that have dominated its work in the past. As Koïchiro Matsuura asserted time and again during his time as Director-General between 1999 and 2009: "UNESCO believes that cultures are not monolithic but interdependent, resulting from mutual exchanges and borrowings" (Matsuura, 2009); "each individual must acknowledge not only otherness in all its forms but also the plurality of his or her own identity, within societies that are themselves plural" (UNESCO,

2001: President's Foreword). Indeed the organisation today promotes a set of principles – hybridity, interculturality, complexity, and so on – that often form part of the conceptual armoury of many of the critiques that we considered above.[12]

To illustrate this very briefly here it is only necessary to consider a few provisions of the Convention. Article 1, for example, refers to the text's objective "to create the conditions for cultures to flourish and to freely interact in a mutually beneficial manner" and "to foster interculturality in order to develop cultural interaction" (UNESCO, 2005a). There was a similar concern running throughout the drafting of the Convention regarding the need to prohibit any invocation of cultural diversity that advances a protective, monolithic or "pure" version of culture in order to justify the intolerance, exclusion or oppression of others: Article 2, for example, takes care to set out the "Principle of respect for human rights and fundamental freedoms", stating that "no one may invoke the provisions of this Convention in order to infringe human rights and fundamental freedoms as enshrined in the Universal Declaration of Human Rights or guaranteed by international law, or to limit the scope thereof" (UNESCO, 2005a). Neither can UNESCO's position on questions of geopolitical conflict and imperial order be subjected so readily to the kind of criticisms that have been directed with such effect at the crude models of "clashes of civilisations" or orientalist orderings such as West and East. UNESCO is an intergovernmental organisation with a mandate to breach such divides and it generally tries to distance itself from them, particularly in the contemporary context of globalisation (however untenable or ideological this position of global neutrality may appear in practice). The meeting of the General Conference which immediately preceded the adoption of the Universal Declaration on Cultural Diversity in November 2001, for example, was permeated with anxiety about the apparent emergence of a new West–East conflict (coming soon after the attacks of 9/11 and the unleashing of the "war on terror"), and the Declaration's adoption was welcomed by UNESCO as an occasion "for States to reaffirm their conviction that intercultural dialogue is the best guarantee of peace and to reject outright the theory of the inevitable clash of civilizations" (UNESCO, 2001: President's Foreword). We will return to these discussions about the normative thrust of the contemporary valorisation of cultural diversity in more detail below, and over the following chapters we will look more closely and critically at the way such principles have been reflected (or not) in the recent work that has come out of the new instruments adopted at UNESCO.

Culture and neoliberal government

For now, however, I want to bring a longer perspective to the discussion and to re-centre on the debates concerning the place of culture within the realms of trade, the market and policy – for this is the key contribution of UNESCO's recent work and the focus of the Convention's core provisions. They are also, of course, questions which have long been under scrutiny in critical theory, notably through the Frankfurt School tradition established by Adorno and Horkheimer earlier in the twentieth century. We will briefly revisit this line of criticism here as a way of further contextualising the contemporary concern for cultural diversity and then situating it within the more nuanced accounts of the relationship between culture and governmentality that have been developed by more recent work in the field of cultural studies.

For Adorno and Horkheimer, the growth of "mass culture" and "the culture industries" in the twentieth century raised the spectres of the standardisation, commodification and degradation of cultural forms and content, along with their potential for aesthetic and moral transcendence in the face of industrial society's ambition of total administration. In his 1960 essay "Culture and Administration", Adorno argued that the tension between culture and administration called for a careful balancing act on the part of cultural experts: on one hand, practices such as painting, literature, theatre and music offered the hope of reaching for a level of freedom and human realisation beyond the parameters set by "mere administration" and "the control of the market" (since, for Adorno, bureaucracy and democracy tend to institutionalise, popularise, or even "serve barbarism"), while the market and dominance of the cultural industries "today unhesitatingly mutilate culture" (Adorno, 2001: 129). On the other hand, however, and despite the prevalence of conceptions which locate the essence of culture in a heroic autonomy from administration (as "the manifestation of pure humanity without regard for its functional relationships within society"; Adorno, 2001: 108), Adorno reflected on the fact that the very concept of culture cannot be disentangled from social management – and, for him, neither should it be: it is precisely the duty of what he saw as "men of insight", "aesthetic personalities" and other experts in cultural criticism, to "uphold the interest of the public against the public itself", to "open perspectives for the protection of cultural matters from the control of the market", and so on (Adorno, 2001: 129–130).[13]

What is most pertinent to the discussion here is how such an understanding of culture has come to be associated with a particular, privileged modern episteme over the second half of the twentieth century. In cultural theory this is a development that has been analysed particularly effectively by Bennett (1998), who has noted, in reference to Adorno, that such positions have largely become untenable in a contemporary context where culture has been relativised in policy procedures and academic debate: we have seen a widespread extension of the ambit of cultural policy in "authorising a democratic expansion of the fields of activity that can be brought within its compass" (Bennett, 1998: 91).

This point is most clearly demonstrated in Bennett's discussion of the development of cultural policy in Britain. This is traced from nineteenth century equations of culture with the high arts and carrying certain values of civilisation (colonial, masculine, bourgeois) juxtaposed to anarchy (as in the paradigmatic work of Matthew Arnold, for whom culture entailed "a conscious striving towards progress or perfection"), to more contemporary attempts to detach the administration of culture from the elitist-universalist biases of such positions and towards the more anthropological conception of culture as it has been expanded to recognise the value of a wider range of social practices and ways of life. Bennett also draws parallels in the field of cultural studies, noting Raymond Williams's attempt to draw out the concept of culture from the "monopolistic clutch of the likes of Arnold ... and so redefining it that it could serve as the basis for a new intellectual and political project" (Bennett, 1998: 87–106; 2003).

To develop this point it also worth considering that neoliberal policy has taken aim precisely at the ambitions of a standardised, mass society that provided the target of critical theory for much of the twentieth century. As Foucault (2008), for example, sought to emphasise in his analyses of neoliberalism that make up the lecture series The Birth of Biopolitics, neoliberalism is driven less by the objective of a society of standardisation (one which is orientated towards the commodity and the uniformity of the commodity, as criticised by theorists such as Adorno or others such as Werner Sombart) but, more fundamentally, by the objective of a society that is oriented towards the *multiplication and differentiation of the enterprise form*, seeking to universalise the enterprise, private property and the market as models of social relations and of existence itself (Foucault, 2008: 145–149). Indeed, it is this multiplicity of diverse enterprises which for neoliberal government provides the opportunity for the reconstruction of a set of "warm" moral and cultural values which are presented as antithetical to the "cold" economic mechanisms of the market and the totalising and homogenising ambitions of the modern state (and which, for all neoliberalism's talk of "rolling back the state", have necessitated a proliferation of juridical mechanisms and policy interventions throughout the social body) (Foucault, 2008: 240–243).

The point here is not to recapitulate debates about Adorno's elitism, nor to revise accounts of the culture industry for the global or post-Fordist era (see, for example, Lash and Lury, 2007),[14] but rather to demonstrate a broader point regarding the ways in which the more democratic and decentralised principles and criteria of access, distribution and entitlement that Adorno among others feared have largely replaced the kinds of privileged frameworks of cultural reform that characterised much of the modern period (Bennett, 1998: 199; 2003). In this scenario, Adorno's fears over the culture industry appear not only as an anachronism but they stand in the way of a progressive and politically engaged form of cultural studies:

It is precisely because we can now, without regret, treat culture as an industry and, in so doing, recognise that the aesthetic disposition forms merely a particular market segment within that industry, that it is a particular form of life like any other, that it is possible for questions of cultural policy to be posed, and pursued, in ways which allow competing patterns of expenditure, forms of administration and support to be debated and assessed in terms of their consequences for different publics, their relation to competing political values, and their implication for particular policy objectives

– and all without lacerating ourselves as lonely subjects caught in the grip of the contradictory pincer of culture and administration.

(Bennett, 1998: 199–200)

The arguments that have been advanced by Bennett have at least two important contributions here. First, they demonstrate that the "anthropological" expansion in the way that culture has been conceptualised in frameworks of policy such as those we have seen at UNESCO is not without its own normative implications and effects – precisely because it has also enlarged the range of activities which are brought into the field of governmental concern and which, as such, can become subjects of politicisation and programmes of reform (Bennett, 1998: 101–106). Indeed, Bennett argues that over recent decades we have seen an increasingly blurred division between the second and third senses of culture that we saw outlined earlier by Raymond Williams (as a way of demarking a "particular way of life, whether of a people, a period, a group, or humanity in general", and as "the independent and abstract noun which describes the works and practices of intellectual and especially artistic activity"; see Chapter 1). This has happened as the relations between commercially produced forms of mass culture and the field of everyday conduct and ways of life have, from a governmental perspective, displaced the significance of the kind of aesthetically-grounded, elitist programmes of cultural reform that have been the legacy of late nineteenth and early twentieth century cultural policies (Bennett, 2003).

A second important implication of Bennett's argument here is to note the ways in which mutations in the meanings and roles ascribed to culture can be understood alongside shifts in the ways that varied governmental aims and programmes seek to define and operationalise culture in order to bring it into a productive relationship with particular social objectives. From an analytical perspective it therefore makes sense to investigate culture's formation as:

[A] distinctive set of knowledges, expertise, techniques, and apparatuses which – through the roles they play as technologies of sign systems connected to technologies of power and working through the mechanisms of technologies of the self – act on, and are aligned in relation to, the social in distinctive ways.

(Bennett, 2003: 59–60)

It is in this concern for the ways in which the governmental or administrative realm of culture comes to be organised and functions as a distinctive body of reforming rationalities and technologies that Bennett distances himself from the kinds of analyses found in the body of governmentality literature (as in the work of Nikolas Rose or Mitchell Dean, for example) or the neo-Gramscian body of cultural studies (for example, Stuart Hall) which have tended to theorise culture as an "amorphous domain" of norms, beliefs, attitudes and values (Bennett, 2003: 55–56). Rather, the focus of analysis is trained within culture's particular discursive and institutional domains – the civic "contact zones" of museums, galleries, media, and so on – and on seeking to make explicit their particular normative dispositions and effects within historically shifting tasks of social reform. Moreover, Bennett argues that it is precisely such attempts to recognise the boundaries of this "distinctive set" and acknowledge its strategic imbrication with the realms of policy and administration which is a necessary condition for effective intervention on the part of cultural theory (Bennett, 1998, 2007b).

It is this broad approach which informs Bennett's account of the contemporary concern for cultural diversity which, agreeing with a range of theorists in the 1990s, he recognised was becoming "the primary cultural challenge of our time" (Bennett, 1998: 102). It is often assumed that the contemporary political elevation of cultural diversity is characterised by a normative relativism or neutrality: for Zygmunt Bauman, for example, it is one which does not involve the kind of legislative and reforming impulses that characterised the universalising projects of modernity, in which cultural difference was conceived less as something to be achieved or reconciled than as something to be reformed or legislated out of existence (reflected in the tendency to single out those ways of life which placed obstacles in the paths of modernity as immature, backward, deviant, primitive, vulgar, and so on) (Bennett, 1998: 102–103). However, Bennett demonstrates more clearly than most that the contemporary concern to promote forms of mutual understanding and tolerance between cultures cannot be a simply "interpretative" or neutral matter: it requires a particular reforming and legislative orientation to culture that can secure the institutional spaces and organisational frameworks within which the mutual interpretation of cultures can take place, while providing a normative framework or gradient in which certain ways of life are to be assigned a reforming role while others are to be targeted as objects of reform (Bennett, 1998: 103–105; 2007a).

It is in this vein that Bennett (1998: 105–106) refers to the UN/UNESCO established World Commission on Culture and Development and its 1995 report *Our Creative Diversity* which, as we will see in later chapters, was an important early landmark in the campaign for the Convention. Among its recommendations, this report reiterated the call for an expansion of cultural policy from a narrow focus on the high arts to a more inclusive concern for cultural diversity and exchange, while urging the condemnation and prohibition of "intolerant, exclusive, exploitative, cruel and repressive" ways of life that stand in the way of the projects of global integration and development, according to what the report referred to as a "new global ethics" and a set of "absolute standards of judging what is right, good and true" (Bennett, 1998: 105–106; UNESCO, 1995).

Bennett presents an insightful analysis on the connections between contemporary governmentality, the expansion of the concept of culture and the contemporary concern for cultural diversity, but it is an account which pays only limited attention to developments happening at the international level and in particular to the kinds of controversies over globalisation, trade and culture that caught fire in the 1990s and in which the recent instruments at

UNESCO have been forged. We should also note here that independent reports commissioned by UNESCO such as *Our Creative Diversity* are rarely indicative of internationally authoritative norms regarding culture or cultural policy. Governments and policy practitioners around the world generally found its conclusions and recommendations too radical and far-reaching for it to have much practical impact (UNESCO Member States rejected most of the report's findings and its recommendations were not adopted; Donders, 2008: 10–11). Moreover, an examination of the ways in which particular aspects of the report were discarded, altered or emphasised by the subsequent campaign for cultural diversity at UNESCO is in itself useful for developing a more grounded and politically engaged analysis of the contemporary discourses of cultural diversity that are circulating internationally today. We will examine these points in more detail in Chapters 3 and 4.

To continue the theoretical discussion here, we might briefly turn to consider a critique of the approach that has been taken within the Foucauldian influenced cultural-policy studies literature more broadly:

> The implicit privilege accorded to disciplinary understandings of power in the cultural-policy studies literature needs to be displaced, because it provides a far too coherent image of governmental practices seemingly constructing subjects. In turn, it supports an over-optimistic image of the extent to which "policy" can serve as a practicable entry-point for the transformation of conduct.
>
> (Barnett, 1999: 389)

Barnett refers, in particular, to two broad "contemporary transformations" in making this claim. First of all, referring to the Deleuzian claim about the shift from disciplinary to control societies, it is argued that it is becoming fruitless to analyse cultural regulation as if it is something that occurs within discrete disciplinary spaces of enclosure: the governmental rationalities and technologies of contemporary capitalism and the reach of contemporary networks of public mediation and communication (referring in particular to electronic media and communications) tend to work with a more diverse and dispersed assemblage of culture that recognises fewer clear boundaries between the roles performed in particular localities and institutions or by distinct ordering categories (cultural, economic, political, social, private, public). Second, Barnett argues that the historical role of culture in mediating the relationships between individual citizens and the state is now "in crisis" in the context of globalisation, as culture can no longer nor is asked to perform its traditional role for the nation state: "processes of global economic and political rescaling are literally relocating the sites of institutionalised decision-making over cultural practices to which transformative political projects need to be addressed" (Barnett, 1999: 390). In this way, it is argued, the assumption of a readily identifiable and coherent body of cultural institutions cultivating or reforming citizens and subjects, which underwrites the claims made on behalf of the embrace of policy as a vocation at the cost of criticism, is "open to considerable question not only on normative political grounds but also empirically" (Barnett, 1999: 390).

In light of the kind of measures that we see taking shape today, following the UNESCO Convention and the cultural turn in development more broadly, it would appear reasonable to posit that cultural policy in the present conjuncture is developing in engagement with the kind of developments identified by Barnett, and that analysis should be attentive to some of the implications and dynamics that may be flowing from this. However, in basing his arguments on such sweeping claims about historical transformation, Barnett perhaps misses a crucial methodological point: the critical strength and thrust of the method developed by Foucault lies precisely in tracing the way that political responses to shifting social phenomena are framed and formed, elaborating how such responses are the outcome of sets of historically contingent and contested political questions and problematisations. By drawing attention to these contingencies, analysis can denaturalise and re-politicise the apparently natural or non-political – a crucial task in politically engaged analysis (Foucault, 1984).

We might therefore suggest, contra Barnett, that rather than reproducing the authoritative account that policy and its domains are being melted down and reshaped as part of the "inevitable" or "irresistible" processes of contemporary globalisation, analysis should begin from the recognition that there have been fewer processes under greater political contestation in the recent period than those going under the term globalisation (despite the attempts that have been made in the neoliberal era to turn it into a historical imperative outside of political and ethical debate). In this sense contemporary globalisation is less a description of an empirical process against which we should measure the veracity of critical commentary or policy intervention, but rather a site in the ongoing problematisation (and reassertion) of the role of the state and its domains of authority, expertise and regulation. As du Gay (1999) or Larner and Walters (2004) have argued in this vein for example, globalisation is most critically approached in this sense as part of the strategic framework of neoliberal governmentality, deployed differently in different contexts and with varying implications as a *dispositif* that ontologises or, in other words, a body of rationalities and technologies that seek to conduct the conduct of states, enterprises and populations through the call to adapt and perform in the global marketplace ("be global!", "think globally!").

Taking such an approach allows us to examine the ways in which cultural policy and its traditional discursive domains (museums, education, galleries, media, and so on) are caught up with responses to globalisation not so much as a symptom of the "erosion" of the state but rather as part of the particular ways in which contemporary governmentality seeks reform in order for the state and individuals to become more competitive, more entrepreneurial, to embrace the "challenges" of market imperatives and opportunities, and so on. Indeed, in Part II I will argue that the emerging framework of cultural development centred on UNESCO is one which, despite the way in which it has been framed by supporters as a rejection of neoliberal globalisation, in fact seeks to intensify neoliberal processes of reform and competitive insertion into the global market. In the process, culture is losing some of its traditional features as a distinct set of knowledges, techniques and apparatuses, particularly as it becomes a central concern of trade negotiators and lawyers, copyright professionals and collection agencies, political economists and international development agencies, and others who seek to break the "monopolistic clutch" of modern cultural policy and its experts in order to more effectively mobilise and manage culture as a resource in international trade, investment and development.

To elaborate on this last point, I would like finally to turn to Yúdice's (2003) work, *The Expediency of Culture*. Yúdice understands the democratic or anthropological expansion of the concept of culture in similar terms to Bennett, noting the ways in which this development has been paralleled in culture's changing relation to government, and pointing out its imbrication with contemporary programmes of social management and administration. For Yúdice (2003: 24) this "anthropological turn" is consistent with what he refers to as "cultural power", or "the extension of biopower in the age of globalization":

> While governmentalisation continues to operate at the level of biopower … it is increasingly the case that cultural power is at work. Perhaps the prime instance of this is the permeation of society by a conventional anthropological definition of groups as defined by cultures, with the political corollary that democracy is to be understood as the recognition of these cultures.
>
> (Yúdice, 2003: 49)

For our purposes here there are at least two aspects of this account that can be brought out in more detail in order to develop some of the insights to be found in the work of Bennett. First, the ways that contemporary changes in the discourses of culture (including the concern for cultural diversity) have been related to the governmental projects associated with neoliberal globalisation, development and related transformations in "cultural" capitalism; and second, how thoroughly intertwined with the *economic* and the *political* – understood not as prior existing realities but in their shifting, governmental senses as technically distinct sectors or domains – the *cultural* has become as part of these processes. Yúdice is not alone in addressing these developments, but he has perhaps gone furthest in elaborating them with theoretical form and, despite the weaknesses of his thesis (which we will consider below), offers greater critical purchase than the kinds of analyses that we considered in the earlier part of this chapter.

The essence of Yúdice's argument is that the neoliberal period has ushered in a new epistemic conjuncture in which culture has increasingly become redefined and redeployed in policy, in an expedient way, as a resource. This is illustrated in reference to a number of developments: it has become a tool for resolving political conflicts or empowering communities in the context of contemporary liberal democracy and international development; it is increasingly conceptualised as something to be tapped into and managed as a key source of value in a capitalism which is increasingly characterised by the immaterial, creative and symbolic as motors of accumulation (expressed in particular by the contemporary importance attached to the enforcement of intellectual property law, or the rise of the content industries and service sectors); and – complementing the roles of human and social capital that have been added to the repertoire of political economy in the last decades – as something to be known, studied, managed and invested in as part of projects of economic competitiveness and development, socio-political and economic amelioration, urban regeneration, and so on.

The museum offers a useful point of reference here. According to Ole Scheeren, the architect at the centre of some of the most iconic international cultural exhibitions and constructions of recent years, the museum's primary role and operations in the context of neoliberal globalisation are being transformed along the lines suggested by Yúdice: its function as a "contact-zone" of national civic or public reform has become blurred with its ability to attract international arrivals, income and publicity; to generate local investment, regeneration and employment; and to safeguard (and, where possible, inflate) the value of its assets. It also involves a reorientation of the spatial organisation of the museum and the way subjects pass through and experience its objects (symbolised for Scheeren in the replacement of the ticket counter by the souvenir shop at the museum entrance) (Scheeren, 2004: 252–255). In Scheeren's words:

> Amid rising economic pressures and shrinking government subsidies, the museum ... has been subjected to market-driven privatization.... The nineties introduced increasing need to "perform", to compete on the basis of economic growth and an associated idea of size and "presence", concerns that had theretofore existed only on the periphery of the cultural sphere.
>
> (Scheeren, 2004: 252)

One of the broader implications of such developments for Yúdice is that culture's utility for power is being transformed: from being a medium for shaping ethical subjects of the nation, culture is being "'freed', so to speak, to become a generator of value in its own right" (Yúdice, 2003: 336). It is argued that the corollary of this transformation in what we understand by the notion of culture and what we do in its name has been the declining relevance and credibility of arguments invoking notions of culture for culture's sake, culture as transcendence or, to take the example of Adorno again, as the medium and process through which "the individual gains freedom by externalising himself" (in contrast to Adorno's philistine, who craves culture for what they can get out of it) (Yúdice, 2003: 10).

As we have seen, alignments between culture and administration are in themselves nothing new. However, Yúdice notes that the nature of this relation in the contemporary context of neoliberal globalisation and the proliferation of governmental and commercial rationalities and technologies that seek to mobilise culture in this way have combined to place a greater instrumental demand upon culture than at any other moment in the history of modernity.

Indeed, it has effectively left "the notion of culture as resource [as] the only surviving definition in contemporary practice" (Yúdice, 2003: 279) and, in the process, has "absorbed and cancelled out hitherto prevailing distinctions among high culture, anthropological, and mass cultural definitions" (Yúdice, 2003: 4). In this sense, it is claimed that the reciprocal permeation of the cultural with economic and political management that we see today goes beyond the kind of commodification or instrumentality that has typically been the target of critiques in the Frankfurt School tradition: it represents a more pervasive mode of cognition and political action in which there is little recognition or relevance for political projects that are pitched outside the episteme of culture as resource.

This last point is developed by Yúdice in particular by noting how the elevation of cultural identity has been simultaneous with neoliberal strategies of withdrawal from forms of social provision, reinforcing the shift to the values of market citizenship and the tendency towards greater material inequalities (Yúdice, 2003: 160–191).[15] In this context the discourse of cultural diversity has been an integral part of managing the social effects of trade liberalisation and economic restructuring, as it has emerged to offer forms of economic revival and political recognition to "people who are losing their jobs to 'developing' countries and to workers earning survival wages in those countries whose *value* is measured in terms of their cultural identity" (Yúdice, 2003: 251, emphasis in original). In this way the turn to cultural diversity as a mode of economic entitlement and political recognition has been subject to the criteria and prerogatives of national and international strategies of market reform. The implications of these developments are contained in the following passage:

> Most of their [NGOs, development agencies, other international organisations] cultural policies have been concentrated in the recognition of cultural differences, on the premise that such recognition will provide access to citizen participation. In other words, the work of these organisations has been limited to opening access to fora of interlocution ... without noticing that these fora have already been structured according to corporate arrangements and protocols, often with their collaboration.
>
> (Yúdice, 2003: 362)

Other work looking at the rise of new social movements in "post-neoliberal" Latin America since the 2000s has generated similar caution regarding the contemporary deployment of claims to cultural and Indigenous rights (for example, Hale, 2005; Stahler-Sholk *et al.*, 2014). Such work has demonstrated some of the ways in which apparently progressive measures related to the (limited) recognition of cultural rights, the strengthening of civil society, and the endorsement of the principle of intercultural equality, have in fact reinforced neoliberal objectives to shape and neutralise political opposition and, in particular, claims to control over the resources (such as land) necessary for those rights to be realised (Hale, 2005: 10–13). Such studies support Yúdice's argument that more critical work needs to be done to disentangle the "hitherto

difficult to understand imbrications of projects for social justice with a neoliber-
alized focus on diversity. Even the antiglobalisation movement has not given
this less visible conundrum its due" (2003: 284).

However, there are two limitations in Yúdice's account that I would like to
draw out here in addressing some of the issues raised earlier in relation to the
Convention and the debates over trade and culture. First, although Yúdice com-
piles some compelling case studies and analyses, they are not given the kind of
historical contextualisation that might substantiate the core of his thesis; they
do not, as Lobo (2004) has argued, count as convincing illustrations of how
culture as a resource gained legitimacy and displaced or absorbed other under-
standings of culture. This thesis remains in need of more detailed historical
exploration – particularly at the kind of international level that Yúdice makes
claims for. A related point is that if UNESCO is, as Yúdice (2003: 25, 251)
argues, the institution that has done most to bring about this transformation in
internationally authoritative definitions and roles of culture, its recent work
would appear to offer an obvious site for beginning such an investigation.
However, Yúdice barely scratched its surface in his analysis, and was writing
prior to the adoption of the Convention's standard setting provisions. Any analysis of UNESCO should also approach it in a way which recognises its nature
as an intergovernmental organisation: one that has not only been struggling for
relevance in recent decades but also one in which some are more able than
others to define the legitimate parameters of the organisation's programmes and
discursive frameworks. Given some of the political differences and commercial
conflicts that have emerged in the debates over the Convention regarding the
appropriate role of UNESCO in relation to other agencies and regulatory bodies
such as the WTO, analysis should clearly not accord too much coherence or
organisation to the international discourses of contemporary capitalism.

A second and related limitation, or at least an area that requires more careful
scrutiny, lies in Yúdice's claims that we have witnessed an "epochal" transformation. As Yúdice himself acknowledged in his conclusion (which he had put on
hold in the light of 9/11 and the subsequent bursting of the new economy
bubble of the 1990s) the kind of claims he had made were premised upon "a
reasonably stable world" which now seemed to be in flux, and he could only
speculate as to what extent they would remain valid in the coming years (see
Yúdice, 2003: 338–362). Nevertheless we might argue that, in light of the adoption of the Convention and the heightened political conflicts and debates that
we have considered in this chapter, the kind of commercial and governmental
investments in culture and cultural diversity that form the more modest observations in studies such as Yúdice's remain something to be reckoned with today.

Summary

In conclusion, we might raise a number of issues which have so far been absent
in approaching the recent work of UNESCO, and the cultural diversity Convention in particular. What normative implications and effects are generated by

this discourse of cultural development policy that has emerged over the last decade? To what extent does UNESCO's recent work represent a post-neoliberal challenge to the primacy of "market culture" in the way it has been framed by its supporters – or, to turn this question around, can UNESCO really be accused of being the institution most responsible for normalising a set of principles that are so central to the strategies of contemporary "cultural" capitalism and neoliberal governmentality? How do the difficulties and controversies over defining and operationalising culture in the Convention and fixing its place in international regulation reflect on Yúdice's claims regarding the emergence of culture as resource as "the only surviving definition in contemporary practice"? The developments of the last two decades, crystallised around the international conflicts over trade liberalisation and the Convention's adoption and implementation, present a rich seam of material through which we can begin to subject such questions to closer scrutiny.

Notes

1 For more detailed coverage, see Footer and Beat Graber (2000), Beat Graber *et al.* (2004); Bernier (2005), Harvey (2006), Voon (2007), Singh (2008), Bartsch (2014) or Richieri Hanania (2014).

2 Examples of such measures include the Canadian Radio-Television and Telecommunications Commission's quotas reserving air-time for Canadian televisual and musical productions; the European Union's Television Without Frontiers and Audiovisual Media Services Directives, through which broadcasters have been required to reserve a majority proportion of their transmission time for European works; Egypt's restrictions on the number of foreign produced films that can be distributed relative to domestic films (and the use of profits from the distribution of those foreign films to finance domestic production), and so on. For more detailed discussions of such measures see, for example, Beat Graber *et al.* (2004) or Voon (2007: 18–23).

3 For more detailed coverage of the "pro-culture" arguments see, for example, UNESCO (1999, 2005b), Bernier (2005) or Voon (2007).

4 The "cultural exception" has gained no legal status under EU law; instead, EU law has come to refer to the concept of "promotion of cultural diversity" (see European Commission, 2014: 4). This evolution from "cultural exception" to "cultural diversity" in the context of international trade is addressed in more detail in Chapter 5. On the evolution of the place of culture in the EU's external relations in particular, see Isar (2015).

5 For example see Beat Graber *et al.* (2004); Bernier (2005); Guerrieri *et al.* (2005); Beat Graber (2006); Hahn (2006); Harvey (2006); Voon (2006, 2007), Van den Bossche (2007); Nenova (2008, 2010); von Schorlemer and Stoll (2012); Richieri Hanania (2014).

6 Relevant notable examples of such work in cultural economics include Throsby (2000, 2008, 2010) and Klamer (2004), who have also both contributed to the recent debates at UNESCO and the World Bank. Also see Towse (2003, 2010).

7 For information on the Toolbox see https://en.unesco.org/creativity/cdis.

8 Albert (2000) writes, for example,

> the view of movements against the WTO should be that social, labor, ecology, cultural, and other concerns take precedence over profit-making everywhere.... The WTO has no rules to guard those who labor or to protect long-term development or to foster cultural sustainability or diversity.

9 Similar observations and lines of critique to those developed by Benhabib have been advanced by Mamdani (2002), Bayart (2005) or Bhatt (2006).

10 Benhabib thus asserts throughout her work that there can be "no single principle of societal culture": inasmuch as such entities can be identified, they are made up of myriad and conflicting narratives and symbolisations; they are multiple practices with a history or narrative of coherence which are "the sedimented repositories of struggles for power, symbolisation, and signification – in short, for cultural and political hegemony carried out among groups, classes, and genders" (Benhabib, 2002: 60).

11 Eriksen makes the critique from the perspective of poststructuralist anthropology, identifying in UNESCO's recent work an emphasis on the "relativist", "functionalist" and "structuralist" ontology of culture as comprising relatively static and bounded systems of traditions, values and expressions (as "islands in an archipelago"), at the expense of the "deconstructivist" and "poststructuralist" ontology of culture as dynamic processes of hybridisation, communication and contestation. Appiah's critique stems from a conventional liberal cosmopolitan position – arguing that the Convention, by taking *groups* rather than *individuals* as "the proper object of moral concern" – is aiming at the wrong target in its efforts to promote cultural diversity and tolerance.

12 It is worth stressing again here that UNESCO commissions reports from some of the world's leading anthropologists and sociologists, and draws on the contributions of staff who are often well-versed in contemporary social and cultural theory. Notable examples include the involvement of Claude Levi-Strauss in the organisation's work on racism in the 1950s and 1960s, and the work of the World Commission on Culture and Development in the 1990s (see Chapter 3). Prominent experts and intellectuals (such as Kwame Anthony Appiah, one of the critics of the Convention that was considered above) therefore in fact often appear as reference points in the organisation's recent work (see, for example, UNESCO, 2006: 10).

13 Adorno writes:

> Whoever speaks of culture speaks of administration as well, whether this is his intention or not. The combination of so many things lacking a common denominator – such as philosophy and religion, science and art, forms of conduct and mores – and finally the inclusion of the objective spirit of an age in the single word "culture" betrays from the outset the administrative view, the task of which, looking down from on high, is to assemble, distribute, evaluate and organise.
>
> (2001: 108)

14 In Lash and Lury's account of *Global Culture Industry*, the products and subjects of Adorno and Horkheimer's culture industry were "determinate" – in the double sense that they were determined by massifying, Fordist processes of production and that they determined their social subjects ("slotting subjects into the reproductive cycle of capitalism" – the nuclear family, the proper place of the home, and so on (Lash and Lury, 2007: 5). By contrast, they argue, the products and subjects of global culture industry are "indeterminate": production and consumption are processes of the post-Fordist and design intensive construction and marketing of *difference*, in an encounter with the "characteristically reflexive individuals of today's informational capitalism" (Lash and Lury, 2007: 5).

15 This is also a point which has been well developed by a number of authors; it is given special treatment in Fraser and Honneth (2003). Also see Hale (2005).

Bibliography

Adorno, T. 2001. "Culture and Administration". In Bernstein, J.M. (ed.). *The Culture Industry: Selected Essays on Mass Culture*. London: Routledge.

Albert, M. 2000. "WTO, World Bank, IMF and Activism: an interview with Michael Albert, January 2000". *Third World Traveler*. Available online at: www.thirdworldtraveler.com/WTO_MAI/Q%26A_WTO_IMF_Activism.html; accessed 20/03/2005.

Albro, R. 2005. "Managing culture at diversity's expense? Thoughts on UNESCO's newest cultural policy instrument". *The Journal of Arts Management, Law and Society.* 35(3).

Appiah, K.A. 2006. *Cosmopolitanism: Ethics in a World of Strangers*. New York: W.W. Norton & Co.

Barnett, C. 1999. "Culture, government and spatiality: Reassessing the 'Foucault effect' in cultural-policy studies". *International Journal of Cultural Studies*. 2(3): 369–397.

Barsh, R.L. 1999. "How Do You Patent a Landscape? The Perils of Dichotomizing Cultural and Intellectual Property". *International Journal of Cultural Property*. 8(1): 14–47.

Bartsch, M. 2014. "The return of the cultural exception and its impact on international agreements". *Global Media Journal*. 4(1), Spring/Summer 2014. Available online at: www.db-thueringen.de/servlets/DerivateServlet/Derivate-29860/GMJ7_Bartsch_final.pdf; accessed 12/07/2015.

Bauman, Z. 2004. *Identity: Conversations with Benedetto Vecchi*. Cambridge: Polity Press.

Bayart, J.F. 2005. *The Illusion of Cultural Identity*. London: Hurst & Company.

Beat Graber, C. 2006. "The New UNESCO Convention on Cultural Diversity: A Counterbalance to the WTO?" *Journal of International Economic Law*. 9(3): 553–574.

Beat Graber, C. 2008. "Substantive Rights and Obligations Under the UNESCO Convention on Cultural Diversity". In Schneider, H. and P. van den Bossche (eds). *Protection of Cultural Diversity from a European and International Perspective*. Oxford: Intersentia.

Beat Graber, C. 2009. "State Aid for Digital Games and Cultural Diversity: A Critical Reflection in the Light of EU and WTO Law". *NCCR Working Paper*. No. 2009/8 (March 2009).

Beat Graber, C., M. Girsberger and M. Nenova (eds) 2004. *Free Trade Versus Cultural Diversity: WTO Negotiations in the Field of Audiovisual Services*. Zurich: Schulthess.

Benhabib, S. 2002. *The Claims of Culture: Equality and Diversity in the Global Era*. NJ: Princeton University Press.

Bennett, T. 1998. *Culture: A Reformer's Science*. London: Sage.

Bennett, T. 2003. "Culture and Governmentality". In Bratitch, J.Z., J. Packer and C. McCarthy (eds). *Foucault, Cultural Studies and Governmentality*. Albany: State University of New York Press.

Bennett, T. 2007a. "Exhibition, Difference, and the Logic of Culture". In Karp, I., C.A. Kratz and L. Szwaja (eds). *Museum Frictions: Public Cultures/Global Transformations*. Durham, NC: Duke University Press.

Bennett, T. 2007b. "Making Culture, Changing Society". *Cultural Studies*. 21(4–5).

Bernier, I. 2003. "A comparative analysis of the Chile-US and Singapore-US Free Trade Agreements with particular reference to the cultural sector". *Media Trade Monitor*. Available online at: www.mediatrademonitor.org; accessed 05/04/2007.

Bernier, I. 2005. "Trade and Culture". In Macrory, P., A. Appleton; and A. Plummer (eds). *World Trade Organization: Legal, Economic and Political Analysis*. Springer Science and Business Media.

Bhatt, C. 2006. "The Fetish of the Margins: Religious Absolutism, Anti-Racism and Post-Colonial Silence". *New Formations*. 59: 98–115.

Bruner, C.M. 2008. "Culture, Sovereignty, and Hollywood: UNESCO and the Future of Trade in Cultural Products". *NYU Journal of International Law & Politics*. 40: 2.

Chakrabarty, D. 1998. "Modernity and Ethnicity in India". In Bennett, D. (ed.). *Multicultural States: Rethinking Difference and Identity*. London: Routledge.

Committee on Culture and Education. 2015. *Draft opinion of the Committee of Culture and Education for the Committee on International Trade on recommendations to the European Commission on the negotiations for the Transatlantic Trade and Investment Partnership (TTIP)*. European Parliament. 2014/2228(INI). Available online at: www.ttip 2015.eu/files/content/docs/Full%20documents/Opinion%20TTIP%20Cult.pdf; accessed 12/07/2015.

Coombe, R. 2003. "Works in Progress: Traditional Knowledge, Biological Diversity, and Intellectual Property in a Neoliberal Era". In Perry, R.W. and B. Maurer (eds). *Globalisation Under Construction: Governmentality, Law and Identity*. Minneapolis: University of Minnesota Press.

Coombe, R. 2005. "Legal claims to culture in and against the market: Neoliberalism and the global proliferation of meaningful difference". *Law, Culture and the Humanities*. 1(1): 35–52.

Cowan, J.K., M.B. Dembour and R.A. Wilson (eds) 2001. *Culture and Rights: Anthropological Perspectives*. Cambridge: Cambridge University Press.

Des Beauvais, S. 2014. "France: Ending the cultural exception". *World Policy Blog*. 3 November 2014. Available online at: www.worldpolicy.org/blog/2014/11/03/france-ending-cultural-exception; accessed 12/07/2015.

De Witte, B. 2001. "Trade in Culture: International Legal Regimes and EU Constitutional Values". In Scott, J. and G. De Burca (eds). *The EU and the WTO: Legal and Constitutional Issues*. Oxford: Hart.

Disdier, A., S. Tai, L. Fontagne and T. Mayer. 2009. "Bilateral Trade of Cultural Goods". *Review of World Economics*. October 2009: *Online First*. Available online at: www.springerlink.com/content/033j37v11815v677/; accessed 30/10/2009.

Donders, Y. 2008. "The History of the UNESCO Convention on the Protection and Promotion of the Diversity of Cultural Expressions". In Schneider, H. and P. Van den Bossche (eds). *Protection of Cultural Diversity from a European and International Perspective*. Oxford: Intersentia.

Donnedieu de Vabres, R. 2005. "La diversité culturelle n'est pas une arrogance". *Le Monde*. 19/10/2005.

du Gay, P. 1999. "In the name of globalisation: Enterprising up nations, organisations, individuals". In Leisink, P. (ed.). *Globalisation and Labour Relations*. Cheltenham: Edward Elgar.

Eriksen, T.H. 2001. "Between Universalism and Relativism: A critique of the UNESCO concepts of culture". In Cowan, J., M.B. Dembour and R.A. Wilson (eds). *Culture and Rights: Anthropological Perspectives*. Cambridge: Cambridge University Press.

European Commission. 2014. *TTIP and Culture*. 16 July 2014. Available online at: http://trade.ec.europa.eu/doclib/docs/2014/july/tradoc_152670.pdf; accessed 12/07/2015.

Farhat, R. 2008. "Neotribal entrepreneurialism and the commodification of biodiversity: WIPO's displacement of development for private property rights". *Review of International Political Economy*. 15(2): 206–233.

Fiegenbaum, H.B. 2007. "Hegemony or diversity in film and television? The United States, Europe and Japan". *Pacific Review*. 20(3): 371–396.

Footer, M. and C. Beat Graber. 2000. "Trade Liberalisation and Cultural Policy". *Journal of International Economic Law*. 3(1).

Forsyth, S. 2004. "Hollywood Reloaded: The Film as Imperial Commodity". In Panitch, L. and C. Leys (eds). *The Empire Reloaded: Socialist Register 2005*. London: The Merlin Press.

Foucault, M. 1984. "Polemics, Politics and Problematizations". Interview with Paul Rabinow (May 1984), in Vol. 1 (Ethics) of Rabinow, P. (ed.). *Essential Works of Michel Foucault 1954–1984*. London: Penguin.

Foucault, M. 2008. *The Birth of Biopolitics: Lectures at the College de France, 1978–1979*. Hampshire: Palgrave Macmillan.

Fraser, N. 1997. *Justice Interruptus: Critical Reflections on the "Postsocialist" Condition*. London: Routledge.

Fraser, N. and A. Honneth. 2003. *Redistribution or Recognition? A Political-Philosophical Exchange*. London: Verso.

Galloway, S. and S. Dunlop. 2007. "A Critique of the Definitions of the Cultural and Creative Industries in Public Policy". *International Journal of Cultural Policy*. 13(1).

Gioia, D. 2005. "UNESCO Cultural Diversity Convention: The US View". *Foreign Press Center Roundtable*. Washington DC, September 27, 2005. Available online at: http://fpc.state.gov/fpc/54039.htm; accessed 03/09/2007 (no longer available; transcript in possession of author, available on request).

Gouvernement du Québec. 2006. "The Issues Regarding Cultural Diversity". Available online at: www.diversite-culturelle.qc.ca/index.php?id=22&L=1; accessed 02/01/2015.

Gray, C. 2007. "Commodification and Instrumentality in Cultural Policy". *International Journal of Cultural Policy*. 13(2).

Guerrieri, P., P. Lelio Iapadre and G. Koopmann (eds) 2005. *Cultural Diversity and International Economic Integration: The Global Governance of the Audio-Visual Sector*. Cheltenham: Edward Elgar.

Hahn, M. 2006. "A Clash of Cultures? The UNESCO Diversity Convention and International Trade Law". *Journal of International Economic Law*. 9(3).

Hale, C.R. 2005. "Neoliberal multiculturalism: The remaking of cultural rights and racial dominance in Central America". *Political and Legal Anthropological Review*. 28(1): 10–28.

Hardt, M. 2009. "Politics of the Common". *ZNet*. 6 July 2009. Available online at: www.zcommunications.org/politics-of-the-common-by-michael-hardt; accessed 10/07/2009.

Harvey, S. (ed.) 2006. *Trading Culture: Global Traffic and Local Cultures in Film and Television*. Eastleigh: John Libbey Publishing.

Inter Press Service. 2005, 19 October. "UN Treaty Challenges 'Planet Hollywood.'"

Isar, Y.R. 2015. "'Culture in EU external relations': an idea whose time has come?" *International Journal of Cultural Policy*. 21(4): 494–508.

Kymlicka, W. 1995. *Multicultural Citizenship: A Liberal Theory of Minority Rights*. Oxford: Oxford University Press.

Kymlicka, W. 2013. "Chapter 3 – Neoliberal multiculturalism?" In Hall, P.A. and M. Lamont (eds). *Social Resilience in the Neoliberal Era*. New York: Cambridge University Press.

Larner, W. and W. Walters. 2004. "Globalisation as Governmentality". *Alternatives*. 29(2004): 495–514.

Lash, S. and C. Lury. 2007. *Global Culture Industry*. Cambridge: Polity Press.

Lobo, G. 2004. "Against Expediency". *A Contracorriente*. 2(1).

Macmillan, F. 2008. "The UNESCO Convention as a New Incentive to Protect Cultural Diversity". In Schneider, H. and P. van den Bossche (eds). *Protection of Cultural Diversity from a European and International Perspective*. Oxford: Intersentia.

Mamdani, M. 2001. *When Victims Become Killers: Colonialism, Nativism and the Genocide in Rwanda*. Princeton: Princeton University Press.

Mamdani, M. 2002. "Good Muslim, Bad Muslim: A Political Perspective on Culture and Terrorism". *American Anthropologist*. 104(3): 766–755.

Martin, R.S. 2005. "Final Statement of the US Delegation at UNESCO. Paris, 3 June 2005". Available online at: http://unesco.usmission.gov/CL_09122006_CLDiversity-Convention.cfm; accessed 29/09/2009.

Matsuura, K. 2007. "Address by Mr Koïchiro Matsuura, Director-General of UNESCO, on the occasion of the first Conference of Parties to the Convention on the Protection and Promotion of the Diversity of Cultural Expressions. 18 June 2007". Available online at: www.unesco.org/culture/culturaldiversity/discours_dg_en_20070618.pdf; accessed 27/06/2007.

Matsuura, K. 2009. "Message from the Director-General of UNESCO, on the occasion of World Day for Cultural Diversity for Dialogue and Development, 21 May 2009". UNESCO: DG/ME/ID/2009/09.

MercoPress. 2013, 14 January. "Major victory for President Morales: UN accepts 'coca leaf chewing' in Bolivia". Available online at: http://en.mercopress.com/2013/01/14/major-victory-for-president-morales-un-accepts-coca-leaf-chewing-in-bolivia; accessed 16/01/2013.

Moghadam, V.E. and D. Elveren. 2008. "The making of an international Convention: Culture and free trade in a global era". *Review of International Studies*. 34(4): 735–753.

Morales, E. 2009. "Letter from President Evo Morales to UN Secretary General". La Paz, 12 March 2009. Available online at: www.boliviaun.org/cms/?p=997; accessed 12/04/2009.

Mukherjee, A., P. Deb Gupta and P. Ahuja. 2007. *Indo-US FTA: Prospects for Audiovisual Services*. India Council for Research on International Economic Relations, Working Paper #192 (February 2007).

Musitelli, J. 2006. "The Convention on Cultural Diversity: Anatomy of a Diplomatic Success Story". *French Ministry of Foreign Affairs*. Available online at: www.diplomatie.gouv.fr/en/IMG/pdf/The_Convention_on_Cultural_Diversity.pdf; accessed 29/09/2009.

Musitelli, J. 2007. "The Convention's success depends on the will of States". Interview with Jean Musitelli during the First Conference of Parties to the Convention on the Protection and Promotion of the Diversity of Cultural Expressions, 14 June 2007. UNESCO Service de Presse. Available online at: www.unesco.org/new/fr/media-services/; accessed 30/09/2009.

Nenova, M. 2008. "Trade and Culture: Making the WTO Legal Framework Conducive to Cultural Considerations". *Manchester Journal of International Economic Law*. 5(3).

Nenova, M. 2010. "Reconciling Trade and Culture: A Global Law Perspective". *Journal of Arts Management, Law and Society*. 40.

New York Times. 2005, 20 October. "U.S. all but alone in opposing Unesco cultural pact".

Nurse, K. 2012. "Creative industries as growth engine". *Policy Innovations*. Available online at: www.policyinnovations.org/ideas/innovations/data/creative_cultural/: pf_printable; accessed 11/08/2015.

Oliver, L. 2005. "Explanation of Vote of the United States on the Convention on the Protection and Promotion of the Diversity of Cultural Expressions". *Statement by Louise V. Oliver, U.S. Ambassador to UNESCO*. UNESCO, Paris, 20 October 2005. Available online at: www.america.gov/st/washfile-english/2005/October/20051020170821GLnesnoM3.670901e-02.html; accessed 14/03/2007.

Reuters. 2006, 15 February. "Bolivia's coca: From cottage industry to mass export?"

Richardson, B.J.K. 2004. "Hollywood's Vision of a Clear, Predictable Trade Framework Consistent with Cultural Diversity". In Beat Graber, C., M. Girsberger and M. Nenova (eds). *Free Trade Versus Cultural Diversity: WTO Negotiations in the Field of Audiovisual Services*. Zurich: Schulthess.

Richieri Hanania, L. (ed.) 2014. *Cultural Diversity in International Law: The Effectiveness of the UNESCO Convention on the Protection and Promotion of the Diversity of Cultural Expressions*. Oxon: Routledge.

Rushdie, S. 1999. "A culture of easy criticism". *The Age*. 10 March 1999.

Scheeren, O. 2004. "Museum: Economy/Museum: Content". In Koolhaas, R. (ed.). *Content*. Köln: Taschen.

Scott, A.J. 2002. "Hollywood in the era of globalization". *Yale Center for the Study of Globalization*. 22 November 2002. Available online at: http://yaleglobal.yale.edu/content/hollywood-era-globalization; accessed 15/03/2007.

Shin-yi, C. 2009. "Liberalization of Trade in Television Services: The Negotiation Dilemma and Challenges for the Future". *Journal of World Trade*. 43(4): 657–681.

Singh, J.P. 2008. "Agents of Policy Learning and Change: US and EU Perspectives on Cultural Trade Policy". *Journal of Arts Management, Law and Society*. 38(2).

Singh, J.P. 2011. *United Nations Educational, Scientific and Cultural Organisation: Creating norms for a complex world*. London and New York: Routledge.

Stahler-Sholk, R., H.E. Vanden and M. Becker (eds) 2014. *Rethinking Latin American Social Movements: Radical Action From Below*. London: Rowman and Littlefield.

Taylor, C. 1992. *Multiculturalism and the Politics of Recognition*. Princeton: Princeton University Press.

Throsby, D. 2000. *Economics and Culture*. Cambridge: Cambridge University Press.

Throsby, D. 2008. "Culture in Sustainable Development: Insights for the Future Implementation of Article 13". Paper presented to the Parties to the UNESCO Cultural Diversity Convention. Available online at: http://unesdoc.UNESCO.org/images/0015/001572/157287E.pdf; accessed 27/06/2008.

Throsby, D. 2010. *The Economics of Cultural Policy*. Cambridge: Cambridge University Press.

Tian, Y. 2009. *Rethinking Intellectual Property: The Political Economy of Copyright Protection in the Digital Era*. Oxon: Routledge-Cavendish.

Towse, R. (ed.) 2003. *A Handbook of Cultural Economics*. Cheltenham: Edward Elgar.

Towse, R. 2010. *A Textbook of Cultural Economics*. New York: Cambridge University Press.

UNESCO. 1982. *Mexico City Declaration on Cultural Policies*. Paris: UNESCO. Available online at: http://portal.UNESCO.org/culture/en/ev.php-URL_ID=12762&URL_DO=DO_TOPIC&URL_SECTION=201.html; accessed 09/07/2007.

UNESCO. 1995. *Our Creative Diversity: Report of the World Commission on Culture and Development*. Paris: UNESCO.

UNESCO. 1999. "CULTURE: A FORM OF MERCHANDISE LIKE NO OTHER? Symposium of Experts on Culture, the Market and Globalisation, 14–15 June 1999". Paris: UNESCO. CLT/CIC/BCI/CMMIDOC.FIN.E.

UNESCO. 2001. *Universal Declaration on Cultural Diversity*. Paris: UNESCO. Available online at: http://unesdoc.UNESCO.org/images/0012/001271/127160m.pdf; accessed 09/07/2007.

UNESCO. 2003. *Desirability of Drawing up an International Standard-Setting Instrument on Cultural Diversity*. 32/C52. Paris: UNESCO. Available online at: http://unesdoc.unesco.org/images/0013/001307/130798e.pdf; accessed 09/07/2007.

UNESCO. 2004. *First Meeting of Experts (category VI) on the First Draft of an International Convention on the Protection of the Diversity of Cultural Contents and Artistic Expressions.* CLT/CPD/2003–608/01. Paris: UNESCO. Available online at: www.unesco.org/culture/culturaldiversity/docs_pre_2007/clt_cpd_2003_608_01_en_20022004.pdf; accessed 09/07/2007.

UNESCO. 2005a. *Convention on the Protection and Promotion of the Diversity of Cultural Expressions.* CLT-2005/CONVENTION DIVERSITE-CULT REV. Paris: UNESCO. Available online at: www.unesco.org/culture/en/diversity/convention; accessed 14/03/2007.

UNESCO. 2005b. "Preliminary report by the Director General setting out the situation to be regulated and the possible scope of the regulating action proposed, accompanied by the preliminary draft of a Convention on the Protection of the Diversity of Cultural Contents and Artistic Expressions". Paris: UNESCO. 4 August 2005. 33 C/23.

UNESCO. 2006. *Innovative Practices of Youth Participation in Media.* Paris: UNESCO.

US State Department. 2005. "LOUISE OLIVER HOLDS A NEWS CONFERENCE ON THE CONVENTION ON CULTURAL DIVERSITY". Paris: QC Transcriptions, LLC. (In possession of author, available on request.)

Van den Bossche, P. 2007. *Free Trade and Culture: A study of relevant WTO rules and constraints on national cultural policy measures.* Amsterdam: Boekmanstudies.

Vlassis, A. and L. Richieri Hanania. 2014. "Chapter 1 – Effects of the CDCE on trade negotiations". In Richieri Hanania, L. (ed.). *Cultural Diversity in International Law: The Effectiveness of the UNESCO Convention on the Protection and Promotion of the Diversity of Cultural Expressions.* Oxon: Routledge.

von Schorlemer, S. and P.T. Stoll (eds) 2012. *The UNESCO Convention on the Protection and Promotion of the Diversity of Cultural Expressions: Explanatory Notes.* Heidelberg: Springer.

Voon, T. 2006. "State support for audiovisual products in the World Trade Organization: Protectionism or Cultural Policy?" *International Journal of Cultural Property.* 13: 129–160.

Voon, T. 2007. *Cultural Products and the World Trade Organization.* Cambridge: Cambridge University Press.

Young, I.M. 2002. *Inclusion and Democracy.* Oxford: Oxford University Press.

Yúdice, G. 2003. *The Expediency of Culture: Uses of Culture in the Global Era.* London: Duke University Press.

Žižek, S. 1997. "Multiculturalism, or, the cultural logic of multinational capitalism?" *New Left Review.* I/225 September/October 1997. Available online at: http://newleftreview.org/I/225/slavoj-zizek-multiculturalism-or-the-cultural-logic-of-multinational-capitalism; accessed 06/08/2015.

Žižek, S. 2013. "It's the *political* economy, stupid!" In Sholette, G. and O. Ressler (eds). *It's the Political Economy, Stupid: The Global Financial Crisis in Art and Theory.* London: Pluto Press.

3 The "last frontier" of development

Exploration and conflict during the World Decade for Cultural Development, 1988–1997

Introduction

If some of the major discussions at UNESCO from the late 1990s came to revolve around the relationship between trade and culture, much of the decade prior to that had been occupied with the relationship between culture and development. 1988 saw the launch of the UN-UNESCO World Decade for Cultural Development, which culminated in the Intergovernmental Conference on Cultural Policies for Development in Stockholm in 1998. These events laid much of the groundwork for the framework of cultural development that would become formalised at UNESCO over the coming years.

The World Decade for Cultural Development also spanned a long and difficult period for UNESCO itself, and paralleled major shifts in the international political context of development associated with the end of the Cold War and the rise to global hegemony of the neoliberal Washington Consensus. It is worth pointing out that the UN resolution that had mandated the World Decade in 1986 had opened by referring to the call that had originally been made for such a decade at the World Conference on Cultural Policies (MONDIACULT) in 1982, and it was hoped that the decade would build on the earlier progress that had been made at UNESCO through the 1976 Recommendation on the Participation by the People at Large in Cultural Life and Their Contribution to it ("the Nairobi Declaration") and the 1982 Mexico City Declaration on Cultural Policies ("the Mexico Declaration") (United Nations, 1986). As we saw in Chapter 1, these were important landmarks in articulating claims for a more holistic, "anthropological" concept of culture, reflecting in particular the way that the new members of UNESCO sought to address colonial biases and legacies as part of post-independence nation-building projects and wider efforts to bring about a New World Information and Communication Order (NWICO) and New International Economic Order (NIEO). However, faced with opposition from the Western bloc no significant or authoritative measures had come out of these campaigns and by the time the work of the Decade got underway in 1988, NWICO and NIEO had faded into history. With the international debt crisis and the reorientation of projects of national development towards the project of neoliberal globalisation and the Washington Consensus, commentators were now speaking of the "end of the Third World" as a coherent actor and ideology in world politics (Harris, 1987; Hoogvelt, 1987), a development that was given added momentum over the following years with the end of the Cold War. UNESCO as an organisation was also in a process of transition, under intense pressures to reform, "depoliticise" its programmes and work around the gaping holes in its budget that had been left by the withdrawal of the US and UK in 1984 and 1985 respectively.

In tracing the contemporary entanglement of the politics of cultural diversity with the neoliberal regime of cultural power that we earlier saw elaborated by Yúdice (Chapter 2), it is useful to revisit the developments at UNESCO over this period. On one hand, through the work of the World Decade for Cultural Development, there was a continuation of the radical calls made in the NWICO period to give wider recognition to culture's place in development. On the other hand, these calls were also reformed to align within the emerging discursive order of neoliberal globalisation and the ideological hegemony of the Washington Consensus. In these ways, the inclusion of the expanded, anthropological concept of culture in trade and development that has been articulated over the 1990s and 2000s has also happened alongside a reframing of the concept of development itself and a delimitation of the legitimate scope in which culture could feature in the work of UNESCO. Whereas the expansion of the concept of culture in the period of decolonisation expressed the ambitions of nationalist claims to difference and autonomy outside of authoritative (neocolonial) international frameworks of trade and development, by the end of the 1990s it had become part of the search for strategies of integration into the new world order of neoliberal globalisation.

In examining these developments in more detail, this chapter is split into three sections. The first section begins by looking in detail at some of the specific contributions that were made by the World Decade for Cultural Development, focusing on its standard-setting report *Our Creative Diversity*. The second section then turns to survey some of the ways in which the Decade's work was initially taken up, lost in translation or simply ignored within frameworks of international development, looking in particular at the work of the World Bank and the emergence of the post-Washington Consensus. Finally, the third section retraces the path of reform and depoliticisation that was taken at UNESCO between MONDIACULT in 1982 and the Stockholm conference of 1998. These analyses prepare the following chapters to examine the particular ways in which the relationship between culture and development that had been set out by the work of the Decade, and in particular its models of cultural diversity and the "dual role of culture", came to take their particular shape over the following years in the instruments on cultural diversity.

The World Decade for Cultural Development, 1988–1997

The UN resolution that proclaimed 1988–1997 as the World Decade for Cultural Development set out four main objectives: "acknowledging the cultural dimension of development", "affirming and enriching cultural identities", "broadening participation in culture" and "promoting international cultural cooperation" (United Nations, 1986). To these ends a number of initiatives involving a range of bodies and expertise came to be drawn up over the following years. UNESCO was the agency placed at the head of this mission, although it was hoped that the work of the Decade would be carried out in a spirit which would try to bridge gaps between UNESCO and its sister institutions in the UN system through joint projects in a range of development areas.

At the launch of the decade in 1988 the new Director-General of UNESCO (Federico Mayor, who served from 1987–1999) was joined by the UN Secretary-General in noting that development programmes had too often failed because "the importance of the human factor – that complex web of relationships and beliefs, values and motivations, which lie at the very heart of a culture – had been underestimated in many development projects.... Clearly there [is] a need to transcend economics, without abandoning it" (UNESCO, 1995: 7–8). The task of integrating these aspects into an enlarged framework of development economics represented what came to be referred to over the Decade at UNESCO as the "last frontier" of development, and opening this frontier up would be no small feat. In being invited by UNESCO half way through the Decade to prepare a synopsis of the work that had been generated so far, Cole (1995: 474) reflected that "practically every conceivable issue in which culture and development might figure was invoked". The scale and complexity of the task had been set out in an address by Mayor in 1993, in which he had urged an examination of the roles that the hitherto underexplored and undervalued domains of culture could play in the following:

> Education, information, communication, maintenance and promotion of cultural forms, choice and development of technology and the economy, exploitation and care of the environment, demographic growth and complexity, political realities, inter-group relations and international relations, and local notions of human rights.
>
> (Mayor, cited in Cole, 1995: 474)

The huge body of theoretical and applied work that was done in this vein between 1988 and 1997 – 1200 projects had been counted by the conclusion of the Decade in 1997 (UNESCO, 1997) – added momentum to an ongoing shift in development theory and practice, so that by the turn of the century it was being remarked that the "cultural turn" that had been unfolding in its various ways in the social sciences had "finally come to economics and the bundle of practices called development" (Nederveen Pieterse, 2001: 60). To begin to unpack how this happened, it is useful to look at the contributions made by a landmark piece of work produced during the Decade, *Our Creative Diversity*.

Our Creative Diversity

The flagship of the fleet of initiatives launched between 1988 and 1997 was the World Commission on Culture and Development (WCCD), assembled as an independent, international and interdisciplinary group in 1992 by the UN and UNESCO to prepare and publicise a report which would consolidate and develop the kinds of links that were now being made between culture and development. The resulting *Our Creative Diversity: Report of the World Commission on Culture and Development* (UNESCO, 1995) was the crowning work of the Decade and presented the most authoritative policy-oriented report to date on these questions. It contained ten substantive chapters of in-depth contributions on a range of topics (the relationship between the state and pluralism; gender and development; media regulation; culture and the environment; tourism and heritage; among others), was translated and circulated widely, and came to be acknowledged even by critics such as Eriksen (2001) as marking a "genuine intellectual contribution to the field … with real-world consequences of a magnitude most academics can only dream of on behalf of their scholarly work". Its ultimate goal was to bring about a shift in international and national practices in development policy, and to this end it concluded with an "International Agenda" of initiatives designed to generate greater international authority and consensus for the issues that it had explored over the previous ten chapters (UNESCO, 1995: 271–288). Among the most significant outcomes of this Agenda was the convening of the Intergovernmental Conference on Cultural Policies for Development in Stockholm in 1998, which was envisaged as an opportunity to follow up on the report's call for the formulation of "new culturally sensitive development strategies".

Our Creative Diversity was placed by the WCCD alongside the ongoing elaborations of the notion of "human development" at the UN (the first of the annual UN Development Program's Human Development Reports was published in 1990)[1] and related evocations of "the cultural dimensions of development" that had been made in other recent forums such as the Brundtland Commission (World Commission on Environment and Development), as well as the South Commission and the Commission on Global Governance (UNESCO, 1995: 7–13). If each of these had broken new grounds on, respectively, the issues of sustainable development, North–South relationships, and world governance and security, the work of the WCCD was heralded by UNESCO as opening "the 'last frontier' of development", seeking to mainstream cultural considerations in international and national policy frameworks.

In this respect the work of the Brundtland Commission and its 1987 report *Our Common Future* were especially influential on the work of the WCCD, for they had demonstrated the possibility of generating greater authority and consensus at an international level regarding the present urgency of integrative thinking towards economic development. This had stressed the need in particular for a greater fusion of environmental and development concerns, for greater political weight behind the principle of sustainable development, and for the necessity of international collaboration and reform in designing policy.[2] The policy impact that had been created by Brundtland was highlighted by the president of the WCCD in his foreword to *Our Creative Diversity*, which stressed that the need to create a practical agenda for cultural development must become the "next step in rethinking development":

> [T]he time had come to do for "culture and development" what had been achieved for "environment and development". This conviction was widely shared. Just as the Brundtland Commission had so successfully served notice to the international community that a marriage of economy and ecology was overdue and had set in motion a new world agenda for that purpose, so, it was felt, the relationship between culture and development should be clarified and deepened, in practical and constructive ways.... We want [the report] to inform the world's opinion leaders and to guide its policymakers.
>
> (UNESCO, 1995: 8–10)

In aiming to set this agenda in motion, most of the links between culture and development that were elaborated in the report were less reflective of any groundbreaking insights than an attempt to crystallise existing work in order to give a state of the art account of cultural development thinking accessible to the international policy community. This was reflected in a number of reviews of the report – with one, Margolin (1996), for example, pointing out that although it contained little that anyone following the changing discourses on gender, heritage and cultural diversity would find entirely new, their inclusion as part of a consciously pragmatic and policy-oriented document such as this "marked a significant advance in the definition of global development requirements". How far and in what directions this advance would actually go in practice of course remained to be seen. Nevertheless, to the extent that *Our Creative Diversity* marked a landmark event of the Decade and sought to provide a guide for subsequent development policies to follow, there are a number of key contributions that it made which are worth considering briefly below.

A new global ethics

As we saw in the previous chapter, Bennett's (1998) brief analysis of *Our Creative Diversity* suggested some of the ways in which it rests on a normative splitting and hierarchical gradation of culture: it sets out principles for identifying which "ways of life" are to be allotted a reforming role and which are to be targeted as objects of reform. We might develop this point by considering a section of the report entitled *No Culture is an Island*, which opens by stating that: "No culture is a hermetically sealed entity. All cultures are influenced by and in turn influence other cultures. Nor is any culture changeless, invariant or static" (UNESCO, 1995: 54). In a rejection of previous, more static, models of culture at UNESCO, it is asserted that cultures are in a constant state of flux, involved in an ongoing process of mutual exchange, discovery and enrichment, and it is in this sense that a peaceful international cultural diversity based on mutual respect, exchange and influence is described in the report as having "benefits comparable to those of bio-diversity" (UNESCO, 1995: 54).

This outlook goes beyond the long-standing principle at UNESCO of promoting inter-cultural dialogue and exchange but is at the core of an attempt to elaborate what is referred to in the report as a "new global ethics". This refers to an attempt to outline a principle of international intervention in which movements trying to pull up the cultural drawbridge and raise the flag of "intolerant, exclusive, exploitative, cruel and repressive" forms of identity must not be tolerated. ("Whatever we may be told about the importance of 'not interfering with local customs', such repulsive practices, whether aimed at people from different cultures or at other members of the same culture, should be condemned" (UNESCO, 1995: 54)). In this way, international intervention has a legitimate role to play in setting and enforcing rules around mutual tolerance and accommodation:

> Intolerant attitudes become particularly pernicious when they become the policy of intolerant governments. Discrimination, segregation and exclusion based on cultural traits then become official policy. In these cases strong international pressures should be used to denounce and punish such policies, including all forms of racism, persecution of people because of their beliefs, and the curtailment of freedom of their own people.
>
> (UNESCO, 1995: 54)

We can see here some of the ways in which culture in the report appears in Bennett's sense as a reforming apparatus – one which differs from the past by marking a shift "from a principle of cultural development which saw diversity as an obstacle to be removed to one dedicated to (within limits) the promotion and celebration of diversity" (Bennett, 1998: 106). Its assertion of a new global ethics also marks an attempt to outline a cause and principle of international regulation that transcends some of the Westphalian limitations set by national sovereignty, in keeping with the emerging post-Cold War regime of international intervention that was elaborated over the 1990s: one in which national sovereignty is contingent upon its ability to maintain certain global requirements of security, and subject to an expanding multi-agency apparatus of international humanitarian intervention and development (Elden, 2006; Duffield, 2007).

However, *Our Creative Diversity*'s elaboration of the roles that culture can play in a more comprehensive development framework is also a critique of the Washington Consensus model of development that had risen to hegemony over the previous decade. In the report's call for the preparation of "new, culturally sensitive development strategies", the lack of cultural considerations in the work of the major development agencies is declared an intellectual, ethical and practical failure that has resulted in not just "distorted models of development" but "development without a soul" (UNESCO, 1995: 273–274).

In setting out these critiques, and in its various explorations of how to build cultural insights into broader development strategies, much of the substance of the report is concerned to alter the priority that continues to be accorded in development policy to "economic" over "cultural" considerations. This partly reflects contributions made by a number of anthropologists, notably Lourdes Arizpe (who supervised the work of the secretariat of the WCCD, and acted as UNESCO Assistant Director-General for Culture between 1994–1998) and Marshall Sahlins, who – along with Claude Levi-Strauss, an honorary member of the Commission with long-standing connections to UNESCO – wrote papers on which many of the key arguments of *Our Creative Diversity* were based. We might call the result an "anthropological critique" of development, and this is evident in two central lines of concern that run through the report.

Development anthropology

First is the matter of more effectively incorporating a wider set of cultural variables into development programmes, since it had become "well known that projects that do not take into account sufficiently the 'human factor' have a greater chance of failing" (UNESCO, 1995: 262). Similarly, the spread of paradigms of sustainable and human development meant that "the notion of development itself had broadened, as people realised that economic criteria alone cannot provide the criteria for human dignity and well-being" (UNESCO, 1995: 8). Opening up the last frontier of development therefore meant opening the practices of development up to an expanded repertoire of concerns and expertise: the kinds of one-dimensional economistic and quantitative frameworks that continued to reign among governments and the institutions of international development are identified as increasingly untenable and requiring a new set of cultural, qualitative sensibilities and variables to become more effective. Despite some recent advances and refinements in the development of social cost-benefit analyses,[3] these are regretted for being too limited in depth and in application, and besides had had great difficulty taking into account

> such cultural variables as attitudes to work, work ethic, group solidarity, interpersonal relationships and people's valuations.... Though it is generally acknowledged that neglect of these variables frequently leads to unforeseen problems in the implementation of a project, no method has been evolved as to how these parameters can be built into models.
> (UNESCO, 1995: 260)

This analysis provokes a series of attempts in the report to show how a greater appreciation and engagement with cultural differences can foster more participatory and sustainable forms of economic growth, build stronger and more stable civil institutions and democracies, help to sustain the physical environment, improve the take-up of technology and agricultural techniques, preserve family values, improve the provision of education and health care, contribute to the alleviation and prevention of conflict, and so on. We might summarise these aspects of the report as its "development anthropology", to borrow a term used by Escobar (1997) – in other words, the application of anthropological knowledge and methods in development projects to focus on the project cycle, to tailor projects to the particularities of beneficiaries' cultures and situations, to assess the possibility of contributing to the needs of the poor, and so on.

Anthropology of development

The second reason for the report's concern to reorder the priorities between economics and culture in development lies deeper in what we might refer to as its "anthropology of development" – that is, the historicisation and relativisation of development itself so as to lay bare its roots in particular (European, Enlightenment) conceptions of progress and rationality – since it is recognised that "all forms of development, including human development, ultimately are determined by cultural factors" (UNESCO, 1995: 24). This recognition is an attempt to provincialise mainstream development, at least insofar as it is an attempt to reconceptualise orthodox development policy by de-emphasising its focus on economic growth and subordinating it to an emphasis on what is referred to in the report as a model of "cultural growth": "Once we shift our attention from the purely instrumental view of culture to awarding it a constructive, constitutive and creative role, we have to see development in terms that include cultural growth" (UNESCO, 1995: 25).

The dual role of culture

This assertion of the centrality of culture's "constructive, constitutive and creative" role in development processes is most clear in the contribution of Sahlins, who had long been associated with work aimed at demonstrating the historical and cultural contingency of many of the assumptions and practices underlying more orthodox and economistic forms of development (see in particular Sahlins, 1972; 1976). It is Sahlins's opening words of the first chapter that set the tone of *Our Creative Diversity*, by foregrounding what he refers to as "the great ideological issue" that had been confronted by the Commission:

> is "culture" an aspect or a means of "development", the latter understood as material progress; or is "culture" the end and aim of "development": the latter understood as the flourishing of human existence in its several forms and as a whole?
>
> (UNESCO, 1995: 21)

The answer, we soon find, is that it must be both: this is described as the "dual role of culture", which is used here to denote its simultaneously "far-reaching instrumental function" and its intrinsic value as "the end and aim of development itself" (UNESCO, 1995: 23–24). We can consider a couple of the examples that are given to illustrate in a little more detail how exactly this works:

> At one extreme of modernity, promotion of creativity is seen as essential for industrial productivity and innovation. A new kind of organization for managing creativity, known as the "entrepreneurial conglomerate", for example, has come into being during the 1980s.... At the other end, where tradition meets modernity, a process of "hybridization" is well under way. Many Latin American Indian populations are seeking deliberately to master both modern technological knowledge and cultural resources, despite strong movements against "Westernization".... They are combining traditional healing techniques with allopathic methods ... adapting to their own ends democratic changes in the economic and political spheres, and aligning their traditional beliefs with Christian movements that generally have a more radical approach to the promotion of modernity.
>
> Many tribal communities in India have age-old technologies and practices in such diverse areas as hill-top agriculture, medicine and health care, community education and socialization. On the surface, their attitudes appear to be to be anti-modern. But a closer look reveals that through a complex process of assimilation they are absorbing and using modern technology and political systems as a path to power and betterment. Society's ritual base is modernized to fit into and serve its political and economic ends. In this way they help, in unobtrusive and effective ways, to bring together the instrumental and constitutive roles of culture.
>
> (UNESCO, 1995: 78–79)

We can see that development here is conceptualised as a complex and productive engagement between "modernity" and "culture": a process of absorption, assimilation and hybridisation that can more effectively realise the creative potential of both modern and traditional forms of knowledge, technology and social organisation. There is an orientalist logic at play in this formula which remains largely intact: fostering productivity and development in this scenario by implication remains an engagement between "modern" forms of rationality, management and progress on the one hand, and the cultures, traditions and creativity of "others" on the other. However, by seeking to recognise the potential of a range of practices that might previously have been denied by development as "anti-modern", and by tradition as "Western", there is some attempt to overcome this binary opposition – and in the process to bring together the dual ("instrumental" and "constitutive") roles of culture.

It is arguably here that we find the key normative thrust of the report, because once this formula is established it becomes clear that cultural development requires a constantly active, careful mediation to be successful. Some groups – those that are dynamic, pluralistic, open to exchange, assimilation, experimentation, hybridisation – are seen to make better use of their cultural differences and creative potential than others, and this forms a key area for contemporary development policy. As the report states: "These capacities can neither be imposed nor taught. But they can be nurtured.... Creative and organizational processes must engage, must mesh with each other if social institutions are to be fully productive" (UNESCO, 1995: 78). It is precisely in designing the right kinds of regulatory frameworks and institutional balances that the productive and developmental potential of culture can be allowed to flourish. Furthermore, this requires that culture be conceptualised in its broad, "anthropological" sense in order to acknowledge the contributions of as wide a range of creative human activities as possible. Such points are laid out, for example, in the following passage:

> There is no such thing as the creative spirit divorced from a particular human group, from specific social institutions and values, even from certain political constraints. Hence creativity is an intangible whose nurture can and indeed must be managed and not squandered.... An over-emphasis on rationality alone, technocratic reasoning, restrictive organizational or community structures and an over-reliance on traditional approaches can restrict or destroy this potential. This is why it is important that the prestige attached to the arts should not lead to the neglect of countless, modest imaginative undertakings that inject a vital substance into the social fabric.
> (UNESCO, 1995: 78–79)

Aside from the measures necessary to ensure the above aims – that is, the proper development of creative and cultural potential and the productive circulation of this "vital substance in the social fabric" – there may also be occasions where a different set of measures is required. We might return at this point to the report's assertion of the need for a "new global ethics" and principle of international intervention. Just as cultural diversity can have benefits to humanity comparable to those of bio-diversity, it can also become harmful if not properly managed: just as it is noted that cultural differences can "encourage creativity, experimentation and diversity, the very essentials of human development", it is equally noted that they "run the risk of cultural conflict", bringing disorder and breeding "hotbeds of disgruntlement rather than a source of productive activity" (UNESCO, 1995: 25–26, 154).

The vital substance in the social fabric, in other words, can also turn poisonous if not administered correctly and carefully. The report makes clear that this is as much a problem stemming from flawed Washington Consensus models of development (which it argues had failed to recognise the salience of cultural and ethnic complexities) as from the efforts of particular groups and elites seeking to manipulate and essentialise cultural differences into principles of exclusion and subordination (e.g. see UNESCO, 1995: 25, 55, 73). In a post-Cold War context of growing ethnic and religious tensions, the failure to properly integrate cultural considerations into international and national development frameworks has not only resulted in the kinds of economic and political failures noted above, it also has given rise to a state of global insecurity which demands a changed role for the UN in managing a proliferation of crises. In brief, the report notes: "Development divorced from its human or cultural context is development without a soul" (UNESCO, 1995: 273).

In summary, we have seen that *Our Creative Diversity* was primarily intended as an appeal to bring culture in from the margins and give it a more central place in contemporary strategies of development and international intervention. In doing so it also set out a case for the role that UNESCO can play in a reformed Washington Consensus. However, these appeals have to be set alongside the organisation's continued position on the sidelines of international administration in the 1990s. As the World Decade for Cultural Development came to a close in 1997 and preparations were being made for the Intergovernmental Conference on Cultural Policies for Development in Stockholm in 1998, it remained to be seen how the WCCD's contributions would be taken up, if at all – particularly given UNESCO's ongoing marginalisation by the US, ongoing controversies over reform (the budget, inefficiency and allegations of corruption) and the ongoing resilience of orthodox development models at national and international levels. In the following section we will therefore turn to examine the ways in which the report's contributions had an impact on the wider practices of international development over the following years.

The revolution in and around economics and the [still]birth of cultural development

The session of the intergovernmental committee held at UNESCO headquarters for the conclusion of the Decade in 1997 began by celebrating *Our Creative Diversity*'s impact on the "evolution in international thinking on development", but the actual evidence that they could refer to in making this claim was in reality thin: a recent Declaration on culture and health, co-initiated by UNESCO and the World Health Organisation, and the UN Environment Program's publication of UNESCO's views on the cultural approach to environmental issues (see the Final Report of the committee in UNESCO, 1997). In relation to the key international development actors the World Bank and IMF it could only refer to "discussion in progress" regarding "the importance of developing human resources and participatory methods" (UNESCO, 1997). Similarly, although *Our Creative Diversity* had undoubtedly sparked discussion in the international development community, governments generally found its implications too radical and far-reaching and rejected most of its findings, with the result that its recommendations were not taken up (Donders, 2008).

The Stockholm intergovernmental conference of 1998 was therefore an opportunity for UNESCO to bring together as many policymakers and stakeholders from the development community together as possible in order to give the work of the Decade more political impact, working with participants to generate practical, policy-oriented responses. The background document UNESCO circulated to participants prior to the conference was less sanguine than the assessments that had been made a year earlier about the impact of the Decade, pointing out that although "culture may appear to be on the ascendant in public awareness everywhere", it remained in "the sphere of low priority politics in most countries, as is often reflected both in the level of resources it is accorded and in the status of the ministries and civil servants who oversee it" (UNESCO, 1998a). It also noted that this situation had been compounded by a general lack of progress in the international arena, where the inclusion of culture in development programmes had made very little progress. Furthermore, where culture had started to filter into national and international policy, this was lamented as being due to its utility as "a mere instrument" of economic growth rather than respect for it as "constitutive of human development" itself (in the way that had been set out in the WCCD's vision of the "dual role of culture").

The outcome of the discussions that took place at Stockholm was the formulation of an Action Plan on Cultural Policies for Development (UNESCO, 1998b), which contained a declaration of unbinding commitment on behalf of participating governments to some of the principles that had been outlined in *Our Creative Diversity*.[4] This at least marked something of a starting point for a more formal international mobilisation around the principles of cultural development, and was received in this spirit by the UNESCO Director-General as the first concrete step in "bridging culture and development" insofar as it meant that governments from all participating countries had, for the first time, recognised that "human beings, hitherto considered as human resources, are at long last recognised as women and men: unique with diverse cultural identities" (UNESCO, 1998c). He added that all that remained to be seen after this was how many states would actually begin to take steps to translate their stated commitment into concrete measures and legislation.

Breaching the economic fortress: the World Bank

The efforts of the Decade were also now starting to be reflected in proliferating references to culture in development at national, regional and international levels. This was most remarkable in the work of the World Bank, which had become perhaps the key source of development orthodoxy around the world since the 1980s through its influence over the processes of structural adjustment. As we saw above, the Bank was also one of the main targets of the WCCD's anthropological critique of development. The need to factor a greater number of social and cultural variables into its work had been recognised to some extent by the Bank since the 1970s, with the employment of a growing corps of non-economic social scientists after Michael Cernea was appointed as the Bank's first anthropologist in 1974: by the mid-1990s the Bank had the largest concentration of anthropologists and sociologists working in the field of development of any institution in the world, while also drawing on the work of hundreds of anthropologist and sociologist consultants in designing and implementing particular development projects (Cernea, 1995). In 1995, Cernea, now Senior Advisor for Social Policy and Sociology of the World Bank, remarked in a lecture to the Annual Meeting of the Society for Applied Anthropologists that as World Bank sociologists and anthropologists had gained critical mass in-house, the institution had been forced to move from its "initial pristine ethnocentricity" to "an expanding hospitality toward social variables and the contemporary variations among existing cultures" (Cernea, 1995: 342).

Their task in bringing about this institutional change, however, remained an uphill one, and Cernea invited his audience to join him in this battle against a largely unreconstructed set of "econocentric" and "technocentric" orthodoxies (likening his work to that of a "Secretary to the Non-Believers" and a crusade to "introduce anthropological knowledge within an economic fortress") (Cernea, 1995). He also referred to the fact that his cause was now being aided by a number of high-profile development anthropologists, NGOs and public interest groups who presented a range of external criticisms of Bank programmes, emphasising in particular the importance of cultural and social issues and the mounting failures and injustices associated with World Bank/IMF Structural Adjustment Programmes since the 1980s.

It is only later in the 1990s that there is a formal acknowledgement within the Bank of the role of culture in development, and the work of the Decade undoubtedly played a part in this, along with the work of influential advocates of cultural and Indigenous rights within the Bank (such as the anthropologist Shelton H. Davis; see Davis, 2011). Under the leadership of Federico Mayor in 1989 UNESCO sought to renew its vows with the Bank after the fallouts of the late 1970s and early 1980s,[5] and an internal Bank report entitled *Culture and the Corporate Priorities of the World Bank* identified the efforts of UNESCO that had culminated in Stockholm in 1998 as an important turning point in Bank management making an active commitment to acknowledge the cultural dimension of development (World Bank, 2003: 2).

The shift in the work of the Bank in the late 1990s was evidenced over the following years in gestures (some more serious than others) towards greater cultural concerns in the design and delivery of its Structural Adjustment Programmes, increased appreciation by the Bank of the value of cultural assets and cultural resources in development (most notably regarding the role of heritage in attracting investment and tourism, forging a link with one of UNESCO's key competencies), and through a growing recognition of the ways that economic models could be improved by taking cultural factors into account (notably by improving accuracy in forecasting and analytical models; World Bank, 2003). A major part of the groundwork for these developments in the work of the Bank had been done in October 1999, when UNESCO worked with the Bank to arrange an international meeting of cultural ministers and experts together with representatives from finance ministries, development agencies, private commercial banks, major multinational companies, foundations, and NGOs under the theme "Culture Counts: Financing, Resources, and the Economics of Culture in Sustainable Development" (World Bank, 2000). Referring to the work done by UNESCO over the World Decade for Cultural Development, the Bank set out its aim here to respond by: 1) promoting the expansion of economic analysis in, and resources available for, culture in sustainable development programmes; 2) expanding the range of institutions and actors involved in culture with a development perspective; and 3) increasing the instruments to be used for these programmes. It sought in particular to impress upon participants the value of investing in culture:

> An effort to preserve and enhance cultural assets and expressions can also provide important economic returns and opportunities for greater social cohesion. Investments in culture – besides generating tourist flows – can help poor communities grow out of poverty and encourage local development by strengthening social capital and expanding opportunities for education.
>
> (World Bank, 2000: viii)

The rationality behind this was set out more explicitly in the opening address by its President James D. Wolfensohn, who set out "a twofold interest" by the Bank in the role of culture in development (the following quotes are taken from World Bank, 2000: 9–13). First, the Bank now recognised that factoring in local cultural considerations in development plans makes them more sustainable and effective: there was mounting evidence that without doing so, development "either fails or does not reach its full potential" ("development effectiveness and sustainability demand that development assistance be integral with the social strengths and traditions, and the local institutions, that are most crucial for the poor"). Second, Wolfensohn noted the ways in which the Bank had come to view culture as "a resource to generate incomes and around which poor communities can organise and establish enterprises", highlighting in particular the importance of working with UNESCO to encourage investment in the heritage and tourism sectors – noting that this was now the biggest industry worldwide – and to build cultural enterprises ("Heritage gives value. Part of our joint challenge is to analyze the local and national returns on investments which restore and draw value from cultural heritage – whether it is built or living cultural expression, such as indigenous music, theater, crafts"). Both aspects of this twofold interest in culture are important in that "one can make actions more effective and meaningful at no extra cost; the other can generate income which is desperately needed in many countries, energize poor communities, and build their self-esteem".

In these ways, the World Bank's particular take on the dual role of culture found its way into the framework of the post-Washington Consensus that was being constructed under Wolfensohn, in a way which complemented the Bank's newfound interest in developing concepts such as social capital, good governance and participation.[6] The Bank utilised these concepts over the coming years not only to rationalise and justify essential continuities in Washington Consensus policies but also to try to address some of its practical failures and blind spots as it sought solutions to a growing number of development failures – and also as it sought to respond to the growing dissatisfaction and protest against its work and the effects of neoliberal globalisation more broadly.

The revolution in and around economics

To situate this cultural evolution in the Bank's policy in the late 1990s and early 2000s it is useful to refer to what Fine (2001) has identified as the "revolution in and around economics" that unfolded in the social sciences over the 1990s. In essence this involved an attempt across the disciplines to transcend one of the defining features of neoclassical economics since the marginalist revolution of the 1870s – namely the particular analytical distinction set up between the economy and the "rest" of society (and that led to the analytical preoccupation with the former as market relations). The result of the attempts to transcend the marginalist revolution in the 1990s was an intensified attention within the discipline of economics to a growing set of "non-economic" activities and concerns that could expand its explanatory and reformatory repertoire: extending the application of market-based schema and grids of intelligibility to the "non-market" arena in new ways and igniting an interest in social, institutional and customary variables and forms of behaviour – embeddedness, trust, social networks, co-operation, and so on – that had hitherto largely been neglected as too complex, irrational or "non-optimising".

Accordingly there has been a search for methods for their measurement and analysis (e.g. Robert Putnam's work on social capital; see Harriss, 2001) and explorations into the possibility of developing a "generalised morality" that can support market mechanisms in processes of development (e.g. Platteau, 1994; Moore, 1994). With mixed results and reception, such intellectual and analytical innovations began to filter into the policies of the World Bank that were adopted under the Wolfensohn presidency (1995–2005). Its effects were also paralleled by the emergence of a whole new range of sub-disciplines and analytical frameworks that were animated by the spirit of "the new economy" (such as the new institutional economics, the new political economy, the new development economics, the new household economics, and so on) (Fine, 2001).

We should be clear here when invoking the "newness" of these developments that economics has long had a concern for the "non-economic". However, it has done so with a new zeal in the contemporary era. One of the defining objectives of neoliberal governmentality, as Foucault recognised in his analyses of the Chicago School, has been this deployment of a certain form of economic analysis to the social and cultural domains: the generalisation of the economic form of the market throughout the social body and to phenomena which, since the nineteenth century, had been defined in opposition to the economy, or otherwise as something that complemented and supported it (Foucault, 2008).

Fine (2001: 11) is also clear on this point: "Only, however, with recent develop-ments within the discipline [of economics] has it been able to offer an analysis of the social, institutional and customary".

In these ways, while echoing *Our Creative Diversity*'s model of a dual role for culture, the cultural awareness in the practices of the Bank largely emerged in a way which did not so much bring the UNESCO report's anthropological cri-tique to bear on a "godless", one-dimensional economics (as Cernea or members of the WCCD might have hoped) but rather signalled the expansion of a set of economic models and techniques into the traditional territories of the "other" social sciences. At the same time, although the number of "non-economists" joining figures such as Cernea on the Bank staff continued to grow, and slowly move up the chain of command, the voting structures within the Bank have remained biased towards the guardians of development orthodoxy, while the top leadership remains bankers whose orientations are legal and economic – and, of course, whose commitment to maintaining the Bank's credibility with its major investors on Wall Street generally comes first (Leaf, 2006).

We might conclude here that at the World Bank economics had effectively beaten anthropology in the race to the last frontier of development. To put it in the terms that had been set out in *Our Creative Diversity*, the primacy of the "instrumental" over the "constitutive" role of culture had been reasserted through the reconstructed neoliberalism of the post-Washington Consensus. There was room here for "development anthropology" but less so for the "anthropology of development", as the *constitutive, constructive and creative role* of culture that had been elaborated by the WCCD effectively became collapsed into the elaboration of a particular model of culture as resource by the Bank and the architects of the revolution in and around economics. This was a model in which culture was conceptualised not so much as a resource for political recog-nition or a basis for the articulation of claims to "cultural growth" that could redeem a "soul" for neoliberal development (along with all the problems con-tained in such a notion), but rather as something to be taken into account in order to improve the effectiveness of economic models and that could provide readily identifiable assets for poverty alleviation by adding value and attracting investment in the increasingly lucrative heritage and tourism sectors. Yúdice's observations on culture as a resource that we considered in the previous chapter are at least partly correct here: in his analysis of the work of the Inter-American Development Bank (IADB), he had already suggested, for example, that such a model is a predictable outcome in such a context given the requirement for hard data and a reliable set of indicators for culture that can offer some form of method for the approval and appraisal of development programmes and invest-ment (Yúdice, 2003: 15–16).

However, this observation is also to gloss over the particular ways in which the nature of culture as a resource has been contested between UNESCO and the more orthodox development institutions. The kind of lament that had been circulated by UNESCO prior to the Stockholm conference in 1998 con-cerning the state of existing measures and priorities for culture in international development was still being echoed several years later by those who remained unconvinced by the advances claimed by the World Bank and the recent revolution in economics, and who continued to point to problems in the ways that the architects of the post-Washington Consensus had attempted to bridge the gap between culture and development.

Their explanations for these problems largely centred on the difficulties with operationalising a "truly" anthropological and holistic concept of culture in policy, alongside the "imperialism" of economic disciplines and the lack of meaningful reform in national and international development projects. Lourdes Arizpe for example, writing for a workshop organised by the World Bank in 2002 on the theme of culture and development,[7] reflected on this lack of action by noting that "ambiguities in the definition of culture" and "the implicit assumptions about culture in economic development models" had produced a series of "culturally blind rather than culturally sensitive development programmes" and led to "generally well-intentioned, yet frequently insubstantial, institutional responses, both nationally and internationally" (Arizpe, 2004: 183). Also in attendance was Michael Cernea, who identified the source of the problem in a widespread inability and reluctance to fuse cultural and economic disciplinary frameworks in a way that retained the anthropological richness and vitality of the former. Cernea put much of the blame on the dichotomy created at the end of WWII between the work of the World Bank and UNESCO which had "put culture in one pot and development in a totally different pot and that wrecked culture and development for five decades and continues to do so".[8]

Despite such laments over the results of the work of the Decade, however, UNESCO was by now finding a more receptive audience for its work. Its embrace of new partnerships among the Bretton Woods institutions and the broader development community of donors, investors and NGOs, as well as its emergence as the platform for the cultural diversity agenda, was symptomatic of a return to relevance in international society and debate. Most symbolic of all was the US's announcement in 2002 of its decision to return to the organisation after an absence of almost 20 years – a decision made all the more remarkable since it was made under the Presidency of G.W. Bush (a Presidency that matched Reagan's in its level of hostility towards international institutions), who endorsed the organisation and the reforms that it had carried out since the 1980s (Bush, 2002). As we will examine in the next chapter, the US re-entry to UNESCO had a double significance: it signalled, on the one hand, UNESCO's comeback as a "universal" point of reference on matters related to international cultural policy, but on the other it exposed the depth of the international fault-line that had emerged on the question of the trade in cultural products. Tracing the rehabilitation of the organisation over the neoliberal era is important in understanding this faultline regarding the framework of cultural development that was ultimately adopted at UNESCO in the decade after Stockholm, and so before going on to examine this in more detail in the following chapter it is worth digging a little further down by examining the reforms that were carried out at UNESCO over the 1980s and 1990s.

Overcoming "cultural misunderstandings" at UNESCO: the road from Mexico City to Stockholm

Action plans

The most significant effect of the Intergovernmental Conference on Cultural Policies for Development in Stockholm in 1998 arguably lay less in the content of the Action Plan that was adopted than in the nature of the gathering itself, since this initiated the kind of political dynamic and impact that was necessary to begin to breathe life into the agenda for cultural development as it had been conceived by the WCCD. Stockholm certainly attracted an impressive number of participants – 2,500 people, from 149 countries – and UNESCO reflected enthusiastically on the wide range of delegations in attendance over the four days: a mixture of representatives not just from governments but also civil society and the private sector (UNESCO, 1998c).

An intergovernmental gathering on this scale and with such a wide range of participants marked something of a coup for UNESCO, which over the 1980s and 1990s had found itself at risk of floating away on a cloud of irrelevance since the high that had been reached at the MONDIACULT conference in Mexico City 1982 and the demands for NWICO. In seeking a greater political impact for the work of the Decade, and indeed for the credibility of the organisation itself, UNESCO was particularly keen to make clear prior to the conference that Stockholm would be a gathering of a different nature to those in the past. It referred here in particular to the turbulent period that had been bracketed by the meetings in Nairobi in 1976 and Mexico City in 1982 (UNESCO, 1998a). Stockholm presented an opportunity for the organisation not only to revive the kind of political scale and ambition of such events, but also to reinvent cultural policy in the contemporary era and to present a new face to delegates:

> The success of future cultural policies will greatly depend on whether the relationship between culture and development can be effectively integrated and on the capacity of policy-makers to achieve results cross-sectorally.... In reviving its own tradition of intergovernmental conferences on cultural policies, UNESCO itself must radically renew that tradition as well. The Stockholm Conference has been designed, therefore, to enable govern-mental delegates to interact more directly with representatives of civil society. By the same token, instead of seeking to adopt solemn declarations and resolutions it will seek practical outcomes.
>
> (UNESCO, 1998a)

This change was partly a sign of the times, reflecting a concern to work more closely with, and through, the new agents of development, namely the "dynamic forces" of international civil society and the private sector. Proceedings were therefore set up to allow government ministers and cultural leaders, artists, intellectuals, scholars, and media personalities, to interact and debate

(UNESCO, 1998a), and in celebrating the adoption of the Plan following the conference Mayor had made a point to "highlight the importance of the Conference in establishing a link with the private sector" (UNESCO, 1998c). These were all key themes at Stockholm, and after the work of the Decade UNESCO was at pains to put them centre stage. By reaching out and seeking partners outside of the organisation in this way, it was hoped that more effective and longer-lasting bridges could be secured between economic and cultural concerns in development policy, and this was now being repeatedly stressed as an imperative if Stockholm was to inaugurate more than just another decade of hot air.

This shift by UNESCO evident at Stockholm – building links with civil society and the private sector, alongside a greater decentralisation and pragmatism in achieving its goals – was also borne out of a more pressing set of concerns, stemming from the ongoing fiscal problems facing the organisation and persistent pressure regarding the need to reform and recover international political credibility. These pressures had been mounting since the last major intergovernmental gathering in Mexico City in 1982 had effectively split the organisation in two, and so Stockholm offered an opportunity to open a new phase in the organisation's work – particularly concerning the relationship between culture and development, which had been at the heart of the disagreements of the 1970s and 1980s. The withdrawal of the US (1984) and UK (1985) following the NWICO period had resulted in a 30% cut in its annual operating funds and put it under a number of pressures to reform at the same time as it found itself struggling for relevance within the international system following the rise of the Washington Consensus under US leadership.

De-politicising culture and development

The marginalisation of UNESCO from the mid-1980s was consistent with the intensification of US policy in this period of denying funding and cooperation to UN agencies and related organisations that operate according to some minimal standard of majority decision making and full participation of their members (Schiller, 1989: 116). The United Nations Conference on Trade and Development (UNCTAD), for example, which had been the Third World platform for the New International Economic Order (NIEO) alongside its calls for a New World Information and Communication Order at UNESCO, was similarly marginalised in this period. At the same time, institutions which could be more easily influenced, notably the World Bank and IMF, were given greater priority – along with the shift to administering a greater proportion of economic and developmental assistance through bilateral channels. In these ways, the US actively sought to prepare the international environment for forms of deregulation and privatisation that would maintain "open doors" for transnational corporate enterprise. As Thomas Gulick, analyst for the Reaganite think-tank The Heritage Foundation had put it on the eve of the announcement that the US would withdraw from UNESCO:

The US must provide a powerful free enterprise alternative to the NIEO – a kind of Freedom in Free Enterprise strategy for free market development in the developing world. ... Funds should be cut to UNESCO programs advocating NIEO concepts, the New World Information and Communication Order, or the New World Culture Order. If these ideologies persist and the UNESCO effort to curtail Western cultural industries and mass communications businesses continues, all US funds to UNESCO, assessed and unassessed funds as well as US funding of UNESCO through United Nations Development Program, international lending institutions, and regional banks, should be discontinued.

(Gulick, 1982)

Following the US's withdrawal, the establishment by the Reagan administration in 1985 of the US Reform Observation Panel for UNESCO ("To assess the reform process in UNESCO and to encourage reform efforts that advance U.S. interests", as a memorandum by William Harley from the US Department of State put it; Harley, 1985) is symptomatic of the hostile atmosphere in which UNESCO came to find itself in this period. By 1989 it was being observed among members of the US scientific community that unless UNESCO was to win the US and UK back soon, "its present state of temporary weakness may degenerate into permanent impotence" (*The Scientist*, 1989: 364).

Mayor was elected in 1987 on a platform intended to address some of these crises gathering at UNESCO, and steps were quickly taken to address many of the key concerns of the organisation's critics, notably in the preparation by Mayor between 1987 and 1989 of the Medium-Term Plan for 1990–1995 (UNESCO, 1990). A range of issues were highlighted, including management structures and efficiency and the holes in the organisation's budget, but at the top of the list was the issue of "politicisation". This is the term that had come to be used to refer to the organisation's alleged departure from its "universal" mandate – an allegation that came most forcefully from the US and UK in complaining of the "anti-Western" and anti-freedom-of-the-press agendas of the organisation's management, appointment and decision-making procedures. The reform measures proposed by Mayor detailed a readiness to take on such issues and prompted calls from a number of groups within the US (such as the National Academy of Sciences, the American Association for the Advancement of Science, the American Bar Association, the American Chemical Society, and the National Education Association) that UNESCO deserved renewed US support (*The Scientist*, 1989: 364). This was echoed by the US State Department, which indicated that the US would rejoin if the general conference approved Mayor's strategic plan (*Washington Post*, 1989).

Such offers of renewed support shifted the pressure to reform within UNESCO onto the supporters of "politicisation", since a key sticking point for the US was a stubborn persistence among some within the organisation for making references to the more radical implications of the MacBride Report, NWICO and NIEO. The removal of such references within the organisation's work had been proposed in Mayor's drafts for the 1990–1995 Medium-Term Plan, and this was a key theme of the General Conference of 1989. Mayor's proposal had initially met some opposition from a number of members on UNESCO's Executive Board, who expressed concerns over the lack of consultation that had been made (particularly among developing country members) and sought to have the references reinstated.[9] Given the internal and external pressures to have them removed, however, references to the objectives of NWICO in the Medium-Term Plan were ultimately only included to the extent that they had been part of a series of "misunderstandings" and that it was now time for the organisation to dispel such misunderstandings by moving on and recovering its properly "universal" mandate in a forward-looking, pragmatic spirit of consensus and reform. In a section dealing with how the NWICO agenda had tarnished the organisation's image, the Medium-Term Plan that was finally adopted noted, for example, that now that UNESCO was

> setting out on a path of innovation, it is perhaps the time to take the lessons of past experience to heart and to explore the possibilities of a new strategy whereby the Organization's global objective may be attained in such a manner as to dispel the misunderstandings.
>
> (UNESCO, 1990: 117)

In other words, NWICO was now officially on the wrong side of history, as were any stragglers who were preventing UNESCO from catching up with it.

This path out of NWICO was also forged by a change of course amongst many of the developing country members in this period, as "the 'triumph' of liberal economics in the developing world" (Biersteker, 1995) saw the replacement of Third World projects of national development with the neoliberal project of global liberalisation, competitiveness and structural adjustment (Hoogvelt, 1987; Harris, 1987). This change of course combined with that of the Eastern Bloc over the 1980s, which had in practice often served to reinforce some the Non-Aligned demands at UNESCO against Western dominance in information and communications. This move away from the oppositional politics of the previous decades at UNESCO was most clearly expressed in the form of the "new strategy" settled upon at UNESCO in 1989 and heralded in the 1990–1995 Medium-Term Plan as pointing the way forward for the organisation in the 1990s: the International Program for the Development of Communication (IPDC). The IPDC provides a useful point of reference in tracing the way in which cultural development emerged from the reforms of the 1980s in "depoliticised" form, and so will be considered below.

The International Program for the Development of Communication

The IPDC was an initiative which came out of one of the recommendations of the MacBride Commission in 1980 for increased cooperation and development assistance in building communications capacity and infrastructure in developing countries (concerning the provision of training, technology transfer, and so on). Most of the rest of the MacBride Commission's recommendations were jettisoned. To the extent that any formal international consensus over the recommendations of the MacBride Commission had been reached – as can be gauged, for example, by the resolution on the report that was adopted at the General Conference in 1980, after difficult and protracted negotiations (UNESCO, 1980) – this involved an acknowledgement of the need for such development assistance alongside a recognition of the importance of cultural identity. It was not possible to achieve substantial acknowledgement in the resolution for the other key recommendations of the MacBride Commission regarding the more sensitive questions related to Western cultural dominance and its control over the administration of development assistance and the free flow of information. The Mac-Bride Report had highlighted five key points for consideration, and these had also featured prominently in the demands of the Non-Aligned movement: "development", "strengthening of independence and self-reliance", "cultural identity", "democratisation (access-participation)" and the "right to communicate". However, the negotiations over the content of the 1980 resolution that responded to the report led only to the adoption of substantive commitments to the concepts of "development" and "cultural identity" (Carlsson, 2003: 20–22).

Therefore, unlike many of the other recommendations presented to the General Conference in 1980, "development" and "cultural identity" were deemed uncontroversial enough to maintain the kind of consensus necessary in order for them to remain on the agenda at UNESCO. Most importantly they had the support of the Western countries, who hoped that focusing the debate on the provision of cooperation, aid and assistance for the development of communications capacity and infrastructure might appease the Non-Aligned countries by meeting one of their demands, bringing them to soften their overall stance and reducing the intensity of ideological confrontations over questions of international order and regulation. The Western bloc countries thus celebrated their role as the "authors" of the IPDC (Carlsson, 2003: 23–26) and, as The Heritage Foundation put it, settling on the IPDC offered Western nations not only a "means to buy peace" but also a commitment to keep the door open for Western-led projects of investment and development:

> The West and the US looked on the IPDC as a means to buy peace. The Western nations agreed to increase foreign aid and the transfer of communications technology and training to the Third World through the IPDC. The G77, in turn, indicated that the Third World would cease its NWICO attacks on the West via UNESCO if the IPDC, backed by Western capital, would start to help the Third World develop modern communications networks.
>
> (The Heritage Foundation, 1983)

Unsurprisingly, interest in the IPDC quickly waned over the following years as it became evident that it was proving to be ineffective, not least because of the lack of funds being made available to it (after the first two years in operation, Norway contributed roughly half of its small budget, with two-thirds of the other half being made up by the developing countries themselves) (Carlsson, 2003: 25). The US was most vocal in expressing concern over majority control by the G77 over the use of parts of the funds (the "Special Account") and withheld contributions until withdrawing from UNESCO altogether in 1984. This combined with the mandate of IPDC chairman Gunnar Garbo – who was praised for seeing out his responsibility of defusing any "ideological" debate during his term of office (UNESCO, 1988b) – to effectively make the IPDC a redundant talking shop, administering the few minor programmes that were able to get off the ground with an increasingly restricted remit and small budget.

Even the little work that had initially come out of the IPDC provoked the familiar criticisms that had been made of NWICO: instead of delivering on its promise to bring peace and respect for Western capital and development assistance, by 1983 it was claimed that the IPDC had become a "a stalking horse for Third World press interests" and a mechanism designed to "to tap the West" for billions of dollars in development assistance free from bilateral conditions (*The Heritage Foundation*, 1983). Furthermore, the IPDC was seen to be "actively supporting liberation movements" and "terrorist groups" (with the proposal of funding for a printing press for the anti-apartheid SWAPO and ANC organisations given as examples) and "proposing to correct the inequalities between the living standards of the Western industrialized nations and the developing countries", thereby continuing to wage "the long-range attack on the ability of the Western press and media to move freely in the Third World" (*The Heritage Foundation*, 1983). Particularly worrying in this scenario was an attempt by some to use the IPDC to gain legitimacy for a redefinition of information, to be "understood as a social good and a cultural product, not as a material commodity or merchandise", and ultimately to have this definition accepted in international law. If that were to happen, it was warned, Western news agencies could

> be accused of having no "right" to sell their international wire services. The information they contain would be regarded as a "social good" and the property of all. This is an overt denial of private property and, by association, of a free enterprise economy.
>
> (The Heritage Foundation, 1983)

In such ways, by the end of the 1980s the debate over NWICO at UNESCO had been displaced by a depoliticised and largely ineffectual concern with projects of development assistance. The "new path" being forged in the 1990s was therefore a circumscribed one, as the organisation experienced demotion and was no longer equipped to deliver any significant programmes of investment or development assistance that did not challenge the supremacy of Western capital and expertise, or which offered an alternative set of regulatory and conceptual underpinnings. Along the way a commitment to the recognition of "cultural identity" had been maintained in its programmes, and although what this meant exactly was yet to be given any substance, it was nevertheless now clear that it could not stand for anything that would present a fundamental challenge to the new liberal consensus: it was either commensurable with the emergent (neoliberal) rules of the global marketplace or it was fit only for the dustbin of history.

From NWICO to New World Order

UNESCO's own internal task of modernisation and reform continued apace over the 1990s, and this theme dominates the organisation's internal records after 1989. Measures focused on management practices and structures, staff policy (a process of far-reaching staff and department cuts was soon underway as well as a review of appointment procedures and criteria, which the critics of politicisation accused of becoming biased to Third World representatives under M'Bow), addressing the shortfall in its budget (and its accumulating debt) and – most importantly and overarching these themes – continuing to work towards the depoliticisation of its programmes (or, in other words, aligning UNESCO more closely with the post-Cold War spirit of universalism and a New World Order). In the 1990–1991 Report of the Director-General (UNESCO, 1992), Mayor was already stressing that the eventual adoption of the Medium-Term Plan in 1989, and its implementation in the first phase of programmes executed in 1990–1991, had finally "put an end to the controversies that had all too often given a distorted image of the Organization as a battle ground rather than a centre for co-operation" – noting in particular that "the misunderstandings connected with the concept of the New World Information and Communication Order have now been sorted out" and that UNESCO had resumed its role as "an international point of reference in the field of human rights and fundamental freedoms" (UNESCO, 1992: XXXV).

Having drawn a line under the past in this way, the next phase in the reform of the organisation was to continue to address its financial difficulties and political limitations through ongoing reform and by seeking to work not just with its member states but also partners in civil society and business, streamlining the organisation and adapting it to a new era. This was the message that was emphasised in the closing points made by Mayor in his 1990–1991 report:

> How can we create new partnerships, not just with governments, which are our natural partners, but with the dynamic forces in civil society: non-governmental organisations, associations, universities, research institutes, private firms?
>
> These questions, which are now concerned with how things are to be done rather than with the nature of the objectives, lie at the heart of the process of reflection which all of us, Member States and Secretariat alike, must continue to pursue if UNESCO is to have the multiplier effect needed to effect the transformations which the present world situation demands.
>
> (UNESCO, 1992: XXXVI)

It was on the basis of the path that was taken up under Mayor in the 1990s that much of the groundwork for Stockholm 1998 was prepared, and in this sense the reinvention of the organisation at Stockholm that we considered earlier was as much a follow-up to the work of the World Decade for Cultural Development as it was a reflection of UNESCO's efforts to reform the organisation and rebuild relations with those governments and organisations that had been broken by the confrontational politics of the previous decades: in particular the major donors among the Western bloc, the World Bank and the private sector. The UK rejoined in 1997, and further murmurs of approval for the organisation's reforms came from the US with calls from Congress over the 1990s for the President to authorise renewed membership (*New York Times*, 1994; *Washington Post*, 2000). Continued external criticism also continued to keep UNESCO under political pressure over this time, backed up by a reliable supply of coverage detailing the organisation's cronyism and bloated bureaucracy (e.g. *The Guardian*, 1999; *The Heritage Foundation*, 2001). Following on and off proposals to rejoin over the 1990s from the US Presidencies of Bush (senior) and Clinton, President G.W. Bush finally announced to the UN General Assembly in 2002 that UNESCO's rehabilitation was complete and that the US was now ready to renew membership (which took effect from 2003) (Bush, 2002). The Bush administration's subsequent attempts at UNESCO to water down and sink the Convention on cultural diversity before it could be adopted was widely seen as a return to the politics of the 1970s and 1980s. However, as we will see in the following chapters this analysis is quite far from the mark since it underestimates the extent to which a productive consensus has come to be forged between the North and South on the question of cultural development, even without US approval.

Summary

In summary, we might pick out a number of key points.

Although the ambitions of the World Decade for Cultural Development to gain wider authoritative recognition for culture as the "last frontier of development" were largely eclipsed by the revolution in and around economics and the designs of the post-Washington Consensus, UNESCO's parallel efforts over this period to emerge from the international wilderness did help to restore some of the organisation's international standing. The Stockholm intergovernmental conference of 1998 was a culmination of both of these developments. It presented an opportunity for an expression of the first international political commitment to the need to take cultural diversity into account in development (however empty of content this commitment remained at this stage). It also helped to clear what was left of the poisonous atmosphere that remained from the Nairobi and Mexico City meetings of the 1970s and 1980s and signalled the organisation's readiness to embrace a new era of international cooperation.

We have also seen how the path to "depoliticisation" that was laid from Mexico City to Stockholm buried beneath it some of the international political fissures that had given rise to NWICO. In the process this established some of the parameters within which culture as concept and political claim could have any place in the new world order of neoliberal globalisation. The ultimate outcome of the struggles over NWICO was a consensus around a set of principles that cultural development only be achieved through participation in international processes of aid, trade and investment that were endorsed by the West.

Nevertheless, over the following years this consensus also provided the basis for a broad North–South alliance that would eventually attempt to turn the tables on Washington at UNESCO. In the following chapter we will look in more detail at the nature of this consensus and examine the particular ways in which the themes of the Stockholm conference were given a more concrete form in the drafting of the Convention on cultural diversity.

Notes

1 The UNDP's (United Nations Development Programme) notion of human development is referred in *Our Creative Diversity* as "a process of enlarging people's choices – that measures development in a broad array of capabilities, ranging from political, economic and social freedom to individual opportunities for being healthy, educated, productive, creative, and enjoying self-respect and human-rights" (UNESCO, 1995: 8). A good summary of the elaboration of the "human development" approach in development economics from the 1970s is given by Qizilbash (2006). Critics have referred to the way that this conception of human development serves to de-politicise questions of international inequality and poverty (see, for example, Duffield, 2007).

2 For a critical overview of the concept of sustainable development that emerged during this period, see Pearce (2006).

3 The report notes, for example, that:

> Income distribution, poverty, employment and environmental objectives have been incorporated, externalities are sometimes accounted for, intertemporal choices and social rates of time discount have been explored in greater depth, and the prejudicial notion that what cannot be counted does not count (or even exist) has been, to some extent, abandoned.
>
> (UNESCO, 1995: 259)

4 The Action Plan contained a recognition on the part of Member States of the need for five broad objectives in policy (themselves subdivided into a total of 51 objectives): 1) To make cultural policy one of the key components of development strategy; 2) Promote creativity and participation in cultural life; 3) Reinforce policy and practice to safeguard and enhance the cultural heritage, tangible and intangible, moveable and immoveable, and to promote cultural industries; 4) Promote cultural and linguistic diversity in and for the information society; 5) Make more human and financial resources available for cultural development (UNESCO, 1998b).

5 Mayor's report of UNESCO activities between 1988–1989 recalled euphemistically that relations between UNESCO and the Bank had "reached the peak of their effectiveness in the late 1970s", and went on to detail some of the joint work that would be undertaken over the following years after the negotiation of a new framework of cooperation between UNESCO and the Bank in 1989. This took cooperation between the two organisations beyond the traditional area of education, extending to the fields of science and technology, the environment, statistics and the development of human

resources, as well as regarding the formulation of Structural Adjustment Policies (UNESCO, 1991: 21).

6 There is already good coverage of the ways in which these particular concepts were taken up and developed in the field of development in this period, and in particular by the World Bank. See, for example, Harriss (2001); Fine (2001); Cooke and Kothari (2001); Kwame Sundaram and Fine (2006).

7 The World Bank made papers and video recordings of the contributions to the 2002 workshop available to view online at: www.cultureandpublicaction.org/conference/conference.htm. Many of the written contributions were also collected in the publication *Culture and Public Action* (Rao and Walton, 2004).

8 Cernea's contribution to the workshop is available to view at www.cultureandpubli-caction.org/conference/conference.htm

9 See the guidelines for redrafting Mayor's Medium-Term Plan that were suggested by the Executive Board in *Item 4* of UNESCO (1988a); and the warnings such as those made in *The Scientist* (1989: 365) regarding the Executive Board's jeopardising of US support for UNESCO – and therefore the future of the organisation itself – by seeking to reinstate references in the plan to NWICO.

Bibliography

Arizpe, L. 1998. "UN cultured". *Anthropology Today*. 14(3).

Arizpe, L. 2004. "The Intellectual History of Culture and Development Institutions". In Rao, V. and M. Walton (eds). *Culture and Public Action*. World Bank/Stanford: Stanford University Press.

Bennett, T. 1998. *Culture: A Reformer's Science*. London: Sage.

Biersteker, 1995. "The 'triumph' of liberal economic ideas in the developing world". In Stallings, B. (ed.). *Global Change, Regional Response: The New International Context of Development*. Cambridge: Cambridge University Press.

Bush, G.W. 2002. *President's Remarks at the United Nations General Assembly*. United Nations, New York, 12 September 2002. White House Office of the Press Secretary. Available online at: http://usiraq.procon.org/sourcefiles/bush.un.9-12-02.pdf; accessed 26/04/2009.

Carlsson, U. 2003. "The Rise and Fall of NWIO – and then?" Paper presented at the EURICOM Colloquium, Venice, 5–7 May 2003.

Cernea, M. 1995. "Malinowski Award Lecture: Social Organization and Development Anthropology". *Human Organization*. 54(3).

Cole, S. 1995. "Contending voices: Futures, culture and development". *Futures*. 27(4).

Cooke, B. and U. Kothari (eds) 2001. *Participation: The New Tyranny?* London: Zed Books.

Davis, P. (ed.) 2011. "Shelton H. Davis (1942–2010)". *Tipití: Journal of the Society for the Anthropology of Lowland South America*. 9(2): Art.11. Available online at: http://digitalcommons.trinity.edu/cgi/viewcontent.cgi?article=1143&context=tipiti; accessed 14/08/2015.

Donders, Y. 2008. "The History of the UNESCO Convention on the Protection and Promotion of the Diversity of Cultural Expressions". In Schneider, H. and P. van den Bossche (eds). *Protection of Cultural Diversity from a European and International Perspective*. Oxford: Intersentia.

Duffield, M. 2007. *Development, Security and Unending War*. Cambridge: Polity Press.

Elden, S. 2006. "Contingent sovereignty, territorial integrity and the sanctity of borders". *SAIS Review of International Affairs*. 26(1).

Eriksen, T.H. 2001. "Between Universalism and Relativism: A critique of the UNESCO concepts of culture". In Cowan, J., M. Dembour and R. Wilson (eds). *Culture and Rights: Anthropological Perspectives*. Cambridge: Cambridge University Press.

Escobar, A. 1997. "Anthropology and Development". *International Social Science Journal*. 154: 497–516.

Fine, B. 2001. *Social Capital Versus Social Theory: Political Economy and Social Science at the Turn of the Millennium*. London: Routledge.

Foucault, M. 2008. *The Birth of Biopolitics: Lectures at the College de France, 1978–1979*. Hampshire: Palgrave Macmillan.

Guardian. 1999, 18 October. "Family and mistresses dip in UNESCO trough; Staff say the UN body is being crippled as its budget is spent on unmonitored projects".

Gulick, T.G. 1982. *UNESCO: Where Culture Becomes Propaganda*. Washington: Heritage Foundation.

Harley, W.G. 1985. "Telecommunications Development: The U.S. Effort". *Journal of Communication*. Spring 1985.

Harris, N. 1987. *The End of the Third World: Newly Industrializing Countries and the Decline of an Ideology*. Harmondsworth: Penguin.

Harriss, J. 2001. *Depoliticizing Development: The World Bank and Social Capital*. New Delhi: Leftword.

Hoogvelt, A.M.M. 1987. *The Third World in Global Development*. London: Macmillan.

Kwame Sundaram, J. and B. Fine (eds) 2006. *The New Development Economics: After the Washington Consensus*. London: Zed Books.

Leaf, M.J. 2006. "Michael Cernea's Excerpt: What it Means for Us". *Culture and Agriculture*. 28(1).

Margolin, V. 1996. "Our Creative Diversity". *The Journal of Developing Areas*. 35(1).

Minister of Foreign Affairs and Foreign Trade of Barbados, Austria Center, Vienna, 20 June 2006. Available online at: www.foreign.gov.bb; accessed 20/02/2010.

Moore, M. 1994. "How difficult is it to construct market relations? A commentary on Platteau". Journal of Development Studies. 30: 818–830.

Nederveen Pieterse, J. 2001. *Development Theory: Deconstructions/Reconstructions*. London: Sage.

New York Times. 1994, 19 February. "Rejoining UNESCO Suggested to US".

Pearce, D. 2006. "Sustainable Development". In Alexander Clark, D. (ed.). *The Elgar Companion to Development Studies*. Cheltenham: Edward Elgar.

Platteau, J.P. 1994. "Behind the Market Stage Where Real Societies Exist". *Journal of Development Studies*. 30: 533–77 (Part I); 753–817 (Part II).

Qizilbash, M. 2006. "Human Development". In Alexander Clark, D. (ed.). *The Elgar Companion to Development Studies*. Cheltenham: Edward Elgar.

Rao, V. and M.Walton (eds) 2004. *Culture and Public Action*. Stanford: Stanford University Press/World Bank.

Sahlins, M. 1972. "The Original Affluent Society". In Sahlins, M. *Stone Age Economics*. Chicago: Aldine-Atherton.

Sahlins, M. 1976. *Culture and Practical Reason*. Chicago: University of Chicago Press.

Schiller, H.I. 1989. *CULTURE, INC.: The Corporate Takeover of Public Expression*. Oxford: Oxford University Press.

The Heritage Foundation. 1983. "The IPDC: UNESCO vs. the Free Press". 10 March 1983. Available online at: www.heritage.org/research/internationalorganizations/bg253.cfm; accessed 26/04/2009.

The Heritage Foundation. 2001. "Not the Time for the United States to Rejoin UNESCO". 17 January 2001. Available online at: www.heritage.org/research/internationalorganizations/bg1405.cfm; accessed 26/04/2009.

The Scientist. 1989. "The Time Has Come For The United States To Get Back Into UNESCO". 3(22): 13 November 1989.

UNESCO. 1980. "Resolution 4/19: International Commission for the Study of Communication Problems". *Records of the General Conference 21st Session, Belgrade 23 September to 28 October 1980. Vol. 1, Resolutions*. Available online at: http://unesdoc.UNESCO.org/images/0011/001140/114029E.pdf; accessed 24/04/2009.

UNESCO. 1988a. *Decisions Adopted by the Executive Board at its 129th Session*. Paris: UNESCO. 129 EX/Decisions. Available online at: http://unesdoc.UNESCO.org/images/0007/000795/079539E.pdf; accessed 24/04/2009.

UNESCO. 1988b. *Address by Mr. Michel de Bonnecorse at the Ninth Session of the Intergovernmental Council of the IPDC*. DG/88/3/MB.

UNESCO. 1990. *Third Medium-Term Plan 1990–1995*. Paris: UNESCO 25/C4 Approved. Available online at: http://unesdoc.UNESCO.org/images/0008/000846/084697eo.pdf; accessed 24/04/2009.

UNESCO. 1991. *Report of the Director-General 1988–1989*. 26 C/3. Available online at: http://unesdoc.UNESCO.org/images/0008/000866/086600eo.pdf; accessed 24/04/2009.

UNESCO. 1992. *Report of the Director-General 1990–1991*. 27 C/3. Available online at: http://unesdoc.UNESCO.org/images/0009/000922/092295e.pdf; accessed 24/04/2009.

UNESCO. 1995. *Our Creative Diversity: Report of the World Commission on Culture and Development*. Paris: UNESCO.

UNESCO. 1997. *Final Report of the Intergovernmental Committee of the World Decade for Cultural Development*. Paris: UNESCO. CLT/MD/6.

UNESCO. 1998a. *The Stockholm Conference – Background Document*. Paris: UNESCO. Available online at: http://portal.UNESCO.org/culture/en/ev.php-URL_ID=18717&URL_DO=DO_TOPIC&URL_SECTION=-465.html; accessed 15/03/2009.

UNESCO. 1998b. *The Stockholm Conference – Action Plan on Cultural Policies for Development*. Paris: UNESCO. Available online at: http://portal.UNESCO.org/culture/en/files/35220/12290888881stockholm_actionplan_rec_en.pdf/stockholm_actionplan_rec_en.pdf; accessed 15/03/2009.

UNESCO. 1998c. *STOCKHOLM ACTION PLAN BRIDGES CULTURE AND DEVELOPMENT*. UNESCO Press Release, No. 98–64e.

United Nations. 1986. *Proclamation of the World Decade for Cultural Development*. United Nations, 8 December 1986. A/RES/41/187.

Washington Post. 1989, 25 February. "UNESCO Chief Vows Major Reforms; Director-General Seeks to Persuade U.S. to Rejoin Agency".

Washington Post. 2000, 20 April. "Riley Seeks Payment of Dues, Return to UNESCO".

World Bank. 2000. *Culture Counts: Financing, Resources and the Economics of Culture in Sustainable Development*. Washington: The World Bank.

World Bank. 2003. *Culture and the Corporate Priorities of the World Bank: Report on progress from April 1999 to December 2002*. Available online at: http://documents.worldbank.org/curated/en/2003/02/8390065/culture-corporate-priorities-world-bank; accessed 04/03/2008.

Yúdice, G. 2003. *The Expediency of Culture: Uses of Culture in the Global Era*. London: Duke University Press.

Part II

4 The rules of the cultural marketplace

Introduction

A new consensus and a new fault line emerge at UNESCO

In the previous chapter we examined the ways in which the World Commission on Culture and Development (WCCD) had set out an ambitious "anthropological" critique of development, challenging the Washington Consensus model that had dominated international development in the 1980s and 1990s. Its 1995 report *Our Creative Diversity* set out the case for a new international framework of cultural policy based on a particular model of "the dual role of culture", while calling for a concern for cultural diversity to be placed at the centre of a new global ethics. In this way the WCCD elaborated some of the intellectual foundations on which a new agenda for cultural development could be constructed, in parallel with the ongoing elaboration of principles of sustainable development and their mainstreaming in policy: "We are providing the groundwork. Our hope is that others will move forward and build on it" (UNESCO, 1995: 11). In the last chapter we also saw, however, how this hope was frustrated over the following years by the particular ways in which culture came to feature in the revolution in and around economics and the reconstructed neo-liberalism of the post-Washington Consensus.

Nevertheless, the dual role of culture and cultural diversity became defining causes at UNESCO following the Intergovernmental Conference on Cultural Policies for Development in Stockholm, 1998. These causes were placed at the centre of a campaign that ultimately secured the adoption of a binding international instrument in the form of the 2005 Convention on the Protection and Promotion of the Diversity of Cultural Expressions ("the Convention"). The legal standing of this instrument is far from what most of its supporters had hoped for. Nevertheless, the fact that it was adopted by an overwhelming majority of states against the wishes of the US, and that it gave formal expression to the principle of cultural sovereignty within the framework of international trade liberalisation, has been seen as expressing a new international consensus around cultural development. The European Commission, which had been delegated to negotiate the Convention on behalf of the European Member

States, referred to the emergence of "a consensus that the international community has never before reached on a variety of guiding principles and concepts related to cultural diversity" (European Commission, 2006).

The process of reform at UNESCO initiated under Director General Federico Mayor has also continued apace following Stockholm, with the tenure of his successor – the Japanese diplomat Kōichirō Matsuura (which ran from 1999 to 2009) – characterised by an intensification of efforts to bring the organisation into line with the new spirit of the times. As we also saw in the previous chapter, the reforms initiated under Mayor were necessary conditions for restoring the organisation's standing in the new world order of US supremacy and neoliberal globalisation. This rehabilitation was consolidated during the tenure of Matsuura, despite facing criticisms from the beginning (protests and hunger strikes from staff at the prospects of deep cuts and reform, and accusations from a number of delegates that Japan had been buying and bullying developing country members in a bid to secure leverage at the organisation). Matsuura was nevertheless successful in achieving the central objectives of the platform on which he was elected by the majority of UNESCO's members: to woo back Washington and restore "the indisputable status of UNESCO as a unique universal organisation" (Ministry of Foreign Affairs of Japan, 1999; UN Wire, 1999).

The two broad developments since Stockholm that are outlined above – the emergence of the campaign for cultural diversity centred on UNESCO, and the organisation's recovery of international political credibility and standing – have brought UNESCO a level of attention and a relevance regarding questions of international governance that it has not seen since the days of NWICO. However, these developments have also served to highlight the emergence of a new faultline of controversy as the organisation has become a platform for the long-standing transatlantic and North American debate over what kind of regulatory framework is most appropriate to govern the trade in cultural products (see Chapter 2). As this debate began to take on an increasingly international character and intensity in the years following Stockholm, driven by the diplomatic initiatives of Canada and France, a powerful coalition began to emerge and assert the need for a new international cultural treaty that could offset the momentum of liberalisation in the cultural sector. They therefore called upon UNESCO to intervene, on the grounds of cultural diversity, in what had previously largely been a matter for dispute in the context of international trade negotiation and adjudication.

These developments were serious enough to provoke the anxieties of the US International Trade Administration which, wary of the potential impact on the American film and television sector, expressed objection to "France and Canada's efforts to remove cultural issues from the WTO and obtain support for their draft of a 'new instrument', possibly to be created within UNESCO" (US International Trade Administration, 2001: 87). The US decision to rejoin UNESCO was received in Canada and France not only as a reflection of the US's approval of the organisation's reforms, but also of its realisation of the need to be within the organisation to fight the Convention as the drafting process formally got underway in 2003 (Byers, 2005; *Le Devoir*, 2005). In the process UNESCO has come to play a renewed role as a "universal" point of reference in matters related to cultural governance, but it has also come to be fractured internally over questions regarding the rules governing the trade in cultural products.

This chapter seeks to draw out the main features of this new politics that has emerged at UNESCO over the 2000s. In doing so it is split into three sections. In the first section it is argued that the political and analytical attention accorded to the adoption of the Convention has over-emphasised the significance of the new fracture at UNESCO over trade and culture while missing what is arguably the more significant development over the previous quarter of a century: the post-NWICO shift in the terrain of controversy concerning questions of cultural development. It is argued that the significance of the recent fallout at UNESCO lies less in reflecting the contemporary salience of conflicts between culture and global capitalism, as is often assumed, but rather in demonstrating the extent of political concern for the stakes that have come to be attached to the management of culture as a resource for industrialisation, trade and development in the global marketplace.

This theme is developed in the second section by examining in more detail how the principle of the dual nature of culture that had been elaborated by the WCCD has been given political and legal content following the Stockholm conference of 1998 as it became articulated in the intensified debates over trade and culture. It notes in particular how France, the European Union and Canada have led this campaign as they have sought to "soften" the application of WTO rules in the cultural sector. However, it also notes that they have been unable to monopolise the drafting process at UNESCO, not only due to US opposition but also due to the presence of a number of other claims regarding the purpose of the Convention.

Finally, the third section turns to demonstrating the broader relevance of these developments at UNESCO by considering the case of contemporary cultural policy reform in China. China became the first major test case for the new rules of the cultural marketplace in 2009 as part of a high-profile dispute with the US at the WTO. This case can be used to draw out a number of aspects of the new politics of cultural development as they are becoming manifest both within China and internationally, and introduces themes that are taken up over the following two chapters.

"The causal link uniting two complementary attitudes": the rapprochement of culture and the market at UNESCO

A new balance between trade and culture

The Canadian trade lawyer, Ivan Bernier, has been one of the foremost experts working on the Convention since his involvement in the first drafts of an international instrument on cultural diversity that began to circulate in Canada in 2002. He has noted that the main task of the groups that worked on finalising the text at UNESCO between 2003 and 2005 was one of "legal rapprochement": to meet the demands of the coalition gathered at UNESCO that were calling for a new balance between trade and culture (Bernier, 2009).

This task of legal rapprochement, however, was also a process of political rapprochement, and its completion was widely heralded as the expression of a new progressive consensus on principles of international cultural governance. The near-unanimous adoption of the Convention had served not only to expose the US's isolation on the question of trade and culture, but also to finally bury some of the divisions of the past in the form of a binding international treaty with significant political support. Through its "dual" economic and cultural provisions, and its attempt to integrate the concerns of both developed and developing countries, as well as civil society and the private sector, the Convention has been celebrated for accommodating a variety of claims in a way that had seemed impossible only two to three decades previously during the international conflicts over NWICO. "The elephants and eagles could converse with mice" was how the Jamaican representative to UNESCO referred to the adoption of the Convention at the 2005 General Conference; "without cultural pluralism, we choke," added Brazil culture minister Gilberto Gil. "It guarantees the survival of minority cultures" (Guyanese cultural minister); "a real antidote to globalization" (Mauritania's cultural minister) (cited in *Le Monde*, 2005). Reflecting on his experience as president of the inter-governmental committee that was responsible for the final stages of completing the draft of the Convention between 2004 and 2005, Kader Asmal noted that its adoption had finally marked not only the first formal step taken to address global inequalities in flows of cultural goods and services, but also a transcendence of previous North–South divisions on cultural matters and "the most innovative platform for international cultural co-operation that the world has ever known" (Asmal, 2006: 355–356).

Underpinning such statements about the new consensus at UNESCO, and at the heart of the provisions making up the new framework of cultural regulation and development, has been the principle of the dual characteristics of cultural products. This was given particular emphasis by Director-General Matsuura in commenting on the significance of the Universal Declaration on Cultural Diversity, which contained among its provisions the first formal international recognition of "the specificity of cultural goods and services which, as vectors of identity, values and meaning, must not be treated as mere commodities or consumer goods" (UNESCO, 2001a: Article 8). Matsuura sought to emphasise in particular that, with the adoption of the Universal Declaration, campaigns for cultural recognition and rights could now be squared with campaigns for the special treatment of cultural goods and services in the context of trade liberalisation. This had provided the common ground on which to construct an agenda for cultural development and begin to cement the efforts of the WCCD and UNESCO over the previous decade:

The debate between those countries which would like to defend cultural goods and services "which, as vectors of identity, values and meaning, must not be treated as mere commodities or consumer goods", and those which would hope to promote cultural rights has thus been surpassed, with the two approaches brought together by the Declaration, which has highlighted the causal link uniting two complementary attitudes.

(UNESCO, 2001a: Foreword by the Director General)

This confluence of agendas has indeed marked an important development in the international debate, with the formulation of the dual nature of cultural goods and services presented as the basis of a set of measures that transcend past divisions over the international regulation of culture. However, it is important here to address a number of claims that have been made about the nature of this new consensus.

The way that the Convention has been framed at UNESCO has tended to present a one-dimensional picture of this consensus and this has been reflected in commentary and analysis. Observers from the field of international relations and communications that have examined the new consensus have often assumed that the US's opposition to the tide of support behind the Convention is a sign of its isolation in the face of a progressive, anti-neoliberal coalition to defend culture from the logics of capitalism and imperialism – or even as a sign that the spirit of NWICO had been reborn at UNESCO (see, for example, Mattelart, 2005; *Inter Press Service*, 2005; Moghadam and Elveren, 2008). Moghadam and Elveren (2008) have interpreted the Convention in this way, for example, as an expression of a conflict between the forces of cultural diversity and alterity on the one hand, and those of capitalism and globalisation (which they largely conflate with US power) on the other. As this conflict reached its climax during the intergovernmental drafting committee, which saw vigorous lobbying by the US delegation and coordinated efforts by US and Japanese delegates to weaken the Convention's standing in international law, they argue that the resulting text is an instrument that sets out a body of provisions on behalf of cultural diversity that have been compromised by a series of "concessions" to "the power of capital" – and thereby giving "economics" the final say over "culture":

The making of the UNESCO convention shows that culture matters, and that member states can go a long way toward addressing liberalisation and cultural invasion. But it also shows that given a capitalist world-system, economics trumps culture – or, to put it less bluntly, cultural concerns end where economic agreements and financial concerns begin. A related conclusion is that although the defeat of the United States over the Convention would suggest its declining hegemony, the compromises that were necessary confirm the power that the financial and trade institutions have in the contemporary world-system, and the way the power of capital is reflected in inter-governmental debates within the UN.

(Moghadam and Elveren, 2008: 751–752)

Such accounts, however, present a profoundly misleading analysis of the Convention, and can be used here to draw attention to a number of points. First of all, by situating the Convention this way, Moghadam and Elveren operate with a problematic concept of culture, as if it is at one end of a spectrum with "economics" and "the power of [American] capital" at the other. One of the implications of such an approach is that it cannot account for the role that has been played by the constellation of interests that have brought the cultural diversity agenda to UNESCO: their concern has not been to "shield" cultural from commercial concerns but precisely to raise the problem of cultural diversity as *simultaneously* a matter of commercial and cultural administration. To illustrate this point here it is only necessary to reiterate that the US position, rather than attempting to water down the instrument in a way which sought to "trump" culture with economics, has been to object to the Convention precisely on the grounds that it establishes a framework of regulation for the trade in cultural products in a way that encroaches into the regulatory domain of commerce and thereby exceeds UNESCO's remit as a cultural organisation. These objections were clearly raised on several occasions by the US State Department (US State Department, 2005), the US ambassador to UNESCO Louise Oliver (US Mission to UNESCO, 2005) and by Robert Martin of the US delegation to UNESCO. Martin, for example, wrote the delegation's final statement of opposition to the draft text by asserting that:

> This convention is not about culture.... In fact, the trade agenda was so compelling that we even had to bend UNESCO's long-established rules to accommodate the participation of the European Commission, which has competency for trade, not culture. Because it is about trade, this convention clearly exceeds the mandate of UNESCO.
>
> (Martin, 2005)

In other words, it is important to be clear that it has been the attempt by the Convention's supporters to create some form of authoritative recognition of the link between the commercial and the cultural – while the US has maintained that they should be kept apart, asserting the need for a division of competencies between UNESCO and the WTO – that has given UNESCO its recent significance as an arena of international norm creation. An instrument dealing only with culture and identity in a way that made no such reference to the rules of international commerce (and that therefore posed no substantive threat to the internationally dominant market positions of major exporters) would have barely sent out a ripple and UNESCO would have likely remained off the international political radar. In a prickly press conference following the adoption of the Convention, the US Ambassador to UNESCO was forced to acknowledge that the US's return to the organisation in 2003, and its subsequent efforts in opposing the Convention, had had the effect of focusing international attention back on an institution which normally produced instruments about which "nobody cares, neither before, neither after" (US State Department, 2005).

Another point that we should emphasise in clearing up some of the misconceptions about the new consensus that has been expressed in the Convention is to note the way that this latest controversy at UNESCO between the US and the Franco-Canadian led coalition has come to revolve around the rules governing the international production and trade of cultural products. In this sense the significance of the recent fallout at UNESCO lies not so much in demonstrating the contemporary salience of conflicts between culture and commerce, but rather in demonstrating the extent of political concern for the stakes that have come to be attached to the management of culture as a resource for investment, industrialisation, trade and development through the medium of the global market. Set against the NWICO period, this represents a significant shift in the terrain of controversy at UNESCO and has involved a change in the organisation's stance towards the long-standing problem of how to define culture and its relationship to global capitalism. Whereas it had previously approached culture and commerce as separate domains, and indeed had come to stand as a buffer between them by the 1970s and early 1980s, through landmark standard-setting instruments such as the Convention it has today become an agency promoting their engagement. In doing so it has taken the opportunity to finally give some form of substantial recognition to the developmental potential of the anthropological and sociological components of culture – what the WCCD referred to as its *constructive, constitutive and creative* role – by emphasising the particular nature of cultural goods and services as carriers of "identities, values and meanings" in the new global economy of cultural production and intellectual property.

The multiplication of the enterprise form

To illustrate this recent shift in UNESCO's approach to cultural regulation and development in greater depth here, it is useful to briefly set it against the pre-reform period of the Nairobi General Conference, MONDIACULT and the Mac-Bride Commission (for background on these, see Chapter 1). Consider, for example, the following, from two of the landmark events at UNESCO in this period: 1) the 1976 Nairobi Recommendation on the Participation by the People at Large in Cultural Life and Their Contribution to it; and 2) the UNESCO report *Cultural Industries: A Challenge for the Future of Culture* (which was circulated at MONDIACULT in 1982 as a document "bear[ing] witness to UNESCO's efforts over the past ten years or so to update its thinking on culture"):

1   The ultimate objective of access and participation is to raise the spiritual and cultural level of society as a whole on the basis of humanistic values and to endow culture with a humanistic and democratic content, and this in turn implies taking measures against the harmful effect of "commercial mass culture" which threatens national cultures and the cultural development of mankind, leads to debasement of the personality and exerts a particularly harmful influence on the young generation.

(UNESCO, 1976)

2   Generally speaking, a cultural industry is held to exist when cultural goods
     and services are produced, reproduced, stored or distributed on industrial or
     commercial lines, that is to say on a large scale and in accordance with a
     strategy based on economic considerations rather than any concerns for
     cultural development.

                                                                (UNESCO, 1982: 21)

We might compare the above examples with examples of work carried out at
UNESCO in response to the adoption of the instruments on cultural diversity
in the 2000s: 3) UNESCO's overview of the contemporary role of cultural
industries in development; 4) the organisation's recent attempts to measure
levels of global diversity in film and video production; and 5) the work of the
UNESCO Global Alliance for Cultural Diversity (GACD), an initiative
responding to the 2001 Universal Declaration and 2005 Convention that assists
attempts to build cultural industries in developing countries by generating international public-private partnerships and programmes of international investment and assistance:

3   The cultural industries, which include publishing, music, cinema, crafts and
     design, continue to grow steadily apace and have a determinant role to play
     in the future of culture.... The world map of these industries reveals a
     yawning gap between North and South. This can only be counteracted by
     strengthening local capacities and facilitating access to global markets at
     national level by way of new partnerships, know-how, control of piracy and
     increased international solidarity of every kind.

                                                                   (UNESCO, 2009a)

4   Film and video production are shining examples of how cultural industries
     – as vehicles of identity, values and meanings – can open the door to dia-
     logue and understanding between peoples, but also to economic growth and
     development. This conviction underpins the UNESCO *Convention on Cul-
     tural Diversity*.

                                                                   (UNESCO, 2009b)

5   In recent years creative industries have become a significant source of social
     and economic development and are now recognized as a powerful driving
     force of world trade and offer great potential for developing economies rich
     in cultural diversity ... Global Alliance projects are therefore underway to
     unlock the potential of local cultural industries. These recognize that a suc-
     cessful cultural industry has a range of needs that span the production chain
     from initial conception through to distribution and they support countries
     in their efforts to develop a conducive business environment necessary to
     allow such industries to grow.

                              (UNESCO-Global Alliance for Cultural Diversity, 2009a)

Examples 1) and 2) above illustrate the ways in which the aims of "humanising" and "democratising" culture that characterised the NWICO and NIEO campaigns at UNESCO stood opposed to the designs of international commerce and its attendant models of the cultural industries. The attempt to broaden the meaning of culture and the scope of cultural policy in this period to encompass a broader array of "ways of life" was part of a search for forms of national political independence and economic development outside of what were perceived to be neocolonial categories and prescriptions (also see Chapter 1).

In the more recent examples of 3), 4) and 5), this unease about the relationship between culture, the market and industrialisation has largely disappeared. The aim here is not so much to insulate culture from processes of industrialisation and marketisation but rather to improve the conditions necessary for the multiplication of cultural industries and their integration into international circuits of production, investment and exchange. With the traditional national cultural policy projects of civic formation increasingly seen to be losing their effectiveness in the context of globalisation, and with cheaper and faster production and distribution systems making it possible, in theory, for producers to market products to overseas diasporas and ever larger audiences, it is recognised that the most effective means of realising the expression of different ways of life today is through the international production, trade and consumption of cultural goods and services. As such, it is stressed by the GACD that effective cultural policies for development should place their emphasis upon remaining open to international flows of cultural content and information while developing the competitiveness of local cultural enterprises and their place in the international market, requiring measures such as improving their access to finance and providing appropriate forms of market policy and infrastructure (with a particular emphasis on providing appropriate frameworks of copyright and neighbouring rights).[1]

This puts the emphasis of cultural policy onto implementing favourable legislative and fiscal reforms for cultural enterprises, building capacity in the cultural sector and reforming the work of cultural institutions and creators so that they are more able to take advantage of the contemporary opportunities that are available to market their work domestically and internationally. The GACD programme Capacity-Building in the Senegalese Music Sector between 2008 and 2009, for example, worked with Senegalese policy makers, musicians and others involved in the development of Senegal's music industry in order to improve knowledge of "how to design and manage websites at lower costs, cultural business administration dealing with legal issues, events driven communication, and management and accounting" (UNESCO-Global Alliance for Cultural Diversity, 2009b). Such efforts have been reinforced by the establishment in 2010 of a UNESCO-EU expert facility project of technical assistance, funded by the EU, which is aimed at creating a pool of experts at national levels in the developing world that can assist in the creation of policy frameworks conducive for the growth of cultural industries.[2]

Measures such as these address real concerns of the cultural sector in developing countries, but have generally been slow to be taken up by governments and cultural ministries in much of the South, where the interests of the cultural sector have tended to be a low priority. This has been a key issue in the Caribbean, for example, where Nurse (2008) has reflected on this lack of priority accorded to culture in the region:

> The Caribbean enjoys a competitive capability in cultural production however the problem is that the creativity of our artists has not been backed up by an entrepreneurial, managerial and marketing capability from within our business sector nor has there been strong state support, facilitation or leadership. This is the essence of the problem that plagues several sectors of the cultural industries in the region.
>
> (Nurse, 2008: 2)

It has been in recognition of similar challenges faced elsewhere in the developing world that complementary strategies have been drawn up the World Intellectual Property Organization (WIPO)[3] and the principal organ of the United Nations addressing trade and development, the UN Conference on Trade and Development (UNCTAD).[4] Other initiatives have taken shape through the Mauritius Strategy for small island developing states (United Nations, 2005) and the Strengthening the Creative Industries programme for developing countries being implemented between the European Commission, the ILO, UNCTAD and UNESCO (UNESCO, 2010; also see Chapter 6). The key theme in these programmes is broadly similar, namely the need to implement careful market reforms that can nurture creativity and empower cultural entrepreneurs:

> Creativity is not a given resource. However, unlike labour or capital, or even traditional technologies, it is a resource that is deeply embedded in a country's social and historical context. As such, it is a ubiquitous asset. This provides new opportunities for developing countries to develop new areas of wealth and employment creation consistent with wider trends in the global economy. However, the nurturing and effective harnessing of this asset may be just as challenging, if not more so, for policymakers.
>
> To strengthen entrepreneurship, a framework must be established to improve the investment climate through appropriate market mechanisms, as well as public-private arrangements. This implies a wider development strategy where the central focus is on the creation of local enterprises with a high propensity to invest as a necessary prelude to closer integration into the global economy. Building cultural entrepreneurship has the advantage of captured local markets, but it must also be outward-looking, both regionally and globally.
>
> (UNCTAD, 2004: 8)

As such initiatives of capacity building have got underway, it has also been stressed that policymakers and cultural enterprises should seek out assistance and synergies through international capital, technology and expertise, particularly by striking public-private partnerships and forging areas of mutual commercial interest. In contrast to the spirit of NWICO, where nationalist claims for cultural autonomy and development resulted in international antagonism and confrontation, this new approach is characterised more by encouraging international cultural cooperation, investment and liberalisation and seeking out areas of mutual interest between developed and developing countries.

For example, as developing and emerging countries seek to expand their cultural and creative economies through media and information and communication technologies (ICT), it has been recognised by the European Commission that opportunities are opened for the European media and ICT sectors in a way which dovetails with its own strategies for commercial expansion, such as the Information Society in Europe (as was set out in the neoliberal framework of the Lisbon Strategy or the i2010 Initiative: "a more ambitious, targeted international EU strategy for ICT that explores new markets for EU industries, improves the competitiveness of Europe's ICT industry in global markets and promotes EU interests worldwide" (European Commission, cited in *Nordicom*, 2007)). Similarly, as cultural and commercial concerns increasingly overlap in the new economy, the commercial significance of international markets reflecting diasporic and linguistic ties has also been heightened: the European Commission's *European Agenda for Culture in a Globalizing World*, for example, advised member states to take advantage of Europe's historic language links with partner countries and regions in order to create opportunities for their cultural and creative sectors (European Commission, 2007). Such opportunities are also seen to exist today for many developing countries, for whom considerable overseas diasporas and linguistic ties offer the possibility of export markets that can help to overcome the limits of small domestic markets and purchasing power.

The Convention has aimed to provide the political and economic resources to encourage and support such measures in a number of ways, in particular by promoting international development cooperation and assistance through Articles 14, 15 and 16, which are aimed at encouraging developed countries to provide preferential market access to cultural exports from developing countries, while also building sustainable capacity in developing countries' cultural industries through mechanisms such as development assistance, technology transfer, investment and the fostering of co-productions in the cultural sector (UNESCO, 2005a). There is also a notable emphasis in the Convention and the other programmes noted above on the role of intellectual property and the private sector, responding to the call made at the end of the Universal Declaration to "Recognize and encourage the contribution that the private sector can make to enhancing cultural diversity and facilitating to that end the establishment of forums for dialogue between the public sector and the private sector" (UNESCO, 2001a).

In short, we can see from the above examples that the consensus on culture and development that has emerged over the last decade is based on a strategy which aims to promote competitive insertion into the global marketplace, accompanied by interventions to support the creation of appropriate market mechanisms and reforms aimed at stimulating the work of entrepreneurs and harnessing international capital, expertise and development assistance. The WCCD's concern for "cultural growth" that we considered in the previous chapter has been translated into an assertion of the role that international agencies and national cultural policymakers have to play in reforming local deficiencies in enterprise and production as a way of addressing global imbalances in the production and consumption of cultural goods and services. After the conflicts of the 1970s and 1980s, this has offered a welcome coincidence of interests in which projects of national cultural development and claims for cultural recognition and growth can be realised within the project of global integration through trade while opening new avenues for international capital and opportunities for market reform. The key normative contribution of the Convention as an international reference point for cultural regulation and intervention lies in this concern to establish a framework in which a multiplication and differentiation of the enterprise form can take place in the cultural sector: diversity is to be achieved here primarily through building the capacity of local enterprises and production and in pursuing increased opportunities for international investment and market access.

In light of this, we can also see that the claim that the Convention has exposed some of the "limits" to the marketisation, industrialisation or commodification of culture is a misleading one, as is the claim that it is American capitalism that is driving these processes forward. Rather than seeing the Convention as a symptom of a revival of some of the themes of the NWICO period, we might note instead that the extent to which its adoption has been celebrated as heralding an international consensus around principles of cultural development in fact reflects the extent to which the market and the enterprise form have been established as universal points of reference.

However, in noting this point it would be equally misleading to understand the recent developments at UNESCO and the broader cultural turn in development by reverting to the kind of critiques of commodification and instrumentality that were developed earlier in the twentieth century. Not only are international political dynamics much transformed today but, as was argued earlier in Chapter 2, it can also be disingenuous of critique to rely on such binary models of culture and administration, particularly where this obstructs a critical evaluation of the effects that flow from contemporary programmes of cultural reform and their consequences for different groups and competing claims to political recognition within and beyond the nation-state. These are both themes that we will return to below in examining the case of contemporary cultural policy reform in China, and again over the following chapters.

Having outlined the broad features of the new consensus at UNESCO we can now turn to examine in more detail the nature of the new fault line that has emerged over culture's status in the contemporary market order. In the following section we will look in particular at the way in which the key principle of the dual nature of culture that had been elaborated as part of the work of the WCCD came to be animated by France and Canada and given broader formal recognition as it was eventually drafted into the Convention against the opposition of the US.

The dual nature of culture after Stockholm and the conflict over Article 20

In the Action Plan that was drawn up in Stockholm in 1998 as a response to *Our Creative Diversity*, governments expressed a commitment to "Promote the idea that cultural goods and services should be fully recognized and treated as being not like other forms of merchandise" but this formed only one amongst 51 other broad policy objectives (UNESCO, 1998: Policy Objective 3.12). In other words, it is worth reflecting on the fact that this particular commitment only became a priority as it was adopted and elaborated as the central cause in the international campaign for cultural diversity at UNESCO over the following years. Tracing this process allows us to more fully grasp the political dynamics that have been obscured by the language of consensus and universality that has surrounded the adoption of the Convention.

Support for the principle concerning the special nature of cultural products gathered momentum through a concerted diplomatic effort from Canada and France, who had one eye on the timeframe of the WTO, and the bilateral efforts being made meanwhile by the US to advance a liberalisation agenda in the cultural sector. These pressures made them determined, as the former French Ambassador and Permanent Delegate to UNESCO Jean Musitelli (2006) has recounted, to work together to wrap up the Convention before the finalising of any further negotiations on the audiovisual and cultural sector at the WTO (the Doha "Development" Round of negotiations that got underway in 2001 were originally scheduled to be completed in 2005). A plan for how this could be achieved at UNESCO was suggested by the calendar of the organisation's activities and biennial General Conferences over the coming years, with the General Conference of 2005 pencilled in by the campaigners as a possible window for its adoption (Musitelli, 2006: 6; INCP, 2003; for a detailed outline of the stages that led up to the adoption of the Declaration and the Convention at UNESCO see UNESCO, 2001b, 2005b).

The first significant response to the Action Plan at UNESCO was the hosting of a symposium on the theme "Culture, the Market and Globalisation" in June 1999, supported and organised at the initiative of France and Canada. This event was framed as a follow up to the Stockholm Action Plan as well as to a number of other, more recent "international factors concerning cultural goods" (UNESCO, 1999: 7). These factors referred, on one hand, to the intensified pressures for trade liberalisation and the growth in the trade in cultural products and, on the other, to the "increasingly major implications of the cultural industries" – which were now noted to be simultaneously "economic, political and cultural" in a way that had not been the case only a decade ago, particularly in light of their contemporary contributions to employment and economic growth (UNESCO, 1999: 7). Emphasising the gravity of such points, the symposium arrived at a consensus view, expressed in language that would be echoed in the text of the Convention, that cultural products were distinguished by an "'essential duality' ... at one and the same time commercial objects and assets which convey values, ideas and a meaning" (UNESCO, 1999: 8). With the reiteration of this principle in closing addresses by the Minister of Canadian Heritage (Sheila Copps) and the French Minister of Culture and Communication (Catherine Trautmann), these became the themes that France and Canada urged should be at the centre of a UNESCO working group on cultural diversity, which was established following the 1999 UNESCO General Conference later that year. The work of this group, reinforced by a coordinated effort by French and Canadian ambassadors at UNESCO, directly resulted in the drafting of the Universal Declaration on Cultural Diversity for adoption at the 2001 General Conference, marking the first formal political step towards the creation of a binding international treaty.

This response to Stockholm – prioritising the question of how to situate cultural goods and services in the context of international trade, and noting the increasing economic, political and cultural importance of the cultural industries – was carried forward to the first meeting of experts delegated with the task of preparing a draft text between 2003 and 2004. During this meeting it was established that the Universal Declaration was too broad in scope to make for an effective instrument and that the specific purpose of the Convention should therefore be clarified from the beginning: to provide for what was identified as "the need for a balance between culture and trade, and thereby the dual nature – cultural and economic – of cultural goods and services" (UNESCO, 2004: 3). This provided the basic parameters of the text that went into the second, intergovernmental drafting stage between 2004 and 2005. Jean Musitelli, who along with Ivan Bernier played the key role in the round of expert meetings between 2003 and 2004, therefore reflected on the work done in the run-up to the Convention's adoption as the "creation of a pre-project conforming to the original Franco-Canadian objectives" (Musitelli, 2006: 7–8).

Although, as we will see below and in the following chapter, the drafting work completed between 2003 and 2005 was by no means free of disagreements over details, nor over the ways in which the trade issue had been foregrounded in the drafting process, the text that was ultimately approved and adopted was announced by its supporters in Canada and France as a coup by their governments and cultural industries: "So, let's salute the negotiating success of our ministers, bureaucrats and cultural industries. International lawmaking requires vision and a willingness to play as a team. It's a Canadian game" (Byers, 2005);

> France was the initiator and leader of this process.... Putting the defense of its national interest under the aegis of collective values, France transformed what was at risk of becoming a lonely battle of the old guard into a universally shared ambition for building the first global pillar of cultural governance.
>
> (Musitelli, 2006: 9)

The US Ambassador to UNESCO reacted to the same process by complaining of the aggressive way that it had been pursued by France, the EU and Canada both inside and outside UNESCO, and how US proposals to amend the text had proven helpless during the final drafting stage because they had worked together to ensure "that nothing in the document could be changed" (US State Department, 2005).

We have already seen that the major problem in the Convention for the US delegation lay in the way in which it blurred the regulatory domains of culture and commerce and potentially threatened the management of international trade. US objections during the drafting negotiations therefore centred on Article 20, which concerns the relationship of the Convention to other international agreements. This issue provided the major source of friction during the intergovernmental drafting phase, also raising the concerns of Japan, which joined the US in leading a diplomatic effort to amend Article 20 so as to weaken the Convention's standing in relation to international trade rules. Elaborating on this discomfort with Article 20, the US Mission to UNESCO stressed that

> Under the provisions of the convention as drafted, any State, in the name of cultural diversity, might invoke the ambiguous provisions of this convention to try to assert a right to erect trade barriers to goods or services that are deemed to be cultural expressions. That term, "cultural expressions," has never been clearly defined and therefore is open to wide misinterpretation. Such protectionism would be detrimental to the free exchange of ideas and images. It could also impair the world trading system and hurt exporters of all countries.
>
> (US Mission to UNESCO, 2005)

In these ways, the campaign for the recognition of the dual role of culture and for its wide international adoption and ratification became part of the increasingly complex political games that characterise contemporary international treaty making. One analyst observed that as Article 20 became the major bone of contention in the negotiations over the drafting, the key disagreement over the Convention was "not about finding the most effective policy for different cultures to flourish.... It was rather about how the new treaty – explicitly permitting the protection of cultural industries – would relate to existing free trade rules at the WTO" (Pauwelyn, 2005). The controversy and attention that has been focused on Article 20 has continued after the Convention's adoption, since it has left a number of questions regarding the relationship of the Convention to WTO rules.

Article 20 states, on the one hand, that the Convention does not modify the rights and obligations of the signatories under any other treaties to which they are party, but also states, on the other, that the Convention should not be subordinated to any other treaty and that Parties shall "foster mutual supportiveness" with other treaties and "take into account the relevant provisions" of the

Convention when interpreting and applying other treaties and when entering into other international obligations (UNESCO, 2005a). Shaffer and Pollack (2008) have observed that this "strategic ambiguity" in Article 20, which was secured in particular by European and Canadian negotiators, is symptomatic of the broader way in which negotiators are seeking to blur treaty regimes by developing international instruments and customary principles in fora outside of the WTO that can be used to strengthen their positions in the rivalries that are now being played out in international trade – particularly given the ever-broadening scope of WTO disciplines and the implications that stem from its significant, hard law dispute settlement mechanisms. As they note in their analysis of the Convention:

> The UNESCO convention could thus have an impact on future WTO negotiations and on future WTO cases involving cultural products, even where they involve a WTO member that is not a party to it. The UNESCO convention can be used, in particular, to attempt to constrain WTO jurisprudence so that WTO panels interpret WTO rules in a manner that treads lightly in this area, with the result that the application of WTO agreements to cultural products will be softened.
>
> (Shaffer and Pollack, 2008: 49)

This "softening effect" on WTO jurisprudence has indeed proven to be one of the Convention's first significant effects, as we will consider below in an examination of the recent dispute between the US and China over Chinese restrictions on the import and distribution of films, DVDs, music and other forms of published audiovisual and entertainment material. However, while such simmering trade conflicts between some of the old and new heavyweights in international trade have undoubtedly provided the main subtext of the Convention and the key political dynamic that has driven it forward, they have also tended to draw attention away from the ways in which the trade–culture problem mutated and broadened to accommodate a number of other concerns and claims as it migrated to UNESCO. The creation of the kind of effective regulatory counterparts to WTO rules discussed by analysts such as Shaffer and Pollack above is dependent on successful campaigns of diplomacy and coalition building among a range of stakeholders and in reference to an increasingly complex web of international legal and institutional frameworks. This means that the final draft of the Convention could not be based around a simple displacement of the concerns of a handful of states. Although French and Canadian willingness to broaden the terms of their campaign so as to garner wider international support and legitimacy was indeed part of their strategy to secure the adoption of the Convention, the resulting agenda for culture and development was also a product of UNESCO's established corpus of work on culture and a reflection of the presence within the organisation of a large number of countries with divergent interests.

Likewise, "cultural diversity" is far too empty a signifier for its meaning to be fixed quite so easily. A reminder of this came at the first of the expert drafting meetings between 2003 and 2004, for example, at which the agreement that the text should focus on giving recognition to the dual nature of cultural products was complicated by controversy over what exactly that should mean in practice (UNESCO, 2004; INCD, 2004). As a result, it was decided that the principles of cultural "exemption" and "exception" were too narrowly focused as a basis for such an international treaty and should be broadened in this context to "cultural recognition" in an effort to follow a more positive approach that recognised the concerns of a broader number of countries and groups (UNESCO, 2004: 3). Such controversies, which are not simple reflections of the heavyweight transatlantic rivalries over trade, arose throughout the drafting process between 2003 and 2005, and it is important to bear this in mind as we turn in the next chapter to discuss the particular ways in which the international campaign for the Convention was built and how it managed to bring other countries and groups on board.

Summary

In light of the analyses so far in this chapter, we might note two main points.

First, we have seen how a new consensus has emerged at UNESCO around a set of measures that are aimed at intensifying and proliferating the production and exchange of cultural goods and services in the global marketplace. This has buried some of the North–South divisions of the past over questions of international cultural regulation and development in a way which has not so much revealed the "limits" to the marketisation of culture (along with many of the analytical confusions that are contained in such a notion) as it has demonstrated the political and economic significance of the stakes that have come to be attached to the definition, management and exploitation of culture as a resource for commercial development in the context of neoliberal globalisation. We have also seen that the measures associated with this new consensus on culture and development should not be seen as a straightforward rejection of the basic principles of neoliberal forms of intervention. They seek to intensify such interventions, promoting a set of policies that are aimed at promoting a multiplication of market-oriented enterprises within the cultural sector.

Second, we have seen how the key principle underpinning the new consensus – the dual nature of cultural goods and services – has been prioritised as part of the strategic webs of international political and legal norm creation that are characteristic of contemporary rivalries over international trade liberalisation and negotiation: in this case in an attempt to "soften" WTO rules regarding the treatment of cultural products and to provide backup when conflicts between trade and culture arise.

In the following section we will turn to consider in more detail how these two broad developments have been playing out by turning to China, which presents a particularly significant and high stake case for the new rules of the cultural marketplace.

China, globalisation and the new cultural revolution

Testing the rules of the cultural marketplace: the WTO ruling of 2009

Since the early 2000s Chinese cultural policy has witnessed some radical changes, encapsulated in the mission set out by the Minister of Culture, Cai Wu: "to build competitive international cultural brands and promote the influence of Chinese culture" (Government of the People's Republic of China (hereinafter "GPRC"), 2009). At the same time this attempt to develop and launch its own "vehicles of identity, values and meaning" onto the global market confronts a number of difficulties – not least the legacies of the old cultural policy which have left a weak base of domestic production unable to compete with the growing presence of imported cultural goods from the US, Japan and South Korea – particularly following Chinese accession to the WTO in 2001.

As the government has sought to develop China's capacity in cultural production and make a transition to a growth model driven by creativity and intellectual property, it has therefore become a significant ally of the campaign at UNESCO. During the drafting process, the Ministry of Culture, the General Administration of Press and Publication, and the Office of Intellectual Property together formed a "Task Force Concerning Participation in the Creation of Convention on Cultural Diversity", which sought to shape an instrument conducive to Chinese interests. This marked a more active phase by the GPRC in participating in the design of international law pertaining to its trade interests in areas related to the cultural sector (Handong, 2010). There were also concerted diplomatic efforts from the treaty's key stakeholders from Europe and Canada, who were keen to bring China on board as part of their campaign to build the Convention's international support and legitimacy (CCD 2006, 2007).

China ratified the Convention in January 2007, and later became the first country to cite the new UNESCO instruments on cultural diversity in a dispute at the WTO, following a complaint that had been filed by the US soon after the Convention's entry into force in March 2007. The US complaint centred on Chinese restrictions on the import of cultural goods and services, and reflected in particular the concerns of the Motion Picture Association of America (MPAA), which had taken the initiative in urging the US Trade Representative to take the case to the WTO in the hope of gaining greater access to the Chinese market by, in particular, challenging the legality of the government's effective monopoly over the distribution of imported films (MPAA, 2009). The case was followed closely around the world by those with an interest in the implications of the UNESCO Convention upon the application of WTO rules regarding the trade in cultural products, and in particular by those with interests in improving access to the vast, and rapidly growing, Chinese market (which became the world's second largest box office territory in 2012 (Zhou, 2015: 4)). Third parties to the US–China dispute at the WTO included the European

Community, as well as neighbouring cultural industry powerhouses South Korea and Japan (WTO, 2009).

The case resulted in a ruling that called upon the Chinese government to lift a number of its restrictions on the import of films, DVDs, music, publications and other copyrighted material, which the WTO panel had found to be in breach of China's WTO commitments (WTO, 2009). When the main points of China's subsequent appeal against the ruling were rejected by the WTO panel later that year, the case was generally received as confirmation that the UNESCO Convention had proven to be a largely ineffective shield of the kind that its supporters had hoped for, while US negotiators and the MPAA hailed the WTO decision as a "big win" for the US (US Trade Representative, 2009; MPAA, 2009). This was a verdict echoed by the *Wall Street Journal* (2009), which responded to the WTO decision with the headline "Hollywood upstages Beijing" and reflected that the WTO had handed China "its biggest defeat yet". Within weeks of the ruling, the US Trade Representative was being lobbied to keep the momentum rolling at the WTO by raising the issue of China's "Great Firewall" (which China also defends on grounds of cultural sovereignty) on behalf of Google, eBay, Yahoo! and the myriad of companies that trade and advertise through the internet (*San Francisco Chronicle*, 2010). This call was quickly echoed across the Atlantic by the European Commission (*Economic Times*, 2010), in the process exposing some of the limits to its alliance with China on the question of trade and culture.

However, the 2009 decision at the WTO also left a number of other issues unresolved, particularly regarding the ongoing controversies over the status of culture in international trade and the right of China to reserve a number of other controls over the import of cultural products (such as caps on the number of films that can be imported into China and a system of content-review). As part of the WTO case, the GPRC had argued that such measures are necessary in order for it to be able to assess the impact of imported cultural material on national "public morals". Working with the following definition of public morals – "the standards of right and wrong conduct maintained by or on behalf of a community or nation ... that can vary in time and space, depending upon a range of factors, including prevailing social, cultural, ethical and religious values" (WTO, 2009: 280) – the WTO panel went on to acknowledge the right of Members to apply "this and other similar societal concepts ... in their respective territories, according to their own systems and scales of values" (WTO, 2009: 281). The Panel made reference to the authority that this right had now been given at UNESCO, but it also noted that China had *not* invoked the UNESCO instruments as a defence to its breaches of trading rights commitments under the Accession Protocol, reflecting the extent to which China had been careful not to undermine the general principle of free trade and WTO membership (WTO, 2009: 279, fn 538).

The acknowledgement by the WTO Panel of China's references to the principles contained in the UNESCO cultural diversity instruments represents a new development at the WTO, and an important moment in the broader trade and culture debate. The key lessons from the China case for evaluating the impact of the Convention were highlighted in a report presented to the Intergovernmental Committee of the Convention in 2014. First, it was noted that an important step had been taken since the last major trade dispute concerning cultural goods and services (between the US and Canada in 1997), in which the judicial bodies of the WTO were committed only to the commercial value of the cultural goods and services. Second, it was noted to be the first time since the adoption of the Convention that the WTO court has acknowledged the "non-commercial" value of audiovisual services (UNESCO, 2014: 23–24).

This apparent "softening" of the WTO's position on culture has therefore left the outcome of the decision somewhat uncertain for future negotiations and disputes in this sector. An analysis of the decision by China Media Monitor Intelligence (an authoritative Beijing-based consultancy for cultural industry exporters to China), for example, was quick to point out that the Chinese strategy of invoking arguments based on the particularity of cultural products had rendered the WTO decision a "half-victory at best" for exporters to China and in fact presented them with a new set of problems: "If experience offers any indication of what we can expect, it is that these sorts of non-tariff, extra-WTO tools will rise in importance for the government" (Wolf, 2009).

Indeed, in December 2009, in a statement responding to the ruling, the Chinese Ministry of Commerce reiterated its position by referring to the principle of the dual role of culture: "China insists that cultural products have both commercial and cultural values which decide that the management of trade on such products should be different from that of general goods" (Liaoning Provincial Online Foreign Trade Information Center, 2009). The following month the government then issued a guideline of ten initiatives to promote the development of its domestic film industry and to increase its international competitiveness between now and 2015, along with a reminder to domestic theatres that they were required to screen a quota of at least two-thirds of domestically produced films – further straining relations with Hollywood in the process (*Xinhua*, 2010; *Wall Street Journal*, 2010). Analysts such as Burri (2013: 362–363) have therefore noted that the US–China case demonstrates the ongoing ambiguity of the relationship between the UNESCO Convention and the WTO: on the one hand, the ability of the Convention to defend protective measures in China had proven to be limited but, on the other hand, the case also signalled a new flexibility of WTO rules in a way that acknowledged, for the first time, some of the claims of "pro-culture" advocates. As we have also seen, it appears to have strengthened the GPRC's resolve to seek ways of managing and developing its domestic cultural sector.

However, and to reiterate the themes that were developed earlier in this chapter, the main point that we should draw attention to in this dispute is that it has not revolved around any straightforward opposition between "culture" on the one hand and the values of "commerce" and the "market" on the other. It has centred rather on the Chinese government's attempt to articulate a new strategy of integration into the global market as it seeks to become an international player in the production and trade of cultural goods and services. As we will see below, this strategy involves an overhaul of its cultural policy based on a reconceptualisation of culture and an active role in designing and implementing market-based reforms and interventions aimed at nurturing the formation of competitive, export-oriented enterprises in the cultural sector. To recall once more the account of Yúdice (2003), the dispute has been an occasion for the articulation of the increasing protagonism of culture as a resource in the context of neoliberal globalisation, as it becomes a simultaneous problem of economic, social and political management. This occasion has come around dramatically in China, where the shift in strategy has been pivotal in effecting a contemporary geographical shift in the locus of debates about the cultural and creative economy from the advanced industrial countries to the developing regions (Flew, 2013).

Chinese cultural policy in the WTO-era and the reconceptualisation of culture

In contrast to the years before the changes initiated under Deng Xiaoping in 1979, when policymakers resisted the idea that cultural undertakings could be considered or operated in such terms, they are now identified as one of the fastest growing and most profitable sectors of the economy. This has required a new approach to cultural policy in which culture has been reconceptualised from "propaganda work" to culture as a "pillar industry" (Keane, 2013). The first official, documented use of the term "cultural industries" (*wenhua chanye*) can be found in 2000 and their identification as an objective of policy was legitimised in 2001 (the year that China entered the WTO), subsequently coming to be a key element of cultural and economic policy in the eleventh Five Year Plan (2005–2010) as senior officials recognised that China needed to accelerate a process of industrialising culture in order to compete in the new global environment (Keane, 2013: 21–27).

This broad shift from propaganda to industry, however, does not mean that there is less governmental attention to it. This is a point that has also been noted by Pang, who reflects that culture has today been elevated to perhaps its highest official status since the Cultural Revolution, and that current reforms are not any less political than those of the previous socialist regime but are characterised by "a more contrived relationship between the political and the economic" (2012: 95–96). It is in this spirit that bodies of cultural industry expertise came to be established in China over the 2000s, and figures began to be released that estimated the total added value of the cultural industries in China (in 2004) at US$42 billion, or 2% of China's GDP, and employed approximately ten million people (*Inter Press Service*, 2006). Much of the focus has been on the "upgrading" and "transformation" of industries, the redevelopment of industrial districts and the provision of infrastructure and incentives that can attract creativity and talent. This has had some success in making China at least an entry-level player for production in media and culture, turning it into an important base for international outsourcing in areas such as design and animation (Keane, 2013). Although statistics can be difficult to verify in China, the available data clearly indicates that the cultural sector has been growing rapidly since the early 2000s (a pattern that has largely been unaffected by the global economic crisis), even though cultural industries still only made up 1% of Chinese listed companies in 2010 (Zhongxi, 2010). The proliferation of independent companies has been most dramatic, with a conservative official estimate of over 4,000 private companies operating in the audiovisual sector in 2009 (Keane, 2013: 78).

Such data is striking, but perhaps more significant here is that such activity is now being conceptualised and measured in this way in the first place. Two milestones in this respect came in November 2012 with the launch of China's first cultural industry index at the Shenzhen Stock Exchange, and the designation of culture as a new "pillar industry" in the twelfth Five Year Plan (for 2011–2015) (Bhattacharya, 2012; *China Daily*, 2012). The origins of this change of approach and subsequent rapid growth in the cultural sector are often traced to the Sixteenth National Congress of the Communist Party in 2002, when non-profit cultural undertakings and commercial cultural industries were separated, initiating widespread reform across the sector and bringing thousands of formerly government-affiliated agencies to the market (*China Daily*, 2012). By September 2012, more than 580 publishing houses, 3,000 bookstores, 850 movie producers and distributors, 57 public TV series producers, 99.5% of the country's art troupes and the marketing sectors of 38 Communist Party newspapers and journals had been restructured into market enterprises, along with over 3,000 government funded non-political newspapers and journals (Bhattacharya, 2012). Meanwhile, although the emphasis in cultural policy has been on such decentralisation and privatisation, many of the more sensitive sectors (such as the main media groups) have remained under closer political control and, through the State Administration of Press, Publication, Radio, Film and Television (SAPPRFT), authorities continue to monitor and regulate the ideological content of communications and audiovisual products.

The result of this ascendancy of market interests and prerogatives alongside the continued supervision of content by the state results in what Niedenführ (2013) has described (in a study of the Chinese television industry) as a "tug of war" between regulatory interventions and market demands, or what Zhou (2015) describes (in an account of the film industry) as the interplay of socialist ideological control and market-oriented economic reforms. Central government also continues to subsidise non-profit and public cultural projects such as free art museums, libraries, cultural centres and protection of intangible cultural heritage; indeed the funding for such operations from the central budget has been increasing in recent years (*Xinhua*, 2014).

These changes reflect the importance that has come to be attached by government to the roles of culture and creativity. On the one hand, it reflects a concern to manage the strains on "national harmony" that are being generated 1) internally, by the social disruptions and inequalities that have come with China's recent period of rapid economic growth, and 2) externally, by the perceived threat to "cultural security" (*wenhuan anquan*) that comes from the growing domestic presence of imported content in sectors such as advertising, media and cinema (particularly following Chinese accession to the WTO in 2001). On the other hand, it is part of a strategy of finding new areas of industrial expansion, since culture is identified by the GPRC as having a strategic significance in making the transition from developing country to world power. These objectives make the reform of the cultural system an important component in the drive to expand the country's international cultural influence or "soft power", a term which officially enters the political lexicon in China in 2007 (the same year in which it ratified the UNESCO Convention). One of the more recent emphases in the new cultural policy therefore has been on the development of cultural industries for export and this is also reflected in the data, with the export volume of China's core cultural products reported to have increased from US$3.08 billion in 2001 to US$18.68 billion in 2011 (Bhattacharya, 2012).

The recognition of the contemporary need to develop the strategic political, economic and social role of culture led the government and Beijing's Tsinghua University to establish the first national Research Centre for Cultural Industry (RCCI) in 2004. Its remit was to look into issues relating to reforms in cultural policy and the parallel elaboration of market rules for the development of a new batch of cultural enterprises and as a way of reforming what were coming to be seen as the "old ways" across the cultural institutions that had been inherited from the planned economy. This was guided by the principle that culture has become one of the "rising industries" of the twenty-first century, generating employment, income and opportunities for the global expression of China's distinctive heritage: "Culture and Industry are from two completely different fields. Today the two fields are merging together and bringing out new energy" (RCCI, 2006). In this spirit, a number of high-profile projects have been carried out through the work of the RCCI and have come to stand as emblems of the new cultural policy:

Set up in Aug. 2004, Beijing Song and Dance Theater Co. Ltd. saw its revenue double in the second half of last year to 3.64 million yuan (US$455,000) from the first half before its restructuring.... Its major shareholder, Capital Tourism Co., has cashed in on its advantage of Beijing's tourist market and the advertising campaign of Beijing TV Station to bring a slew of visitors to the theater by having it sign performance contracts with over a dozen Beijing hotels.... In Shanghai, a grand art center was established by incorporating six institutions including the Shanghai Theater, Concert Hall and Shanghai Symphony Orchestra, an epitome of cultural resources merging in the country.

(*Xinhua*, 2006)

The cultural policy reforms were given momentum in September 2006 through a Five-Year Program for Cultural Development, China's first middle- and long-term programme focusing on cultural development. This has been implemented in a tone set by Li Changchun, a senior figure in the Political Bureau of the Central Committee, who "urged society to break away from all the ideologies, practices, regulations and drawbacks of the system that hinders cultural development" (GPRC, 2006a). The key theme is that cultural policy and the subjects it aims to act upon must radically adapt to the imperatives of market reform and competitive insertion into the global economy, generating "cultural companies with capacities for independent innovation, famous brands and proprietary intellectual property rights" (GPRC, 2006b). Effective cultural policy in this context must therefore widen its traditional concerns to overlap with industrial policy by setting the right regulatory environment for the formation and work of cultural enterprises – decentralisation and privatisation, improved access to finance and technology, the extension of copyright protection and enforcement, and so on – in short, to transform the work of cultural institutions and companies through the competitive pressures and opportunities offered by market reforms and international flows of trade, investment and tourism.

As decentralisation and privatisation have been pursued, one of the key issues has been improving the access of reformed cultural enterprises to finance and designing financial products and information specifically tailored to the cultural sector. To this end, the Ministry of Culture has established strategic partnerships with financial institutions to provide capital for projects (such as the dance show *Tea* or the cultural theme park *Song City* in Hangzhou), as well as developing financial consulting services on loans, trust funds, securities and insurance for the cultural sector (Zhongxi, 2010). By the end of 2013, the credit balance of cultural industry loans was 157.4 billion yuan (US$25.3 billion), up by 36.3% annually (*Xinhua*, 2014); meanwhile, between 2009 and 2014 20 billion yuan/US$2.94 billion of loans was dedicated to help a number of flagship cultural enterprises mount productions overseas (GPRC, 2009).

A series of expos in China (notably the International Cultural Industries Fair, held annually since 2004) and overseas have also been held for the showcasing of production, the exchange of expertise and the fostering of international partnerships and investment in the cultural sector. Such events are envisaged not only as opportunities giving greater international exposure for Chinese cultural industries and for expressing China's soft power on the international stage (Bell, 2010; *China Daily*, 2010) but they are also envisaged as sites in which the Chinese population can benefit from exposure to the global village of enterprise and production. As the spokesperson for the lavish 2010 World Expo in Shanghai explained:

> It is a big platform, a big event for cultural exchanges. We are bringing the whole world – different countries, different peoples – to this area, so it's a good opportunity for Chinese people to have "face to face" contact with international society.
>
> (Wei, quoted in Hogg, 2010)

The emphasis on the creation of recognisably Chinese brands for insertion in the global marketplace and communicating the country's growing international presence has also extended the remit of cultural policy to fostering innovations in technology, design and marketing beyond the traditional domains and contact points of cultural reform and propaganda (media, theatres, galleries, museums and so on) to a more generalised concern for the role of culture and creativity in economic development through activities such as intellectual property creation and industrial design. In this way, brands such as Lenovo (PCs, laptops, tablets), Li Ning (sportswear) and BYD Auto (automobiles, producer of the world's first mass-produced plug-in hybrid vehicle) have been developed over the last decade to become recognised internationally as distinctively Chinese brands and signifying the country as a culturally advanced and competitive participant in the world market (*Global Times*, 2010). In this context, cultural policy also therefore extends to impressing upon citizens the value of innovation, creativity and intellectual property – such as through dedicated history and television programming (see, for example, Bell, 2010: 19) or through exhibitions and events such as the World Expo, showcasing the latest innovations from around the world (against a backdrop of tight security aimed at rooting out intellectual property thieves and removing those "undesirables" that jeopardise China's new image by gathering to sell illegal fake merchandise) (Hogg, 2010).

The strategy of cultural system reform sketched out above has, of course, not proceeded without tensions and debates. A key point of recent debate centres on the role of creativity. Although it is increasingly recognised that it is necessary to harness creativity to industry and national development, this has also been a source of unease where it is seen to pose a challenge to the national government's attempts to maintain central control over ideology.[5] The proliferation of "informal" user-generated content in the digital domain has provided one recent source of such insecurity (a large-scale government crackdown on peer-to-peer video-sharing sites occurred in 2008, for example), because it threatens ideological centralisation and cannot be accounted for in official statistics (although, as Zhao and Keane (2013) have noted in their study of the online video industry in China, there is increasing rapprochement between formalised professional industry and informal user-created content).

Another set of tensions regarding the role of creativity centres on the expansion of intellectual property rights, particularly in a society with long-established traditions of appropriating and reappropriating existing designs and brands (often referred to as China's "shanzhai" culture). In a detailed study of this theme, Pang (2012) has drawn attention to some of the contradictions in the contemporary promotion of the cultural and creative economy in China by national and international agencies. In particular, she notes how the expansion of "Western" norms, policies and laws related to intellectual property in China as a route to economic and cultural development undermines important traditional sources of innovation and creativity (which are often predicated precisely on the absence or even subversion of such copyright protections, such as in

China's dynamic *anime* or art scenes). Although Pang's equation of intellectual property with "Western" culture here is problematic, she raises important observations regarding the contemporary governmental tendency to fetishise "creativity" and use the language of the creative economy to obscure dynamics of capitalist appropriation and the intensification of patterns of exploitation and precarity amongst workers in the cultural sector.

Mindful of such tensions, the broad thrust of policy in the recent period can be summarised as responding to contemporary globalisation through an intensification, rather than any uncomplicated resistance to, processes of industrialisation, commercialisation and marketisation. Central to this shift has been a reconceptualisation of the nature and role of culture itself as a resource to be harnessed to economic and political development. The UNESCO Convention has played a role in this as a means by which the government has sought to carve out a space in which it can further these aims (with only partial success, as we witnessed earlier in looking at the dispute with the US at the WTO), and bolstering the objectives of cultural security, soft power and sustained industrial expansion.

Building a rival to Hollywood?

China's efforts to nurture and develop its film industry as part of the reforms underway since the early 2000s can be used to develop a number of points regarding contemporary shifts in cultural policy, and the roles that culture as a resource is being expected to play more broadly. As China has achieved some successes in the first wave of cultural system reforms designed to upgrade industry and foster capacity in the cultural and creative industries, it has also stepped up its ambitions in line with the soft power drive. This has brought with it greater focus on the significance of finished products such as feature films and blockbusters that might actually begin to compete with the cultural superpowers of East Asia and the US.

This represents a formidable challenge, however. In comparison with countries such as Canada or the European states which spearheaded the campaign for the UNESCO Convention, or with China's emerging country peers in Asia (notably India and South Korea), China is working with a relatively weak domestic base of production that has been further eroded as a result of the liberalisation of the last decades. Although the number of films produced in China has grown massively over the last decade, along with the size of the Chinese market (in 2014, films generated a revenue of almost 30 billion yuan (US$4.8 billion), which was 32 times that of 2002), the domestic film industry has been developing unevenly, and still performs poorly when it comes up against competition from overseas (Zhou, 2015: 4; *Xinhua*, 2015). 2015, in fact, saw the number of screenings of foreign films in Chinese cinemas surpass those of domestic films for the first time, according to official statistics (*Xinhua*, 2015). Meanwhile Chinese-language or Chinese-themed films have so far generated very little international commercial appeal (with some exceptions in Vietnam and the Philippines) and international box office revenue from Chinese films remains relatively small (indeed it declined dramatically between 2011 and 2013 (Zhou, 2015: 4)).

Hollywood, dominant in China before the 1949 revolution but subsequently expelled by the revolutionary government, has worked particularly hard to re-establish its position following the restoration of US–China relations in 1979, gaining growing market access over the coming decades as China has negotiated reciprocal access to US markets and gained WTO membership (Zhao, 2004). The sensation caused in China by *Rambo: First Blood* in 1985 was a symbol of the spectacular comeback that Hollywood was making in China and a portent of the deep crisis that would face the domestic film sector by the early 1990s as it came to be abandoned by domestic audiences and effectively crippled against its competitors by the combination of ideological control, underinvestment and lack of reform that had been the legacy of the planned economy.

The international film industry's growing presence in China since the 1980s – not only from the US but also from the imports and investment now coming from Japan, Hong Kong, Taiwan and South Korea, as well as from transnational conglomerates such as Sony (a committed member of the MPAA since the late 1980s) – then made another advance in 1994. Under pressure in particular from the MPAA and the US Trade Representative, and in exchange for market access in other sectors, China agreed to accept an annual importation of ten first-run Hollywood films on the basis that these could only be imported through the state-run distribution network the China Film Group (CFG). There was also an agreement that these imported films would be subject both to a box-office revenue sharing system and a process of content review. While the Chinese government therefore retained a degree of control and oversight, the door had been opened enough to let in the "cultural insecurity" that would be felt by conservatives over the coming decades.

The effect over the 1990s was that Chinese distributors and cinemas came to ignore domestic productions (in 1995 more than 70 were denied distribution) while eagerly promoting the latest imported films, which now generated huge revenues for both Hollywood and the CFG and met the expectations of an expanding urban middle class that had come to regard seeing the latest imports at the cinema as an entitlement of their new cultural citizenship (see Zhao, 2004). In 1998, the Hollywood blockbuster *Titanic* took a record 25% of the year's total Chinese box-office revenue – the same year in which the number of domestic Chinese productions hit a record low of 37 – and this pattern was entrenched with China's entry into the WTO in 2001 and the next set of gains secured by the MPAA in the form of a US–China bilateral agreement (which included increasing the Hollywood import quota to 20).[6] By 2003, 80% of box-office revenue came from the quota of Hollywood films and official statistics showed that copyright earnings on imported films were ten times more than those received from domestic productions (Keane, 2006). Meanwhile, international pressures for improved access to the Chinese market intensified, with the US complaint against China at the WTO in 2007 taking aim at the effective monopoly that had been retained by the CFG over the distribution of imported films (with some success, as we have already seen). Herein lies one of the main difficulties in developing an internationally competitive film industry in China, because China has to balance its ambition to address the cultural trade deficit and become a centre of production with the commitments that it has made to international liberalisation and existing trade agreements – agreements which have been a key factor in China's growth and in which it has come to have a considerable stake.

China's support for the UNESCO Convention on cultural diversity, along with other informal mechanisms of protection (such as using censorship mechanisms to delay the release of Hollywood blockbusters until after the golden holiday season (Zhou, 2015: 7)), do provide some protection to domestic production. However, the development of the sector is further complicated by at least two factors. On one hand, the pattern of liberalisation in the newly emerging cultural sector has happened in a particular way in China, under careful management and with the Chinese state effectively acting as the dominant domestic capitalist. As Zhao (2004) has pointed out, the increased integration between international and domestic capital that has emerged as a result of the gradual liberalisation of the last 30 years has complicated any notion that China can achieve success "all on its own". This has been evident, for example, not only with the domestic distribution of imported films but in the trend for domestic production to become increasingly entwined with transnational investment and co-production. Meanwhile, a combination of lack of finance and ongoing ideological supervision by state agencies such as SAPPRFT has, at least until recently, made it difficult for domestic filmmakers to develop the kind of internationally marketable creative content and long-term business models that are key to making the leap into high value-added "winner-takes-all" branded products of the kind envisaged by the new strategy (Keane, 2006; Zhou, 2015).

One of the consequences of the above noted challenges for the film industry in China is that a generation of Chinese filmmakers has been taken under the wing of international investors and distributors in order to find commercial success and circumvent regulatory controls. Although the measures introduced over the last decade have been partly designed to tackle this, policymakers remain faced with what Keane (2006) has referred to as a "conundrum of creativity": the development of a viable film industry in China and its capacity to create exportable content is ultimately dependent on deep institutional reforms that can both channel a significant increase in finance while stimulating new models of internationally oriented cultural production, distribution and marketing strategies that are not hampered by government oversight and requirements. Yueh (2014) and Zhou (2015) have suggested that it is this restriction on creativity and experimentation with new ideas and themes, rather than lack of finance or access to technology, that has now become the most significant obstacle to China's soft power strategy of developing an internationally competitive film industry.

It would be misleading to contrast this situation in China too dramatically with elsewhere: it is no secret that Hollywood, for example, for all the discussion and posturing that there has been over its superiority against a bureaucratically stifled Chinese film industry, has maintained close links with US governmental, military and foreign policy objectives (producing films which, in the words of Forsyth (2004) are "always blatantly political, always about international power, and mostly uncritical"). One of the key differences, however, is that the versions of imperialist militarism and other forms of propaganda that are often served up by Hollywood are generally in the form of populist fun, just as the East Asian pop culture that is perceived by cultural conservatives within China as a threat to cultural security is generally dynamic, youthful and devoid of overt political posturing: these are not the soft power formulae that currently pertain in mainland China, where TV and film production privilege history, and domestic and international audiences have tended to find this a turn-off (Keane, 2013: 189–194).

More recent rounds of cultural system reform have begun to address some of the abovementioned limitations by promoting greater autonomy of the cultural sector from the state while also reforming tax and fiscal policies, extending intellectual property protections, streamlining the process by which state-owned film companies are listed on the stock market, and improving the access of reformed, export-oriented filmmakers to bank lending, bond issuance and venture capital financing (*Xinhua*, 2010; *Wall Street Journal*, 2010). As a result, Chinese film production companies are mounting ever larger productions and industry analysts have been prompted to consider the possibility that China could one day rival Hollywood after all (*Guardian*, 2010). There has also been some relaxation of the censoring of film scripts following reforms in 2013 (Zhou, 2015: 8) and calls from the Minister of Culture, Cai Wu, for the government to reduce "administrative interference … when it comes to the development of various art forms and their industries" and not "go beyond its duties to intervene in the commercial cultural market" (cited in *ECNS*, 2013).

Although it still remains to be seen what kinds of effects these more recent reforms will have, their overall objective has a clear set of motifs: the reconceptualisation and management of culture as a resource for the country's next phase of development, competitive insertion into the global market and greater presence on the international stage. The next section develops this theme by looking more closely at the political and ideological drivers involved in the transformation of culture into a resource in the Chinese context.

First blood: Confucius vs Avatar

In taking stock of how far China has travelled with the reforms over the last decade, it is perhaps indicative that in January 2010, not long after the WTO ruling of the previous year, the CFG pulled the Hollywood blockbuster *Avatar* from nearly 1,600 2-D screens across China in order to make room for its own US$23 million blockbuster telling the life of Confucius, in what was described by domestic theatres and officials as "a commercial decision" (to the watching horror of Hollywood executives and many within China – not least because *Avatar* had been causing a sensation, already becoming the highest grossing film of all time in China) (*Wall Street Journal*, 2010; *LA Times*, 2010; LaFraniere, 2010). The result of a co-production between the CFG and the Dadi Culture and Media Group (a Beijing-based corporation specialising in the latest audio-visual technology), the release of *Confucius* had initially been planned to coincide with the sixtieth anniversary of the revolution and to form part of the wider attempt by the Communist Party to resuscitate Confucius's legacy for building the "harmonious society" of market socialism.

The film represents one of the trophies of the reforms undertaken since the early 2000s and was released amidst the national hubris that came with a series of other blockbuster events at the end of the decade (the 2008 Beijing Olympic Games and the 2010 World Expo in Shanghai; the completion of the landmark construction projects the China Central Television (CCTV) Headquarters Building and Cultural Centre; and massive investments in media and news networks, including the launch in 2010 of a global English language news network to rival CNN and BBC World). Starring the global superstar Chow Yun-Fat and a theme song by pop star Faye Wong, *Confucius* the movie was launched in this spirit as an attempt to present the face of the new China to the population and the wider world: released on more than 3,000 screens on mainland China – another new record – and with a series of deals struck for international release (Shackleton, 2009), it aimed to send out a powerful message about China's efforts at cultural transformation and growing international presence – even if that message proved something of a bore for domestic audiences and flopped at the box office (LaFraniere, 2010). Such a landmark event can help to put some of the developments since the early 2000s into wider perspective.

First of all, it is worth recalling that only a few decades ago Confucius's legacy in Chinese society was being targeted for destruction by the Communist Party as part of the Cultural Revolution – quite literally in the case of the cemetery, temples, libraries and thousands of artefacts that were damaged and destroyed in Confucius's home town Qufu and neighbouring Zoucheng (Liang, 2002). In his study *China's New Confucianism*, Bell (2010) notes that the contemporary revival of Confucius in Chinese culture has served two main purposes in the revision of official Marxism that has come in the wake of the post-Deng reforms: 1) by calling for peace and harmony at home in the face of a sharp rise in inequality and the number of so-called "mass incidents" (strikes, protests and so on) across the country; and 2) by attempting to extend China's international soft power by dispelling growing international insecurities about the country's rise and emphasising its commitment to the peaceful resolution of conflicts.

As far as the film adaptation is concerned, however, Bell argues that its primary function is a commercial one: fictionalising and romanticising Confucius's life and dwelling on epic CGI battle scenes in an attempt to enthuse audiences and generate revenue at the box office. To the extent that the movie has a political agenda, he argues, it is that it does not "rock the boat": at the end of the film we see Confucius returning to a life of peaceful contemplation in his home state of Lu and the impression of him that we are left with is of a peace-loving patriot attached to his native land, immortalised as part of the eternal foundations of Chinese society (Bell cited in Ash, 2010). For Wasserstrom (2010), the key theme of the film and the broader revival of interest in Confucius is its attempt to cater to a broader nostalgia for the past amidst the dramatic changes occurring in China: it can be read, he argues, as part of a "rebranding effort" and "a makeover of the image of the country (and the Party) that is helping persuade many overseas Chinese that they can identify with and invest in today's People's Republic 2.0, even if they hated Mao". We could extend these interpretations here by noting that, in the form of the *Confucius* production, the sage has been resurrected to serve a simultaneously economic and cultural role as both the carrier of a new Chinese brand of identity, values and meanings to the global market, and as a prophet of China's ability to become an economic powerhouse in the twenty-first century in a slick, high-value added commodity fit for competitive domestic and international distribution.

The monuments to Confucius's home and resting place that were destroyed and damaged during the Cultural Revolution have also become part of this attempt to reincarnate Confucius in this "dual role". Following careful reconstruction, they have appeared on UNESCO's World Heritage List since 1994, where their legacy has been earmarked to become one of China's most valuable resources of cultural patrimony (boosted by their reference in the film) (World Bank, 2010). Attracting steadily growing national and international arrivals over recent years – reaching 9.7 million visitors in 2008 and generating revenues of US$635 million – and yet located across a particularly poor and undeveloped area of Shandong province, it is also noted by prospectors and developers that the monuments of Qufu and Zoucheng are only realising a fraction of their potential. Roads and transport, accommodation, restaurants, tour guides and companies, marketing, signs and information are all underdeveloped and, as identified in a World Bank report on the project, visitors "have little information, incentive or opportunity to spend more time and money" (World Bank, 2010). Addressing these deficiencies through developing sustainable programmes of asset preservation and presentation, upgrading infrastructure, attracting inward investment and building capacity for sustainable tourist enterprises in the region, it is added, can multiply arrivals whilst creating spinoff benefits for the local population by generating employment, income and access to improved infrastructure (although the local population have seen little of such benefits so far; indeed, work on one of the major components of the project – urban regeneration and infrastructure upgrading – had still not started as of the latest report produced in 2015) (World Bank, 2010; 2015). We can see here how the legacy of Confucius has become involved in a set of governmental concerns associated with how to manage culture as a resource, and how to position it most effectively in circuits of investment, marketing and world heritage tourism, as well as how to manage its effects on material distribution and sustainable development in the provinces (even if the latter concerns with regard to material distribution and sustainable development appear to be underprioritised).

If the kind of developments in China noted above offer some demonstration of the contemporary transformation of culture into a resource, we might also begin to elaborate in greater depth on some of their implications and effects, both internationally and nationally. First of all, while *Confucius* raised a budget of US$23 million, its rival *Avatar* is estimated to have raised anything upwards of US$200 million[7] and was able to draw on ground-breaking technology and expertise from a bewildering array of locations around the world (see *New York Times*, 2009). Even after the millions spent on *Confucius*, it enters this profoundly asymmetrical arena of cultural production and expression. At the same time, however, it would be misleading to situate the film as a response to "cultural imperialism" in the kind of terms that were used as part of the Non-Aligned Movement's calls for NWICO at UNESCO in the 1970s and 1980s, or during China's Cultural Revolution in the 1960s. Hollywood's success in China before 1949 and after the reforms of the 1980s is today described by policy-makers as evidence of "the radiating power of global audiovisual products" and as the triumph of "advanced culture" over the "backward culture" of others (just as General Secretary Jiang Zemin openly expressed admiration for *Titanic* in 1998 as it was winning over Chinese audiences and sinking what was left of the old Chinese film studios) (Zhao, 2004: 199). A measure of this shift was evident in January 2010 when the decision by theatres and officials to replace *Avatar* with *Confucius* was reversed within one week once the box-office figures became clear: *Avatar* had been grossing nearly two and a half times more money per day, whilst measurements of audience responses to *Confucius* in China, coupled with the expressions of discontent from Chinese audiences regarding the removal of *Avatar*, showed that *Confucius* had largely fallen flat (LaFraniere, 2010). At the same time, in Hunan Province, officials held a ceremony involving hundreds of locals dressed in the region's ethnic Tujia costumes, to rename mountain peaks in the Zhangjiajie national park (a UNESCO World Heritage site) as the "Avatar Halleluah Mountains" – reportedly because they had inspired the CGI floating mountains that had featured in *Avatar* (*Telegraph*, 2010). Criticisms from some within China that officials had "forgotten their cultural roots" fell on deaf ears, since the government responded by saying that the *Avatar* connection would increase tourism to the park (LaFraniere, 2010).

In these ways the continued dominance of Hollywood in China is today received not so much as the harbinger of a "harmful", commercial mass culture and bringer of predatory capitalist values and business practices (in the kinds of terms that it has been referred to in the past), but as an exemplary paradigm for development, demonstrating the latest technology and marketing strategies. Indeed, as we saw earlier, the growing presence of the international film industry in China since the 1980s has become an integral part of the new strategy of cultural development – in particular, by providing the revenues, investment and audiences that have been necessary to construct theatre complexes and stimulate domestic capacity, while also bringing the kind of competitive pressures necessary to root out the inefficient and unpopular studios, directors and cultural policies that were left over from the era of the planned economy. The moral of *Confucius's* defeat at the box-office and the rapid turnaround by theatres over the screening of *Avatar* has been to highlight the market ethics informing the new cultural policy: if you live by the market, you also have to die by the market – or, in the now ubiquitous advice of Confucius as it has been mobilised in contemporary China, "he who does not economise will have to agonise".

Moreover, if it seems that the traditional concerns about the discourses of cultural imperialism may be losing their relevance in China in this context of culture as resource, *Confucius* nevertheless highlights some of the ways in which culture has become a source of new and often intensified tensions in the international arena today. In this respect, Mao's assertion that "political power grows out of the barrel of a gun" has been tempered by the new emphasis on soft power and the cultural export drive in China's foreign policy. The advice of Confucius on the art of power was also clear – "lead by moral authority, not force" – and the past glories of Chinese cultural influence in countries such as Japan, Korea and Vietnam (which it was mostly unable to conquer physically, but developed strong linkages through the take-up of Confucianism, as well as forms of Chinese government, art and literature) have come to offer guiding examples in developing the contemporary strategy of extending political and commercial influence in the region and overseas by exporting what has come to be referred to as "the Confucius brand" (Kuhn, 2008; Bell, 2010).

This attempt by China to project greater international influence comes not only in the form of its cultural industry exports and the staging of globally significant blockbuster projects, but also in the establishment of Confucius Institutes, modelled on the expansion of the British Councils of the 1930s and seeking to extend Chinese cultural and linguistic ties in countries with particular commercial significance, as well as "third-tier" countries in Africa, Latin America and Central Asia (*Global Times*, 2010; Lien *et al.*, 2012). By the end of 2013, China had set up 440 such Confucius Institutes (mostly in tertiary institutions) and 646 Confucius Classrooms (in primary and secondary educational institutions) in 120 countries (Lo and Pan, 2014: 2).[8] This has presented a disturbing development for some in the West, such as Halper (2010) who observed in *Foreign Policy* that, since the late 1990s, Beijing has been working to build

> a coalition of countries – a great many of them in Africa – that can be trusted to vote China's way in an increasingly clogged alphabet soup of international fora. It's a bloc reminiscent of the one the Soviet Union assembled during the Cold War, though focused on economic and trade advantages, not security issues.

With the renewed confidence and capacity that has been provided through increased ties with China, an African voting bloc has emerged under Chinese leadership within the WTO and this has provided one of the key factors in the standoff between the North and South in the Doha Round – particularly over the key question of agricultural liberalisation (Halper, 2010).

Giving a contemporary twist to the racist and ideological discourses of "yellow peril", commentators in Europe and the US have responded to this development by warning of Chinese "cultural imperialism", both in the West and in the South, and the threat that the Chinese cultural drive is coming to pose to the West's diplomatic influence on questions of trade rules and the international balance of power (including, crucially, the status of Taiwan) in international fora (see, for example, Follath, 2010; Halper, 2010; *Global Times*, 2010). In other words, it appears that as the economic and political importance of cultural policy has risen, along with the stakes that have come to be attached to the cultural sector in trade negotiations and disputes of the kind considered earlier, many of the distinctions between "high" and "low" politics have also begun to lose some of their utility for grand strategists. As Follath (2010) puts it in his nightmarish account of China's cultural expansion: "soft is the new hard".

Such emerging international rivalries, however, should not be allowed to obscure developments within China itself – nor the considerable overlap of interests that exist between Western capitalism and the Chinese "market authoritarianism" which is denounced by neo-Orientalists today. It is important to remember here that China's references to the UNESCO instruments on cultural diversity in its submission to the WTO in 2009 only referred to the country's right to reserve particular policies of public morals and cultural sovereignty based on the specificity of cultural products: they made no reference to matters of China's internal cultural or ethnic diversity, nor to any concept of a "new global ethics" as it had been articulated by the WCCD (see the Chinese submissions to the Panel in WTO (2009: 18–31, 271–309)). Predictably enough, the invocation of cultural diversity in this context has functioned as little more than a reassertion of national sovereignty, while its accompanying claims about the privileged place of cultural products have been part of a recognisable pattern of integration into the global economy: one in which the concerns of a relatively privileged bureaucratic and economic strata are anointed with a position in the vanguard of national development. One of the motifs of the cultural system reform among policy officials and the RCCI is that the development of the cultural industries must keep up in order to satisfy the demands of the new middle class that would deliver China's prosperity in the twenty-first century:

> In view of China's rapid urbanization and economic expansion [the] cultural sector has failed to keep pace. Economically better off Chinese people now desire better and richer cultural activities, yet the domestic cultural industry is unable to meet that demand.
>
> (*Xinhua*, 2006)

It may be here that the new Chinese strategy of cultural reform has failed in this respect to emulate one of the key factors that gave the American cultural industries their launchpad for global success: it was in part their ability to develop a strong domestic market and enfranchise the diverse US immigrant population that was crucial to their eventual global expansion and universal appeal. In contrast, the Chinese cultural industry, despite "its dreams of global market success, has largely been unwilling to reach China's vast numbers of internal migrants and the urban poor, not to mention the rural population [of 900 million]" (Zhao, 2004: 202).

There are some indications that the government stance on these issues has shifted in recent years, as it has sought to foster greater national cultural unity whilst also extending some recognition of the rights of minority groups in Chinese society (see, for example, Lim, 2013; *Xinhua*, 2013). Such efforts, however, remain limited and ultimately subordinated to the overriding concerns with the legitimacy and objectives of the Communist Party. As far as they have featured in China's cultural development strategy, the "native" or "ethnic" populations, cities and villages across China's cities and provinces have tended to be either targets for removal by property developers (or for assimilation and/or "cultural genocide", in the words of the exiled Dalai Lama (*Independent*, 2008)), or encouraged to transform into areas of cultural relics, consumption and leisure for international tourists and the new Chinese urban middle class – rather than the sites of dispossessed and displaced farmers, villagers or laid-off and migrant workers (Zhao, 2004: 205–208), or the sites of an intensifying series of conflicts between workers, peasants, farmers and the state (Buckley, 2010; Bell, 2010).

The conflict between *Avatar* and *Confucius* has also drawn attention to these sensitive issues, since *Avatar*'s central theme evoked memories of a series of controversial, often brutal, forced evictions from a number of China's urban districts and rural villages at the hands of property developers and local governments during the construction boom of the 2000s. The plot of *Avatar* revolves around a quest by a team of anthropologists from planet Earth to persuade a mythical population of blue-skinned aliens ("the Na'vi") on a faraway fictional planet to make way for mineral prospectors from Earth, ultimately resulting in a tactic of military annihilation and forced removal. One commentator in China reflected on the *Avatar* phenomenon by noting that "All the forced removal of old neighbourhoods in China makes us the only earthlings today who can really feel the pain of the Na'vi", while another reflected that *Avatar* had effectively implied to Western audiences that "such brutal eviction could only take place on another planet – or in China" (cited in *The Straits Times*, 2010). Some reports have implied that it was governmental concerns over such parallels that were a contributing factor in the initial decision to pull the film from the screens. One source in Hong Kong noted, for example, that

> authorities have two reasons for this check on *Avatar*: first, it has taken in too much money and has seized market share from domestic films, and second, it may lead audiences to think about forced removal, and may possibly incite violence.
>
> (*The Times*, 2010)

If *Avatar* offered spectacular 3-D reminders of the brutality and dispossession that are the necessary conditions of capitalism, right from its opening act of primitive accumulation, *Confucius* tried to cover them up with its 2-D narratives of national harmony – and readily conceded defeat after just one week of humiliation at the box office. It nevertheless appeared to fire a shot at the West's cultural hegemony – and stands as one of a number of such moves that are causing many to reflect that China's soft power drive could seriously challenge the West's influence in the South over the coming decades.

Finally, it is important to put the Chinese case into perspective. China's turn to culture as a resource for market-led development and international soft power has been conceived as part of a strategy to shift to a new phase of development after the expansion of the late twentieth century, and to make the transition to an advanced economic powerhouse and world power in the twenty-first century (with all the trappings that such a dramatic rise brings with it, including rising tensions at home and scrambles for resources, markets and political influence across the South). However, China has also arguably been unique amongst developing countries in finding itself in such a position and being able to steer a course through the global transformations of the last decades – carefully maintaining controls on its currency and the pace of liberalisation, while utilising its vast reserves of labour and the prize of its internal market to position itself strategically as the global hub of investment and production, as well as an international player in its own right (officially the world's second largest economy after overtaking Japan in 2010). This Chinese experience has, of course, not been the experience of most developing countries in the recent round of globalisation. This is a point developed further in Chapter 6 by examining the way that the turn to culture as a resource in the Caribbean over the 2000s has been more a reflection of the region's subordination in the global political economy.

Summary

The broad argument developed in this chapter is that the forging of the new framework of cultural development has been based on a "rapprochement" between culture and the market – and not, as has sometimes been claimed, on the kinds of antagonisms between them that we have seen in the past (such as in the NWICO era at UNESCO or the period of the Cultural Revolution in China). The conflicts over the Convention that have taken place at UNESCO over the rules of the cultural marketplace have served to illustrate the extent of the stakes that have come to be attached by governments to the management of culture as a resource for trade and development in the context of globalisation – and have, in fact, helped to forge a new consensus between the rest of the North and the South on the question of cultural development. In the example of China we have seen how the new international framework of cultural policy has reinforced the government's attempts to secure the policy space in which it can develop its own strategy of market-led cultural policy reform, in a way which seeks to overcome some of the traditional distinctions between cultural and economic policy and that is also part of the ongoing attempt to become a global player in its own right. In the following chapter we will turn to look in greater detail at the nature of the international consensus that has been forged by focusing on the precise points of convergence between North and South as well as the lines of tension and divergence that have been obscured by the language of consensus.

Notes

1 For more information on the GACD, see www.unesco.org/new/en/culture/themes/cultural-diversity/cultural-expressions/programmes/global-alliance-for-cultural-diversity/about-us/.
2 Details of the UNESCO-EU expert facility project are available at www.unesco.org/new/en/culture/themes/cultural-diversity/cultural-expressions/programmes/technical-assistance/.
3 A Creative Industries Division was established in WIPO in 2005 to address the economic developmental impact of intellectual property policies and practices on the sector (WIPO, 2010).
4 See, for example, UNCTAD's Creative Economy and Industries Programme, which has been underway since 2008: http://unctad.org/en/Pages/DITC/CreativeEconomy/Creative-Economy-Programme.aspx.
5 According to Keane (2013: 35–43), unease about the use of the term "creative industries" amongst local and municipal governments, entrepreneurs, academics and reformers has been most keenly felt amongst more conservative policy officials closer to the heart of power in Beijing (for example, in the Ministry of Culture and the Propaganda Department), where there is a preference for the less threatening term "cultural industries" (which tends to feature more in national policy statements).
6 Measures also included reducing tariffs on audiovisual imports, opening up its consumer market for audiovisual products to foreign distributors and allowing foreign investors to own up to a 49% share in companies that build, own and operate cinemas in China.
7 This is in fact a minimum estimate since, when global marketing expenses are added, it appears that *Avatar* cost its various backers closer to US$500 million – even after the plans for investment in marketing were scaled down due to the recession (*New York Times*, 2009).
8 For more detailed analysis and coverage of debates regarding the role of Confucius Institutes in China's "soft power" drive, see Lo and Pan (2014).

Bibliography

Ash, A. 2010. "A Conversation on 'Confucius' with Daniel A. Bell". *The China Beat*. 4 February 2010. Available online at: www.thechinabeat.org/?p=1455; accessed 18/02/2010.
Asmal, K. 2006. "What the Convention means to me". In Obuljen, N. and J. Smiers (eds). UNESCO's Convention on the Protection and Promotion of the Diversity of Cultural Expressions: Making it Work. Zagreb: Institute for International Relations.
Beat Graber, C. 2008. "Substantive Rights and Obligations Under the UNESCO Convention on Cultural Diversity". In Schneider, H. and P. van den Bossche (eds). *Protection of Cultural Diversity from a European and International Perspective*. Oxford: Intersentia.

Bell, D. 2010. *China's New Confucianism: Politics and Everyday Life in a Changing Society*. Oxfordshire: Princeton University Press.

Bernier, I. 2009. "Les Relations Entre la Convention de l'UNESCO sur la Protection et la Promotion de la Diversite des Expressions Culturelles et les Autres Instruments Internationaux: L'Emergence d'un Nouvel Equilibre dans l'Interface entre la Commerce et la Culture". Available online at: www.diversite-culturelle.qc.ca/fileadmin/documents/pdf/Les_relations_entre_la_convention.pdf; accessed 16/07/2009.

Bhattacharya, S.R. 2012. "New culture index signal's China's shift in growth model". *Gulf News*. 7 December 2012. Available online at: http://gulfnews.com/business/markets/new-culture-index-signals-china-s-shift-in-growth-model-1.1115604; accessed 18/06/15.

Buckley, C. 2010. "China's farmers mount movement against land grab". *Reuters*. 3 August 2010. Available online at: http://uk.reuters.com/article/idUSTRE6721DW 20100803; accessed 10/08/2010.

Burri, M. 2013. "The UNESCO Convention on Cultural Diversity: An appraisal five years after its entry into force". *International Journal of Cultural Property*. 20: 357–380.

Byers, M. 2005. "This round in the cultural protection fight goes to Canada". *The Globe and Mail*. 20 October 2005.

CCD. 2006. "China, India Figure Prominently in CCD International Missions". Available online at: www.cdc-ccd.org/ccd_enews/06_march/ccd_update_March06.html#2; accessed 12/01/2010.

CCD. 2007. "CCD Maintains Intense Schedule of Missions to Promote Ratification". Available online at: www.cdc-ccd.org/ccd_enews/07_march/ccd_update_March07.html; accessed 12/01/2010.

China Daily. 2009, 17 November. "Sino-US co-operation in filmmaking is on the rise". Available online at: www.china.org.cn/arts/2009-11/17/content_18902113.htm; accessed 18/06/2015.

China Daily. 2010, 28 April. "Shanghai World Expo showcases China's soft power". Available online at: www.chinadaily.com.cn/opinion/2010-04/28/content_9785158.htm; accessed 12/08/2010.

China Daily. 2012, 23 October. "China's cultural industry reform pays off". Available online at: http://europe.chinadaily.com.cn/business/2012-10/23/content_15839948.htm; accessed 19/06/2015.

ECNS. 2013. "Minister urges less government meddling in cultural development". Available online at: www.ecns.cn/2013/04-17/59130.shtml; accessed 12/07/2015.

European Commission. 2006. "Summary: FAQ: UNESCO Convention on Cultural Diversity – a new instrument of international governance (19 December 2006: Brussels)". Available online at: http://eu-un.europa.eu/articles/en/article_6630_en.htm; accessed 18/06/15.

European Commission. 2007. *European Agenda for Culture in a Globalized World*. Brussels, 10 May 2007. COM(2007) 242 final.

Flew, T. 2013. *Global Creative Industries*. Cambridge: Polity.

Follath, E. 2010. "The Dragon's Embrace: China's soft power is a threat to the West". *Der Spiegel*. (International edition). 28 July 2010.

Forsyth, S. 2004. "Hollywood Reloaded: The Film as Imperial Commodity". In L. Panitch and C. Leys (eds). *The Empire Reloaded: Socialist Register 2005*. London: The Merlin Press.

Foucault, M. 2008. *The Birth of Biopolitics: Lectures at the College de France, 1978–1979*. Hampshire: Palgrave Macmillan.

Global Times. 2010. "Cultural exports can reshape China's image". 7 April 2010. Available online at: http://en.people.cn/90001/90782/6944365.html; accessed 18/06/15.

GPRC. 2006a, 30 March. "Senior leader calls for promoting reform of cultural system". *Government of the People's Republic of China*. Available online at: www.china-embassy.org/eng/xw/t243200.htm; accessed 18/06/15.

GPRC. 2006b, 31 March. "China to carry out more cultural reform". *Government of the People's Republic of China*. Available online at: www.gov.cn/english/2006-03/31/content_241047.htm; accessed 18/06/15.

GPRC. 2009, 5 August. "Chinese cultural industry maintains growth via government-supported loans". *Government of the People's Republic of China*. Available online at: http://news.xinhuanet.com/english/2009-08/04/content_11826618.htm; accessed 18/06/15.

Guardian. 2010, 13 September. "Chinese film industry aims to challenge Hollywood".

Halper, S. 2010. "Beijing's Coalition of the Willing". *Foreign Policy*. July/August 2010.

Handong, W. 2010. "Chapter 10 – Intellectual property law as China moves toward an innovation oriented society". In Dingjian, C. and W. Chenguang (eds). *China's Journey Toward the Rule of Law: Legal Reform 1978–2008*. Lieden: Brill.

Hogg, C. 2010. "Shanghai expo is China's new showcase to the world". *BBC News, Shanghai*. 29/4/2010. Available online at: http://news.bbc.co.uk/1/hi/world/asia-pacific/8651057.stm; accessed 10/08/2010.

INCD. 2004. *INCD Newsletter – February 2004*. 5(2).

INCP. 2003. *Framework for Cooperation Between the International Network on Cultural Policy and UNESCO in Support of an International Instrument on Cultural Diversity*. Available online at: http://incp-ripc.org/w-group/wg-cdg/paris2003/framework_e.shtml; accessed 07/01/2009.

Independent. 2008, 17 March. "Dalai Lama attacks 'cultural genocide'". Available online at: www.independent.co.uk/news/world/asia/dalai-lama-attacks-cultural-genocide-796795.html; accessed 10/08/2010.

Inter Press Service. 2005, 19 October. "UN Treaty Challenges 'Planet Hollywood.'"

Inter Press Service. 2006, 28 July. "CHINA: From Cultural Revolution to Cultural Exports".

Keane, M. 2006. "Exporting Chinese Culture: Industry Financing Models in Film and Television". *Westminster Papers in Communication and Culture*. 3(1): 11–27.

Keane, M. 2013. *Creative Industries in China*. Cambridge and Maldon: Polity Press.

Kuhn, A. 2008. "China tries to export culture as influence increases". *NPR*. 2 April 2008. Available online at: www.npr.org/templates/story/story.php?storyId=89306145; accessed 27/01/2010.

LA Times. 2010, 18 January. "'Avatar' pulled from 2-D screens by Chinese government". Available online at: http://latimesblogs.latimes.com/entertainmentnewsbuzz/2010/01/avatar-pulled-from-2d-screens-by-chinese-government.html; accessed 18/06/2015.

LaFraniere, S. 2010. "China's zeal for 'Avatar' crowds out 'Confucius.'" *New York Times*, 29 January 2010. Available online at: www.nytimes.com/2010/01/30/business/global/30avatar.html?_r=1&partner=rss&emc=rss; accessed 18/06/2015.

Le Devoir. 2005, 18 October. "Diversité culturelle: c'est oui à Paris".

Le Monde. 2005, 18 October. "UNESCO adopts the Convention on the Diversity of Cultural Expressions".

Liang, W. 2002. "The Confucius temple tragedy of the cultural revolution". In Wilson, T.A. (ed.). *On Sacred Grounds: Culture, Society, Politics and the Formation of the Cult of Confucius*. Cambridge: Harvard University Press.

Liaoning Provincial Online Foreign Trade Information Center. 2009. "MOC Spokesman Talked on the WTO Ruling on China Publishing Market Access Appeal". 25/12/2009. Available online at: www.china-liaoning.gov.cn/lnftec/portalpubsys/pubsys.jsp?subjectID =0000000ad000ff9a37cacc&articleID2=00000035a00125c2809db1; accessed 12/01/10.

Lien, D., C. Hoon Oh and W.T. Selmier. 2012. "Confucius Institute effects on China's trade and FDI: Isn't it delightful when folks afar study Hanyu?" *International Review of Economics and Finance*. 21(1).

Lim, K. 2013. "China's shift in cultural policy and cultural awareness". In Park, J.J. (ed.). *Multimedia and Ubiquitous Engineering; Lecture Notes in Electrical Engineering*: 601–609.

Lo, J.T. and S. Pan. 2014. Confucius Institutes and China's soft power: practices and paradoxes. *Compare: A Journal of Comparative and International Education*. Published online 30 May 2014. Available online at: www.tandfonline.com/doi/abs/10.1080/0305 7925.2014.916185#.VaE7U3vCZ5w; accessed 11/07/2015.

Martin, R.S. 2005. "Final Statement of the US Delegation at UNESCO, Paris, 3 June 2005". Available online at: http://unesco.usmission.gov/CL_09122006_CLDiversity-Convention.cfm; accessed 29/09/2009.

Mattelart, A. 2005. "Cultural Diversity Belongs to Us All". (trans. Harry Forster) *Le Monde Diplomatique*. November 2005.

Ministry of Foreign Affairs of Japan. 1999. "Points concerning the UNESCO Director-General election and the nomination of Ambassador Matsuura". Press Conference by the Press Secretary, 22 October 1999.

Moghadam, V.E. and D. Elveren. 2008. "The making of an international Convention: Culture and free trade in a global era". *Review of International Studies*. 34(4): 735–753.

MPAA. 2009. "MPAA Hails WTO Ruling". Press Release, 21 December 2009. Available online at: www.mpaa.org/press_releases/mpaa%27s%20glickman%20hails%20 wto%20ruling.pdf; accessed 12/01/2010.

Musitelli, J. 2006. "The Convention on Cultural Diversity: Anatomy of a Diplomatic Success Story". *French Ministry of Foreign Affairs*. Available online at: www.diplomatie. gouv.fr/en/IMG/pdf/The_Convention_on_Cultural_Diversity.pdf; accessed 29/09/2009.

New York Times. 2009, 8 November. "A movie's budget pops from the screen".

New York Times. 2010, 29 January. "China's zeal for 'Avatar' crowds out 'Confucius.'" www. nytimes.com/2010/01/30/business/global/30avatar.html?_r=1&partner=rss&emc=rss; accessed 02/02/2010.

Niedenführ, M. 2013. "The Tug-of-War between Regulatory Interventions and Market Demands in the Chinese Television Industry". *The Political Economy of Communication*. 1(1).

Nordicom. 2007. "Cultural Industries: Opportunities in Developing Countries". *Nordic Media Policy*. No. 1, December 2007. Available online at: www.nordicom.gu.se/eng_ mt/minletter.php?id=89#Opportunities in Developing Countries; accessed 14/01/2008.

Nurse, K. 2008. "The Cultural Industries and Sustainable Development in Small Island Developing States". *Creative Industries Exchange*. Available online at: http://portal. unesco.org/en/files/24726/110805219811CLT3.doc/CLT3.doc; accessed 23/03/2010.

Pang, L. 2012. *Creativity and its Discontents: China's Creative Industries and Intellectual Property Rights Offences*. Durham, NC: Duke University Press.

Pauwelyn, J. 2005. "The UNESCO Convention on Cultural Diversity, and the WTO: Diversity in International Law-Making?" American Society of International Law. 15 November 2005. Available online at: www.asil.org/insights051115.cfm; accessed 19/03/2007.

RCCI. 2006. "From the Director". *Tsinghua National Research Centre for Cultural Industry*. Available online at: www.rcci.org.cn/en/fd.htm; accessed 07/01/2010.

San Francisco Chronicle. 2010, 24 January. "China's Great Firewall Impedes Foreign Trade".

Shackleton, L. 2009. "Dadi seals Asian deals on $23million biopic Confucius". *Screen Daily*, 9 November. Available online at: www.screendaily.com/festivals/afm/dadi-seals-asian-deals-on-23m-biopic-confucius/5007862.article; accessed 11/11/2009.

Shaffer, G.C. and M.A. Pollack. 2008. "How hard and soft law interact in regulatory governance: alternatives, complements and antagonists". Paper presented at the inaugural conference of the Society of International Economic Law, Geneva, 15–17 July 2008. Available online at: www.ssrn.com/link/SIEL-Inaugural-Conference.html; accessed 07/01/2009.

Telegraph. 2010, 26 January. "Avatar: China changes name of peak to 'Hallelujah Mountain'". Available online at: www.telegraph.co.uk/culture/film/7078150/Avatar-China-changes-name-of-peak-to-Hallelujah-Mountain.html; accessed 11/07/2015.

The Economic Times. 2010, 17 May. "Chinese Firewall a Barrier Under WTO: EU". Available online at: www.forexyard.com/en/news/China-Web-firewall-should-be-WTO-issue-Kroes-2010-05-17T054257Z-UPDATE-1-EU; accessed 09/08/2010.

The Straits Times. 2010, 5 February. "All hail the aliens". Available online at: http://blogs.straitstimes.com/2010/2/4/all-hail-the-aliens; accessed 10/08/2010.

The Times. 2010, 19 January. "Confucius says 'no' to subversive blockbuster Avatar". Available online at: http://entertainment.timesonline.co.uk/tol/arts_and_entertainment/film/article6992685.ece; accessed 10/08/2010.

UNCTAD. 2004. *Creative Industries and Development*. United Nations Conference on Trade and Development. TD(XI)/BP/13. Available online at: www.unctad.org/en/docs//tdxibpd13_en.pdf; accessed 14/06/2010.

UNESCO. 1976. *Recommendation on Participation by the People at Large in Cultural Life and Their Contribution to it*. Paris: UNESCO. Available online at: www.UNESCO.org/culture/laws/nairobi/html_eng/page1.shtml; accessed 09/07/2007.

UNESCO. 1982. *Cultural Industries: A Challenge for the Future of Culture*. Paris: UNESCO.

UNESCO. 1995. *Our Creative Diversity: Report of the World Commission on Culture and Development*. Paris: UNESCO.

UNESCO. 1998. *The Stockholm Conference – Action Plan on Cultural Policies for Development*. Paris: UNESCO. Available online at: http://portal.UNESCO.org/culture/en/files/35220/12290888881stockholm_actionplan_rec_en.pdf/stockholm_actionplan_rec_en.pdf; accessed 15/03/2009.

UNESCO. 1999. "CULTURE: A FORM OF MERCHANDISE LIKE NO OTHER? Symposium of Experts on Culture, the Market and Globalisation, 14–15 June 1999". Paris: UNESCO. CLT/CIC/BCI/CMMIDOC.FIN.E.

UNESCO. 2001a. *Universal Declaration on Cultural Diversity*. Paris: UNESCO. Available online at: http://unesdoc.UNESCO.org/images/0012/001271/127160m.pdf; accessed 09/07/2007.

UNESCO. 2001b. *Draft Universal Declaration on Cultural Diversity*. Paris: UNESCO. Available online at: http://unesdoc.unesco.org/images/0012/001234/123405e.pdf; accessed 09/07/2007.

UNESCO. 2004. *First Meeting of Experts (category VI) on the First Draft of an International Convention on the Protection of the Diversity of Cultural Contents and Artistic Expressions*. CLT/CPD/2003–608/01. Paris: UNESCO. Available online at: www.unesco.org/

culture/culturaldiversity/docs_pre_2007/clt_cpd_2003_608_01_en_20022004.pdf; accessed 09/07/2007.

UNESCO. 2005a. *Convention on the Protection and Promotion of the Diversity of Cultural Expressions*. CLT-2005/CONVENTION DIVERSITE-CULT REV. Paris: UNESCO. Available online at: www.unesco.org/culture/en/diversity/convention; accessed 14/03/2007.

UNESCO. 2005b. "Preliminary report by the Director-General setting out the situation to be regulated and the possible scope of the regulating actions proposed, accompanied by the preliminary draft of a Convention on the Protection of the Diversity of Cultural Contents and Artistic Expressions". Paris: UNESCO. 4 August 2005. 33 C/23.

UNESCO. 2009a. *Creative Industries*. Available online at: http://portal.unesco.org/culture/en/ev.php-URL_ID=35024&URL_DO=DO_TOPIC&URL_SECTION=201.html; accessed 19/12/2009.

UNESCO. 2009b. "Nollywood rivals Bollywood in film/video production". Available online at: www.unesco.org/new/en/media-services/single-view/news/nollywood_rivals_bollywood_in_filmvideo_production/#.VZw1S3vCZ5w; accessed 07/07/2015.

UNESCO. 2010. *Strengthening the Creative Industries* in Five ACP Countries Through Employment and Trade Expansion. Paris: UNESCO. Available online at: http://portal.unesco.org/culture/en/ev.php-URL_ID=39091&URL_DO=DO_TOPIC&URL_SECTION=201.html; accessed 18/02/2010.

UNESCO. 2014. *Report prepared for the Eighth Ordinary Session of the Intergovernmental Committee for the Convention on the Protection and Promotion of the Diversity of Cultural Expressions*, 9–11 December 2014. Paris: UNESCO. CE/14/8.IGC/11. Available online at: http://en.unesco.org/creativity/sites/creativity/files/8IGC_11_impact_articles_16_et_21_fr_EN.pdf; accessed 17/08/2015.

UNESCO-Global Alliance for Cultural Diversity. 2009a. "Promoting Cultural Diversity Through Cultural Industries". Available online at: http://portal.unesco.org/culture/en/ev.php-URL_ID=24507&URL_DO=DO_TOPIC&URL_SECTION=201.html; accessed 20/10/2009.

UNESCO-Global Alliance for Cultural Diversity. 2009b. "Training of cultural entrepreneurs in Senegal 2008/2009". Available online at: http://portal.unesco.org/culture/en/ev.php-URL_ID=39895&URL_DO=DO_PRINTPAGE&URL_SECTION=201.html; accessed 24/10/2009.

United Nations. 2005. *Draft Mauritius Strategy for the further Implementation of the Programme of Action for the Sustainable Development of Small Island Developing States*. A/CONF.207/CRP.7. Available online at: www.un.org/smallislands2005/pdf/sids_strategy.pdf; accessed 27/07/2007.

UN Wire. 1999. "Japan Frets About Reaction to Winning Top Post". *United Nations Foundation*, 22 October.

US International Trade Administration. 2001. "Impact of the Migration of U.S. Film and Television Production". Available online at: www.ita.doc.gov/media/migration11901.pdf; accessed 06/07/2007.

US Mission to UNESCO. 2005. *Intervention by Ambassador Louise V. Oliver, Permanent Delegate of the United States of America*. As delivered at 33rd UNESCO General Conference, October 17, 2005. Available online at: www.unesco.usmission.gov/GC_09082006_Item83DR_10172005.cfm; accessed 21/03/2007.

US State Department. 2005. "LOUISE OLIVER HOLDS A NEWS CONFERENCE ON THE CONVENTION ON CULTURAL DIVERSITY". Paris: QC Transcriptions, LLC. (In possession of author, available on request.)

US Trade Representative. 2009. "Trade Rep. Praises WTO Decision Against China on Movies, Music". Available online at: http://iipdigital.ait.org.tw/st/english/article/2009/12/20091222103457dmslahrellek0.2171137.html#axzz3dVbahiPc; accessed 19/06/2015.

Wall Street Journal. 2009, 13 August. "Hollywood Upstages Beijing". Available online at: www.wsj.com/articles/SB125008679464026013; accessed 18/06/15.

Wall Street Journal. 2010, 25 January. "China Unveils Measures to Boost Domestic Film Industry". Available online at: http://online.wsj.com/article/BT-CO-20100125-700952.html; accessed 26/01/2010.

Wasserstrom, J. 2010. "'Confucius' and 'Avatar' at the Chinese multiplex". History News Network. 8 February 2010. Available online at: http://hnn.us/articles/122922.html; accessed 13/08.2010.

WIPO. 2010. "Creative Industries". *World Intellectual Property Organization, Program Activities*. Available online at: www.wipo.int/ip-development/en/creative_industry/; accessed 14/06/2010.

Wolf, D. 2009. "The WTO Ruling on China's Regime for Distributing and Importing Entertainment Products: What Does it Mean for You?" China Media Monitor Intelligence. Available online at: www.danwei.org/china_books/the_wto_ruling_on_chinas_regim.php; accessed 18/06/2015.

World Bank. 2010. *PROJECT INFORMATION DOCUMENT (PID): China: Shandong Confucius and Mencius Culture Heritage Protection and Development Project*. World Bank, Report No: AB5520, 28 February 2010. Available online at: http://documents.worldbank.org/curated/en/docsearch/projects/P120234; accessed 10/07/2015.

World Bank. 2015. *Implementation Status Results Report: China: Shandong Confucius and Mencius Culture Heritage Protection and Development Project: P120234*. World Bank, Report No: ISR17944, 20 March 2015. Available online at: http://documents.worldbank.org/curated/en/docsearch/projects/P120234; accessed 10/07/2015.

WTO. 2009. *China: Measures Affecting Trading Rights and Distribution Services for Certain Publications and Audiovisual Entertainment Products. Panel Report, 12/08/2009.* WT/DS363/R. Available online at: www.wto.org/english/tratop_e/dispu_e/cases_e/ds363_e.htm; accessed 18/06/2015.

Xinhua. 2006, 5 January. "Cultural Sector to be Reformed". Available online at: www.china.org.cn/government/central_government/2006-01/05/content_1154147.htm; accessed 26/01/2010.

Xinhua. 2010, 26 January. "China to Boost Domestic Film Industry". Available online at: http://news.xinhuanet.com/english2010/entertainment/2010-01/26/c_13150435.htm; accessed 11/07/2015.

Xinhua. 2013, 14 May. "China protects cultural rights of ethnic minority groups: white paper". Available online at: http://news.xinhuanet.com/english/china/2013-05/14/c_132380800.htm; accessed 18/06/2015.

Xinhua. 2014, 15 May. "China releases report on cultural development". Available online at: www.china.org.cn/china/Off_the_Wire/2014-05/15/content_32398695.htm; accessed 18/06/15.

Xinhua. 2015, 15 June. "Domestic competitiveness key to development of China's film industry". Available online at: http://usa.chinadaily.com.cn/life/2015-06/15/content_21011805.htm; accessed 12/07/2015.

Yúdice, G. 2003. *The Expediency of Culture: Uses of Culture in the Global Era*. London: Duke University Press.

Yueh, L. 2014. "Is it a golden age for Chinese cinema?" *BBC News Business.* 14 October 2014. Available online at: www.bbc.co.uk/news/business-29834530; accessed 18/06/15.

Zhao, Y. 2004. "The Media Matrix: China's Integration into Global Capitalism". In L. Panitch and C. Leys (eds). *The Empire Reloaded: Socialist Register 2005*. London: The Merlin Press.

Zhao, E.J. and Keane, M. 2013. "Between formal and informal: the shakeout in China's online video industry". *Media Culture and Society*. 35(6).

Zhongxi, R. 2010. "Cultural industry seeks financial support from banks". *China.org.cn*. 15 April 2010. Available online at: www.china.org.cn/china/2010-04/15/content_19828525.htm; accessed 18/06/2015.

Zhou, Y. 2015. "Pursuing soft power through cinema: censorship and double standards in mainland China". *Journal of Chinese Cinemas*. Published online 17 June 2015. Available online at: www.tandfonline.com/doi/abs/10.1080/17508061.2015.1049878#.VaF-HMnvCZ5w; accessed 11/07/2015.

5 Cultural exceptions and exclusions
The other sides of the consensus

Introduction

The adoption of the UNESCO Convention on the Protection and Promotion of the Diversity of Cultural Expressions ("the Convention") gave expression to a broad North–South consensus on questions related to sustainable cultural development and drew a line under the international political divisions of the 1970s and 1980s around calls for a New World Information and Communications Order (NWICO). The emergence of this consensus had been all the more remarkable given that during the Uruguay Round (1986–1993) of trade negotiations, and for much of the 1990s, France and Canada had had comparatively little success in convincing the rest of the international community about the importance of the "cultural exception" in international trade. Indeed France's insistence on this principle in this period had led to it being described by observers as occupying the "lunatic fringe" on this issue (Bruner, 2008). The near unanimous support that they were able to gather behind the approval of the Convention when it was put to vote in 2005 goes some way to demonstrate how international opinion had changed over this period, with the French culture minister reflecting on the text's adoption by announcing that: "We are no longer the black sheep on this issue" (Donnedieu de Vabres, cited in the *Guardian*, 2005).

In this chapter we will explore in greater depth how exactly this new consensus was achieved politically and pinpoint some of the areas of convergence and divergence, as well as some of the omissions and exclusions, that characterise the new consensus. We have already seen (in Chapter 3) how the controversies of the NWICO period at UNESCO came to be settled over the 1980s and 1990s through a jettisoning of its more radical demands, preparing the possibility for a less confrontational and more pragmatic approach by the time of the Stockholm Intergovernmental Conference on Cultural Policies for Development in 1998. We have also seen how Canada, France and the EU were largely successful in building on particular points of the agreements reached at Stockholm – notably, regarding the uniquely "dual" nature of cultural products, and regarding the international political commitment to work towards a binding international instrument on cultural diversity – in a bid to secure a treaty that is primarily aimed at bolstering their disputes with the US. In the process this bid has created a new coincidence of interests with emerging countries, such as China, which have come to have a considerable stake in the provisions that are offered by the new instruments. However, these observations do not account for the ways in which the campaign for the cultural exception was able to generate such wide support in the South as the debate over trade and culture began to migrate to UNESCO from the late 1990s.

Accounts of the Franco-EU–Canadian campaign for the adoption of the Convention have framed it as a successful campaign of trade diplomacy. For analysts such as Bruner (2008) or Shaffer and Pollack (2008), for example, the adoption of the Convention reflected a successful diplomatic campaign by French, European and Canadian diplomats and negotiators to "internationalise" their particular regulatory concerns over the trade and culture issue and to generate wider political support amongst key stakeholders in a bid to bolster their position against the US. This strategy is reflective of a broader pattern in the post-Cold War period whereby Canada and European member states have generally expressed commitment to multilateral processes and institutions when this route has suited their objectives. Where their interests have diverged from each other, or from the US, they have attempted to isolate their rival on the particular issue at hand by invoking an idealised vision of international relations and treaty making that a broad alliance of countries can rally around, find common points of interest and generate a critical mass (Gowan, 2001; Welsh, 2004; Carmody, 2007).

A similar pattern of coalition building to that which has been evident in the formation of the UNESCO Convention has been evident, for example, with the adoption, in 2003, of the Cartagena Protocol on Biosafety (a complement to the 1992 Convention on the Protection of Biological Diversity). The EU has pursued the adoption of this protocol as a matter of international diplomacy amongst developing countries in an attempt to counter the attempt at the WTO by the "Miami Group" of biotechnology-exporting countries (led by the US and Canada, along with China, Brasil, India and Argentina) to gain access to the European market. For Schaffer and Pollack (2008), the adoption of the Convention has been analogous to the adoption of the Cartagena Protocol, in this case with Canada and the EU successfully building the support of a critical mass of states from the South that share their regulatory objectives.

These observations undoubtedly capture an important aspect of the campaign for the Convention, but in focusing on the achievement of the objectives of the more powerful states such as Canada or the EU they leave little room for an account of the reasons why the majority of member governments gathered at UNESCO, most of whom have had relatively little at stake in the debates over trade and culture, came to add their support behind the campaign from the late 1990s. Nor can they account for how it was that the leaders of the campaign were able to maintain the centrality of the cultural exception in creating an instrument addressed to the goal of cultural diversity (a concept which, after all, is so notoriously empty a signifier that it could have been used to generate a variety of possible instruments). In this respect the triumphant claims from French, European and Canadian ministers and diplomats that followed the Convention's adoption, or the parallel observations of trade policy analysts such as those considered above, only paint a partial picture. This requires that we pay closer attention to the ways in which the campaign has been willing to broaden the terms of the debate, including its cry of cultural exception, so as to bring a wider group of countries and interests on board and, in the words of one the key architects of the strategy, rid the debate of its stature in the South as "nothing more than transatlantic rivalry" (Musitelli, 2006: 2).

In addressing these points, this chapter is split into four sections. The first section looks at the ways in which the framing of the problem of cultural diversity by the EU and Canada has in fact had the effect of marginalising other claims for cultural recognition in international fora over the same period. Just as Canada and the EU have invested significant political capital into raising the profile of the trade and culture issue at UNESCO, widening international support behind the principle of the dual nature of cultural products and ensuring its rapid entry into force as the defining international instrument on cultural diversity after Stockholm, they have simultaneously withheld support from a number of other initiatives over the same period, such as the UNESCO Convention for the Safeguarding of Intangible Cultural Heritage or the UN Declaration on the Rights of Indigenous Peoples. At the same time, however, this stance on the Convention has been complicated by the emergence over the 1990s of a distinctive legal vocabulary turning on the rights and values of diverse cultures and ways of life. International concerns over biodiversity and the sustainability of "intangible" and "traditional" heritages, knowledges and practices have provided opportunities across a variety of struggles for articulating claims to recognition through the discourse of human rights and the expanded, "anthropological" concept of culture. Where questions of culture are concerned, this development has changed the dynamics of international treaty making, posing both opportunities and problems for the expansion of capitalist protocols and the consolidation of international and national hierarchies.

These themes are taken up in the second section, which examines some of the ways in which the strategists of the Canadian, French and European campaigns set out to turn their positions into "the rule not the exception" by attempting to give the cultural exception a more universal dimension that could gain wider support in the South and thereby gain broader legitimacy in their dispute with the US. I look in particular at the genesis of the campaigns in the late 1990s and how they began to take shape through the work of the Canadian Department of Foreign Affairs and International Trade (DFAIT) and French leadership of the *Organisation International de la Francophonie* (OIF). Referring back to the arguments of Yúdice that we considered in Chapter 2, it is also noted that the strategy has relied not only on the contemporary protagonism of culture as a resource for trade, development and political recognition, but has in fact looked for its most potent arguments in the notion of culture's irreducible contribution to "the dignity of humanity" – an ideological formula through which France has attempted to consolidate postcolonial linkages in the OIF and reinvigorate the organisation's role in the era of globalisation.

The third and fourth sections then go on to look in more detail at the precise mechanisms through which the campaign gathered international support and forged alliances and common points of interest. The third section looks in particular at how the campaign sought to mobilise what it referred to as "the cultural milieu", striking strategic alliances amongst cultural ministries, professionals and industry stakeholders around the world. With particular reference to the campaign in Morocco in 2004, I also note how the international cultural diversity campaign has simultaneously tended to marginalise the diffuse "pluralism of opinions and lifestyles" that it has deemed surplus to the formulation of an effective international treaty in the context of transatlantic rivalry. The final section then goes on to look at what happened after the first draft was put on the table at UNESCO in 2003 by the campaign as the basis for a binding international instrument. It refers in particular to the records of the intergovernmental drafting negotiations that took place between 2004 and 2005, examining some of the processes of North–South negotiation and compromise that allowed the Convention to proceed to the vote in 2005 with sufficient international support.

Intangible heritage, biological diversity and the right to land, tenure and place

The Intangible Cultural Heritage Convention and the Convention on Biological Diversity

To contextualise the Euro-Canadian campaign for cultural diversity that took shape from the late 1990s, it is useful to begin by considering an alternative instrument that was under discussion at UNESCO at the same time but that had been on the table long before the cultural diversity Convention: the Convention for the Safeguarding of Intangible Cultural Heritage ("the ICH Convention"). The road to the adoption of this instrument at UNESCO in 2003 was a long one. After some largely fruitless initiatives in the 1970s (notably a campaign led by Bolivia for the recognition of oral traditions), momentum began to build within UNESCO after a set of recommendations was issued at the 1982 MONDIACULT (World Conference on Cultural Policies, Mexico City), which was eventually followed by the formal adoption at UNESCO of a Recommendation on the Safeguarding of Traditional Culture and Folklore (1989) and the creation of a new programme on "Intangible Cultural Heritage" in 1992.[1]

This slow progress on the creation of an instrument on intangible cultural heritage contrasts with the speed at which the Convention on cultural diversity came into existence once it was put on the international agenda. One of the reasons for this has been a relative lack of political support, particularly from the more powerful states that have backed the Convention on cultural diversity (neither Canada, France nor the EU has ratified this instrument and they have shown relatively little support for it). While the Canadian government made a point of being the first to ratify the cultural diversity Convention (and Canadian representatives have flown around the world in a bid to secure support and widen the number of ratifications), when asked about its position on the ICH Convention representatives responded by noting that they were unaware even of "any research reports that have been undertaken by the Government of Canada or its agencies that address the [ICH Convention]" (IFACCA, 2009: 4). On this occasion Canada and Europe have therefore found themselves more aligned with the position of the US, which has also not ratified the instrument.

This relative lack of political investment, along with some of the more practical and legal-technical difficulties that have been involved in drafting a treaty on intangible heritage (which we will explore below), means that the ICH Convention has taken much longer to get off the ground and its standing in comparison to the cultural diversity Convention remains relatively low. This is significant in the context of discussions surrounding cultural development because the ICH Convention has been of particular interest to those countries that have less at stake in creating an instrument to protect the kind of cultural resources that are the focus of the cultural diversity Convention. In the case of intangible cultural heritage (hereinafter "ICH"), the weight of support has been located further "south" (from governments in Africa, Latin America, Eastern Europe, Central Asia and the small island developing states, such as those in the Pacific). The ICH Convention's provisions, programmes and activities have less of an emphasis on the creations of the cultural industries (or the "tangible" monuments listed on the World Heritage List, which have tended to reflect a bias towards the more developed regions) than on those aspects hitherto referred to as the "traditional" or as "folklore".[2] In parallel to the negotiation of the ICH Convention, the African Group of WTO Members also made an attempt under the auspices of the Doha Development Round for greater protection and intellectual property recognition at the WTO for the kinds of traditional knowledges and practices that are covered under the framework of ICH (WTO, 2003).

The ICH Convention therefore offers some useful points of comparison with the cultural diversity Convention in assessing some of the broader international stakes over the question of cultural diversity as it rose on the international agenda towards the end of the 1990s. The main objective of the ICH Convention has been the creation of a set of internationally recognised provisions covering the intangible "living expressions", practices and knowledges that "countless groups and communities worldwide have inherited from their ancestors and transmit to their descendants", such as (to give the specific examples referred to in the text of the ICH Convention): oral traditions, performing arts, rituals, festive events, knowledge and practices concerning "nature and the universe" (covering among others agricultural, ecological, medicinal and botanical knowledges) and the knowledge and skills involved in crafts – in short, those aspects of human activity that were not covered by the authoritative definitions of culture at UNESCO prior to MONDIACULT (UNESCO, 2003a).

The emergence of the notion of ICH at MONDIACULT was part of the attempt in this period to expand the definition of culture to incorporate its more "anthropological" dimension and to gain wider legitimacy for its role in democratising cultural policy (and, as we saw in Chapter 2, to simultaneously bring a wider field of human activities under the concerns of government). UNESCO notes, for example, in its account of the development of the concept of ICH since the MONDIACULT Conference that:

> One of the main achievements of the Conference was its redefinition of culture. It stated that heritage now also covered all the values of culture as expressed in everyday life, and growing importance was being attached to activities calculated to sustain the ways of life and forms of expression by which such values were conveyed. *The Conference remarked that the attention now being given to the preservation of the "intangible heritage" may be regarded as one of the most constructive developments of the past decade. It was one of the first times that the term "intangible heritage" was officially used.*
>
> (UNESCO, 2010a; emphasis in original)

The subsequent attempts to elevate the legal and political stature of ICH at UNESCO have, particularly since Stockholm, sought to expand the concept further by noting that it represents a particularly "fragile" resource in the contemporary context of globalisation, drawing attention to its simultaneously economic, political and cultural roles in realising the objectives of social cohesion and economic development, as well as the right to cultural expression and the objective of global cultural diversity (see, for example, UNESCO, 2002; UNESCO, 2003a). The preliminary work for the ICH Convention, for example, referred to this need to develop the legacy of MONDIACULT by continuing to expand the concept of culture in order to more fully account for its roles in social, cultural and economic development (UNESCO, 2002: 3). It goes on to note that:

> [I]ntangible aspects of cultural heritage can play an important role in economic and social as well as cultural terms for a given society. The Action Plan from the Stockholm Conference [UNESCO, 1998] makes this point clear when recommending to Member States to promote cultural and linguistic diversity as well as local cultures and languages and encourage cultural diversity and traditions as part of their development strategy.
>
> (UNESCO, 2002: 6)

We can see here that the value of ICH has been framed at UNESCO in broadly similar terms to those that have been used for cultural goods and services over the same period. By giving greater formal recognition to particular knowledges and practices hitherto under-acknowledged within frameworks of political inclusion and economic development, and backing this up with international development assistance and expertise, the broad aim is to safeguard cultural expressions deemed to be under threat and to improve the conditions for a pluralised international expression of cultural forms. This is also seen as a way to meet the aspirations of particular social groups by improving the safeguarding and, where possible, the effective exploitation and marketing of their distinctive knowledges and practices so as to generate revenue streams and other material benefits (even if it is also asserted that this should not go so far as to lead to "unsustainable" or "inappropriate" forms of commercial development that would threaten their long term sustainability; see UNESCO, 2010c).

On the face of it, such an instrument appears to hold out greater potential to a wider number of groups than those that are the focus of the cultural diversity Convention (cultural industry sectors such as audiovisual, publishing, and so on). However, there are at least two main differences between ICH and cultural goods and services as they have featured in the campaigns for the respective instruments:

1   the relative lack of international political backing or interest behind the attempt to articulate ICH's role as a resource for trade and development; and
2   the particular difficulties related to situating ICH within existing international legal and developmental frameworks. These two points will be explored in more detail below.

1) On the first point, it is important to note that although the campaign for ICH has received less backing from the more powerful states, it has nevertheless had the effect of continuing the ongoing expansion and legitimisation of the anthropological concept of culture in international fora. In her study of the campaigns and discussions that led to the adoption of the Convention on Biological Diversity, Coombe (2003) has argued that the assertion of the value of "traditional" knowledges and identities provided a means to turn around colonial categorical frameworks of intellectual property (in which the "uncultivated" aspects of human activity, information and ideas created by "pre-moderns" are earmarked to be transformed into "cultivated" expressions, inventions or innovations that can be alienated and exploited as "works" of intellectual property for commercial exploitation). The sense of global urgency amongst Northern governments and corporations over the loss of cultural and biological resources has provided a strategic opportunity for Southern governments, as well as some of the world's most marginalised populations – from Indigenous groups, developing country farmers and peasants, to rain-forest inhabitants (along with the scientists, environmentalists, and NGOs that support them) – to invert the terms of this framework. In this way, she suggests that "'the South' has potentially effected a rhetorical sea change in global legal discourse" (Coombe, 2003: 291).

The Convention on Biological Diversity marked at least three landmarks in this respect. First, it was the first time that Indigenous groups had been given supported standing in a UN forum over the creation of a treaty (other than those specifically addressing an autonomous set of human rights). Second, it created a binding legal instrument that reflects not only a neocolonial concern to gain access to genetic resources, local knowledge and ecosystem expertise in the South, but also sets up mechanisms of concession and reciprocity by specifically requiring that parties "respect, preserve, and maintain knowledge, innovations, and practices of Indigenous and local communities embodying traditional lifestyles" (Convention on Biological Diversity, cited in Coombe, 2003: 275). In such ways, it is argued that the negotiation of the Convention on Biological Diversity demonstrates the increasing ability of Southern governments, Indigenous groups and international NGOs to put issues of cultural integrity, democratic decision-making, accountability, and self-determination squarely on the bargaining table (assisted by the rhetorical leverage provided by expanding international human rights norms) and the central (although ambiguous) place of culture within these (Coombe, 2003: 286).

Third, the global biological diversity agenda and its accompanying fora of participation, funding and publicity opportunities have provided an opportunity for Indigenous groups to negotiate and campaign independently from the states with which they have long had relationships of distrust, betrayal and violence in the context of colonialism and modernisation. As WIPO has begun to bypass state jurisdictions to broker and negotiate contracts between bio-prospectors and the inhabitants of some of the untapped "goldmines" of capitalist development (rich in biological and genetic resources awaiting commercial exploitation), these developments have indeed begun to create significant benefits and revenue streams for those groups that have been able to put themselves forward as bearers of distinct cultural identities and alienable traditional knowledges. This has also brought some reversal of processes of international "biopiracy" (whereby international bioprospectors and corporations have hitherto been able to exploit local knowledges without any form of remuneration accruing to those that originally developed them) (Farhat, 2008). The ICH Convention contributes to this growing and distinctive legal vocabulary of representations and claims turning on the rights and values of diverse cultures and ways of life – and as this vocabulary is reiterated in authoritative contexts it is raising the possibility that it could over time become a feature of customary international law (Coombe, 2003: 287–302; Anaya and Wiessner, 2007).

2) However, we should also note that it has proven more problematic to situate ICH within the same kind of international legal framework of rights to political recognition and economic remuneration that can be extended to activities contributing to the cultural and creative industries or to the alienable knowledges, codes and compounds of biotechnology. This is because most of the activities covered under the term ICH have relatively little international concern or value as potential objects of alienation and exchange (other than as marketable handicrafts or niche tourist curios).[3] Furthermore, when dealing with ICH it has proven extremely difficult to reliably identify factors that can be captured within the logic of intellectual property: such as the originality of their effects; their final forms and fixation; the clear identification of an author;

or the duration of their protection (see, for example, the deliberations presented to the UNESCO Executive Board, 2001: 3–4). UNESCO has therefore noted that

> applying intellectual property rights with the current legislative framework is not satisfactory when dealing with intangible cultural heritage. Main difficulties are related to its evolving and shared nature as well as to the fact that it is often owned collectively.
>
> (UNESCO, 2010c)

The fact that requests to the funds and assistance that are available under the ICH Convention can only be made by governments, in accordance with existing international frameworks and in agreement with UNESCO, reinforces this tendency for ICH to be defined and operationalised according to state objectives and internationally authoritative frameworks of recognition – in which, of course, some claims to culture have more legitimacy or value than others.[4]

Some critics of the ICH Convention have therefore argued that it "supports an obliteration of local rights in preference to state and global interests" (Kearney, 2009: 220). Although that is perhaps to overstate the case, it is nevertheless clear that in the absence of any clarification of the status of Indigenous groups and other communities as bearers of intangible heritage in the ICH Convention, it is the state which ultimately retains discretionary power in the pursuit of safeguarding mechanisms. In other words, the language of culture as a resource for development and intellectual property exploitation has relatively little international protagonism or currency here, other than how it can augment international and state development priorities. In this framework, there remains little room for claims from some of the most marginalised communities who seek to link economic and political struggles with the language of cultural recognition or cultural rights – for example, those that seek to link cultural preservation to disputes covering issues such as land tenure and reform, forestry, fisheries, mining or agricultural liberalisation.

The right to land, tenure and place and the Declaration on the Rights of Indigenous Peoples

It has been in recognition of these difficulties in articulating a broader and more effective treaty in respect of the activities covered under the terms of intangible culture that campaigns have sought to develop alternative instruments to those that have been negotiated under the terms of the new world economic order of neoliberal globalisation. Alongside the attempts to draft the ICH Convention, one such attempt was made by a network of Indigenous groups to draft an approach to cultural development outside of the inter-governmental treaty-making framework: the International Covenant on the Rights of Indigenous Nations (in 1994). This sought to give recognition to the links between ICH and "collective" (rather than "individual") property rights such as "the right to land, tenure and place" – by which is meant "the total environment of the land space, soils, air, water, sky, sea, sea-ice, flora and fauna and other resources which Indigenous peoples used historically and on which they continue to depend to sustain and evolve their culture" (International Covenant on the Rights of Indigenous Nations, 1994). However, drafted outside of the arena of inter-state agreements this presented little more than a "pseudo-treaty", with no real international standing (Chartrand, 1999).

A more successful attempt has come in the form of the UN Declaration on the Rights of Indigenous Peoples (hereinafter "UNDRIP"), which was adopted at the UN General Assembly in 2007 after a campaign that, like the ICH Convention, can be traced back several decades and gained momentum in 1982 through the establishment of a UN Working Group on Indigenous Populations (United Nations, 2007). Among other things the UNDRIP notably calls upon governments to recognise the rights of Indigenous populations by working to give them more control over the land and resources they traditionally possessed, to return confiscated territory or to pay compensation (United Nations, 2007).

UNDRIP has only declarative rather than legally binding status, however, and indeed it is unlikely that it would have got off the ground diplomatically if it was seen to have posed a serious challenge on matters related to ownership and control over territory and resources. Nevertheless, its elevation on the international agenda is another reflection of the growing recognition and legitimacy of the vocabulary and claims attached to cultural rights. It stands as the most comprehensive answer yet to the demands of Indigenous peoples, providing a yardstick by which states can be judged internationally (for example, by the UN Special Rapporteur on the rights of Indigenous peoples) and becoming mainstreamed into the policies of the major development organisations (Wiessner, 2011). Like the UNESCO Convention on cultural diversity, its passing has also been reflective of the diplomatic initiatives of particular governments – notably the Indigenous government of Bolivia, which was a political spearhead for the campaign and responded quickly to the adoption of UNDRIP by working to write the declaration into the new Bolivian Constitution of 2008. The Bolivian President, Evo Morales, has also made reference to UNDRIP in the campaign at the UN over the criminalisation of the use and cultivation of the coca leaf, noting in a letter to the UN Secretary General in 2009 that the UNDRIP now sat alongside a growing corpus of international treaties and agreements concerning culture that had rendered coca's ongoing prohibition "an attack on the human rights of Indigenous communities" (Morales, 2009).

The starkest divisions over UNDRIP have reflected lingering colonial tensions, particularly as UNDRIP touches on questions related to the control and development of land and resources. The four countries that voted against its adoption were Canada, Australia, New Zealand and the US, former settler colonies that have been involved in ongoing disputes over territory with historically marginalised and disenfranchised minority and Indigenous populations (and, in the case of the latter three, have received warnings over their treatment of Indigenous groups by the UN Committee on the Elimination of Racial

Discrimination) (*Survival International*, 2007). Assurances over UNDRIP's merely declarative status and its subordination to national jurisdiction, along with pressure applied by domestic and international human rights organisations, have meant that all four countries that initially opposed UNDRIP have since reversed their position and endorsed it. In doing so, however, they have been careful to make a number of reservations. For example in Canada's statement announcing that it was joining the other countries of the world in supporting UNDRIP, it added the disclaimer that the declaration remained "a non-legally binding document that does not reflect customary international law nor change Canadian laws" (Government of Canada, 2010). This position has been described as "manifestly untenable" by the UN Special Rapporteur on the rights of Indigenous peoples, and was quickly criticised in a joint statement issued by a number of Canadian and international networks and NGOs in response to the Canadian government's statement (Cultural Survival, 2010).

The opposition to UNDRIP has parallels with ILO Convention 169 (the "Indigenous and Tribal People's Convention", adopted in 1989), the only legally binding international treaty addressed to Indigenous rights. One of its most notable provisions is the requirement on parties to recognise the connection between the cultural identities of Indigenous communities and control over land and resources, in particular by obliging states to seek "free, prior and informed consent" from Indigenous communities when making decisions that affect them and the territories that they have claims over. To date, however, only 22 of the ILO's 186 member states have signed and ratified this instrument (15 of which are in Latin America). Canada, the US and Australia have been notable opponents, as well as France and the United Kingdom (who have both been concerned in particular with the implications that it could have for their significant commercial investments on Indigenous lands), making these countries the focus of campaigns for wider international ratification (UNPO, 2009).

Some of the key state sponsors of the UNESCO Convention on cultural diversity have therefore been reluctant to lend their support to a legally binding instrument related to Indigenous rights, particularly under more conservative governments. The position of Canada is worth focusing on here since it illustrates the selective nature of Canada's stance in the international debate and its prioritisation of a set of principles related to cultural goods and services in the campaign for the Convention on cultural diversity. It also demonstrates the shallow commitment of Canada in practice to some of the other principles that found their way into the Convention regarding the recognition of minority and Indigenous groups at national level (e.g. UNESCO, 2005a: Article 2).

Although Canada has a long-established legal and policy framework addressing Indigenous ("Aboriginal") concerns, this has been subject to a number of criticisms both within Canada and internationally. The 2014 report of the UN Special Rapporteur on the rights of Indigenous peoples noted, for example, that "It is difficult to reconcile Canada's well-developed legal framework and general prosperity with the human rights problems faced by indigenous peoples in Canada, which have reached crisis proportions in many respects" (Anaya, 2014: 6).

Canada's position on UNDRIP was subject to further criticism in 2014 when it filed objections to the Outcome Document of the first UN World Conference on Indigenous Peoples – the only member state to do so.[5] Since the Outcome Document was intended to express commitment to what UN Secretary General Ban-Ki Moon described as a set of "minimum standards for the survival, dignity and well-being of indigenous peoples", there has been much domestic and international criticism of Canada's position, with Assembly of First Nations (AFN)[6] leaders protesting that there had been no communication from the government prior to the Conference and describing Canada's stance on the Outcome Document as unjustified and "deeply concerning", adding that "Canada continues to embarrass itself and isolate itself on the world stage" (cited in Lum, 2014).

The controversies over Canada's international stance on the question of Indigenous rights have come in the context of a growing strain in relations between the recent Stephen Harper government (2006–2015) and First Nations groups on domestic issues. One of the sources of this is the contemporary intensification of government and business plans to open up resource development projects across First Nations territories. The federal government's aim over the next decade is for US$600 billion of investment to flow into mining, forestry, gas and oil projects, much of which will implicate First Nations communities (as of March 2013, 94 of 105 projects under federal review are recognised to be located on reserve, within an historic treaty area, or in a settled or unsettled claims area; Lukacs, 2015). Mindful of the growing activism around Indigenous rights and mounting protests against developments in resource extractions and pipeline construction, the government has noted that it "can no longer afford the investment uncertainty created by issues around Aboriginal participation", and responded by undertaking a series of risk evaluations and seeking new channels of engagement between government, businesses and First Nations communities (notably through the creation of a Working Group on Natural Resource Development in 2013) (Lukacs, 2015). In the process this has opened a divide between grassroots activists (expressed in the formation of movements such as "Idle No More", who are opposed to increased investments on cultural and environmental grounds and accuse the government of seeking to undermine First Nations rights claims)[7] and some leaders within the AFN (who have entered into dialogue as part of this process in the hope of securing potential royalties and development opportunities from increased investment).

One striking aspect of this new approach in Canada is a drive to detach the agenda for economic development from the Indigenous rights agenda, based on the argument that separating a rights-based agenda (politics) from economic development (business) is key to wealth generation in First Nations communities (Lukacs, 2015). The promotion of business-to-business relationships between First Nations leaders and industry proponents, based on a search for mutual financial interests and shared stakes in resource development projects, is envisaged here as a way to generate much needed financial resources for First Nations communities while overcoming growing Indigenous opposition to such projects and avoiding the potential for lengthy and obstructive judicial proceedings over land claims. This has allowed the Canadian government to square an essentially neoliberal economic agenda with a commitment to negotiation with, and recognising the needs of, First Nations. Grassroots activists have therefore accused AFN chiefs and council members of engaging in a process that is aimed at "sacrificing our [First Nations] rights and our lands at the altar of profit", and ultimately removing the basis for sustainable development within First Nations communities (Clayton Thomas Mueller, cited in Lukacs, 2015). Other critics have described the contemporary strategy of the Canadian government as a colonial agenda to "terminate" the constitutionally protected and internationally recognised rights of First Nations (Diabo, 2012).

At the time of writing it remains to be seen what the outcome of these discussions in Canada will be. Negotiations and increased investments into First Nations communities could indeed provide much-needed boosts to socioeconomic development but they could also be part of a package of "neoliberal multiculturalism" (Hale, 2005; see Chapter 2) which offers some acknowledgement of First Nations rights while in fact emptying those rights of meaningful content – and ultimately entrenching the disadvantaged and disenfranchised status of First Nations communities.

What does emerge more clearly from the above discussions, however, is a sense of how some of the limits to a politically acceptable international treaty on cultural diversity have been staked out and contested since the 1990s, and how these are contingent upon the priorities of powerful states and particular civil society groups. In this sense it is important to put the conflicts over trade and culture within the context of a much broader set of conflicts in this period over defining culture's place in the authoritative vocabulary of political and economic rights and entitlements. Global concerns over biodiversity and the sustenance of "intangible" and "traditional" heritages, knowledges and practices have provided opportunities across a variety of struggles and conflicts for articulating claims to recognition that turn on the growing international legitimacy of the language of human rights and an expanded, "anthropological" concept of culture. Alongside this development, however, we have also seen an ongoing attempt to contain these claims within terms commensurable with capitalist protocols and colonial hierarchies that seek to manage and contain the scope of culture as a resource for political recognition and economic development. This is striking when looking at the debate within Canada, where on one hand the government and cultural industry stakeholders have been able to successfully mobilise behind the principle of the "dual" nature of cultural goods and their links with the realisation of cultural identity and cultural rights (in the form of the UNESCO Convention on cultural diversity), while on the other there has been a government-industry bid to separate economic development from cultural rights on issues pertaining to Indigenous and First Nations populations. In the following section we will draw these themes out in more detail by examining the way that the cultural exception began to evolve in the international campaign from the late 1990s.

The rule not the exception: Canada, France and the reinvention of the cultural exception

In the months following the Stockholm conference in 1998, French and Canadian representatives joined forces to position themselves at the helm of an international campaign with the objective of securing a binding international instrument that would reassert the sovereignty of cultural policy and put the principles of the "cultural exception" and the "dual nature" of cultural goods and services at the centre of the agenda for cultural diversity and cultural development at UNESCO. Mindful of the spirit of international cooperation and urgency that had been summoned during the negotiation of the Convention on Biological Diversity in 1992, and against the backdrop of a growing sense of international unease over the pace and direction of globalisation over the 1990s (expressed dramatically with the collapse of the negotiations over the Multilateral Agreement on Investment in 1998 and the protests at the WTO Ministerial Conference in Seattle in 1999), they capitalised on an opportunity to generate a broad and fast-moving campaign.

On the eve of the Convention's adoption in October 2005, the Canadian Heritage Minister Liza Frulla spoke in Ottawa to praise the efforts of those representatives from across the country, both French- and English-speaking, that had successfully pursued "an aggressive international strategy, taking advantage of major events to advance our objectives. Canada has been at the forefront of a well-orchestrated diplomatic offensive" (Frulla, 2005). Across the Atlantic, the French representative at UNESCO during the key stages of the Convention's drafting celebrated a "diplomatic success story", pointing out that while Canada had provided the original idea of developing an international instrument to defend the cultural exception, France had "provided the script" by utilising its ties within the *Organisation International de la Francophonie* (OIF) and its knowledge of the workings of UNESCO in order to breathe political life into the campaign (Musitelli, 2006). What has been remarkable about this campaign is the way in which has been able to incorporate a broader number of claims and concerns to those that had originally animated it. In this section we will look at how this strategy was developed following Stockholm, and then go on in the following sections to examine how it proved attractive (or not) to particular governments and stakeholders as a framework for the conduct of cultural policy.

Canada, the WTO ruling of 1997 and the formation of the international cultural diversity campaign

> Culture is the heart of a nation. As countries become more economically integrated, nations need strong domestic cultures and cultural expression to maintain their sovereignty and sense of identity.... Canadian books, magazines, songs, films, new media, radio and television programs reflect who we are as a people. Cultural industries shape our society, develop our

understanding of one another and give us a sense of pride in who we are as a nation. Canada's cultural industries fulfil an essential and vital role in Canadian society.

New Strategies for Culture and Trade: Canadian Culture in a Global World. The Cultural Industries Sectoral Advisory Group (SAGIT, 1999)

Canada took the diplomatic lead in building the international campaign for an international treaty on cultural diversity in the late 1990s and demonstrated its commitment to the cause by being the first country to ratify the Convention after its adoption at UNESCO in 2005. The urgency with which it has pursued the cultural diversity agenda at the international level was triggered by a series of developments in the 1990s that gave the trade and culture debate a particular resonance in Canada: the completion of the North American Free Trade Agreement (NAFTA) in 1994; the controversial negotiations between the OECD countries over the Multilateral Agreement on Investment (MAI) (1995–1998, which broke down in large part due to French and Canadian opposition regarding its proposals on the treatment of the cultural industries)[8]; and, most significantly, a decision by the WTO in 1997 which ruled against Canadian content requirements for magazine advertising (following a case brought by the US government representing the concerns of *Time* and *Sports Illustrated*) (WTO, 1997; Carmody, 1999). The WTO ruling was particularly significant because it rejected the cultural arguments with which the content requirements had been defended by Canada in the dispute. This raised the alarm amongst a range of stakeholders in Canada that the momentum of international trade disputes and negotiations, backed up by the kind of powerful international regulatory frameworks that had been created by the WTO, could begin to strip away the significant measures of domestic support that had been built up around its cultural sector by the federal government over the previous century (Acheson and Maule, 2005).[9]

The debate over the future of Canadian cultural policy that was sparked in Canada over this period has been analysed by Allor and Gagnon (1997), who noted that as the topic of free trade and the exemption of cultural products rose to become the central issue facing stakeholders and policymakers, the concern for culture as a question of national civic identity and social cohesion became framed equally in terms of economic development and how to secure the presence of Canada's cultural and creative industries on the domestic and international market. While discussions in Canada around culture during the debate that was sparked in the late 1990s were therefore careful to "steer away from endorsing free market mechanisms", they simultaneously invoked the utility of culture "as a resource to be developed and exploited for the sake of economic development" and to "enhance the international profile" of the country and its provinces (Allor and Gagnon, 1997: 43). Yúdice (2003: 224) similarly reflected on the debate in Canada in the 1990s by noting that free trade was not the central issue: it was more significantly an "occasion for discussion of the increasing protagonism of culture in the articulated management of the economy, mediated representation and citizenship".

Equally significant here is that this was also an occasion that prompted Canada to begin to internationalise these discussions in a bid to create wider international support and legitimacy for its domestic policy objectives. In this spirit, the WTO ruling was followed by a series of coordinated responses from the Canadian government (at both federal and regional levels, encompassing both English and French-speaking Canada), civil society and private sector: notably the formation of the International Network on Cultural Policy (INCP) (in 1998), the formation of the Coalition for Cultural Diversity (CCD) (in 1998) and the adoption, by the Department of Foreign Affairs and International Trade (DFAIT), of a strategy that was set out in a report by the Cultural Industries Sectoral Advisory Group (SAGIT) (in 1999). Together these groups worked to put the question of the trade in cultural products at the centre of the intergovernmental response to the Stockholm conference of 1998 and have provided the defining follow-up to the work that had been undertaken at UNESCO over the previous decade. In the rest of this section we will look at the strategy developed by SAGIT and DFAIT and how this was complemented by France and the EU, and in the following section we will go on to look more closely at the international efforts of the INCP and CCD.

SAGIT: New Strategies for Culture and Trade

The strategy that was pursued by Canadian representatives in securing the adoption of the Convention in 2005 was set out in 1999 when the Canadian government adopted a set of recommendations drawn up by SAGIT (a policy-oriented group of Canadian film, TV, music, publications, arts, new media and communications industries, along with experts in cultural policy and international trade law) who worked closely with DFAIT and the Department of Canadian Heritage. The central theme of these recommendations was the need to set out a strategy for "internationalising" the Canadian campaign for the recognition of the cultural exemption in international trade in a way that could strengthen Canada's position in negotiations and disputes affecting the cultural sector (SAGIT, 1999). Against the backdrop of national and international controversy over the MAI and WTO negotiations, SAGIT highlighted the political opportunity that had been presented by "a growing concern worldwide about the impact of international agreements on trade and investment on culture" (SAGIT, 1999). Pointing in particular to the way that different countries and groups had come together in recognition of the urgent need to protect and promote biodiversity with the adoption of the Convention on Biological Diversity in 1992, SAGIT therefore called upon the Canadian government to gather wider international support behind a new instrument that could be used to further cultural diversity in the context of trade negotiations by asserting the threat now being posed to the role of the cultural industries in development: not only on economic grounds, which it noted were becoming increasingly important (both as a percentage of GDP and as a driving force of the new economy), but also for their role at what it referred to as "the heart of a nation" (SAGIT, 1999). The essence of the new strategy was set out in the following passage:

> The tools and approaches used in the past to keep cultural goods and services from being subject to the same treatment as other goods and services may no longer be enough. As is clear from events over the past few years, the cultural exemption has its limits.
>
> Just as nations have come together to protect and promote biodiversity, it is time for them to come together to promote cultural and linguistic diversity. As Sir David Puttnam, President, Enigma Productions, wrote:
>
> Stories and images are among the principal means by which human society has always transmitted its values and beliefs, from generation to generation and community to community. Movies, along with all the other activities driven by stories and the images and characters that flow from them, are now at the very heart of the way we run our economies and live our lives. If we fail to use them responsibly and creatively, if we treat them simply as so many consumer industries rather than as complex cultural phenomena, then we are likely to damage irreversibly the health and vitality of our own society.
>
> (SAGIT, 1999)

It was also this theme that was subsequently developed by SAGIT into a draft proposal for an international instrument on cultural diversity in September 2002 (SAGIT, 2002). This draft provided a model for domestic and international discussion through Canadian advocacy, and was the template for the draft that was ultimately presented at UNESCO in 2003 as a basis for the negotiations of the text of the Convention. Although these two drafts differed on a number of points, they were largely identical in their language and central objectives and this was emphasised in the preamble to the draft that was presented at UNESCO in 2003 ("What is most remarkable about these three initiatives is how much they have in common. It is unusual to find that governments, civil society and key business groups agree on an important international legal initiative" (INCD, 2003: 3)). Carefully crafted in the terminology of international trade law they set out templates for an internationally binding treaty that recognises the special status of cultural goods and services while asserting that it is the right of states to maintain policies based on this recognition, in the face of international pressures for greater liberalisation, that offers the key regulatory measure for achieving global cultural diversity and cultural development. At the same time, they make a point of balancing provisions for the protection of domestic productive capacity with provisions that ensure the maintenance of an open regulatory environment for international trade that not only benefits Canada in other sectors but that can ensure access to markets for its cultural exporters (SAGIT, 2002: 1).

Above all, the three texts noted that although the instrument should leave no ambiguity as to these objectives, it should also seek to broaden the relevance of the principle of the cultural exception as a matter of international urgency and concern, so as to generate wider international support and to resonate with UNESCO's mandate. In introducing the draft proposal SAGIT therefore pointed out that:

> [T]here may be a serious danger of weakening the instrument itself in adopting an approach that is too wide, such as the one that extends the meaning of "cultural diversity" to include pluralism of opinion and lifestyles and other aspects outside the realm of cultural expression.... However, it is important to continue work on a future-looking approach that would establish a wide positive recognition of the value of cultural diversity as opposed to the implication that because culture is exempted from free trade agreements it is being sheltered behind old-fashioned protectionism.
>
> (SAGIT, 2002: 2–5)

This theme was taken up in particular by the International Network on Cultural Diversity (INCD)[10], which presented the draft at UNESCO in 2003 along with a preamble that situated it within the emerging framework of cultural rights ("The importance of cultural expression is rooted in the Universal Declaration of Human Rights, the United Nations International Covenant on Economic, Social and Cultural Rights, and in declarations of UNESCO, the International Organization of the Francophonie, and the Council of Europe") and went on to conclude by emphasising that:

> Our vision includes the flourishing of cultures, locally, regionally and globally, shared by all. During a time when cultural divisions and intolerance has spawned the most egregious assaults on human dignity and security, the INCD believes that this modest initiative may also offer a guidepost to a peaceful path for resolving our most pressing challenges.
>
> (INCD, 2003: 7)

In other words, we can see how the strategy set out to strengthen the legitimacy of the cultural exception principle in trade negotiations from the late 1990s by situating it within a more diffuse set of international concerns over the pace and direction of globalisation, and rearticulating it through the language of cultural diversity and rights as it had gained international currency and urgency over the previous decade. This has proven to be an extremely fruitful formula, allowing Canadian representatives to strike strategic alliances amongst cultural ministries and industry stakeholders that had previously had comparatively little connection with the global trade and culture debate (even as it simultaneously marginalised the diffuse "pluralism of opinions and lifestyles" deemed surplus to the campaign and to the formulation of an effective international treaty). Before going on to examine in more detail how this strategy was pursued at the international level, and the kind of alliances and overlapping interests that it created amongst different countries and groups, we will first consider how the Canadian strategy was complemented from across the Atlantic.

France, Francophonia and the European Union

> There is no European conscience, emotion nor identity if we don't keep in mind the specific histories of each country, that is to say if we don't watch European films in order to discover the soul of Europe.
>
> Doris Pack, President of the Committee on Culture and Education of the European Parliament (European Parliament, 2009)

Canada found powerful allies to lead its international campaign in Europe, where stakeholders and trade negotiators sought to address a similar set of problems following the end of the Uruguay Round of negotiations in 1994 and as part of the attempt by European institutions and member states to implement policy measures aimed at preserving the international viability and competitiveness of Europe's cultural sector (through measures such as the Television Without Frontiers Directive and, subsequently, the Audiovisual Media Services Directive).[11] It was in light of these concerns, and the ongoing attempt to develop a coherent Europe-wide cultural policy, that the Council of Europe adopted the first Declaration on Cultural Diversity in 2000, which UNESCO subsequently welcomed for "highlight[ing] the distinctive feature of the audiovisual sector in relation to other industrial sectors, stating in particular that 'cultural and audiovisual policies which promote and respect cultural diversity are a necessary complement to trade policies.'" (UNESCO, 2003b).

The concern was most acute in France, where it had become increasingly apparent that the validity of "l'exception culturelle" not only appeared under threat faced with the scheduled resumption of WTO negotiations in Seattle in 1999, but had become "a standard that did not inspire much call to action" among other countries, as the former French diplomat and UNESCO representative Jean Musitelli recalls (Musitelli, 2006: 2). The isolated position of the French negotiating team had been confirmed during the negotiations between the OECD countries over the MAI between 1995 and 1998, where it became clear that French proposals for an inclusion of an exception for cultural goods and services in the proposed agreement were going to be rejected by the other negotiating countries. This prompted France's withdrawal from the negotiations (bringing them to an end, since procedures required unanimity) and led to the search for a new strategy by its negotiators (Musitelli, 2006; Bernier, 2004).

Reflecting on the political opportunities that had been presented by the outburst of international public opposition against the MAI negotiations (largely over labour and environmental standards), as well as the standard-setting work that had been done at UNESCO over the previous decade on cultural development, France therefore joined Canada at the end of 1998 in settling on cultural diversity as a more useful banner in the campaign to maintain support mechanisms in the face of trade liberalisation – one which could overcome the limitations of l'exception culturelle by offering a more universal principle around which greater consensus could be built at an international level. Against the backdrop of the MAI, cultural diversity began to make its first appearances in the official French vocabulary on the international stage, notably with the Franco-Mexican Declaration on Cultural Diversity (in November 1998) and the joint communiqué of the Canadian and French Prime Ministers in Ottawa the following month on The Importance of Cultural Diversity in a Global Economy (Voon, 2007: 32; Musitelli, 2006: 2, 9).

Like Canada, this turn to cultural diversity aimed to transform the French position, according to the key architect of the French strategy, "into the rule not the exception" by seeking to make "the rebalancing of culture/commerce a pillar of construction of the new international judicial order destined to regulate globalisation" (Musitelli, 2006: 2). This involved broadening the concept of cultural exception to the concept of cultural diversity, based on the premise that the defensive posture of "exception" was too explicitly couched in "commercial" rather than "cultural" arguments, and that it was necessary to enlarge the issue to "a universal dimension" so as to rid it of it stature amongst the majority of countries watching the American and European disputes at the WTO as primarily a transatlantic spat (Musitelli, 2006: 2). As Musitelli went on, it was hoped that this turn to the expanded concepts of culture and diversity would prepare the ground for a new consensus:

> The notion of diversity afforded the benefit of opening up the narrow field of vision of exception onto a broadened horizon. It rehabilitated the anthropological and sociological components of culture which had been ignored in commercial negotiations. When it published its report entitled [Our] Creative Diversity, UNESCO had stressed the role of identity and cultural creativity as levers of economic and social development. All the same, held at bay from negotiations on cultural goods and services, it hesitated to confront head on the question of the impact of globalisation on cultural expression and practices. The idea of organizing the convergence of these two ways of looking at the issue, one of them, coming out of the debates on exception and centred on the theme of culture/commerce and cultural industries, and the one suggested by UNESCO, centred on the culture/ development tie and safeguard of creative expression, would allow the practical and theoretical political debates of the North–South Alliance to turn to cultural diversity. It was from this fertile ground of supposition that the "invention" of cultural diversity sprung.
>
> (Musitelli, 2006: 2–3)

The development of this strategy has involved a shift in French foreign policy, particularly regarding the role expected of the *Organisation International de la Francophonie* (OIF). Traditionally, the OIF has been seen as a strategic bulwark against "Anglo-Saxon" cultural, economic, political and military influence in areas of

French interest, particularly in Paris's "African backyard" where postcolonial Francophone ties have been cultivated in reference to the defence of French universalism and civilisation against its British, or more recently American, rival.[12]

Although this role of Francophonia undoubtedly remains a central one (see, for example, Bagayoko, 2009), the elevation of cultural diversity as a point of French diplomacy since the 1990s has also involved seeking alliances outside its traditional spheres of influence, turning to the non-Francophone South as well as to Eastern and Central Europe – with the campaign for the Convention at UNESCO emerging as an occasion for what Glasze (2007: 672) has described as the transformation of Francophonia into "a huge political alliance ... apart from the centre of 'anglo-saxony', the United States". With the UK also becoming a key player in the campaign for the Convention (notably by holding presidency of the EU as it negotiated the text and playing a key role in forging a common position amongst the other member states), traditional inter-imperial or "civilisational" rivalries have made way for a more pragmatic approach based on overlapping political, strategic and commercial interests. Requirements for membership or observer status in the OIF over this period have changed to reflect this shift in the identity of Francophonia as a geopolitical bloc that is united less through allegiance to the common ties of French language and institutions than through a looser commitment to the principle of the protection and promotion of cultural diversity. Since the late 1990s, the OIF has therefore expanded to incorporate a number of countries where French linguistic or institutional ties have played no significant historical role.[13] Affiliation is rather through, as the Austrian foreign ministry put it, for example, "commitment to cultural diversity and intercultural dialogue" (cited in Glasze, 2007: 670). Former President Jacques Chirac set out this new role of the OIF in 1997:

> Francophonia has a vocation to invite all the other languages of the world to reunite so that cultural diversity, which results from linguistic diversity that this diversity [*sic*] is protected. Beyond French, beyond the Francophonia, it is necessary for us to be the militants of multiculturalism in the world to fight against the smothering, by a single language, of various cultures, which make the richness and the dignity of humanity.
>
> (Chirac, cited in Glasze, 2007: 672)

It has been in this spirit that France and other European countries have brought significant diplomatic clout to Canada's attempts to generate support behind a binding legal instrument on cultural diversity. One of the fruits of the new OIF strategy, the OIF's Cotonou Declaration (in June 2001), therefore expressed a wide commitment to the principle that "cultural goods and services should be given special treatment and that the free determination by States and governments to adopt their cultural policies constitutes the best guarantee of the plurality of cultural expression": this Declaration was subsequently referred to by UNESCO in its preliminary drafting work for the Convention as presenting a complement to the draft proposal that it had been presented in 2003, since together they had contributed to a growing corpus of work that had paved the way towards the creation of a binding international instrument (UNESCO, 2003b). More broadly, the strategy has involved waging a *mission civilisatrice* under the banner of "protecting" vulnerable countries from the [real or imagined] steamroller of US-led trade liberalisation and its effects on cultural development – what the Quai d'Orsay (French Ministry of Foreign Affairs) described in 2005 as Francophonia's mission to "help the countries from the South to structure their mind" on the question of cultural diversity (Milhaud, 2006).[14] This is how *Le Monde* reacted, for example, to the adoption of the Convention in 2005, and how the OIF summarised its work in the run-up to the Convention's adoption:

> The more countries that ratify it, the more real weight it will have.... Time is [now] of the essence, as the U.S. is taking advantage of every minute to sign as many bilateral trade agreements as possible with "fragile" countries that do not have strong cultural industries.... [D]espite U.S. ire, the convention to enshrine the uniqueness of culture has been adopted. But, far from being out of options, the Americans are still trying to include culture in bilateral agreements. They did so with South Korea, Chile, and Morocco in exchange for trade favors, but not without resistance. France intervened for Morocco to ensure it stayed the course. Culture can also be war.
>
> (*Le Monde*, 2005)

> The ongoing transition toward a global knowledge society in which creative works are a source of wealth highlights the fact that the production of cultural goods can contribute to economic development. The adoption of the Convention on the Protection and Promotion of the Diversity of Cultural Expressions at UNESCO on 20th October 2005 reflects the dedicated efforts of the OIF in this field.
>
> (OIF, 2009; author's translation)

The prominence given to culture's place in development here marks one of the most important contributions to the Canadian campaign from Europe, which traditionally has much stronger ties to the South in its trade and development policy, particularly amongst the political grouping of the African, Caribbean and Pacific (ACP) states (79 in total, a trade and development grouping formed largely from former European colonies). With the ACP states involved in negotiations with the European Commission over a series of Economic Partnership Agreements (EPAs) at the same time as the Convention has been on the table at UNESCO, this has been an opportunity for discussions between European and ACP governments to turn on questions of market access and development assistance and to find common points of interest regarding the treatment of cultural products. The European Commission's Directive for the EPA negotiations that was approved by the European Council in 2002 set out this objective of the agreements to provide for a distinct treatment of AV [audiovisual] services that would guarantee the possibility of the EU and its Member States as well as ACP states to preserve and develop their capacity to elaborate and implement their AV and cultural policies aimed at preserving their cultural diversity, [while simultaneously] acknowledging, preserving and promoting ACP cultural values and identities, in order to support intercultural dialogue through an improvement of the possibilities of access of ACP cultural goods and services to the market.

(European Commission, cited in Salmon and Lesales, 2008: 11)

In this context, the campaign for the Convention has provided opportunities to strike an alliance with countries in the South on the question of the treatment of cultural products by offering preferential access to the European market for ACP cultural producers, as well as the possibility of development assistance and cooperation. We will return to this point further below in discussing the negotiations over the drafting of the Convention, and in the next chapter we will look in greater detail at how it has played out in practice through a case study of the EPA that was negotiated between the EU and the Caribbean states over the 2000s.

Summary

In summary, we have seen in this section how the Canadian and Franco-European responses to the challenges of the 1990s sought to give a new lease of life to the cultural exception by rearticulating it on the international stage through the language of cultural diversity as it had gained wider currency and urgency over the previous decade. One of the striking features of the campaign when we set it against arguments such as Yúdice's regarding culture as resource becoming "the only surviving definition" today (see Chapter 2) is the way that particular arguments have been deployed by the architects of the campaign. In fact we have often seen the opposite to Yúdice's observations on this point, as claims invoking culture's irreducible value as the "heart" and "soul" of society and as contributing to the "richness and dignity of humanity" have come to be foregrounded by the campaign: indeed such claims have been used both to bolster culture's "instrumental" protagonism as a source of economic development, as well as being a necessary condition for generating the kind of support and legitimacy needed to approach UNESCO with a proposal for an international treaty. On the other hand, however, we have also seen that the campaign has *not* sought to reinforce the protagonism of the kinds of elitist concerns that have characterised cultural policy in the past. Instead, it has sought to raise the banner of the more anthropological and democratic concepts of culture in a bid to widen the relevance of the campaign amongst a broader number of groups while simultaneously elevating the value of the cultural industries in national and international development as they have emerged as one of the strategic considerations of policymakers in the contemporary global economy. In the following section we will look at some of the main vehicles through which the campaign has travelled beyond Europe and Canada, and go on to examine some of the dynamics of the campaign as it played out in Morocco in 2004.

The INCP/CCD networks and the campaign in Morocco, 2004

Extending the existing international linkages within the OIF, two Canadian initiatives – the International Network on Cultural Policy (INCP) and the Coalition for Cultural Diversity (CCD) – have played a key role in the kind of governmental, non-governmental and industrial coalition-building and advocacy that have been necessary to bring the campaign to more formal international prominence. These groups have rallied international support amongst cultural policymakers and industry stakeholders, and raised the international profile of the trade–culture problem in matters of international regulation. In this section we will begin by giving a brief overview of these groups, and then go on to consider the example of the campaign in Morocco, which can be used to illustrate the simultaneously inclusive and exclusive approach to cultural diversity that characterises the strategy that has been set on since the late 1990s.

The International Network on Cultural Policy (INCP)

Although the strategy set out by SAGIT that we considered earlier was only formally adopted by the Canadian government in 1999, it was in fact already underway in the months following the Stockholm conference in 1998, when the Canadian Heritage Minister Sheila Copps took the diplomatic initiative by assembling the INCP. The aim of this was to bring national cultural ministers from around the world together in order to build on the legacy of Stockholm by developing an instrument aimed specifically at checking the momentum of US-led pressure on cultural policy through the WTO. Working in parallel at this objective has been the International Network on Cultural Diversity (INCD), a non-governmental network of cultural industries, arts and heritage institutions and others, backed by those national ministries involved in the INCP.

Of all the groups that worked to define an intergovernmental and civil society response to Stockholm and to build a campaign to secure an international instrument along the lines suggested by SAGIT, the work of the INCP/ INCD has been the most decisive: widening support, generating consensus and developing the kinds of practical strategies necessary to advance the adoption and subsequent ratification of a binding international treaty. Its most notable contribution was to submit the first draft of a possible instrument for consideration to the UNESCO Director-General in February 2003, along with a request that the task of drawing up a binding international treaty along the lines that they had proposed be put on the agenda at UNESCO later that year (INCD, 2003; INCP, 2003; UNESCO, 2003b).

Canada has played the lead role in expanding membership of the networks (by the time of the Convention's adoption, INCP membership had grown to 72) and coordinating the campaign: hosting the headquarters of both networks, providing resources, organising regular meetings and maintaining the focus of the campaign on the question of trade liberalisation. In parallel with France's diplomatic clout in the South through the OIF, the INCP/INCD networks extended the campaign by focusing diplomatic efforts on those governments and sectors with an emerging stake in the trade in cultural products or that were involved in trade disputes that had the potential to impact the international standing of the cultural exception principle (notably Argentina, Brazil, Mexico, Jamaica, Barbados, South Africa, Morocco, South Korea and China) (Musitelli, 2006). The INCP/INCD has also provided organisational capacity and a focal point for the creation of regional networks in an attempt to generate greater local momentum behind the Convention's ratification and implementation – for example, with the establishment of the African INCD in 2007, which brought together a network of cultural entrepreneurs centred in Dakar (Senegal) keen to widen civil society support in the continent and to press for greater influence in the Convention's implementation (Busari, 2007).

However, the INCP/INCD lost much of its purpose following the Convention's adoption and the required number of ratifications necessary for the treaty to enter into force. A change of government in Canada in 2006 also confirmed the ultimate dependence of the networks on Canadian priorities, with the Department of Canadian Heritage announcing in 2006 that it would withdraw the funding that it had provided to the INCD since the start of the campaign in 1998 (there were also cuts to the Coalition for Cultural Diversity; see below). The network has subsequently lost capacity and been forced to reorganise, while meetings have become infrequent and activities such as the circulation of regular newsletters have ceased. Although the INCP/INCD continued to issue warnings over the potential for aspects of cultural services to become offered as part of the bargaining process during the Doha Round, it has been recognised that with negotiations becoming preoccupied with other matters (in particular agricultural subsidies and market access for industrial goods), the cultural services sector was subsequently unlikely to become the focus of negotiations (INCD, 2008).

Coalition for Cultural Diversity

Also founded in Canada in 1998, and working closely with the INCP/INCD in support of the Convention's adoption and ratification, has been the Canadian Coalition for Cultural Diversity (CCD). This is an alliance of producers, broadcasters, distributors, publishers and others working in the fields of publishing, film, television, music, performing and visual arts with the mission to gain wider international support behind the principle that "cultural policy must not be subject to the constraints of international trade agreements", based on the argument that "cultural diversity is a fundamental human right and that countries and governments must be entirely free to adopt the policies necessary to support the diversity of cultural expression and the viability of enterprises that produce and distribute this expression".[15]

From its headquarters in Montreal, the CCD soon attracted support from other cultural sector groups within Canada and then served as a vehicle to encourage and support the formation of a network of other nationally based CCDs around the world by working directly with cultural industry lobbyists in other countries. Although the nature of this network of nationally based CCDs has made it more dispersed than the internationally organised INCP/INCD, it has also provided a more direct route to key stakeholders and governments by liaising directly with cultural producers around the world while simultaneously harmonising a powerful advocacy and lobbying campaign behind the trade–culture issue (in the words of the Canadian CCD's Executive Vice Chairman, Robert Pilon, "working from local levels so leaders become aware of the issues in their countries to advance the convention"; cited in McDowell, 2006). In this spirit, the CCD backed up the efforts of the INCP/INCD by amplifying the call for the creation of a new international legal instrument for cultural diversity, along with issuing warnings to other countries that until this had been achieved, they refrain from making trade liberalisation commitments in the cultural sector whether in the context of negotiations within the WTO or within any other international trade negotiations (CCD, 2000).

The ability of the CCD to rally such support was aided in 2003 by the creation of an International Liaison Committee (ILC), which provided greater coordination among its members and also sent a number of delegates to the intergovernmental drafting negotiations between 2004 and 2005 (CCD, 2005). Its ability to ensure that the voice of the cultural sector has been heard during these various stages at UNESCO has also been aided by UNESCO's new eagerness to involve civil society and the private sector in its activities, both during the drafting stages and subsequently with the deliberations over the Convention's implementation. Following the Convention's entry into force in 2007, the ILC became the International Federation of Coalitions for Cultural Diversity (IFCCD): shifting the focus of its lobbying activity to the promotion of the Convention's ratification and implementation by individual governments, and coming to aggregate over 600 cultural producer organisations, incorporated in Montreal (while the French CCD has represented the IFCCD at UNESCO in Paris).[16] It has nevertheless retained the core mission of supporting the formation of national constituencies and lobby groups amongst cultural ministries, industries and professionals – in short, working for what it refers to as "mobilization and vigilance by the cultural milieu" (IFCCD, 2009).

Like the INCD/INCP, the Canadian CCD's "international missions" (sending representatives to foster the organisation of CCDs in other countries) have tended to concentrate on cultural sectors and ministries in countries with a strategic significance, particularly among those actively seeking a growing international presence for emerging cultural sectors or that have been involved in bilateral negotiations with the US that impact on the liberalisation of cultural services – such as in China, India and South Korea (see CCD, 2006), or in Morocco in 2004 (CCD, 2004).

The campaign in Morocco, 2004

The campaign in Morocco was undertaken in the context of a series of attempts in this period by the US to schedule commitments from a number of countries to liberalise audiovisual services. This "new generation" of bilateral FTAs was seen as a way to circumvent the Doha deadlock at the WTO while advancing interests in strategic sectors such as audiovisual by countering the Franco-Canadian campaign to widen international support and legitimacy behind the cultural exception (Bernier, 2003; also see Chapter 2).[17] Morocco, an OIF member, had been involved in bilateral negotiations with the US since January 2003 and became a lightning rod for the international campaign in January 2004 when a demonstration organised by the Moroccan branch of the CCD (which had formed over the previous month in cooperation with visiting representatives from Canada and support from France) was broken up by police, allegedly causing a number of injuries in the process (CCD, 2004). The aim of their protest, as set out by the Moroccan CCD founder and filmmaker Nabil Ayouch, had been to draw attention to the lack of transparency from the Moroccan government regarding how the cultural sector was being addressed in the FTA – amidst suspicions expressed by the INCD and observers in France that the audiovisual services sector was being "treated in the same manner" as normal goods and services, particularly agriculture, in the negotiations (INCD, 2004). Ayouch went on to reflect on the events by noting that "In other countries, cultural professionals are consulted in the context of negotiations of this nature. In some cases, they even participate actively in the negotiations.... In Morocco, we are refused access to information and beaten" (CCD, 2004). Statements released by the Canadian CCD following the events in Morocco reflected on the response of the police by highlighting its wider ramifications as part of the international campaign, noting that it had "only show[n] how high the stakes are for culture in negotiations like these.... The issue of whether countries will be able to retain the right to have policies to promote a space for their own cultural production is one of the key debates of our time" (CCD, 2004).

This may have been the view from France, Canada and the representatives of the cultural milieu that make up the Moroccan CCD, but for most of the population the key debate over the FTA negotiations with the US was in fact played out over the issue of agriculture, and this is central to understanding the way that culture came to feature in the negotiations and the campaign as a point of wider international concern. With approximately 40–50% of the Moroccan workforce engaged in agriculture, controversy over the negotiations centred on the way that the FTA would lead to a collapse in domestic production – as had indeed been projected by the World Bank.[18] Negotiations mandated substantial reductions of export subsidies and price supports for grains, the exposure of domestic farms and employment to competition from imports, and a continuation of the ongoing enclosure of collective rangelands following nearly three decades of restructuring in the agricultural sector. This process of restructuring has been rationalised by resurrecting the same discursive strategy that had been deployed in the colonial period regarding "native improvidence" and the land-degrading effects of "traditional" production systems in rural areas – narratives that have been used to justify an ongoing process of dispossession of rural populations in strategic territories, while extending control over Berber, pastoral and nomadic groups in the countryside long deemed problematic by the Moroccan monarchy (Davis, 2006).

It is relevant to note here that this restructuring, and its related assaults on the rural population and those involved in the agricultural sector (as well as the swelling urban population, since the FTA measures have contributed both to urbanisation and to a painful inflation in the price of basic foods, provoking a series of riots and bloody clashes with government and contributing to the ferment that would become the "Arab Spring" in 2011), has been driven as much by European as American pressure. The EU negotiated a similar bilateral FTA with Morocco over the 1990s (entering into force in 2000), in the course of which the two parties had had serious differences over Morocco's priority of gaining access for its agricultural products to the EU market, which the EU refused despite gaining significant concessions from Morocco in other sectors (tightening the squeeze on the population in the cities and countryside in the process) (Damis, 1998; El Ouali, 2008).

In this context, the subsequent agreement between the US and Morocco took on a particular significance in Europe because the US had not only gone further than European negotiators in offering reciprocal access to its own market, but in the process it had also managed to gain a strategic advance against Europe in a country that is seen as crucial in the rival attempts to establish a US-Middle East Free Trade Agreement (MEFTA) and a Euro-Mediterranean Free Trade Area (EMFTA) across North Africa and the Middle East. This is what provoked the French reaction at the start of the FTA negotiations in January 2003, when the French Foreign Trade Minister stated that Morocco "cannot say that [it] want[s] a close partnership with the European Union and at the same time sign a Free Trade Agreement with the United States": as Brunel noted, this statement illuminated a concern that has been regularly raised by Moroccan diplomats and negotiators in the neoliberal context – namely that as Morocco deepens it relations with the US, it must at the same time take care to preserve its ties with Europe (Brunel, 2009: 235).

There are a number of points to draw out here. First is the fact that the Moroccan government's willingness to grant concessions to the US on the principle of audiovisual services liberalisation in exchange for "trade favours" in other sectors was seen as problematic for observers in Europe not only out of a concern for the international standing of the cultural exception, but also out of concern to maintain strategic and commercial influence in the region. What concerned observers in France above all regarding the controversy over culture's place in the negotiations, was that Morocco was prepared to jettison one of the principles binding Morocco to Francophonia and the EU – a commitment to cultural diversity (or, at least, to the principle that the audiovisual services sector should not be surrendered to the US) – in exchange for improved access in other ("normal") sectors and closer ties to Washington.

At the same time, we can see how the alliance that was forged between the Canadian, French and Moroccan cultural milieu in the form of the CCD only extended the concern for cultural diversity as far as their particular concern with the treatment of the audiovisual sector. Since questions of agricultural reform or land enclosures have little cultural significance from the point of view of the international campaign, those other populations who have stood to be displaced and dispossessed by the FTA have had little relevance to the campaign. As we have seen, however, it is not self-evident that questions of agricultural and land reform are not also questions of cultural recognition or diversity: for many in Morocco, the land is both a source of food and other material necessities (agricultural and livestock production, gathered foods and medicines, materials for building and fuel), as well as being integral to a distinctive patchwork of "ways of life" that are defined and expressed through resistance to dispossession, enclosure and assimilation (Bouderbala, 1997; Davis, 2006).

In this context, the claims from movements representing the Berber (Amazigh) populations in Morocco, such as the National Popular Movement, that they constitute "people who don't exist" in the eyes of government (Mahjoubi Aherdan, cited in Prengaman, 2001) have been made with increasing frequency in the recent period of land enclosures and FTAs with the US and EU. Other movements such as the Amazigh Commission for Development and Human Rights (ACDHR) or the Amazigh Democratic Party (PDAM) have therefore turned to other fora for recognition (such as attending the 2001 UN World Conference on Racism in Durban South Africa, or writing directly to the European Parliament in 2008), in an attempt to deploy the language of human and cultural rights, although so far this increased activism has had limited success (Prengaman, 2001; Adghirni, 2008; Bennis, 2009; Raymond, 2014).[19]

The reason such campaigns have had relatively little political traction is not because cultural arguments have been deployed in a way which is incommensurable with the episteme of culture as resource (indeed the Berber movements have attempted to do precisely that, aligning their claims for recognition within the language of political and economic entitlement and human rights; for example, see the letter written to the European Parliament by Adghirni, 2008). Rather, it is because their attempt to deploy such cultural arguments comes with claims which are fundamentally opposed to the neoliberal FTA and the administration in Morocco – and also because they "consider all this land their land" (Lachgar, speaking on behalf of the ACDHR, cited in Prengaman, 2001). We might note again here how the "anthropological" component of culture can for some have relatively little political or economic protagonism: in this case, it has had little use for the Moroccan CCD faced with a government keen to forge ties with the US and that has little interest in developing domestic capacity in its audiovisual sector, but it has had even less protagonism for those outside the particular dynamics of European-American contests for influence in Morocco (such as the rural populations and Amazigh groups, not to mention those who are not represented by formal opposition movements such as PDAM).

Finally we might also note here that, since Morocco ultimately slipped through the net of the campaign and sided with the US on the question of the cultural exception in the FTA, this case also demonstrates that the diplomatic efforts of Canada, France, the EU and groups such as the INCP/INCD/CCD/ IFCCD or the OIF have not been a sufficient condition to bring particular governments on board, even if they have been able to link up with and give greater organisational capacity to local stakeholders and pockets of industry support amongst the cultural milieu.

However, Morocco is not necessarily representative and the broadened concept of cultural diversity has elsewhere proven successful in allowing a broad coalition of governments to add their support to the campaign. In the following section we will therefore turn to consider some of the key points on which a consensus was struck between the North and South in the form of the Convention, focusing on the process of negotiation and compromise as it played out during the drafting work undertaken at UNESCO between 2003 and 2005. Since each individual government clearly has its own motivations and circumstances in showing support for the Convention, it is not possible to examine each case. Nevertheless, we can draw out some broad observations, and this will allow us in the next chapter to go on to contextualise the particular responses to the cultural diversity campaign across the governments of the Caribbean region (some of whom have shown support for the Convention while others have shown little or no interest at all).

North–South negotiation and compromise at UNESCO, 2003–2005

Culture on the table

Once on the table at UNESCO in 2003, the draft proposal that had been presented by the INCP as the fruit of the SAGIT strategy and the Franco-Canadian campaign began to take on a life of its own. From instruments that had been drafted by international trade lawyers and that were designed to leave no doubt about their objective of protecting cultural policy and the cultural exception from the pressures of (US-led) trade liberalisation (even if they also framed this in the "universal" language of cultural diversity and rights), they became instruments that emphasised a much broader set of concerns (international cooperation and assistance, sustainable development, minority rights). McDowell (2006) has observed that as the drafting process proceeded between 2003 and 2005, there was a shift in the early drafts from a "focus solely on the international trade and investment dimensions of cultural diversity" to the inclusion in later drafts of "more commitments to diversity, human rights, and minority rights at the national and sub-national level". Similarly, the title of the first draft only referred to the "protection" of the diversity of cultural expressions (UNESCO, 2004a), with "and promotion" added later. This was paralleled by a shift in the way that the Universal Declaration on Cultural Diversity and early drafts of the Convention referred only to the formula "cultural goods and services", with "cultural goods, services and activities" becoming the formula that was eventually settled on in the final text of the Convention.

In accounting for such shifts, McDowell (2006) suggests that "this may be a reflection in part of the range of issues in UNESCO's mandate, and the need to recognise certain principles as part of an international agreement dealing with ideas and expression" (in particular, the need to be careful not to clash with states' existing commitments under international trade and human rights agreements). This account undoubtedly captures an important aspect of the drafting process. Many of these concerns were clearly evident, for example, at the first expert drafting meeting that was held at UNESCO in December 2003 (see UNESCO, 2004a; also see Chapter 4).

However, to end the explanation there would be to neglect the ways in which the instrument also evolved as a process of negotiation and conflict, particularly during the intergovernmental drafting sessions that took place between 2004 and 2005. Significant differences played out not only in the US–Japanese opposition to the European–Canadian coalition (notably over Article 20, as we also saw in Chapter 4), but also within the European-Canadian coalition itself, as well as between the different bodies of development and trade expertise that were involved in the drafting process. A key issue at stake was how far the concept of culture would be allowed to stretch on the terms that had been set for the instrument by European and Canadian experts, negotiators and stakeholders. Given that they recognised the need to broaden the concept of the cultural exception in order to gain international support (particularly from the numerical majority of governments located in the South) and to ensure the instrument came into force quickly (with one eye on ongoing WTO negotiations and the bilateral deals being pursued by the US), European and Canadian negotiators were also prepared to offer some concessions during the later drafting stages.

However, many of these have not been backed up with substance or commitment. One of the key developments during the drafting process was the assertion from international development organisations such as UNCTAD and the majority of developing countries that if the cultural diversity Convention was going to be an instrument dealing primarily with the cultural industries – a sector which is dominated internationally by the developed countries and a handful of emerging sectors in Brazil, South Korea, Nigeria, India, Turkey and China – then the instrument's focus on reasserting the right to national protection should not come at the expense of international development assistance and market access for developing countries. For the majority of countries in the South the task of developing a viable domestic cultural sector faces a formidable set of obstacles. These include competition and "dumping" from Northern imports, underinvestment and lack of finance, small domestic markets and heavily protected markets in the lucrative North (not least in Europe and Canada). In addition, for many of the Latin American and ACP countries the markets in the North are identified as areas of huge potential for expansion given the presence of diaspora populations and common linguistic ties. These have been guiding concerns of a number of policymakers and cultural sector stakeholders in the Caribbean for example, as we will see later.

Such concerns, therefore, began to be articulated by a number of developing countries during the drafting process at UNESCO, with the backing of organisations such as UNCTAD.[20] This created a powerful argument for expanding the scope of the instrument to cover international development assistance and market access. The argument was also reinforced by articulating it through the increasingly authoritative language of cultural diversity, the dual nature of cultural products and the need for greater balance in international exchanges of cultural products. The most significant provisions that ultimately found their way into the text as a result of these concerns expressed by developing countries and international organisations are Articles 16 and 18. The formation of these key development provisions is considered below.

Development provisions in the convention

Article 16 requires that "developed countries facilitate cultural exchanges with developing countries by granting, through the appropriate institutional *and legal* frameworks, preferential treatment to artists and other cultural professionals and practitioners, as well as cultural goods and services from developing countries" (UNESCO, 2005a; emphasis added) Article 18 sets out a requirement that parties to the Convention provide contributions to an "International Fund for Cultural Diversity" (IFCD) that can be used to support projects aimed at developing cultural sector capacity in developing countries (UNESCO, 2005a).

The records from the decisive third intergovernmental drafting meeting that finalised the text in 2005 show that these two provisions provoked particular controversy due to the priority that had been attached to them by the developing countries (UNESCO, 2005b: 6–7). On Article 16, after negotiations that involved in particular Canada on one hand and, on the other, the African Group alongside members of the Latin American and Caribbean Groups, it was ultimately agreed that the phrase "and legal" should be inserted so that real, binding commitments on market access would be made from developed to developing countries (UNESCO, 2005b: 6–7). On Article 18, a proposal from the African Group to include a new subparagraph calling on parties to provide regular voluntary contributions to the IFCD was ultimately accepted "as a tool aimed at securing the financial resources needed to give life to this Convention" (UNESCO, 2005b: 6–7). These were important concessions that allowed the Convention to proceed to the vote with sufficient international support from the South and they provide the key substantive basis for the claims that the resulting text marks a breakthrough in North–South relations on the matter of cultural development. Articles 14 and 15, which are aimed at promoting international cooperation for the development of the cultural sector in developing countries (through mechanisms such as technology transfer, development assistance, investment and co-productions), also allowed for an overlap of North–South interests in ways we explored in the previous chapter.

In addition to the support from the African, Latin American and Caribbean countries that was secured through Articles 16 and 18, the centrepiece provision of the Convention regarding the sovereignty of cultural policy proved attractive to a number of governments around the world on other grounds, grounds not directly related to the development of the cultural sector. Ultimately, the assertion of the principle of state sovereignty (Article 6) was the only substantial right that actually found its way into the Convention, and this emphasis of the text not only offered the means for defending the cultural exception but also offered a mechanism that could potentially be used by a number of countries to counter international interference on internal matters of governance and human rights, particularly among those governments who for one reason or another have found themselves in trouble with international society over human rights violations, narcotics, restrictions on press freedoms, or treatment of minority sexual, ethnic and religious groups (this is to say nothing of the way that international society has applied these criticisms selectively). As the Cuban Minister of Culture, Rafael Bernal Alemañy, noted, for example, at a meeting on the Non-Aligned Movement, the adoption of the Convention has offered an opportunity to reassert the need for "strict observance of the aims and principles of the UN Charter", particularly on matters related to the state's sovereign authority over matters related to the treatment of media and minorities (Alemañy, 2010).

Such examples should come as no surprise, given that the Convention's provisions on minority rights only assert that they are to be realised through state action. The drafting process also avoided establishing specific rights for media organisations and journalists (Nenova, 2010). In other words, the prioritisation of the principle of states' cultural sovereignty has also been a factor in bringing a wider group of governments on board, despite all the (largely hortatory) references to universal principles of human rights that emerged during the drafting process, and also despite the earlier attempts in the 1990s by the World Commission on Culture and Development (WCCD) to elaborate a "new global ethics" addressed to limiting state sovereignty on such matters (see Chapter 3).

Aside from the rights on states' cultural sovereignty, however, most of the provisions that have given the instrument wider international relevance beyond the cultural exception are couched in language that marks little advance on the kind of unbinding initiatives and declarations that have been made on these areas at UNESCO in the past. Chi Carmody, who has followed the legal aspects of the text from an early stage, has therefore noted that, apart from the right to sovereignty, obligations in the Convention are less well-defined, and "many are exceedingly vague and inconsequential" – drawing particular attention in this respect to the provisions regarding international cooperation and the establishment of the IFCD (Carmody, 2007: 299). This raises significant questions here regarding the development components of the Convention, because as we saw above such provisions came to represent key points around which a North–South consensus could be found. The IFCD in particular has been highlighted as one of the key provisions of the Convention aimed at supporting sustainable development, as an innovative tool for international cultural cooperation and, as noted by the chairman of the sixth meeting of the Intergovernmental Committee of the Convention in December 2012, as being "essential for the implementation of the Convention" (cited in Albornoz, 2015: 16). It therefore deserves closer scrutiny.

International Fund for Cultural Diversity (IFCD)

The broad remit of the IFCD is set out by UNESCO as follows: "The IFCD is a multi-donor fund established to promote sustainable development and poverty reduction in developing countries through support to projects that aim to foster the emergence of a dynamic cultural sector".[21] Although the African Group was successful during the drafting process in securing a commitment from Parties to provide donations to the IFCD, the actual outcome in Article 18 was that Parties should "*endeavour* to provide *voluntary* contributions on a regular basis" (UNESCO, 2005a, emphases added). In other words, the result is that the text expresses a very weak obligation, and it has become clear several years after its creation that this weakness threatens the fund's viability (Albornoz, 2015).

In understanding this here, it is worth returning to the records of the intergovernmental drafting meetings that took place prior to the final third session, which show that the request for voluntary contributions that was made by the African Group was in fact a demand that had been scaled down over the course of the previous meetings: during the earlier rounds of negotiations it had been suggested that contributions be compulsory, a position supported by the Plenary which pointed out to participants that "voluntary contributions would not be enough to make [the IFCD] operational" (UNESCO, 2005c: 31–32). There were also differences between Parties during the negotiations over how the IFCD would be managed and implemented and, with these questions subsequently left unresolved in the final text, it became difficult to operationalise the fund (a pilot phase only got underway in 2010) (UNESCO, 2008; UNESCO, 2010d).

It is unsurprising, therefore, that contributions to the IFCD have been extremely low. At the time of writing, the data showed that a total of just under US$7.5 million had been donated to the IFCD between 2010 and 2015, with a relatively small number of countries providing most of the funding (mostly in Western Europe, and notably France and Norway, who have contributed around 40% of the total contributions so far; outside of Europe, the other main contributors have been Canada, Mexico, Brazil and China).[22] To put this figure of US$7.5 million into perspective, we might note that the EU provided over €500 million of support to its audiovisual sector in the period 2001–2006 under the MEDIA programme, which increased to €755 million for 2007–2013; the current EU programme for culture and audiovisual (Creative Europe) has a budget of €1.46 billion.[23] Meanwhile, although Article 18 encouraged contributions to the IFCD "on a regular basis" (which has been interpreted to mean at least once every one or two years), actual contributions have generally been sporadic or on a one-off basis. The fragility of the funding was demonstrated in 2012 when there was a 34% drop in contributions from the previous year as the major donors responded to the effects of the economic crisis (Albornoz, 2015: 5–6).

It was hoped that funding would be topped up with industry, civil society and other charitable support (Article 18 of the Convention also invites donations from other public and private bodies or individuals) but, aside from some very small individual donations, the fund has remained almost entirely reliant on contributions from state parties. No major media-cultural conglomerates have contributed, even though some have incorporated the promotion of cultural diversity as a strategic issue (such as the French multi-media multinational Vivendi) (Albornoz, 2015: 7). The interest of the European culture lobby in the IFCD has largely been restricted to a concern for building political momentum behind the Convention and strengthening its international standing. The film and television lobby group Eurocinema, which represents largely French industry interests in Brussels, expressed its concern to the European Parliament in 2008 about the lack of support that European governments were showing to the IFCD in its early stages, and pointed out that developing countries were now "looking for practical effects to come out of [the Convention] which they unanimously supported at the urging of some EU countries, Canada and the institutions of the European Union" (Eurocinema, 2008). Similarly, the commitment of civil society appears to have been largely testimonial, given that no international or national NGO acting in the cultural field has designed activities to raise money for the IFCD (Albornoz, 2015: 7).

This relative inertia and lack of funds does not mean that nothing has come out of the IFCD. The latest figures show that the fund has been used to support 80 projects in 47 developing countries, in areas such as the development and implementation of cultural policies, capacity-building of cultural entrepreneurs, mapping of cultural industries and the creation of new cultural industry business models.[24] These measures have been consistent with the underlying logic of supporting the creation of effective markets and multiplying enterprise forms in the cultural sector that was outlined in the previous chapter. An evaluation of the pilot phase of the IFCD noted that much had been achieved in its early work, although it also pointed out that projects have also been relatively local in scale and have received limited financial assistance, whilst concerns have also been expressed about their longer term sustainability and impact (Torggler *et al.*, 2012: 25; Albornoz, 2015).

Aside from these projects, however, the lack of commitment to the fund from the Convention's most powerful backers casts doubt upon the role of the IFCD in the Convention and the nature of the consensus around cultural development more broadly. Albornoz (2015) concludes that, on the basis of the nature of the projects that have been undertaken so far, there is no indication that the IFCD can alter the circulation of audiovisual content on anywhere near the kind of scale that would be required to address the imbalances that exist in international and regional flows of culture. It should be remembered that the IFCD has only been operational for a short time and, as such, its significance so far is to be evaluated in terms of its potential to support and showcase relevant examples of the Convention's implementation, rather than as a funding mechanism (a point raised by Torggler *et al.*, 2012). However, the relative impotence of the IFCD so far is also predictable in light of the lack of genuine political will that we have also considered above, and there is certainly little evidence to support some of the claims that we have seen around the contribution of the IFCD to the broader culture and development agenda. It is reasonable to argue that the IFCD has so far reflected its nature as something of an appendix to the negotiations that took place over the drafting of the Convention, as the developing world sought to draw some concessions from the instrument's more powerful sponsors in exchange for their support behind a treaty that is primarily geared to defending the trade and industry interests of a number of countries in the North.

In short, the above discussions on the way that provisions related to development found their way into the Convention suggest that we should be sceptical about the substance that is accorded to points other than those that have been prioritised by the Franco-European–Canadian campaigns (namely those relating to the renewed and international authority that it gives to the cultural exception, and the scope that it gives these countries to address their own concerns in cultural policy). Despite this, there are some measures relating to matters of international cooperation and development that have had some impact and are worth looking at more deeply. In the following chapter, we will explore in more detail the obligation that is contained in Article 16 that developed countries provide legally binding market access to developing countries' cultural sectors. This does represent something of a breakthrough, particularly as it offers the potential for access to the EU's tightly protected cultural market, and it had an important role to play in the creation of the EPA between the EU and the Caribbean states.

Summary

We began this chapter by comparing the new consensus around cultural diversity at UNESCO with the relative lack of consensus that has been struck on alternative international cultural instruments that have been proposed over the same period. By contrasting the relative success of the campaign for the Convention with the campaign for instruments such as the ICH Convention or the UNDRIP this chapter has sought to draw attention to some of the opportunities and exclusions that are contained within the Convention's model of cultural diversity. Despite the emergence over the 1990s of an authoritative legal vocabulary turning on the rights of diverse ways of life and the currency of the expanded, anthropological concept of culture, there has remained very little leverage in the new framework of cultural development – both internationally and at the level of state development strategies – for claims that relate cultural recognition to claims such as the right to land, tenure and place, or that cannot easily be translated into alienable and internationally marketable expressions.

As we have also seen, however, it would be wrong to interpret this development as a simple reflection of the claims of a small group of states and interests, because it has also reflected the emergence of a dynamic whereby the creation of a binding international treaty must now accommodate a number of claims from other, often previously unheard, groups in the global debate. In the case of the formulation of the Convention on Biological Diversity, the language of cultural diversity, rights and entitlements has provided potentially lucrative openings for groups who are able to come forward as bearers of internationally valuable "traditional" knowledge, practices or biological resources. In the case of the formulation of the UNESCO Convention on cultural diversity, the concern to create a binding international instrument on the part of the key stakeholders in the North, faced with intensified US pressure, has meant that the campaign has widened to accommodate and amplify the claims of a range of cultural producer organisations around the world concerned to gain a foothold in the new economy and attract forms of national and international support. It also opened opportunities for governments in the South to extract some concessions during the drafting process on development assistance and market access (as well as providing an opportune moment for some governments to reassert their sovereign right to be exempted from international human rights obligations and other international pressures). Of course, these alliances and concessions have also been limited in their scope, as we saw in the example of the campaign in Morocco and the weakness of the concessions that were ultimately extracted during the drafting process between 2003 and 2005. In the next chapter we will go on to consider in more detail how this dynamic of international cultural cooperation has played out following the Convention's entry into force by looking at one of the first major cases of implementation of the Convention's development provisions, the cultural cooperation protocol of the EPA that was concluded between Europe and the Caribbean in 2008.

Notes

1 On the MONDIACULT conference, see Chapter 1. On the stages that led to the ICH Convention's adoption see Aikawa (2004); UNESCO (2010a, 2010b).
2 For more details of the programmes and activities related to the ICH Convention, see www.unesco.org/culture/ich. Over the course of the ICH Convention's drafting the term "intangible cultural heritage" came to replace the terms "traditional culture" and "folklore", partly because these terms have been viewed as demeaning and pejorative by many groups (see UNESCO, 1999: 270; UNESCO, 2010b). This has, however, created a new problem, since the phrase "intangible cultural heritage" has been unfamiliar to both international experts and to community members around the world, raising questions over the instrument's operationalisation and international currency (Kurin, 2004).

3 According to UNESCO, for example, the economic value of the intangible cultural heritage for a specific community is "twofold: the knowledge and skills that are transmitted *within* that community [giving the example of the consumption of traditional, non-patented medicines], as well as the product resulting from those knowledge and skills [giving the example of selling a ticket to a tourist]" (UNESCO, 2010c). The potential of traditional handicrafts as marketable expressions of ICH was picked out in the preliminary study for the ICH Convention:

> It has been estimated that handicrafts represent almost a quarter of the micro-enterprises in the developing world, getting money directly into the hands of producers, and providing the means of empowerment to millions of people, many of them women, particularly in rural areas.
>
> (Throsby, cited in UNESCO, 2002: 4)

4 To return to the example of Bolivia used in Chapter 2, while Guarani Indians in the Izogog region are "showered with NGO funding to represent their practices as integral to their cultures and encouraged to develop products based on their traditional knowledge", their mestizo neighbours possess little culture deemed worthy of preservation, with "international organisations deaf to their cries that the harvesting of coca leaves is itself a traditional Inca practice that sustains biodiversity" (Coombe, 2003: 299). Also see Rosaldo (1988); Farhat (2008).

5 Canada's rejection of the Outcome Document centred on the provision that states should seek "free, prior and informed consent" from Indigenous communities when making decisions that affect them and their territories, since this was seen to potentially give Indigenous communities a "veto" over government actions in a way that could interfere with Canadian law and Parliamentary supremacy (Government of Canada, 2014).

6 The AFN is a government-funded national advocacy organisation representing Canada's 634 officially recognised "First Nations" communities or reserves. The term First Nations emerged as a self-designation amongst Native Canadians in the 1970s as part of campaigns to assert the right to be recognised as one of the "founding nations" of Canada (alongside and indeed prior to the English and French) as opposed to the official (colonial) designation "Indian". First Nations does not include the Inuit or Metis populations of Canada, who are also often considered as Indigenous but have a distinct status under Canadian law. For more info on the AFN, see www.afn.ca.

7 On the aims and objectives of the Idle No More movement, see www.idlenomore.ca. The movement came to prominence in December 2012 through protests, flash mobs and online activism, soon attracting support from the wider Canadian population (and beyond). For analysis, see Barker (2015).

8 For more detail on role of culture in the breakdown of the MAI, see Voon (2007: 31–32); Musitelli (2006).

9 Driven by the particular dynamics of Anglophone federation and Francophone nationalism and the requirement that policy proceed with an eye to "the preservation and enhancement of the multicultural heritage of Canadians" (as expressed in the country's Constitution), Canada has also been a pioneer in developing internal policies of multiculturalism and multilingualism in the affected sectors through mechanisms such as broadcast and content quotas, and these have similarly seen to be under threat by the WTO ruling (this particular emphasis on multiculturalism in Canada also often renders minorities that do not fall within the Anglophone-Francophone framework invisible in the national discourse, as Tamang (2010) has noted for example).

10 The INCD is a non-governmental network of cultural industries, arts and heritage institutions and others, backed by some of the key national ministries that have campaigned for the creation of the Convention. It is discussed in more detail later in the chapter.

11 For an analysis of the evolution of European cultural policy and how it has been developed in relation to the problem of globalisation, see de Vinck and Pauwels (2008). The Television Without Frontiers and Audiovisual Media Services Directives are discussed briefly in Chapter 2.

12 According to Gérard Prunier (1995), the Francophone tie in Africa sustains remnants of colonial influence and grandeur, as well as a high degree of symbiosis between French and Francophone African political elites. This tie has been a strategic one since the "Fashoda Incident" during the Scramble for Africa, and often resurfaces in grand strategy on the continent and elsewhere (Bayart, 2005: 19–25; Prunier, 1995; *Independent*, 2007).

13 The recent wave of new members/observers includes Armenia, Austria, Croatia, Cyprus, Czech Republic, Ghana, Greece, Georgia, Hungary, Latvia, Lithuania, Mozambique, Serbia, Slovakia, Slovenia, Thailand, Ukraine. See www.francophonie.org.

14 I am grateful to Olivier Milhaud here for providing me with information from the Quai d'Orsay.

15 For more information on the history and activities of the CCD, see www.cdc-ccd.org

16 On the IFCCD, see www.ficdc.org.

17 The INCD noted in regard to the US-Morocco FTA negotiations that:

> The speed and confidentiality of the bilateral talks result from the failure of the United States to achieve its trade objectives in the multilateral arenas such as the WTO. Additionally, some believe the US government is concerned that the movement for a new international Convention on Cultural Diversity will limit its ability to achieve concessions in the cultural sector.
>
> (INCD, 2004)

18 The World Bank projected that poverty in rural areas would increase from 28% to 34% as a result of the FTA and extreme poverty in rural areas would double from 6% to 12%, meaning that a significant number of the four million Moroccans involved in agriculture in rural areas (as well as their dependents), would be severely adversely affected (Davis, 2006).

19 One breakthrough came in the wake of the Arab Spring, with official recognition of Amazigh language and culture in a new constitution after months of protests by the "20 February Movement" (a broad coalition in which Amazigh activists played a key role). However, it remains to be seen what practical implications this will have, with many activists pointing out that parliament has still not passed legislation specifying how Amazigh will be used in public life. Others have noted that the concession to provide constitutional recognition has simply served the purpose of coopting and defusing the Amazigh element of 20 February and thereby keeping the status quo largely intact (while improving Morocco's image in the face of external criticism) (Raymond, 2014).

20 See, for example, UNESCO (2003b: Reference to other relevant international instruments); UNESCO (2004b: Presentation of Comments and Amendments, Part IV: Comments Proposed by the IGOs).

21 For more details on the IFCD, see http://en.unesco.org/creativity/ifcd.

22 Latest data on donations is available at http://en.unesco.org/creativity/ifcd/fundraising/donations/parties. Albornoz (2015) provides a detailed analysis of the different contributions and funding cycles.

23 On the MEDIA support programme, see http://ec.europa.eu/culture/tools/media-programme_en.htm; on the Creative Europe Programme: http://ec.europa.eu/programmes/creative-europe/.

24 See http://en.unesco.org/creativity/ifcd. Albornoz (2015) has also undertaken detailed analyses of the kinds of projects that have been undertaken so far.

Bibliography

Acheson, K. and C. Maule. 2005. "Canada: Audiovisual Policies: Impact on Trade". In Guerrieri, P., P. Lelio Iapadre and G. Koopmann (eds). *Cultural Diversity and International Economic Integration: The Global Governance of the Audio-Visual Sector*. Cheltenham: Edward Elgar.

Adghirni, A. 2008. *Letter to Mr. Hans-Gert POTTENG, President of the European Parliament, and the Members of the European Parliament, on behalf of Le Parti Démocratique Amazighe Marocain, concerning human rights violation in Morocco*. Rabat, Morocco, 10 September 2008. Available online at: www.amazighworld.org/eng/human_rights/index_show.php?id=22; accessed 12/12/2009.

Aikawa, N. 2004. "An Historical Overview of the Preparation of the UNESCO International Convention for the Safeguarding of the Intangible Cultural Heritage". *Museum International*. 56(1–2): 137–149.

Albornoz, L.A. 2015. "The International Fund for Cultural Diversity: a new tool for cooperation in the audiovisual field". *International Journal of Cultural Policy*. Available online at: www.tandfonline.com/doi/full/10.1080/10286632.2015.1008467#.Vctvj3v CZ5w; accessed 12/08/2015.

Alemañy, R.B. 2010. "Address by the head of the delegation of the Republic of Cuba, Rafael Bernal Alemañy, First Deputy Minister of Culture, at the general debate of the Non-Aligned Movement Ministerial Meeting on Interfaith Dialogue and Cooperation for Peace and Development". Ministry of Foreign Affairs of Cuba. Available online at: www.cubaminrex.cu/english/Multilaterales/Articulos/Politicos/2010/address.html; accessed 12/06/2010.

Allor, M. and M. Gagnon. 1997. *L'État de culture: Généalogie discursive des politiques culturelle québécoise*. Montréal: GRECC.

Anaya, J. 2014. *Report of the Special Rapporteur on the rights of indigenous peoples, James Anaya. Addendum: The situation of indigenous peoples in Canada*. United Nations Human Rights Council. A/HRC/27/52/Add.2. Available online at: http://unsr.jamesanaya.org/docs/countries/2014-report-canada-a-hrc-27-52-add-2-en.pdf; accessed 06/09/2015.

Anaya, S.J. and S. Wiessner. 2007. "The UN Declaration on the Rights of Indigenous Peoples: Towards re-empowerment". *Jurist*. 3.

Bagayoko, N. 2009. "French Reactions to AFRICOM: An Historic Perspective". *Contemporary Security Policy*. 30(1): 28–31.

Barker, A.J. 2015. "'A Direct Act of Resurgence, a Direct Act of Sovereignty': Reflections on Idle No More, Indigenous Activism, and Canadian Settler Colonialism". *Globalizations*. 12(1): 43–65.

Bayart, J.F. 2005. *The Illusion of Cultural Identity*. London: Hurst & Company.

Bennis, S. 2009. The Amazigh Question and National Identity in Morocco. *Arab Reform Initiative*. July 2009. Available online at: www.arab-reform.net/amazigh-question-and-national-identity-morocco; accessed 07/09/2015.

Bernier, I. 2003. "A comparative analysis of the Chile-US and Singapore-US Free Trade Agreements with particular referefence to the cultural sector". *Media Trade Monitor*. Available online at: www.mediatrademonitor.org; accessed 05/04/2007.

Bernier, I. 2004. "A UNESCO Convention on Cultural Diversity". In Beat Graber, C., M. Girsberger and M. Nenova (eds). *Free Trade Versus Cultural Diversity: WTO Negotiations in the Field of Audiovisual Services*. Zurich: Schulthess.

Bouderbala, N. 1997. "La modernisation et la gestion du fancier au Maroc". *CIHEAM – Options Mediteranneenes*. Available online at: http://ressources.ciheam.org/om/pdf/a29/CI971511.pdf; accessed 25/08/2010.

Brunel, C. 2009. "Morocco–EU Trade Relations". In G.C. Hufbauer and C. Brunel (eds). *The Morocco–US Free Trade Agreement*. Washington DC: Peter G. Peterson Institute for International Economics.

Bruner, C.M. 2008. "Culture, Sovereignty, and Hollywood: UNESCO and the Future of Trade in Cultural Products". *NYU Journal of International Law & Politics*. 40: 2.

Busari, L. 2007. "UNESCO launches cultural diversity network". *Sunnewsonline*, 28 March. Available online at: www.sunnewsonline.com/webpages/features/arts/2007/mar/28/arts-28-03-2007-003.htm; accessed 04/04/2007.

CanWest News Service. 2007. "Native Rights Declaration Inconsistent With Legal Tradition: Stahl". Available online at: www.canada.com/nationalpost/news/story.html?id=23df9769-3423-4f43-b828-a755725c2719&k=23677; accessed 20/08/2010.

Carmody, C. 1999. "When 'cultural identity was not at issue': Thinking about Canada – certain measures concerning periodicals". *Law and Policy in International Business*. 30(2).

Carmody, C. 2007. "Creating 'shelf space': NAFTA's experience with cultural protection and its relevance to the WTO". *Asian Journal of WTO & International Health Law and Policy*. 2(2): 287–311.

CCD. 2000. "CCD Mission". Available online at: www.cdc-ccd.org/main_pages_en/mission_en.htm; accessed 07/01/2009.

CCD. 2004. "NEWS RELEASE: Canadian Coalition for Cultural Diversity Backs Moroccan Colleagues in Campaign To Keep Culture Out of Bilateral Trade Talks With United States". *Coalition for Cultural Diversity*. Montreal.

CCD. 2005. *Coalition Update*. Vol. 3, No. 5, November 2005. Available online at: www.cdc-ccd.org/ccd_enews/05_nov/ccd_update_November05.html; accessed 12/01/2010.

CCD. 2006. "China, India Figure Prominently in CCD International Missions". Available online at: www.cdc-ccd.org/ccd_enews/06_march/ccd_update_March06.html#2; accessed 12/01/2010.

Chartrand, H.H. 1999. "Copyright and the New World Economic Order". *Compiler Press Review #3* (July).

Compendium of Cultural Policies. 2008. Canada/ 1. Historical perspective: cultural policies and instruments. Council of Europe/ERICarts. Available online at: www.cultural-policies.net/web/canada.php; accessed 20/06/2009.

Coombe, R. 2003. "Works in Progress: Traditional Knowledge, Biological Diversity, and Intellectual Property in a Neoliberal Era". In Perry, R.W. and B. Maurer (eds). *Globalisation Under Construction: Governmentality, Law and Identity*. Minneapolis: University of Minnesota Press.

Cultural Survival. 2010. *Joint Statement in Response to Canada's Endorsement of the UN Declaration on the Rights of Indigenous Peoples*. Available online at: www.culturalsurvival.org/news/canada/joint-statement-response-canada-s-endorsement-un-declaration-rights-indigenous-peoples; accessed 30/08/2015.

Damis, J. 1998. "Morocco's 1995 association agreement with the European Union". *Journal of North African Studies*. 3(4): 91–112.

Davis, D.K. 2006. "Neoliberalism, environmentalism, and agricultural restructuring in Morocco". *Geographical Journal*. 172(2): 88–105.

de Vinck, S. and C. Pauwels. 2008. "Cultural Diversity as the Final Outcome of EU Policymaking in the Audiovisual Sector: A Critical Analysis". In Schneider, H. and P. van den Bossche (eds). *Protection of Cultural Diversity from a European and International Perspective*. Oxford: Intersentia.

Diabo, R. 2012. "Harper launches major First Nations termination plan as negotiation tables legitimise Canada's colonialism". *Intercontinental Cry*. 9 November 2012. Available online at: https://intercontinentalcry.org/harper-launches-major-first-nations-termination-plan-as-negotiating-tables-legitimize-canadas-colonialism/; accessed 24/02/2015.

El Ouali, A. 2008. "Morocco: Anger Rises with Prices". *Inter Press Service*. 21 February 2008. Available online at: www.bilaterals.org/spip.php?article11216; accessed 13/03/2008.

Eurocinema. 2008. "UNESCO Convention on the protection and promotion of the diversity of cultural expressions: International Fund for Cultural Diversity". Submission to European Parliament, 30/04/2008.

European Parliament. 2009. *2009 LUX Prize Award Ceremony*. European Parliament, Strasbourg, 25 November 2009.

Farhat, R. 2008. "Neotribal entrepreneurialism and the commodification of biodiversity: WIPO's displacement of development for private property rights". *Review of International Political Economy*. 15(2): 206–233.

Frulla, L. 2005. "Speaking Points for The Honourable Liza Frulla P.C., M.P., on the occasion of a Roundtable on the Convention on the Protection and Promotion of the Diversity of Cultural Expressions". *Canadian Heritage*. Ottawa, Ontario.

Glasze, G. 2007. "The Discursive Constitution of a World-Spanning Region and the Role of Empty Signifiers: The Case of Francophonia". *Geopolitics*. 2007(12): 656–679.

Government of Canada. 2010. *Canada's Statement of Support on the United Nations Declaration on the Rights of Indigenous Peoples*. Available online at: www.aadnc-aandc.gc.ca/eng/1309374239861/1309374546142; accessed 30/08/2015.

Government of Canada. 2014. *Canada's Statement on the World Conference on Indigenous Peoples Outcome Document*. Available online at: www.canadainternational.gc.ca/prmny-mponu/canada_un-canada_onu/statements-declarations/other-autres/2014-09-22_WCIPD-PADD.aspx?lang=eng; accessed 21/08/2015.

Gowan, P. 2001. "Neoliberal Cosmopolitanism". *New Left Review*. September–October 2001: 79–93.

Guardian. 2005, 19 October. "Global plan to protect film culture".

Hale, C.R. 2005. "Neoliberal multiculturalism: The remaking of cultural rights and racial dominance in Central America". *Political and Legal Anthropological Review*. 28(1): 10–28.

IFACCA. 2009. "Defining and Mapping Intangible Cultural Heritage". *International Federation of Arts Councils and Culture Agencies*. D'Art Report Number 36 (February 2009).

IFCCD. 2009. "The importance of Affirming the Principles and Objectives of the UNESCO Convention on the Diversity of Cultural Expressions in Other International Forums". *International Federation of Coalitions for Cultural Diversity*. Available online at: www.ifccd.com/content/importance-affirming-principles-and-objectives-unesco-convention-diversity-cultural-expressi; accessed 12/12/2009.

INCD. 2003. *Proposed Convention on Cultural Diversity*. Available online at: www.incd.net/docs/CCDJan2003Final.pdf; accessed 07/01/2009.

INCD. 2004. *INCD Newsletter – February 2004*. 5(2).

INCD. 2008. *INCD Newsletter – May 2008*. 9(1).

INCP. 2003. *Framework for Cooperation Between the International Network on Cultural Policy and UNESCO in Support of an International Instrument on Cultural Diversity*. Available online at: http://incp-ripc.org/w-group/wg-cdg/paris2003/framework_e.shtml; accessed 07/01/2009.

Independent. 2007, 3 July. "Mitterand's role revealed in Rwandan genocide warning".

International Covenant on the Rights of Indigenous Nations. 1994. Authorised Version, Initialled 28 July 1994, Geneva, Switzerland. Available online at: http://cwis.org/icrin-94.htm; accessed 23/07/2010.

Kearney, A. 2009. "Intangible cultural heritage: Global awareness and local interest". In Smith, L. and N. Akagawa (eds). *Intangible Heritage*. New York: Routledge.

Kurin, R. 2004. "Safeguarding intangible cultural heritage in the 2003 Convention: A critical appraisal". *Museum International*. 56(1–2): 66–77.

Le Monde. 2005, 18 October. "UNESCO adopts the Convention on the Diversity of Cultural Expressions".

Lukacs, M. 2015. "Canadian government pushing First Nations to give up land rights for oil and gas profits". *Guardian*, 3 March 2015. Available online at: www.theguardian.com/environment/true-north/2015/mar/03/documents-harper-pushing-first-nations-to-shelve-rights-buy-into-resource-rush; accessed 5/3/2015.

Lum, Z. 2014. "Canada is the only UN member to reject landmark indigenous rights document". *Huffington Post*, 10 February 2014. Available online at: www.huffingtonpost.ca/2014/10/02/canada-un-indigenous-rights_n_5918868.html; accessed 30/08/2015.

McDowell, S. 2006. "States and Civil Society Groups: Canada's Promotion of Cultural Diversity and UNESCO's Convention on the Protection and Promotion of the Diversity of Cultural Expressions". Paper presented at the annual meeting of the International Communication Association, Dresden International Congress Centre, Dresden, Germany, 16 June 2006.

Milhaud, O. 2006. "Post-Francophonie?" *EspacesTemps.net*, Actuel, 07.08.2006 http://espacestemps.net/document2077.html; accessed 01/12/2009.

Morales, E. 2009. "Letter from President Evo Morales to UN Secretary General". La Paz, 12 March 2009. Available online at: www.embolchina.com/newsXe.asp?id=69; accessed 08/07/2015.

Musitelli, J. 2006. "The Convention on Cultural Diversity: Anatomy of a Diplomatic Success Story". *French Ministry of Foreign Affairs*. Available online at: www.diplomatie.gouv.fr/en/IMG/pdf/The_Convention_on_Cultural_Diversity.pdf; accessed 29/09/2009

Nenova, M. 2010. "Reconciling Trade and Culture: A Global Law Perspective". *Journal of Arts Management, Law and Society*. 40.

OIF. 2009. "Diversité culturelle et linguistique". *Organisation International de la Francophonie*. Statement issued following the Ministerial Conference, December 2009. Available online at: www.francophonie.org/-Diversite-culturelle-et-.html; accessed 14/01/2010.

Prengaman, P. 2001. "Morocco's Berbers Battle to Keep From Losing Their Culture/ Arab minority forces majority to abandon native language". *Chronicle Foreign Service*. 16 March 2001. Available online at: http://articles.sfgate.com/2001-03-16/news/17588658_1_arabic-official-language-morocco-s-berbers; accessed 14/03/2005.

Prunier, G. 1995. *The Rwanda Crisis, 1959–1994: History of a Genocide*. London: C. Hirst & Co.

Raymond, P.A. 2014. Morocco's Berbers urge broader reforms. *Al Jazeera*. 6 May 2014. Available online at: www.aljazeera.com/indepth/features/2014/03/moroccos-berbers-urge-broader-reforms-2014357321228806.html; accessed 07/09/2015.

Rosaldo, 1988. "Ideology, Place and People Without Culture". *Cultural Anthropology*. 3(1): 77–87.

SAGIT. 1999. "New Strategies for Culture and Trade: Canadian Culture in a Global World". *The Cultural Industries Sectoral Advisory Group on International Trade*. February 1999. Available online at: www.international.gc.ca/trade-agreements-accords-commerciaux/fo/canculture.aspx?lang=en; accessed 20/04/2009.

SAGIT. 2002. *An International Agreement on Cultural Diversity: A Model for Discussion*. Available online at: www.international.gc.ca/assets/trade-agreements-accords-commerciaux/pdfs/sagit_eg.pdf; accessed 14/03/2007.

Salmon, J.M. and M. Lesales. 2008. "Market access issues for cultural goods and services in the European Union: another story of luck and burden". *Caribbean Regional Negotiating Machinery*. Available online at: www.crnm.org; accessed 13/05/2010.

Shaffer, G.C. and M.A. Pollack. 2008. "How hard and soft law interact in regulatory governance: alternatives, complements and antagonists". Paper presented at the inaugural conference of the Society of International Economic Law, Geneva, 15–17 July 2008. Available online at: www.ssrn.com/link/SIEL-Inaugural-Conference.html; accessed 07/01/2009.

Survival International. 2007. "After 22 years, UN votes on indigenous peoples declaration". 10 September 2007. Available online at: www.survivalinternational.org/news/2499; accessed 14/08/2010.

Tamang, R. 2010. "Culture, Politics and Ethics: Media representation of immigrants and policy in Canada". Paper presented at the *2nd Global Conference on Culture, Politics and Ethics*, Salzburg, Austria, 12–14 March 2010.

Torggler, B., E. Sediakina-Riviere and M. Ruotsalainen. 2012. *Final Report: Evaluation of the pilot phase of the International Fund for Cultural Diversity*. IOS/EVS/PI/116, September 2012. UNESCO. Available online at: http://unesdoc.unesco.org/images/0021/002184/218443e.pdf; accessed 13/08/2015.

UNESCO, 1998. *The Stockholm Conference – Action Plan on Cultural Policies for Development*. Paris: UNESCO. Available online at: http://portal.UNESCO.org/culture/en/files/35220/12290888881stockholm_actionplan_rec_en.pdf/stockholm_actionplan_rec_en.pdf; accessed 15/03/2009.

UNESCO. 1999. "Final Conference Report". From the *Global Assessment of the 1989 Recommendation on the Safeguarding of Traditional Culture and Folklore: Local Empowerment and International Cooperation*, held in Washington, DC, 27–30 June 1999. Available online at: www.unesco.org/culture/ich/doc/src/00111-EN.pdf; accessed 18/08/2010.

UNESCO. 2002. *Developing a new standard setting instrument for the safeguarding of intangible cultural heritage: Elements for consideration*. Paris: UNESCO. CLT-2001/WS/8 Rev. Available online at: http://unesdoc.unesco.org/images/0012/001237/123744e.pdf; accessed 03/08/2010.

UNESCO, 2003a. *Convention for the Safeguarding of Intangible Cultural Heritage*. Paris: UNESCO. Available online at: www.unesco.org/culture/ich/index.php?lg=en&pg=00006; accessed 14/03/2007.

UNESCO, 2003b. *Desirability of Drawing up an International Standard-Setting Instrument on Cultural Diversity*. 32/C52. Paris: UNESCO. Available online at: http://unesdoc.unesco.org/images/0013/001307/130798e.pdf; accessed 09/07/2007.

UNESCO. 2004a. *First Meeting of Experts (category VI) on the First Draft of an International Convention on the Protection of the Diversity of Cultural Contents and Artistic Expressions*. CLT/CPD/2003–608/01. Paris: UNESCO. Available online at: www.unesco.org/culture/culturaldiversity/docs_pre_2007/clt_cpd_2003_608_01_en_20022004.pdf; accessed 09/07/2007.

UNESCO. 2004b. *Preliminary Draft Convention on the Protection and Promotion of the Diversity of Cultural Contents and Artistic Expressions*. CLT/CPD/2004/CONF.607/6. Paris: UNESCO.

UNESCO. 2005a. *Convention on the Protection and Promotion of the Diversity of Cultural Expressions*. CLT-2005/CONVENTION DIVERSITE-CULT REV. Paris: UNESCO.

Available online at: www.unesco.org/culture/en/diversity/convention; accessed 14/03/2007.

UNESCO. 2005b. "Oral report of the Rapporteur, Mr Artur Wilczynski at the Closing of the Third session of the Intergovernmental Meeting of Experts on the Draft Convention on the Protection and Promotion of the Diversity of Cultural Expressions". UNESCO, 25 May–3 June 2005. Paris: UNESCO. Available online at: www.unesco.org/culture/culturaldiversity/docs_pre_2007/oral_report_wilczynski_en_03062005.pdf; accessed 18/07/2006.

UNESCO. 2005c. "Preliminary report of the Director-General containing two preliminary drafts of a Convention on the Protection of the Diversity of Cultural Contents and Artistic Expressions". Paris: UNESCO. 3 March 2005. CLT/CPD/2005/CONF. 203/6.

UNESCO. 2008. *Medium Term Strategy for 2008–2013*. Paris: UNESCO.

UNESCO. 2010a. *Intangible Heritage, 1982–2000: From MONDIACULT to Our Creative Diversity*. Paris: UNESCO. Available online at: www.unesco.org/culture/ich/index.php?lg=en&pg=00309; accessed 05/05/2010.

UNESCO. 2010b. *Intangible Heritage, 2000 onwards and the drafting of the Convention*. Paris: UNESCO. Available online at: www.unesco.org/culture/ich/index.php?pg=00310; accessed 05/08/2010.

UNESCO. 2010c. *Intangible Cultural Heritage: Frequently Asked Questions*. Paris: UNESCO. Available online at: www.unesco.org/culture/ich/index.php?lg=en&pg=00021; accessed 05/08/2010.

UNESCO. 2010d. *International Fund for Cultural Diversity*. Paris: UNESCO. Available online at: www.unesco.org/culture/culturaldiversity/IFCD_ExplanatoryNote_EN.pdf; accessed 05/09/2010.

UNESCO. 2014. *Item 7a of the provisional agenda: Quadrennial periodic reporting: new reports and analytical summary*. CE/14/8.IGC/7a. Paris: UNESCO. Available online at: http://en.unesco.org/creativity/sites/creativity/files/8IGC_7a_analysis_periodic_reports _EN.pdf; accessed 12/08/2015.

UNESCO Executive Board. 2001. "REPORT ON THE PRELIMINARY STUDY ON THE ADVISABILITY OF REGULATING INTERNATIONALLY, THROUGH A NEW STANDARD-SETTING INSTRUMENT, THE PROTECTION OF TRADITIONAL CULTURE AND FOLKLORE". 161EX/15, 16 May 2001. Paris: UNESCO. Available online at: http://unesdoc.unesco.org/images/0012/001225/ 122585e.pdf; accessed 05/08/2010.

United Nations. 2007. *Declaration on the Rights of Indigenous Peoples*. Available online at: www.un.org/esa/socdev/unpfii/en/drip.html; accessed 29/12/2007.

UNPO. 2009. "ILO Convention 169: 20 years later". *Unrepresented Nations and Peoples Organisation*. Available online at: www.unpo.org/article/9746; accessed 02/01/2015.

Voon, T. 2007. *Cultural Products and the World Trade Organization*. Cambridge: Cambridge University Press.

Welsh, J.M. 2004. "Canada in the 21st Century: Beyond Dominion and Middle Power". *The Round Table*. 93(376): 583–593.

Wiessner, S. 2011. "The Cultural Rights of Indigenous Peoples: Achievements and Continuities in International Law". *European Journal of International Law*. 22(1): 121–140.

WTO. 1997. *Dispute DS31: Canada: Certain Measures Concerning Periodicals*. Available online at: www.wto.org/english/tratop_e/dispu_e/cases_e/ds31_e.htm; accessed 15/03/2009.

WTO. 2003. "Taking forward the review of article 27.3(b) of the TRIPS agreement: Joint Communication from the African Group, 26th June 2003". *Council for Trade-Related Aspects of Intellectual Property Rights*. IP/C/W/404. Available online at: www.wto.org/english/tratop_e/trips_e/art27_3b_e.htm; accessed 20/08/2010.

Yúdice, G. 2003. *The Expediency of Culture: Uses of Culture in the Global Era*. London: Duke University Press.

6 A blueprint for cultural development?

The EU–CARIFORUM Economic Partnership Agreement

Introduction

In October 2008, after several years of negotiation, the 15 governments that make up the regional trade grouping of Caribbean states known as the CARIFORUM signed an "Economic Partnership Agreement" (EPA) with the governments of the European Union (EU) (CARIFORUM-EU, 2008).[1] Under the provisions of this EPA approximately 92% of bilateral CARIFORUM-EU trade is due to be liberalised over a 25-year period, with the process of adjustment and implementation facilitated through a programme of European development assistance. The integration of development provisions in a trade agreement such as this marks something relatively novel in North–South relations. Similar agreements have been under negotiation between the EU and the other regional groupings across the "ACP" Group of African, Caribbean and Pacific states (79 in total). Progress on these parallel negotiations has been slow, however, and has taken place against a backdrop of opposition and controversy.[2]

The stated objective of these EPAs has been to set out a partnership for development and trade liberalisation that is consonant with the general pattern of neoliberal globalisation: deepening the integration of ACP states into the global economy by harmonising regional regulation, committing signatories to the widening and deepening of trade liberalisation and in the process bringing trade relations into conformity with WTO rules by removing the preferential arrangements that have been granted by European countries to the ACP since 1975 under the "Lomé" agreements. The Lomé agreements have been the cornerstone of EU trade and aid relations with the developing world in the post-independence period, and the framework in which Europe has maintained favoured trade relations with its former colonies by granting preferential market access to the ACP's tropical agricultural commodities (such as, in the Caribbean case, bananas and sugar).

The CARIFORUM–EU EPA has particular significance here as the first international trade agreement that makes reference to the provisions of the UNESCO Convention on cultural diversity (hereinafter "the Convention"), notably through the inclusion of a novel Protocol on Cultural Cooperation (hereinafter "Protocol"). UNESCO (2014: 22–23) has recognised the EPA as a key instance of implementation of the Convention, since the ability of cultural aspects to influence trade negotiations is seen as a "touchstone on which the Convention's ultimate effectiveness is to be judged". The Protocol was also highlighted in the first official five year report on the implementation of the EPA as a "major innovation in North–South FTA practice" (Singh *et al.*, 2014: 49).

The Protocol has therefore been of particular interest to a number of policy and industry stakeholders in Europe and the Caribbean and its inclusion in the EPA attracted wider attention as a sign of what to expect of the EU's new agenda for culture and development in its external relations based on the new UNESCO instruments on cultural diversity (e.g. see CCD, 2009; FERA, 2008). This has formed part of a broader search in this period within Europe to formulate the EU's policy position on the incorporation of culture in its external relations (Council of the European Union, 2008; Isar, 2015). The European Commission referred to the Protocol as a "showcase of implementation" for the Convention and suggested that it could provide a model for future negotiations not only with the other negotiating regions across the ACP but also further afield: for example, South Korea and India as well as the regional trade blocs ASEAN (South-East Asia), the Andean Community (North-East Latin America) and Central America (European Commission, 2008a; Loisen and de Ville, 2011). In giving its account of the inclusion of the Protocol in the CARIFORUM EPA, the Directorate-General for Trade of the European Commission also explained that this was because they wanted to "move early" in order to signal Europe's commitment to the Convention and reinforce its international standing.[3] The EU subsequently included a Protocol on Cultural Cooperation in the FTA that was concluded between the EU and South Korea in 2009 (see EU–Korea, 2009). Vlassis and Richieri Hanania (2014: 30) have commented that the emergence of these Protocols are a sign of the strong political influence of the Convention and that they mark an evolution of the broader trade and culture debate by reflecting a more proactive agenda by governments on the promotion of cultural diversity (who have begun to *include* the issue of culture in trade agreements rather than *exclude* it).

There has, however, been some unease amongst a number of European member states and cultural sector stakeholders about the precedent that such Protocols have set by bringing culture back into the sphere of trade negotiations, particularly where this involves countries with more developed cultural sectors than the Caribbean region, such as South Korea (Loisen and Ville, 2011; European Coalitions for Cultural Diversity, 2009). This unease has led to some rethinking of the European strategy and the negotiation of subsequent Protocols has not proceeded at the pace that had initially been suggested following the conclusion of the CARIFORUM–EU EPA (Souyri-Desrosier, 2014).

The key theme of the Protocol in the EPA is the affirmation of the principle of the dual nature of cultural goods and services (with an emphasis on the audiovisual sector) and the recognition of the special place of culture in trade and development cooperation between the two regions. The Protocol has also made the first formal references to the Convention's provisions on international cooperation, which are of particular interest to developing countries. Notable in this regard is the reference to Article 16 of the Convention. As we saw in the previous chapter, Article 16 requires developed country parties to the Convention to grant legally binding preferential market access to developing countries in the trade of cultural goods and services. In the case of the CARIFORUM–EU EPA, the Protocol specifically involves improving access to the European audio-visual market – a considerable concession, since this is historically one of Europe's most fiercely protected sectors – and easing the movement of professionals supplying cultural services (including theatre, live bands and circus services, news agency services and library, archive and museum services; see CARIFORUM–EU, 2008: 1770–1772). These provisions in the Protocol were highlighted by the Intergovernmental Committee of the Convention at UNESCO as offering the first evidence of the implementation of Article 16 and an important precedent in the emerging international framework of cultural development inspired by the Convention (UNESCO, 2009).

In light of the above, the Protocol presents an important milestone for those that have been following the contemporary direction of cultural policy and the ongoing attempts to formulate the relationship between culture, trade and development. Before going on to examine the contents of the EPA's cultural provisions in more detail, it is necessary first to understand the broader issues that have been at stake in the agreement's completion. Since the Protocol signals an evolution in the trade and culture debate by integrating culture within a trade agreement, it follows that any attempt to critically situate the cultural provisions in the EPA must begin by considering how they sit in the text as part of a framework of trade and development relations. The first section of this chapter therefore sketches out the background to the EPA's negotiation, considering the debates and analysis that have surrounded it and looking at the way in which a series of provisions on cultural cooperation and development came to offer a point of convergence alongside the other measures in the agreement. Although the bullish conduct of the European Commission over the negotiation of the EPA has tended be emphasised in the critical accounts of the EPA (for good reason), I also argue that it is crucial to examine the motives of CARIFORUM negotiators, looking at the ways in which the cultural components of the text came to offer an important concession on the part of the EU in what is otherwise an extremely one-sided agreement. The inclusion of the Protocol was referred to as a coup by the Caribbean negotiating team and has been presented to the region's governments, industries and populations as a mechanism that can support a strategy of economic diversification in order to offset the loss of preferential market access for tropical agricultural commodities while adjusting to intensified international economic competition in sectors such as tourism and clothing.

This theme is developed in the second section, which goes on to look at the way in which the EPA negotiations have been related to an attempt to reconceptualise culture in the Caribbean, as the value of culture as a resource for export development has been elevated as a key concern in the region's search for a new strategy of integration into the post-Lomé global economy. This section then goes on to look at some of the attempts that have been made by regional and international policymakers and development agencies to mobilise Caribbean governments, industries and the wider population behind the new cultural development strategy.

The third and final section then turns to look at how these efforts have begun to unfold through some of the responses – or lack of responses – that have been evident among the various stakeholders that are involved in this attempt to redefine the role of culture in the region's development strategy. Although there are a number of measures now underway that can be used to give an insight into some of the practical implications of the new strategy, it is equally significant that the call for regional consolidation and adjustment in the cultural sector has only found resonance among a relatively small group of countries and well-positioned cultural producers and professionals. These themes are developed in reference to a number of examples, looking in particular at some of the measures of policy reform that are now underway in Barbados and Trinidad & Tobago, as well as examining some of the other responses in the region from industry and civil society. This allows us to begin to take stock of the new culture and development strategy as it is taking shape in the region, and to consider some of its implications in the context of the broader debates about culture's transformation into a resource in the context of neoliberal globalisation.

Background to the EPA

Banana wars and sugar coatings

The first official five year report on the implementation and results of the EPA was produced in 2014 (Singh *et al.*, 2014). Although it reported on some reductions in tariffs and the setting up of institutions tasked with guiding implementation at national and regional levels, it drew few conclusions on the economic impact of the EPA so far since ratification has been slow (with less than half of the CARIFORUM states ratifying the agreement). Similarly, implementation remains limited and at a largely provisional level. With the EPA signed on the eve of the global economic crisis and downturn (which brought significant repercussions for both regions), it is unsurprising that the political commitment, initiative and resources necessary for implementation have so far been scarce.

However, the relative inertia in implementing the provisions of the EPA so far is also an outcome of the negotiation process itself and the nature of the agreement that resulted. In many ways the EPA is reminiscent of the one-sided "bargain" that was struck between the North and South during the Uruguay Round of trade negotiations that gave birth to the WTO, where developing countries agreed to take on binding commitments to implement agreements on market access and tariff reductions in exchange for unbinding commitments of assistance from developed countries that were often delayed or not forthcoming (although some of the European Development Fund (EDF) shortfalls under the EPA have been made up by bilateral donors such as Germany and the UK) (Heron, 2009; Singh *et al.*, 2014). References in the EPA text to development cooperation and assistance are in fact stated in very general terms and backed up with little or no time-bound or specific measures (a point which was later acknowledged by the European Commission, despite the high-profile that it gave to the place of development in the EPA during the negotiations; see Directorate-General for the External Policies of the Union, 2009: 10). In contrast, and as one of the most persistent and active critics of the EPA in the Caribbean, Norman Girvan, has pointed out, cooperation measures on market liberalisation are spelled out in considerable specificity in areas of especial interest to European negotiators and exporters (Girvan, 2008).

Numerous critics of the EPA therefore appear justified in drawing attention to the lack of substance behind the cooperation and assistance components of the EPA (see, for example, Goodison, 2007; Brewster, 2008; Brewster, Girvan and Lewis, 2008; Hurt, 2010; World Development Movement, 2010). Girvan (2013: 99–100) argues that the EPA is characterised by "sweetification": the highlighting of potential (and largely empty) benefits and the downplaying of certain costs of the EPA in order to sell it to stakeholders. A number of other analyses have pointed out that the EPA looks set to worsen the Caribbean's already disadvantageous terms of trade, while also leading to a reduction in policy space through the removal of tariffs (themselves significant sources of revenue for several of the small states in the region) and other policy mechanisms that could be used to spur diversification in the region.[4] As the global economic downturn began to bite following the completion of the EPA, a number of further questions have been raised regarding the administrative capacity needed in the region for EPA implementation. One former trade negotiator even suggested that Europe's trade policy in the region was turning the Caribbean into another constellation of globalisation's failed states, as abandoned farms and rocketing poverty and unemployment were precipitating a slide into a morass of narcotics and firearms trafficking, adding "this is what happens when you lose a trade war" (Walker, 2010). Less pessimistic observers of the EPA have themselves acknowledged in the light of available evidence that the expected benefits of the agreement had not materialised several years after its completion and that a rethinking of the EPA is now required in the region (Jessop, 2015).

The negotiations that ultimately led to the completion of the EPA in 2008 received relatively little media coverage in the region and proceeded with little or no consultation with Caribbean civil society. This generated some controversy and an acrimonious public fracturing of elite consensus over the direction of CARICOM's future development and the nature of its international economic relations (Girvan, 2013). A number of civil society organisations also orchestrated opposition to the EPA's signing and ratification, both within the Caribbean and internationally. Opposition came from a number of groups, including the International Trade Union Confederation, the Caribbean Labor

Council, the Caribbean Policy Development Center, the Caribbean Association for Feminist Research and Action, international NGOs such as Oxfam, Action Aid and the World Development Movement, and a number of protest movements in both the EU and the Caribbean – notably the Bare APE ("Block the EPA") coalition in Haiti, whose mass mobilisations were a factor in persuading the Haitian government not to participate in the initial signing in October 2008 (Haiti Support Group, 2007). In Jamaica, where the administration had played an active and prominent role amongst the region's governments in brokering the deal, the opposition staged the first walk-out of parliament for over 30 years during the debate that preceded the EPA signing, against the backdrop of fierce opposition from the Jamaica Confederation of Trade Unions (JCTU) and the National Workers' Union (NWU, whose president had suggested that signing the EPA would be "the worst thing that could happen to us since slavery") (*Radio Jamaica News*, 2008).

In explaining the passage of the EPA and the subsequent reluctance to sign across the rest of the ACP, critics have accused European negotiators of seeking to strong-arm ACP negotiators (a claim that has been echoed by ACP negotiators themselves, e.g. Miller, 2006). One former Caribbean diplomat noted that, by threatening to apply much higher levels of tariffs on exports of the region's key commodities and light manufactures – all major employers of labour and well organised politically – if it did not sign the EPA according to the schedule set out by the WTO, European negotiators had effectively "[held] a gun at the heads of Caribbean governments" to sign up for an agreement which was heavily weighted on European terms (*Inter Press Service*, 2010a). It was such threats that ultimately proved decisive in the conclusion of the CARIFORUM negotiations (Girvan, 2009a: 5–6). One exception was Haiti, which under the EU's Everything But Arms initiative is entitled to duty free access to European markets, thus reducing the EU's ability to threaten Haiti with disruption to its exports if it refused to sign the EPA.

The EU's neocolonial strategy in pursuing such an agreement has been provoked by the stepped-up international rivalry in the region that has followed the advances made by the US since the 1990s in the "banana trade wars". Acting on behalf of its agricultural giants exporting from tropical Latin America – notably Chiquita and Dole's trade in "dollar bananas" – the Clinton administration spearheaded a successful campaign in the 1990s by the banana multinationals and client regimes in Central and Latin America to challenge the legality of the EU–ACP Lomé agreements at the WTO and gain improved access to the EU banana market (Canterbury, 2009). Wary of the loss of existing trade privileges and influence in the region that will result from the eventual phasing out of the Lomé agreements following the WTO's banana ruling in 1997, the EU subsequently turned to the asymmetry of bargaining power that it can rely on in regional/bilateral trade agreements to strike a deal over the EPA with the Caribbean Regional Negotiating Machinery (CRNM)[5] in areas that far exceed what the region has been prepared to agree to at the WTO. In this way the EU has sought to secure advantageous access and conditions for European companies, notably in finance and investment, intellectual property, government procurement and competition policy.

Such liberalisation commitments in a bilateral context are highly significant in the context of the deadlocked Doha "Development" Round of WTO negotiations, since they offer a breakthrough in areas (the so-called "Singapore Issues") which developing countries have otherwise refused to negotiate on so far out of concern for a loss of policy space and a determination not to repeat the experiences of the Uruguay Round (Gallagher, 2008; Heron, 2009). Such offensive moves in external trade policy allow the EU to stay on the heels of the US and its other competitors in the intensified scramble for market access that has characterised the post-Uruguay Round era, while establishing precedents that will position the EU well for future trade negotiations. This is consonant with the Global Europe strategy that was unveiled by the European Commission in 2006: a "tough new approach" by European negotiators "to improve the competitive position of EU industry [and] open new markets for its exporters" (European Commission, 2008b). In this context, the EU's recent drive to conclude bilateral FTAs – in which the EU–CARIFORUM EPA represented an important breakthrough – has not only been motivated by immediate concerns for market access but also by wider competing attempts among negotiators representing the developed regions to establish a "spiral of precedents" which could then be deployed as the baseline for subsequent multilateral and extraregional negotiations (as has been demonstrated in the tendency for the developed countries to seek strategic FTAs with developing countries that are often peripheral to their main commercial interests) (Heron, 2009: 17; Phillips, 2005: 9).

So far, the focus in the literature on the inter-imperial trade rivalries that have played out over the EPA has left a number of gaps in the critical analysis. In particular, by focusing on EU strategy it has tended to neglect or downplay the calculations of the members of the Caribbean governmental and negotiating elite in negotiating and signing the EPA (such as, as we will see below, regarding the inclusion of provisions on cultural diversity). The tendency for analysis to remain within the frameworks of international relations and political economy has also left unexplored some of the ways in which the EPA has been related to a reconfiguration of domestic rationalities and technologies of government in the Caribbean. These themes are therefore taken up below.

The place of culture in the EPA: the view from CARIFORUM

Heron (2009) has conducted the only study to date regarding the motives of the CARIFORUM negotiating team. He notes that although the EPA was concluded on largely European terms, the CRNM was nevertheless able to extract a number of concessions from European negotiators, who were themselves keen to conclude a first EPA within the ACP. Among the most significant of the CRNM's calculations was a recognition of the region's particular dependence on agricultural commodities combined with the fact that, by the late 2000s, more than half of Caribbean export revenue was now coming from non-traditional industries, such as tourism, that were not covered under the Lomé agreements. Several Caribbean governments and officials within the CRNM and the secretariat of the Caribbean Community (CARICOM) therefore perceived the EPA not only as an opportunity to improve access to the EU for non-traditional exports, but also a means of fostering economic diversification and lessening the region's long-standing vulnerability to preference erosion and declining terms of trade in tropical agricultural commodities.

This analysis, however, neglects the role that the Protocol on Cultural Cooperation played in the calculations of the region's negotiators, along with a smattering of other provisions in the text related to market access in the cultural sector. During the negotiations, the CRNM Director-General had referred to the Protocol as a historic concession on the part of the EU that could open unprecedented opportunities to the Caribbean's cultural producers (CCIN, 2007), and this sentiment was echoed by the Caribbean Export Development Agency (CEDA) immediately following the conclusion of the EPA, which emphasised the cultural industries as one of two priority sectors earmarked for expansion as part of the new trade and business relationships set to be built with Europe (CEDA, 2008). The Director of the Caribbean Council[6] referred to the Protocol as "the most innovative part of the whole 1,000-plus pages of the text", going on to note that it reflected the way in which a number of Caribbean states with interests in improving international market access for their cultural sectors had made the Protocol a key bargaining point in the drafting of the EPA:

> In the closing days of the negotiations, achieving European agreement on this issue became central to the region's willingness to compromise on other matters. Then, Barbados' Prime Minister, Owen Arthur, made clear that liberalizing access for the export of Caribbean cultural and entertainment products was "a line in the sand" for the Caribbean.
>
> His remarks reflected recognition by Jamaica, Trinidad and other more developed regional economies that without access to the EU market for those involved in the region's hugely valuable creative industries there would be no EPA: the Caribbean had to see gain in a sector in which it excelled. The high profile given to the issue was also intended to ensure popular political backing should the negotiations fail.
>
> (Jessop, 2008)

Given the significance attached to the cultural provisions by the CRNM, it is worth looking at their content in more detail. They are mainly found in the Protocol on Cultural Cooperation (CARIFORUM–EU, 2008: 1938–1941), with further provisions found throughout the text. The Protocol begins by making explicit reference to the UNESCO Convention: "notably Articles 14, 15 and 16" (which concern international cooperation and collaboration, as well as preferential access for developing countries) and "the importance of the cultural industries and the multi-faceted nature of cultural goods and services as activities of cultural, economic and social value" – which is then followed by nine articles setting out what is referred to as a "framework within which the Parties shall cooperate for facilitating exchanges of cultural activities, goods and services, including *inter alia*, in the audiovisual sector" (CARIFORUM–EU, 2008: 1938). This reference to the audiovisual sector is an indication of what has been one of the most noted contributions of this framework: the extension (in Article 5) of preferential access to the European market for audiovisual works that are produced according to certain co-production arrangements between European and Caribbean firms. Such co-productions will qualify as European works and, therefore, satisfy the content and quota requirements of Europe's member states. To be eligible for preferential market access, co-productions must be between Caribbean and European producers who contribute shares of the production cost not less than 20% and not more than 80% of the total respectively: a formula that was described by the CRNM as "generous" on the part of the EU (CRNM, 2008: 5).

Another benefit of the Protocol highlighted by the CRNM is the possibility for the Caribbean cultural sector to access forms of technical assistance and funding from Europe (CRNM, 2008). However, it should be noted that such funding was in fact already available to the region prior to the EPA in the form of the EU–ACP Support Programme for the Cultural Industries and the EU–ACP Film Fund.[7] This casts some doubt over the way that the EPA has been presented as a breakthrough in cultural cooperation and development, and has led some to query why such mechanisms of funding and cooperation came to be emphasised in the agreement in the first place (Thiec, 2009).

Other provisions of note aim at facilitating the importation of workers, material and equipment for the purpose of shooting cinematographic films and television programmes (Articles 3 and 6 of the Protocol) – issues which have been identified as real concerns of the struggling Caribbean movie industry (Warner, 2005). There are also a series of provisions aimed at promoting wider exchanges and cooperation in the arts, publishing and heritage (Articles 7, 8 and 9), although these are without the kind of substance accorded to the other articles in the Protocol and have generated less interest.

Outside of the Protocol, there are a number of other points in the EPA addressing the cultural sector that were welcomed by the CRNM. These involve the protection of Caribbean intellectual property throughout Europe, the movement of Caribbean cultural practitioners in Europe for business purposes (in the jargon, as "Contractual Service Suppliers"), and improved market access in Recreational, Cultural and Sporting Services (Other than Audiovisual).[8] In particular, the extension of legally binding and significant market access to cultural practitioners supplying entertainment services was highlighted by the CRNM as a significant concession by Europe: "this level of market access in the entertainment sector by so many EU states has never been granted before to any other country or regional grouping" (CRNM, 2008: 2–3). These provisions, which unlike the Protocol are covered in the body of the EPA text and therefore governed by the binding rules of the Services and Investment chapter and the general provisions of the EPA, also mark a significant departure from the kinds of vaguer agreements to promote "cultural exchanges" that have tended to result from previous work at UNESCO and which, in practice, have tended to have little substantive significance (as is largely the case with Articles 7, 8 and 9 of the Protocol that we considered above).

Although this improved access granted to Caribbean cultural practitioners also comes with certain conditions, which the EU insisted upon in exchange for its commitment to ease its quota requirements on market access, the commitments that have been made by the EU to the Caribbean cultural sector in this regard do potentially offer important gains, even if these appear likely to be limited to a relatively privileged few.[9] In its own analysis of the EPA, the CRNM favourably compared the way in which this provision on the movement of cultural practitioners for business purposes had gone beyond the kind of limited cultural provisions contained in previous agreements: such provisions, it noted, were generally couched in general or hortatory diplomatic language and "culture was treated in a traditional sense of merely cooperation between nations and did not really address market access for cultural products and services" (CRNM, 2008: 1). This was a point echoed by the Caribbean Council in its analysis of the EPA, which went on to draw attention to the challenges and opportunities that the Protocol had opened up for the Caribbean cultural sector:

> Previous EU trade agreements had almost nothing on cultural cooperation, a sector in which the Caribbean is globally competitive. This level of market access is a first for any trade agreement signed by any nation or group of nations with the EU and offers significant commercial opportunity. It is now up to those in the creative sector to explore through CARIFO-RUM, their governments and with those who negotiated the agreement how to take advantage of the opportunities that will soon be on offer.
>
> (Jessop, 2008)

The Caribbean cultural sector, accustomed to years of neglect by policymakers, has reacted with some caution to such claims that they are now a key source of comparative and competitive advantage and a key priority in the region's development strategy. The founder of the Caribbean Creative Industries Business Network (CCIBN, which formed in 2004 in response to the EPA negotiations and the initiatives of the CRNM), has, for example, described the cultural components of the EPA as part of a "happy-ever-after fairy tale" about the prospects for creators and creative enterprises (Leonard, 2009). There has also been frustration at the way in which the EPA negotiations and related initiatives aimed at building the cultural sector have proceeded without consulting them (CCIN, 2007; CCIBN, 2008). Such scepticism is well founded, because there has been very little to report in terms of actual benefits accruing to the region's cultural sector from the EPA. Implementation of the cultural components of the agreement has been limited by inertia and largely remains at the stage of initial discussions, while there has been barely any interest expressed so far for in nego-tiating bilateral co-production arrangements in the audiovisual sector (Singh *et al.*, 2014: 49–50). Such inertia, along with the way that the cultural compon-ents of the EPA have rather misleadingly been packaged as a radical break-through in North–South relations, casts doubt over the meaning of the broader culture and sustainable development agenda as it has been expressed through the EPA. On the face of it, it is difficult to see how provisions such as the Protocol are anything more than a "sweetener" aimed at tying the negotiations up and selling the EPA to the region.

It would, however, be premature to dismiss the EPA's cultural components altogether. Implementation is likely to take some time to work through, and meanwhile the priority that culture is now coming to be accorded in the region's development strategy is indicative of a shift that has got underway in the kind of role being envisaged for culture in the region by a number of policymakers and cultural sector stakeholders. Figures in the sector who have followed the debates over the EPA negotiation and implementation are aware of the poten-tial opportunities that CRNM negotiators have opened up through the agree-ment, and have sought to rally support and advocate reform across the region in order to take advantage (e.g. see Leonard, 2009). Such lobbying efforts have been bolstered by the creation, in 2009, of the Caribbean Coalition for Cultural Diversity ("Caribbean CCD"), a branch of the International Federation of Coalitions for Cultural Diversity (IFCCD; see Chapter 5) and funded under the Commonwealth's Culture Programme.[10] The Caribbean CCD has had some success in its objective to widen ratification and awareness of the Convention in the region: at the time of the completion of the EPA in 2008, only two of the 15 members of CARICOM had ratified the instrument (Jamaica and St. Lucia); by the time of writing this had grown to 13. UNESCO representatives in the region have expressed concern that many of the states that have ratified the Convention since the conclusion of the EPA have done so out of a concern only to access any funds that may become available under the IFCD, without taking steps to reform their cultural policy (OneCaribbeanLtd, 2010). Never-therless, the formation of groups such as the Caribbean CCD and the CCIBN do suggest the emergence of a more coherent and focused regional lobbying capacity on the part of the cultural sector. This has been paralleled by the cre-ation of regional industry associations following the completion of the EPA, such as the Caribbean Music Industry Networking Organisation (CaMINO, aimed of pooling efforts to achieve greater international market penetration and royalty collection, particularly in the EU) and the Caribbean Audiovisual Network (CAN, the region's first network of representatives from the audiovis-ual sector).

The high profile that negotiators and stakeholders have given to the poten-tial of the cultural provisions contained in the EPA, and their attempts to gear the region up to take advantage and implement reforms, should alert us to another blind-spot in the critical analyses of the EPA that we considered earlier. Such analyses help to shed light on some of the international asymmetries and neocolonial dynamics that have been defining features of the CARIFORUM–EU EPA. However, they tend to obscure the way that the negotiations over the EPA have been related to an attempt to reconfigure rationalities and technologies of government within the region. As discussed in Chapter 2, the attempts that have been made to bring insights from the governmentality literature to bear on the processes of neoliberal globalisation as they are instantiated – and contested – in particular contexts offer a useful framework for analysis here. Along with the programmes of liberalisation and restructuring through which states engage with the project of globalisation, it is also important for analysis to remain sensitive to the moments in which people and places are exhorted to confront the "challenges" of economic liberalisation and dislocation by applying economic disciplines, developing creative and entrepreneurial capacities, seeking out new opportunities, adapting, competing and adjusting themselves in the context of evolving strategies of social management and regimes of accumulation.

These points are helpful for opening up an analysis of the ways in which the field of cultural policy is being reproblematised and redefined in the Caribbean today as the cultural sector is being identified as a new base of comparative advantage and as the region's elites struggle to articulate a post-Lomé strategy of integration into the global economy and sell this to the public. In the next section we will begin to draw these themes out by turning to consider in more detail the way in which the negotiation of the EPA has hastened an attempt in the region to redefine the role of cultural policy.

The EU, CARICOM and cultural development in the Caribbean

The potential benefits of the EPA's cultural provisions for the formulation of a new cultural development strategy across CARICOM appear clear enough. The negotiation of the EPA over the last decade has coincided with a growing recognition in the region of the potential of the cultural sector and the need for provisions that could be used to develop a new strategy of engagement with the global economy in the region as part of its adjustment to the expiration of preferential access to the European market in tropical agricultural commodities. Against the backdrop of the formation of the UNESCO Convention, and in particular its provisions on preferential treatment for developing countries, the negotiations with the EU over the EPA presented an opportunity for the CRNM to begin to put in place some of the pillars of such a strategy. At the same time, the CRNM and CARICOM Secretariat have sought, working in cooperation with international experts and agencies such as UNESCO and European development programmes, to impress upon the region the potential of the new global cultural economy and the need to take advantage of this by transforming culture's place in policy.

In the remainder of this chapter we will therefore look at the ways in which this strategy has unfolded through the responses – or lack of responses – of the various agencies, governments and stakeholders that have been involved in this effort, and we will attempt to draw out some of the defining social and political dynamics of the new culture and sustainable development strategy as it is taking shape in the region. We will begin by looking at some of the key elements of the strategy as it has been framed in response to the EPA negotiations.

Caribbean cultural resources and the post-Lomé global economy

Attempts to articulate the new strategy across the region got underway in October 2004 at a rallying of Caribbean cultural industry representatives in Trinidad, organised jointly by the CRNM and the European Commission's PRO€INVEST/TRINNEX development programme that was aimed at assisting particular sectors in the ACP countries as part of the EPA transition.[11] To an audience of eager, if sceptical, figures from the motion picture, music, video, and related industries, the Services Trade Specialist at the CRNM spoke of the now central role of the cultural industries in light of the region's declining competitiveness in basic and traditional goods and the erosion of preferential treatment in key markets following the WTO banana ruling of 1997 and the mandate of the EPA (Chaitoo, 2004). Aside from presenting an impressive set of figures that demonstrated the economic and societal potential of harnessing the cultural sector to development (based on its strengths in areas such as music and entertainment), the central point made by the CRNM representative was that, since reliance on traditional tropical commodity exports was no longer viable, particularly in light of the impending expiration of the Lomé agreements, culture could no longer be treated as a peripheral concern in the region's development strategy nor, in particular, as a domain of policy that is separate from political economy: it now had a vital importance in the imperative to "diversify exports, add new value, create jobs and stimulate growth" (Chaitoo, 2004). For these reasons he also stressed that there is an onus on Caribbean governments and the CRNM to develop a "formal regional policy position on [the] culture-trade issue" that could be asserted in negotiations in order to both augment the region's policy-making capacity (referring favourably to the Euro-Canadian campaign then underway at UNESCO) and secure greater levels of international market access, investment and development assistance. These sentiments were echoed in a subsequent set of recommendations drawn up between the CRNM and the cultural industries (CRNM, 2004).

A period of research, consolidation and reform in the region has followed that echoes some of the efforts that we have seen taken by China over the last decade in shifting the focus and the nature of cultural policy (Chapter 4). The first major step taken by the CRNM at the end of 2004 was to commission a team of consultants, led by international trade specialist Keith Nurse (a long-standing advocate in the region for giving greater priority to the cultural sector) and funded by the EDF/PRO€INVEST, to begin the process of building an intervention strategy for the region's policymakers based on definitive assessments of the state of the cultural industries, the particular factors constraining the sector's global competitiveness, and related trade and investment issues relating to necessary reform. Cultural industry representatives and culture and trade officials also provided input through a series of interviews and further CRNM-organised meetings between 2004 and 2006. The final analysis and recommendations – The Cultural Industries in CARICOM: Trade and Development Challenges (Nurse *et al.*, 2006) – were then presented to the CRNM in December 2006, setting out the policy changes required in the region while also providing a focus for the CRNM's strategy in the ongoing EPA negotiations (which included seeking an audiovisual co-production treaty between the CARIFORUM and EU).

The central task put before the region's policymakers and stakeholders is the need to reorient their approach to culture and to create mechanisms that can harness and manage the Caribbean's significant, but hitherto largely untapped, pools of creativity in order to take advantage of the possibilities offered for exporters by the new global economy and by the region's considerable overseas diaspora markets. As set out in the executive summary of Nurse *et al.*'s work for the CRNM, culture now holds out considerable comparative advantage for the region relative to its size, emerging as one of the "prime areas for development" in the new global economy: "The conclusion is that the cultural industries should be viewed as a critical strategic resource in the move towards creating sustainable development options" (Nurse *et al.*, 2006: 6–11). Given the ongoing erosion to the Caribbean's prominence in the trade of traditional products such as sugar, bananas and bauxite, as well as the growing international competition from East Asia in low-cost assembly production, the cultural industries have emerged as one of the region's most promising commercial asset bases and, as such, should be prioritised by elevating the status of the region's cultural ministries and pursuing a programme of radical reform of, and through, cultural policy. These have also been the key themes communicated to the region's policymakers and stakeholders through international organisations such as UNCTAD and WIPO as part of the Mauritius Strategy (United Nations, 2005; Nurse, 2008; also see Chapter 4) as well as initiatives under the UNESCO Convention such as the Cultural Diversity Programming Lens (CDPL) (UNESCO, 2010a).

It is often pointed out that many aspects of Caribbean culture are ideally suited to the generation of content that can be marketed across platforms and generate the kind of spin-offs and synergies with other sub-sectors – in particular audiovisual and entertainment – that increasingly hold the key to capturing the most significant gains from rapid innovations in technology, marketing and intellectual property. The oral tradition communicating regional folklore, for example, is seen as lending itself naturally to audiovisual formats and the kind of work that is now required for marketing a major film: "a novelisation, a graphic novel or comic version, a soundtrack album, a video game, a model, toys, and endless promotional publications" (Nurse *et al.*, 2006: 93).

Above all, it is noted that the region's world famous heritage in carnival and in music has so far realised only a fraction of its potential. In the music industry this has been recognised for a while now within the region and internationally:

centres of production such as Kingston in Jamaica are renowned as world-class and highly competitive centres of innovation and creativity generating huge global commercial value, yet most of the value chain remains outside the country and economic benefits, where recorded, generally accrue to international players or otherwise leak away due to weak domestic frameworks of intellectual property recognition and enforcement (Power and Hallencreutz, 2004; Nurse *et al.*, 2006: 30–37).[12] Caribbean Carnival has meanwhile become a regional and worldwide phenomenon (with Trinbagonian carnivals, for example, creating hugely successful spin-offs in North America and Europe and creating potentially huge opportunities for the region's costume designers, performing arts groups, musical and visual artists), yet efforts are only recently underway to provide a framework within which analysts and policymakers can begin to make a notable contribution to the industrial development of carnival (Tull, 2009: 9).

The task of reform across the Caribbean, therefore, not only means improving domestic capacity in sub-sectors such as music, film/television, fashion or book publishing, but also developing the regulatory structures that can transform creative activity into the kind of branded, tradable content that can multiply value across platforms and target the "tie in" market opportunities that hold the key to success in the contemporary global economy. From festivals, carnivals and heritage to music, publishing and film, the call is that the region's cultural endowments must be mapped in greater detail and mobilised more effectively as part of the effort to develop a new basis of comparative advantage. The analysis for the CRNM on trade issues therefore emphasised in particular that "the introduction of culture into global trade rules and governance is an issue of immense concern for the Caribbean", raising the vital importance of maintaining policy space in the face of WTO pressures and seeking support "from those countries in the trading system, like Canada and the European Union, that are promoters of special rules for cultural goods and services" (Nurse *et al.*, 2006: 208).

In this way, the concerns that we have seen expressed in the strategy that has unfolded alongside the EPA negotiations since 2004 – to defend and strengthen the region's capacity to manage culture as a critical strategic resource for export and development in the global economy, under the banner of cultural diversity and in the face of pressures for liberalisation – has formed a key point in the consensus that was reached with the EU in the EPA, and indicates some of the ways in which the Caribbean has come to share a stake in the role of cultural goods and services as a resource for political and economic development in the contemporary global economy. It is also a measure of this new strategic importance attached to culture that CARIFORUM negotiators were willing to accord it a priority in negotiations while sacrificing, as we saw earlier, a great deal of policy space in other areas.

It is nevertheless noted in the strategy set out for the CRNM that ultimately no international framework can legislate who will get into the market or proliferate in the global, regional or national cultural economy: "The point must be reinforced that while policy space is created to foster development of the sectors involved, it is critical to engender entrepreneurship within the territories" (Nurse *et al.*, 2006: 6; 208). It is therefore stressed that the efforts of the CRNM and the CARICOM Secretariat in trade negotiations and securing development assistance need to be matched by the implementation of regional measures in industrial, innovation, marketing, human resources and intellectual property if the region is to meaningfully participate in the expanded role of cultural goods and services in the global economy. This is particularly the case with the cultural provisions that have been provided in the EPA, since it is recognised that their effectiveness will ultimately depend on the region's governments and cultural sector taking the initiative to develop appropriate measures and projects consistent with its aims and that can be supported by international cooperation from the EU and other international development agencies (Leonard, 2009; IFCCD, 2008).

Changing the mindset: redefining cultural policy, mobilising industry and engendering entrepreneurship

One of the first domestic tasks facing the region stems from its geographical, political and linguistic fragmentation which has left a legacy of small domestic markets and a fractured, archipelagic regulatory environment. Together these factors have tended to act as a disincentive to investment and have made the import, export and distribution of content cumbersome and inefficient; at the same time, they make exports to more lucrative diasporic, regional and extra-regional markets critical in order to overcome the islands' lack of economies of scale (Nurse *et al.*, 2006: 11). Echoing the project of European integration, there is therefore an emphasis throughout the strategy on strengthening the international competitive position of the Caribbean's cultural enterprises through regional industrial synergies while simultaneously accelerating and reinforcing the construction of regional liberalisation and distribution networks within the framework of the Caribbean Single Market and Economy (CSME).

A number of steps in this direction have been taken in cooperation with international agencies and development assistance, notably the creation of the Creative Industries Exchange (CIE) and a Regional Task Force on Cultural Industries (RTFCI).[13] The former is funded by UNESCO and based at the region's Centre for International Trade Law at the University of West Indies (UWI), with the principal aim of generating and disseminating data and information in order to provide a stronger regional framework for the measurement and management of the cultural sector. The RTFCI was established following the conclusion of the EPA in 2008, financed by UNESCO and the EU's Hub and Spokes Programme (an "aid for trade" programme which provides support to policymakers and key stakeholders in ACP countries in the formulation of trade and development policy). The RTFCI gave 20 individuals from across the region (Ministers of Culture, Trade and Finance, representatives from regional organisations such as the CRNM and Caribbean export, and a cross section of representatives from industries such as audiovisual, music and festivals) the mandate to gear the region up to respond to the cultural provisions of the EPA and to fold these provisions into a coherent policy across the Caribbean Community and the CSME. The RTFCI presented its draft Action Plan to the CARICOM's Council for Human and Social Development in 2012, although take-up of its recommendations across the region has been slow and CARICOM Heads of Government continue to be urged to implement legislative, policy and institutional responses (Patterson, 2015).

This points to a deeper problem facing the development of such a strategy, which is that the Caribbean's traditional governmental orientation has meant that it has hitherto been slow to recognise and leverage its endowments in culture in the ways now required if it is to successfully reposition itself in the post-Lomé global economy. For some, this has become a matter of urgency as the region faces the erosion of its traditional bases of economic activity (one prominent commentator in Guyana put it in particularly stark terms in 2010: "The Caribbean is still largely unaware that the livelihood of so many could depend on art" (Creighton, 2010)). This turns the problem into one of how to bring about a more fundamental reorientation towards the cultural field itself because, despite what is now increasingly acknowledged as the potential of the Caribbean's vast, "untapped" cultural reserves, in practice there has been an absence of practical interest and advocacy across the region for this new role expected of culture, leaving it underutilised and lacking relevant programmes of data collection and knowledge. Jamaica is the only Caribbean country to date to have undertaken a full assessment of the contribution of the copyright and creative industries to GDP and employment, while a few others (Barbados and Trinidad & Tobago) have developed some partial estimates (Hendrickson *et al.*, 2012: 29–31).

Earlier initiatives taken in the 1990s, such as the development of a CARICOM Regional Cultural Policy (1996), are generally recognised to have been ineffective: as both the CRNM and RTFCI have noted, this is framed in terms of unbinding goals and short/medium term actions which have neither been adopted at a higher level within CARICOM nor translated into specific policy proposals for the cultural sector across the region. At the same time, the policy is seen to have had an outdated focus on culture "as education", failing to address the now pressing issue of creating the kind of regulatory and fiscal environment which is necessary to recognise and develop culture as a viable sector for export in line with the cultural industries agenda (RTFCI, 2009: 8–9). There were also attempts in the 1990s by stakeholders and trade and investment agencies to increase the regional profile given to culture in a reconfigured political economy: following the annual Caribbean Music Expo of 1999, for example, music industry stakeholders (producers, artists, distributors, media practitioners, attorneys and industry analysts) began to articulate a collective position on the development of the regional music industry, requesting five areas for immediate regulatory action aimed at the consolidation of regional industry. Of these requests, however, only one – a regional system for collective management of copyright and related rights – was subsequently taken up (Nurse, 2005: 332–333). It is the need to address such shortcomings which therefore forms the basis of the central recommendation put forward for the CRNM's strategy:

> Governments and the corporate sector in most Caribbean countries have not fully appreciated the new directions in the global economy and the ways in which their economies can diversify to meet new challenges and take advantage of emerging opportunities. In addition, the cultural industries are not seriously regarded as an economic sector, the key stake-holders in the industry are poorly organised and the sector's economic value remains largely undocumented. Changing the mindset of the governments and the corporate sector is key for transforming the sector's viability, but it is equally important for the industry stakeholders to become better organised and provide a more sustained and cohesive advocacy capability.
>
> (Nurse *et al.*, 2006: 8–9)

Here is the root of perhaps the most significant obstacle in the way of redefining and repositioning culture in the region: an entrenched antipathy towards the value of political investment and corporate sponsorship in the domestic cultural sector, or what Nurse has elsewhere described as the particular "cultural industry problématique" in the Caribbean (Nurse, 2005: 324–333). This antipathy is seen to spread from the top to the bottom of Caribbean societies, presenting a huge task for those attempting to implement the new strategy. Among the governing and economic elite, the antipathy is often seen to be rooted in the cultural legacy of colonialism that has tended to inform authoritative attitudes towards the cultural domain: historically, the kinds of activities that have now emerged as the region's prime areas for development and diversification – musical forms such as dancehall, zouk, merengue, bachata, calypso and soca, for example – have tended to be associated with marginalised groups embodying anti-establishment themes. These have therefore generally been dealt with by the region's elite as, on one hand, problems to be denigrated or reformed away, and on the other hand as less worthy than the traditional domains of cultural policy and investment (heritage and museums, the fine arts, deference to imported cultural products, and so on).

The musical genre of dancehall, for example, has typically been stigmatised by the region's elite as violent, threatening, uncivilised and over-sexed (Nurse, 2005: 333–335); similarly, in sectors such as publishing and audiovisual production, an intellectual or "high culture" bias has typically tended to choke domestic creativity and restrict the exploitation of production and marketing opportunities (Nurse *et al.*, 2006: 93–94; Warner, 2005).[14] The most lucrative areas for expansion and diversification are to be found precisely in those expressions which the Caribbean elite have historically been loathe to acknowledge, never mind invest in. Nurse therefore suggests that this has held back such expressions of Caribbean culture from achieving their "globalising potential" and from "the process of becoming commodified", arguing that "the *probléma-tique* is not external but systemic, in that the interplay between global social forces/discourses and internal periphery sources of imperialism stymie growth and development" (Nurse, 2005: 335, emphasis in original).

There is a striking redeployment of cultural criticism here, as it becomes dovetailed with a contemporary problem of economic reform: how to recognise and mobilise the potential of hitherto under-valued, counter-hegemonic and popular practices in order to develop new areas of productivity and deepen their commercial linkages with the global economy. At the same time, cultural policy's relation to the social is framed less in terms of the devaluation and reform of the habitus or conduct of others previously deemed as in need of improvement or as dangerous to social order: rather, there is an attempt to reconfigure the role of cultural policy as part of the contemporary task of engaging the productive potential of aspects of that conduct in light of the need for economic diversification and the search for new technologies of social management and productivity. As the CRNM and RTFCI have both sought to emphasise to the region's governments, the Caribbean's wealth in culture, if managed in this way, can bring greater economic benefits than traditional sectors such as agriculture (in terms of employment, foreign direct investment and foreign exchange earnings) and can open up increasingly scarce avenues out of poverty (particularly for Caribbean youth) as well as new solutions in the ongoing concern in the region for "guarding against hopelessness and crime in some societies" (CRNM, 2004; RTFCI, 2009: 8–9).

Of course, this reconfigured discourse of cultural development relies on certain limitations and hierarchies, both old and new, of useful and permissible conduct. Prominent among the targets of reform is the informal and unprofessional character of the cultural field understood as a pool of underexploited immaterial resources characterised by low levels of intellectual property recognition, entrepreneurship and international commercialisation and distribution (at least among those who have not left to establish bases overseas or have forged links with major international industry players). This is how the essence of the problem was captured following a series of discussions between policymakers and stakeholders in 2008:

> At the core of the problem is that Caribbean society is not yet accustomed to seeing art as an industry.... Because of this the market is largely undeveloped, marketing is unsophisticated and inefficient, artists are hardly seen as worthy of their hire, and the society is still not ready to pay for it. The notion of copyright is hazy, intellectual property is a new concept to the wider population and piracy is the accepted norm.... Among the many reasons these industries are under-developed is that the workers are individuals working on their own outside of the establishment. They have no representation and exist in a framework in which people do not generally recognise that they are part of cultural industries.
>
> (Creighton, 2010)

The issues identified above are evident in looking at what could be one of the jewels in the region's export crown, the Jamaican music industry. The international success of the country's reggae and dancehall contrasts with the low returns actually accruing to the island and its artists and firms, and presents an important focus for the strategy now being developed. The country's trade and investment promotion agency JAMPRO has long lamented the difficulty of developing reggae music for export, faced with the lack of connections that domestic artists have had with government policy and formal channels of production, performance and distribution. Indeed, the problem as JAMPRO has formulated it is precisely the fact that the genre's vibrancy has traditionally had little to do with government policy or incentives and more to do with the struggles of poverty and hardship and the use of informal channels to market local music products (JAMPRO, 1996: 62).

In light of this, the Jamaican government has more recently been one of the furthest ahead in attempting to address the historical lack of attention to music as a viable sector. This has come through the efforts of agencies such as JAMPRO and initiatives in the 1990s such as bringing the island's copyright law up to international standards while putting greater emphasis on the music and entertainment sectors in industrial policy (OPM, 1996). The significance of the music industry was then highlighted in the country's 2002 National Development Plan and this was followed over the next decade by a series of measures aimed at supporting the development of the sector (notably through a series of tax concessions), and the drafting of the Entertainment Industry (Encouragement) Act, which seeks to extend the existing support of the film industry to a wider range of activities, in particular music (Hendrickson et al., 2012: 41–42).

However, it is also recognised that such a reorientation on the part of the Jamaican government itself is only half of the problem since it needs to be matched by measures addressing what is seen as the lax attitudes to entrepreneurship, musical ownership and property rights that prevail amongst the country's producers and the wider population (Nurse et al., 2006; Power and Hallencreutz, 2004). Such attitudes are far removed from the view that prevails in the global industry and this is seen to stem from a number of "socio-cultural" factors that need to be targeted through a combination of legislative-institutional reforms and targeted human resource and education policies (Nurse et al., 2006: 201–207; Power and Hallencreutz, 2004: 234–237). Prominent among these socio-cultural factors that are identified as standing in the way of developing the potential of popular Jamaican music are its roots in Rastafarianism ("the problems many artistes and firms have had with copyrights, particularly with pre-1980s recordings/compositions, can be related to Rastafarian anti-property attitudes" and "the religious beliefs that [they] had thought of as central to musical expression") and the dense, interactive and transactional mode of production that tends to prevail in creative centres such as Kingston (where musical creation and commercialisation happens rapidly through largely informal channels, so that one day is not an uncommon time for new "riddims"[15] to be widely copied by other artists) (Power and Hallencreutz, 2004: 234–237).

There is, in other words, a delicate balancing act involved in realising the productive and innovative value of culture here, since again we see how some forms of activity are clearly held to contain more value than others in such strategies: namely, that which can readily be harnessed and converted into marketable content and intellectual property. This is why the open intertextuality and creative appropriation of others' music that, according to Paul Gilroy, are the keys to the creation of value in modern Jamaican dancehall (Gilroy, 1987: 104, 164), must today be nurtured and managed within appropriate regulatory frameworks, strengthened professional and Collective Management Organisations (CMOs), and through carefully designed reforms in industrial, cultural and human resource policies. Again, we might take note of the central theme here: cultural development is to be achieved through the formation of enterprise and private property in the areas of greatest potential for international trade expansion. At the same time, while creating new possibilities for cultural recognition, it simultaneously seeks to reform those forms of conduct that stand in the way of these aims.

By extension, although the more traditional concern for the defence of society from politically subversive, dangerous, violent or sexual content in the region's popular musical forms is now being tempered in recognition of their role as sources of cultural expression and productive commercial activity, these concerns have also been given a new emphasis with the attention that has come to focus on the dual roles of the music and entertainment industries. This is particularly the case where content is seen to have a damaging effect on social order and international circulation and promotion. It was emphasised by the acting Prime Minister, Bruce Golding, in a communiqué concerning the EPA negotiations in 2008, for example, that:

> We have left ourselves exposed for a while, to the extent that our music has never been promoted and marketed in the way that tourism is. For example, whenever there is negativity in the marketplace that affects tourism, we have a strategy to address that. Reggae music is too important for us to allow it to become victim of the actions of [a] minority of artistes who have allowed their own passions to overflow to the extent that they could damage an entire industry.
>
> (Jamaican Prime Minister Bruce Golding, in *Trade Updates*, 2008)

These concerns reached a peak in 2009 when the Jamaican Broadcasting Commission (JBC) reacted to the latest dancehall, soca and calypso craze of "daggering" with a series of directives aimed at videos and songs which it deemed promoted "violent sexual behaviour", "gunmanship" and the "explicit public simulation of various sexual positions".[16] Under these directives, musicians were effectively prohibited from recording material which contains what is deemed to be excessively or explicit sexual or violent content, and there are recommendations that these measures be extended to cover a wider range of content (some of which – such as the recommendation to prohibit musical expressions of "hostility" – have been interpreted by critics as part of a wider shift on the part of government to reassert authority over the island's so-called "garrison communities", which have effectively begun to go to war with a state which is increasingly perceived as an enemy). Responding to concerns over the dual impact of the daggering saga on "the value of Jamaica's music" and "the psyche of the people", Prime Minister Golding addressed representatives from the industry by announcing the establishment of a programme that would work to develop further mechanisms that could be used to generate appropriate content (while also "ostracising those who step beyond the boundaries of what is decent and uplifting") (*Jamaica Information Service*, 2009; *Inter Press Service*, 2009).

These concerns among the JBC, industry and government followed a series of high-profile controversies in which a number of international Caribbean dancehall stars have faced an international boycott organised by the "Stop Murder Music" campaign protesting violent, racist and homophobic themes in their song lyrics. It has been estimated that this boycott cost affected artists in excess of US$5 million in cancelled tours, lost concert revenue and sponsorship deals across the Caribbean, Europe and North America (*Jamaicans*, 2007; *Guardian*, 2007). Meanwhile a number of Jamaican producers and booking agencies have cited the controversies as causing wider damage to the Jamaican music brand, particularly as increasing numbers of high-profile musicians have subsequently had visas revoked in key markets (*Jamaica Observer*, 2010).

These cases highlight another of the difficulties faced by policymakers in cultivating Jamaican culture for export, because there may be a contradiction in seeking to harness the "dual" economic and social roles of musical expressions such as dancehall. Just as the Jamaican government and industry, for example, have expressed the need to regulate musical content in order to restrict expressions of homophobia and maximise the industry's export potential, this is contradicted by the government's refusal to overturn legislation prohibiting open displays of homosexuality (despite protests in Jamaica and internationally against this legislation) on the grounds that, in the words of Golding, this would be to "overturn [Jamaican] tradition and culture" (cited in *Jamaica Observer*, 2007). In other words, it appears in this case that the concern for the health of the music industry and its ability to realise international economic value in the global cultural economy comes before the kind of other concerns we have seen stressed in the Convention regarding the "universality" of the right to expression of identity. We might note again that, since this right ultimately rests with the state, it is unsurprising that this has been the order of priority here.

Summary

We have seen in this section how the negotiation of the EPA, and the parallel materialisation of the Convention at UNESCO, has begun to reorient and intensify the attention given towards the cultural domain in the Caribbean. A number of cultural forms that have hitherto been neglected, and indeed frowned upon, by the region's policymakers are coming to be identified as strategic resources in the region's search for a new base of comparative advantage in the post-Lomé global economy. Alongside the provisions that have been secured in international trade and development assistance, a series of regional initiatives on the part of the CARICOM Secretariat and in cooperation with international agencies and assistance are also now underway in an attempt to bring about a reorientation of cultural policy in the region. The onus has therefore fallen on Caribbean governments and industries, as well as the wider population, to adapt to the challenges and opportunities presented by the post-Lomé global economy by recognising, managing and exploiting the potential value contained in the region's cultural resources. In the example of the Jamaican music industry we have also seen how the attempt to cultivate a particular set of cultural expressions requires a tricky balancing of national and international concerns and requires a reorientation in the cultural outlook of both the region's elite and cultural practitioners in order to engender outward looking, entrepreneurial exploiters of intellectual property and bearers of (carefully managed) expressions of the region's internationally marketable cultural forms.

It would be misleading, however, to view this example as representative of any wider trend across the region. As we will see in the following section, the responses across the region to the EPA, and to the new strategy of sustainable cultural development that has been set out by regional and international agencies, have been mixed.

Cultural diversity and cultural indifference in the Caribbean

As we have seen above, the EPA negotiations have played an important role over the last decade in sparking an interest in the potential of culture as a sustainable resource for addressing some of the most pressing challenges facing the Caribbean region. This has led to the creation of a number of institutions and policy initiatives aimed at the development of the cultural sector. However, arguably the most striking overall feature of the measures being introduced in the region is that they are proceeding slowly and remain in an embryonic stage, with relatively little support outside of a vanguard of policymakers and regional and international agencies. Meanwhile, responses have been concentrated among the larger economies: notably Jamaica, Barbados and Trinidad & Tobago, although some of the smaller countries have more recently begun to introduce reforms. The general lack of political commitment across the region also limits the picture that is available of the state of implementation of the Convention, with the majority of countries in the region to date not having submitted a periodic report to UNESCO (UNESCO, 2014).

This scenario is not only a reflection of the fact that the strategy is in its early stages but is also, and more fundamentally, indicative of the fact that it has been the CARICOM Secretariat and regional negotiating machinery, in response to the EPA negotiations and in cooperation with international and European development agencies, that have carried the cultural diversity agenda to the region. This reflects the gap that exists between agencies such as the CRNM, the European Commission and UNESCO on the one hand, and the region's governments and cultural producers on the other – not to mention the divide that often exists between governments and those involved in the cultural sector. Although, as noted earlier, a regional cultural industry lobby has begun to emerge over the last decade, most of the region's governments and cultural sectors have had little prior investment in the international cultural diversity agenda (in contrast to the kind of roles we have seen played by a number of industry organisations, such as SAGIT and the CCD in Canada, for example; see Chapter 5). There was little domestic pressure on the part of the cultural sector in the negotiation of the EPA: most of the major Caribbean industry practitioners have based themselves in the OECD countries and the negotiations largely proceeded without consultation with the domestic cultural sector.

The tentative response in the region is also a reflection of the fact that some territories in the region have more developed cultural sectors and longer connections with export markets than others (Jamaica, Barbados, Trinidad & Tobago and St Lucia – in contrast to Guyana, Suriname, Haiti and the other six members of the Organisation of Eastern Caribbean States that come under the CARIFORUM grouping), while export capacity is further restricted to a few sub-sectors (music, book publishing, visual arts and film/television) which are better placed for development since they are, as the report commissioned for the CRNM in 2006 pointed out, "more commodified or commercialised and have had a longer experience of exporting goods, services, and intellectual property" (Nurse *et al.*, 2006: 6).

For these reasons, the call for regional consolidation and adjustment in the cultural sector has found resonance among a relatively small group of countries and well-positioned cultural producers and professionals. We can bring these points out by considering a number of examples, beginning with Barbados and Trinidad & Tobago, and then moving on to some of the other responses in the region.

Barbados and Trinidad & Tobago

Alongside Jamaica, which was considered briefly in the previous section, it is useful to consider some of the responses taken in Barbados, where the cultural industries have come to attract growing attention from government since the early 2000s, particularly as the EPA negotiations have unfolded. Mounting evidence of the commercial potential of the Barbadian cultural sector over the 1990s, alongside the growing international discourse on cultural development promoted by agencies such as UNESCO, have brought about increased recognition of the need for policy to evolve with globalisation and the accelerated transformation in culture's role as a resource for development. Although some of the responses will be examined below, it is important to note that the new strategy has borne relatively little fruit so far and has drawn a lukewarm response from practitioners in the sector – who, if anything, have been more resentful of all the talk of their new importance as generators of national wealth (Best, 2012: 141–144).

Nevertheless, the new strategic focus placed upon the sector marks a notable change in a country where governments have been among the most conservative in the region in their attitudes towards popular cultural forms and their potential as a pillar of national development. As elsewhere in the region, this situation is a legacy of the country's colonial history and the negative attitudes that it left amongst the county's elite towards popular cultural forms. For its part, the cultural sector has traditionally had little grounding in the conceptual and practical aspects of Barbadian, regional and world entertainment culture

Important initiatives were driven forward by Prime Minister Owen Arthur, who took on personal control of the Ministry of Culture in 2001. These included the creation of a National Task Force on Cultural Industries (NTFCI), which in 2004 recommended an overhaul of "the entire environment within which the cultural industries subsist in the country" (NTFCI, 2004). The NTFCI stressed the need for active involvement on the part of the Barbadian government to preserve policy space for the development of the sector and seek forms of international assistance through the new cultural diversity Convention being drafted at UNESCO (NTFCI, 2004), and this also moved PM Arthur to take an active stance on this issue in the negotiations with the EU over the EPA (Jessop, 2008).

The trajectory of the National Cultural Foundation (NCF) of Barbados is indicative of the shift that has been underway in the management of the cultural sector in this period: initially established as a statutory body in 1983 to oversee cultural affairs (focusing primarily on community engagement and development through seven community centres around the island), over the 2000s its management structure and the focus of its activities have become increasingly entrepreneurial and commercially focused (coming to manage and promote many of the island's major cultural events and festivals for example) in recognition of the new role and expanded focus on the cultural and creative industries in national and international policy (NCF, 2010).

This shift in the work of the NCF is reflective of a broader shift from the kinds of measures that characterised cultural reform in the decades following independence (in 1966), which had the broad aim to bring about the kind of "democratic expansion" of the fields of activity within the ambit of government that was one of the defining features of cultural policy in the second half of the twentieth century (see Chapter 2; Bennett, 1998). Such measures sought as their primary aim to address biases of symbolic representation in the conventional theatres and "contact zones" of national cultural formation – museums, art galleries, radio broadcasting, and so on. As an example we might refer to the measures taken at the National Museum in the 1980s after the Barbadian government required it to improve its function as what it described as "an instrument of national identity" and an "institution in the service of national development": alongside changes to make administration and staffing policy more representative of the makeup of Barbadian society, the key emphasis of this policy was to reorder the museum's privileging of the lifestyles and paraphernalia associated with the European merchant and plantation class by increasing the visibility of previously overlooked and marginalised stories and artefacts in the national historical record (survivals of African material culture; the historical records of slaves, plantation workers, peasant farmers and fishermen; traditional and vernacular crafts, architecture and means of transportation, and so on) (Barbados Ministry of Information, 1982; Cannizzo, 1987). These measures were also to be taken beyond the museum through public mobile exhibits, radio broadcasts and school tours, and therefore overlapping with the earlier work of the NCF in the island's community centres.

If we follow the analysis of these measures in the terms used by Cannizzo (1987), cultural policy here sought to operate on culture as a distinct plane or arena for assembling an authoritative ideology and "visual schematic image" of the Barbadian social order consonant with the national developmentalism of the era. The measures being introduced today, by contrast, seek to operate on a number of different planes: they not only seek to give governmental and commercial attention to a wider field of cultural activities but also to dissolve traditional boundaries between industrial, trade, human resources and cultural policies in order to harness the potential of those activities as a source of comparative advantage, capital accumulation and social inclusion for the challenges being posed by the new global economy. In the process, it is hoped that this can contribute to broader social aims by boosting revenues and providing new sources of employment and productive activity, particularly among the young and the working class whose situation in the process of restructuring and the ongoing demise of the traditional plantation economy has emerged as a particular concern. There is also a broader international concern, expressed in the discourses and ideologies of cultural diversity and cultural development, to expand the representation of Barbadian culture within the international marketplace and to add to the momentum of the broader cultural diversity agenda.

A number of areas are seen as particularly ripe for export development, notably fashion, the visual and performing arts, and musical and audiovisual production – particularly where these can be developed through spin-offs from the annual Crop Over Festival. Originally held to celebrate the end of the sugar cane harvest during the colonial period, Crop Over has been transformed since the 1990s to become a significant source of revenue in its own right, bringing in US$50 million in a four week period in 2001 and expanding yearly since then to become one of the major commercial festivals in the region (Walcott, 2007; NCF, 2010; Best 2012: 131–132).

A driving force in the attempts to articulate this new strategy in Barbados is recognition of the country's relative lack of natural resources and the need to "recognize and nurture human creativity and expression (cultural capital), as one of its most valuable assets/resources worthy of significant and long term investment" (NTFCI, 2004: 69). This sense has been heightened in light of the negotiation and completion of the EPA, adding pressure for such arguments to flow through into policy as part of the search for new sources of economic advantage. In 2009 the new Barbadian PM David Thompson (cited in Lashley, 2009) announced the completion of the drafting of the country's new cultural policy and noted that its central objective is to cement the role of culture as a pillar of economic development ("just like you have the sugar industry or manu- facturing sector, international business or the tourism sector") that can support the work of the administration's youth projects and the broader efforts now underway to develop post-Lomé generators of income, employment and foreign exchange. The focus of the policy and its accompanying legislation (the Cul- tural Industries Development Act, which eventually entered into force in 2015 after a series of delays) is on generating domestic cultural entrepreneurship through a variety of measures in education (developing creativity, awareness of issues related to intellectual property and cultural enterprise management, careers in the cultural sector), legal and tax incentives (notably income tax con- cessions for approved projects, as well as the removal of certain duties on inputs into the cultural industries, particularly where these result in the generation of foreign exchange earnings) and the encouragement of private sector support (in particular through seeking co-productions and making better use of diasporic linkages, particularly in the UK) (for further detail see Parliament of Barbados, 2013; Deane, 2015).

The development of this strategy is also seen to require a number of social and attitudinal changes. In diversifying from tropical agriculture, there is a need to tap into and mobilise what is described as an "innate, distinctive and creative capacity" to be found among the young and the working class who, it was pointed out by the cultural minister in 2006, should no longer be motivated "[only] to make a living or to survive and especially in a seasonal context, but they need to be motivated to think in terms of wealth creation" (Atherley, 2006: 5). At the same time, however, it is this focus on acknowledging and har- nessing the immaterial and creative potential of hitherto neglected and mar- ginal activities in Barbadian society that poses one of the most difficult challenges for those now seeking to expand the cultural sector. Indeed, this focus is seen to set the cultural industries apart from other sectors of economic activity such as insurance, banking or construction:

> [In these industries] enormous levels of capital are necessary when you come to the table; and therefore the class which is allowed to benefit with respect to those areas of economic enterprise and endeavour is the capital class, those who have it. With respect to the cultural industries the story is different … when we talk about the development of cultural industries, we need to speak in terms of wealth creation at the level of the working class.
>
> (Atherley, 2006: 4–5)

On the face of it, such statements appear to reinforce Yúdice's observations regarding the role that the discourse of cultural diversity has come to play as a point of reference in the neoliberal context, emerging as a response to the effects of trade liberalisation for those bearing the brunt of restructuring whose value has come to be measured in terms of their cultural identity (Yúdice, 2003: 251; Chapter 2). The new cultural policy also reiterates an essentially neoliberal emphasis on the expansion of those technologies of government aimed at transforming the conduct of potentially burdensome populations into wealth creators and "entrepreneurs of the self", in a move which is presented as being socially progressive.

It is equally important to note, however, that very few of the initiatives underway in Barbados since the 2000s have actually been translated into substantive action on the part of government, the cultural sector or civil society. Alongside this slow and shallow process of implementation there has been very little involvement of Barbadian society and the majority of those involved in the cultural sector, who generally have little sense that they are involved in an activity that is of economic value or interest to policymakers. In light of this, the NCF and Commonwealth Foundation have led calls for public awareness campaigns to address the general lack of knowledge and interest that there has been for the Convention and the cultural diversity agenda more broadly (Commonwealth Foundation and NCF, 2008). However, this simply highlights the fact that the attempts to articulate a new strategy of cultural development have largely been an initiative reflective of international and elite concerns with little input from practitioners. This has generated a sense among many within the sector that the discourse of the cultural and creative industries has been of more concern to a handful of policymakers and the few stakeholding companies, and their interlocking directorships, that control and manage the Barbadian economy (Best, 2012: 141).

This situation came to be compounded over the 2000s as the two major political parties looked to draw on popular music and entertainment as part of their political campaigns, particularly the governing Barbados Labour Party as they have made the case for an elevated social and economic role for music and entertainment as a means for coping with the "harsh global realities" of the early twenty-first century and the implications of the EPA. The result has been the cultivation of linkages between the government and a relatively small troupe of performers while many artists have consciously kept themselves at a distance from the official arts and entertainment sector and the governmental discourse of the expansion of the cultural industries, particularly where this involves being subjected to the continued censure directed against what are perceived to be the transgressive and risqué content of forms, such as reggae and dancehall, that are popular amongst the young in the country (Best, 2012: 130–144).

A similarly slow pattern and rate of progress is evident in the steps that have been taken in Trinidad & Tobago, which is one of five ACP countries (along with Fiji, Mozambique, Senegal and Zambia) to have taken part in a pilot project for cultural and creative industry development, funded by the European Commission as part of the EPA adjustment and implemented jointly by the ILO, UNCTAD and UNESCO between 2008 and 2011. The aim of this project is to strengthen the trade and employment contributions of the cultural sector through policy guidance and entrepreneurship training – what UNESCO has described as "the first large-scale poverty-reduction initiative targeting the creative industries in developing countries" (UNESCO, 2010b). The key message for Trinbagonian policymakers and stakeholders in consultations with UNESCO is the need to build a sustained advantage in sectors such as film production, music and tourism by deploying the "biggest asset [which] is our rich, diverse and warm culture" (Joseph, 2009). This work has been undertaken alongside export diversification strategies targeting the film industry (SCBD, 2005), the music and entertainment industry (SCBD, 2006) and culture and tourism (Nunez-Tesheira, 2009; Joseph, 2009) in light of the expiration of Lomé and the country's dependence on depleting reserves of oil and gas. Again, the emphasis is on the ways in which these sectors are poised to capitalise on the international appeal of the country's cultural resources, and the expanding participation by the young in music and entertainment (SCBD, 2006: 8–9).

So far, however, there are few measures comparable to those that have been developed by Barbados, although responses by the Trinbagonian government – such as the formation of the Trinidad & Tobago Film Company (TTFC) in 2006 – have had some success and led to the country's strategies being seen as a potential model for wider adoption across the region (see, for example, Nurse *et al.*, 2006: 8, 65–67; Farrell, 2010). In contrast to Barbados, however, where measures are aimed at developing domestic capacity in production, the Trinbagonian strategy is aimed more at developing an incentives regime to attract international producers (the introduction of the TTFC's Production Expenditure Rebate Program, for example, provides cash rebates of up to 30% for expenditures accrued while filming in the country).[17] A similar set of fiscal incentives in the audio-visual sector are offered to international producers by Jamaica, and have now also been drawn up by the Dominican Republic.

Despite such measures, it should be emphasised that capacity in audiovisual production generally remains thin and concentrated among a handful of CARICOM countries, a factor which is likely to be important when it comes to seeking forms of international co-productions and assistance, which tend to favour more established operations. Of the three awards that went to the Caribbean region in 2009 under the EU–ACP Film Fund, for example, it is indicative that these went to proposals from partnerships involving groups working across Jamaica, Trinidad & Tobago, Barbados and the UK (CEDA, 2009).

Industry and civil society responses

The interest that has been expressed in the EPA by industry and civil society groups in the region has largely come from a cluster of lobby groups and industry associations that have formed in the region over the last decade, such as the Caribbean CCD, CCIBN, CaMINO and CAN (considered earlier), as well as more established groups such as the Caribbean Copyright Link (CCL).[18] Together these groups can be considered to form a Caribbean "cultural milieu" (see Chapter 5) that have come to hold a stake in the widening of support behind the international cultural diversity agenda in the region and the activation of the cultural provisions in the EPA. As such, they tend to represent a particular vision of cultural diversity rooted in the interests of the cultural sector: as the co-chairman of CaMINO noted following the group's inauguration in 2009, although in principle it is "open to everyone that has a stake in the music industry", he qualified this by adding that "it is more focused on entrepreneurs and business people" (*Jamaica Gleaner*, 2009).

In this respect, the Caribbean cultural milieu have not only positioned themselves as models of reform for the kinds of subjects that are required as part of the reordering of the Caribbean political economy, but they have also brought into relief some of the features of a new cultural politics in the region as the cultural domain is being redefined as an object of political and commercial attention. In this context a political opening has been created for hitherto neglected cultural practitioners articulating claims to recognition through the discourses of accelerated internal restructuring and reform, intellectual property formation and entry into international circuits of production and distribution. However, if these are symptoms of the emergence of a regime of "cultural power" in the region, as we earlier saw formulated by Yúdice (see Chapter 2), then they need to be put in the context of what is otherwise a general indifference towards its realm. Cultural power as it is formulated by Yúdice as a performative field of force can only extend as far as the call to perform, and so far this has barely carried beyond a relatively small group of regional and international agencies, political representatives and industry stakeholders clustered around the cultural provisions that formed part of the pact between the CRNM and the European Commission in the EPA.

This point can be developed by returning to consider the opposition that there has been to the EPA from civil society across the region. For those involved in the Bare APE (Block the EPA) coalition in Haiti, for example – where worker and peasant organisations were joined by groups such as the Dahomey Dance Troupe, the peasant musical group AWOZAM, artists from the Chandèl organisation for popular education and awareness, musicians from the popular protest group Boukman Eksperyans – the cultural provisions contained in the EPA were not even the "fairy tale" referred to earlier by sceptical industry representatives from the CCIBN but were received instead as part of an ongoing bid to assert imperial authority in the region. As they have sought to point out in their campaign, for all the EPA's gestures towards cooperation, its basic contribution to the region has been to further the aggressive international strategy that has been pursued in the region in the neoliberal period (Haiti Support Group, 2007). The international programme of restructuring in Haiti since the 1990s has involved reconfiguring the country's place within the global political economy through the deliberate destruction of agriculture to provide an urban wage labour force for export-oriented assembly plants and sweatshops (which, like culture today, were then hailed as a new basis of comparative advantage for Haiti and much of the rest of the Caribbean basin) (Shamsie, 2009; Heron, 2006; Edmonds, 2010). The fruit of these policies was an intensification of poverty and hunger, prompting a level of political mobilisation against the established order that was met by a coup and counterinsurgency campaign sponsored by the US, France and Canada (Hallward, 2008; Haiti Support Group, 2007). These experiences over the last two decades have been a driving influence on those involved in the Bare APE protests. As they set out in their joint statement addressing the EPA:

> We cannot accept a continuation along the same path. Agreements like the EPA will accelerate the destruction of our economy.... It is clear that this agreement represents a threat to food sovereignty of ACP countries by leading to an extension of the practice of large monoculture plantations. The brutal proletarianization of an important part of the small peasantry will cause social problems on a large scale. Why jeopardize the future of more than 60% of the Haitian population to satisfy the desire of the European powers?
>
> (Haiti Support Group, 2007)

The response from groups such as Bare APE helps to bring some perspective to the analysis of the cultural provisions in the EPA. By including the cultural sector as part of the bargaining repertoire in the EPA negotiations, and offering the "sweetener" of market access and assistance (to what is a relatively small group of stakeholders in the region), culture has become part of such struggles and calculations over who will bear the brunt of economic restructuring and liberalisation. In this sense we might say that the expediency of culture, as it has been written into the framework of the EPA, lies most significantly in the role that it has played in forging a new sphere of mutual political and economic interest between the EU and the CARIFORUM as the traditional colonial linkages and alliances based on tropical commodity preference have been phased out. For European negotiators the cultural provisions have offered a bargaining chip to gain significant market access in other areas and secure precedents for future negotiations, while also widening the formal legal and political recognition of the exceptional place of the audiovisual sector in international trade (which was, after all, the objective that has been set out in the Directive for the EPA negotiations that was approved by the European Council in 2002; see Chapter 5). For the CRNM, the cultural provisions have presented an opportune solution to the contemporary imperatives of diversification and the search for new domestic levers of wealth creation and social management, as well as offering a trophy concession that could be presented in the face of the widespread criticism and hostility in the region directed at the agreement and its implementation. Unlike in China, where the contemporary industrialisation of culture is part of a strategy to put the country on a level footing with the most powerful countries, in the Caribbean it is more of a reflection of the region's ongoing subordination in the world order.

Summary

In this chapter we began by putting the cultural provisions to be found in the EPA in the context of the asymmetrical nature of the relations between the EU and the CARIFORUM. The special measures reserved for culture sit alongside a range of provisions in a way which is broadly reflective of the strategic priorities of European negotiators pursuing market access in the region as well as precedents for future liberalisation in light of the ongoing WTO deadlock. The main contribution of the Protocol on Cultural Cooperation in this context has been as a "sweetener" in the conclusion and implementation of the agreement, and reflects in particular the EU's ongoing concern to widen the authority behind the cultural exception in the context of trade regulation. As Souyri-Desrousier (2014: 212) summarises in an overview of the EU's formulation of such Protocols so far, they have been promoted as a means of encouraging trade partners to ratify and implement the Convention, whilst also broadening the scope of the community that shares the same conception of cultural diversity.

At the same time, however, the EPA negotiations have provided an opportunity for Caribbean negotiators to extract some concessions from the EU on cultural development, bolstered by some of the cooperation and development provisions of the UNESCO Convention and taking advantage of the EU's own sense of urgency to move early with the Convention's implementation and the completion of a first EPA within the ACP. Subsequently, a vanguard of regional and national administrations, professionals and industry representatives in the region, working closely with international agencies and assistance, have sought to sensitise the region to the potential of culture as a resource and are beginning to develop measures that can be used to manage it as a viable, outward-looking sector as part of the search for solutions to some of the challenges associated with the demise of traditional exports and heightened international competition in other areas.

In this way we have seen some indications of a transformation in the role of culture in a form which is broadly consistent with the episteme of culture as resource: less concerned with the modern project of forming civilised subjects of the nation (although this of course remains important, as we have seen in the case of Jamaica, for example) than with the formation of entrepreneurial, marketable identities and forms of intellectual property. As a concern of government, the cultural field has tended to lose its distinction here as it has become part of the expertise and repertoire of the new political economy which, while seeking to overcome some of the limitations of traditional colonial and elite attitudes concerning political and economic investment in the region's popular cultural forms, also, of course, draws up its own hierarchies and grids of value that set out which kinds of conduct are to be assigned a reforming role and which are to be targeted as objects of reform.

However, it is also worth reiterating that these developments have ultimately been contingent upon the strategic priorities of the EU as well as wider changes in the international political economy. The strategy of culture as a resource for development appears precarious in the region due not only to superficial levels of social and political commitment but also because the EPA demonstrates the continued dependency of development strategies upon the paths taken by the major international players and the fortunes of the global political economy. It is worth remembering that, relatively recently, the future competitive advantage of much of the Caribbean, reinforced by international advice, was seen to lie in its ability to provide attractive regulatory environments and low-cost labour for assembly plants servicing the globalising textile and garment industries. This strategy has proven increasingly futile given the combination of the phasing out of the Multifibre Agreement and intensified international competition from East Asia. In addition, following the completion of the EPA the EU soon reneged on commitments made to CARIFORUM in assisting with major adjustments in agriculture and concessions in areas such as rum production, while striking trade deals with Peru and Colombia that, in the words of one former ACP negotiator, confirmed the European Commission's calculated move to "sell the Caribbean banana industry down the river" (Walker, 2010).[19] In response, a number of stakeholders that had formerly highlighted the potential that the cultural provisions in the EPA had for transforming the basis of the region's political economy are now expressing doubts over the substance of the EPA's provisions on development and cooperation, as well as the commitment from CARIFORUM and EU governments to see them through (*Inter Press Service*, 2010a; 2010b; Jessop, 2015).

In this context it is unsurprising that doubts are emerging about the utility of the cultural provisions in the EPA, including UNESCO representatives who have expressed unease over the way in which the region's governments have, in the words of UNESCO's Caribbean Culture Consultant Kris Rampersad, had "the wool pulled over their eyes" (cited in OneCaribbeanLtd, 2010). It remains unclear, for example, how exactly the preferential access and co-production arrangements that have been cited as a breakthrough provision of the Protocol can bring any substantially new gains in this context. Confusion on these points arose during a CARIFORUM-EU business forum responding to the conclusion of the EPA, where it was pointed out to the region's producers by one European delegate that co-productions in the cinematographic and audiovisual sector are not a European competence since they are bilateral agreements "under which a state gives advantage to another state and vice-et-versa. A co-production agreement is sometimes settled for political reasons and their 'raison d'être' is therefore sometimes mysterious" (Thiec, 2009). In practice, this is likely to mean that any co-production arrangements will likely come with certain strings attached. One of the few precedents to refer to in co-production arrangements between the regions involves Jamaica and the UK, which predates the EPA: the original advantage of this arrangement was that Jamaican producers would be able to benefit from international cooperation and market access while being eligible to access British funds such as those available from the Lottery Fund and the Film Council. However, some of the funds in the Jamaica-UK agreement subsequently became restricted to acquiring British goods and services as well as requiring the filming to be done in England (Nurse *et al.*, 2006: 69–70).

Finally, we should also take note of the fact that the original aims of those who initialled the campaign at UNESCO have taken an unintended turn in the EPA. Although the leaders of the international cultural diversity agenda in Europe and Canada have generally welcomed the progress that has been made through the inclusion of such Protocols in trade agreements as a way of widening the international legitimacy and application of the Convention, they have also expressed concern over the precedent that has been established of using culture as a bargaining chip in brokering such deals – particularly where this involves countries and regions with more developed cultural sectors (such as South Korea, which represents more of a competitive threat to European stakeholders than the Caribbean region). As such concerns have caused EU negotiators to revise their stance, and as the negotiations with the other ACP regions have continued to stall, it is therefore unclear whether the new "blueprint for cultural development" will extend much beyond the CARIFORUM EPA. Its momentum has already lost support among the key stakeholders in Europe, and if the Protocol was intended as a showcase of implementation of the Convention's provisions on development, as was widely suggested following its completion, then so far it has hardly offered an attractive proposition for other regions looking to gain something from trade and development relations with Europe.

Notes

1 These 15 countries are: Antigua & Barbuda, the Bahamas, Barbados, Belize, Dominica, the Dominican Republic, Grenada, Guyana, Haiti, Jamaica, St. Kitts & Nevis, St. Lucia, St. Vincent & the Grenadines, Suriname and Trinidad & Tobago. Haiti did not sign the EPA until December 2009. Cuba is formally part of the Caribbean Community of states but does not participate in the CARIFORUM and therefore had no part in the EPA negotiations.

2 For analysis of the broader failure to conclude EPAs across the ACP, see Heron (2014). For up-to-date overviews and analyses of the state of the play of the EPA negotiations, see http://ec.europa.eu/trade/policy/countries-and-regions/development/economic-partnerships/ and www.bilaterals.org/spip.php?rubrique17.

3 The Trade DG's explanation of the Protocol was referred to in a hearing on the implementation of the Convention at the European Parliament, 27 February 2008.

4 See, for example, Brewster *et al.* (2008); Canterbury (2009); Gallagher (2008); Gordon (2007); Heron (2009); Haiti Support Group (2007); World Development Movement (2010).

5 The CRNM refers to the team of negotiators that worked on behalf of the Caribbean states during the EPA negotiations. The CRNM became absorbed within the Caribbean Community Secretariat in 2009 as the "Office of Trade Negotiations" (OTN). For clarity I refer throughout to the CRNM, which includes its work as the OTN.

6 This is a European-based trade, development and investment consultancy focused on the Caribbean and Central American region. Available online at www.caribbean-council.org/.

7 For details on these programmes see, respectively, www.acpcultures.eu and www.acp-films.eu.

8 This latter provision on Recreational, Cultural and Sporting Services (Other than Audiovisual) covers, among others: theatre; live bands and circus services; news agency services and library; and archive and museum services. For more details see CARIFORUM–EU (2008: 1770–1772).

9 The improved access requires that Caribbean applicants for entry to the EU have completed a "bona fide contract" to supply an entertainment service, and that they fulfil the same criteria as other Caribbean business professionals that are granted improved access to the EU. As Girvan (2009b) has pointed out, this grants new access to Caribbean professionals, but there is also a double standard here in that the FTA mandates the countries of the Caribbean to open the majority of their markets to imports of European goods and employees of European firms, while reserving Europe's right to maintain tight restrictions on the inflow of Caribbean workers and visitors.

10 The Culture Programme was established by the Commonwealth's civil society arm, the Commonwealth Foundation, in 2005 in light of the adoption of the Convention at UNESCO.

11 PRO€INVEST is an EU–ACP partnership programme administered by the European Commission as part of the EDF. TRINNEX is a project under PRO€INVEST aimed at facilitating trade and investment. The stated objective of PRO€INVEST is to assist the ACP countries in adjusting to the EPA transition by promoting investment and technology flows to enterprises operating within key sectors in ACP countries. With a total budget of €110 million over seven years, however, it appears miniscule compared to the likely adjustment and implementation costs (which one study has placed close to €1 billion for the Caribbean region alone (Heron, 2009: 27)). For more information on these programmes see www.proinvest-eu.org.

12 UNCTAD has calculated the recorded musical product of Jamaica, in the main reggae music, to have had a worldwide wholesale value of at least US$1.2 billion in 1994 whilst exports of recorded music from Jamaica itself totalled a relatively minuscule US$291,000. A WIPO study commissioned by the Jamaican government to look into the economic contribution of copyright-based industries calculated that in 2005 they contributed 4.8% to GDP: this is not only a higher proportion than in countries such as Canada, but it could also be significantly higher if the country's informal activities in music, entertainment and related sectors were more effectively managed (Daley and Foga, 2009).

13 See, respectively, www.creativeindustriesexchange.com and CARICOM (2008).

14 In his analysis of the problems facing the Caribbean film industry, Warner (2005: 246–248) notes that the historical reluctance of the Caribbean's middle and upper classes to support popular forms stems from the fact that they were cultural expressions closely associated with the African-descended lower classes. As a result, those in control had always "admiringly turned their attention to extra-Caribbean cultures, and fed themselves and the lower classes a diet of things foreign". Perry Henzell's *The Harder They Come* (1972) remains the only feature film from the region to achieve anything close to international acclaim (even if its commercial success was extremely limited by Hollywood standards) and has widely been seen as a launchpad for reggae music's international popularity (despite, again, the distaste with which the film was generally received by the Jamaican middle and upper classes). As such, it has come to stand as a symbol of the potential of the film industry in the region.

15 "Riddim" here refers to a particular configuration of drums and bass that form the distinctive rhythmic composition or "DNA" of a piece of reggae music (or one of its derivative genres). Ironically, Jamaican musicologist and producer Dermot Hussey once remarked that "you can copyright a song, but you can't copyright a rhythm".

16 See the JBC's Directives on the Transmission of Explicit Sexual Content, the Transmission of Soca/Calypso Content and the Transmission of Violent Content (www.broadcastingcommission.org/broadcasting_laws_regulations_codes). The Commission's

Chairman has since also called for the government to amend the 1946 Television and Sound Broadcasting Regulation Act to take into account

> requirements around playlists and music sheets; vetting and approval of songs by station managers prior to transmission by DJs; non-transmission of songs that condone or encourage hostility or violence; the encouragement or glamourising of use of illegal drugs or misuse of alcohol.
>
> (JBC Chairman Dr. Hopeton Dunn, cited in *Inter Press Service*, 2009)

Critics of the directives in Jamaica and beyond have cried censorship and reaction towards what is, after all, just another in a long tradition of rapidly shifting music and dance crazes (for examples of commentary see Tutweiler, 2009; Evans, 2007). In the British press one commentator suggested ironically that:

> With naughty behaviour inspiring much of the past 50 years of popular music, there may not be much left on Jamaican radio by the time the Broadcasting Commission has its way. We can imagine the charts now – a little classical music, part of Tiny Tim's discography, and some soca tunes about taxes.
>
> (*Guardian*, 2009)

17 For information on the work of TTFC, see www.trinidadandtobagofilm.com.
18 This is an umbrella organisation for the region's copyright management that was founded with the assistance of WIPO in 2000 by the Caribbean's four major CMOs (from Trinidad & Tobago, Jamaica, Barbados and St. Lucia) concerned in particular to establish some form of region-wide collective management infrastructure in the music industry. It has been estimated that the CCL's members represent approximately 5,300 writers, performers, producers and publishers (CARICOM, 2010).
19 As the former Caribbean diplomat, Ron Sanders, has noted: "Informed observers in Europe are convinced that the European Commissioners believe that Caribbean governments are supine and therefore the EU can carry on stitching-up deals with Latin America that leave the Caribbean on the sidelines" (Sanders, 2010).

Bibliography

Atherley, J.J.S. 2006. "Feature Address". Caribbean Regional Negotiationg Manchinery (CRNM) Workshop on Promoting Creative Industries: A Trade and Investment Strategy of the Caribbean. Barbados, 25 October 2006. Available online at: www.crnm.org/index.php?option=com_docman&task=cat_view&gid=165&Itemid=116; accessed 20/02/2010.

Barbados Ministry of Information. 1982. *Final Report of the Museum Development Plan Committee*. Government of Barbados.

Bennett, T. 1998. *Culture: A Reformer's Science*. London: Sage.

Best, C. 2012. *The Popular Music and Entertainment Culture of Barbados: Pathways to Digital Culture*. Plymouth: Scarecrow Press, Inc.

Brewster, H. 2008. "The Anti-Development Dimension of the European Community's Economic Partnership Agreement for the Caribbean". Paper presented at the Commonwealth Secretariat High Level Technical Meeting: *EPAs: The Way Forward for the ACP*. Cape Town, South Africa. 7–8 April 2008.

Brewster, H., N. Girvan and V. Lewis. 2008. "Renegotiate the CARIFORUM EPA". *Trade Negotiations Insights*. 7(3): 8–10.

Cannizzo, J. 1987. "How sweet it is: cultural politics in Barbados". MUSE. 4(4): 22–27.

Canterbury, D.C. 2009. "European bloc imperialism". *Critical Sociology*. 35(6): 801–823.

CARICOM. 2008. "REGIONAL CULTURAL INDUSTRY TASK FORCE LAUNCHED". CARICOM Press release 313/2008, 23 October 2008. Available online at: www.caricom.org/jsp/pressreleases/pres313_08.jsp; accessed 07/01/2009.

CARICOM. 2010. "Intellectual Property Rights and the Cultural Industries in CARICOM". Presentation by Dr. Hilary Brown, CARICOM Secretariat, as part of the World Intellectual Property Day, Guyana, 26 April 2010. Available online at: www.caricom.org/jsp/community_organs/cohsod_culture/intellectual_property_rights_ cultural_industries_caricom_brown.pdf; accessed 02/05/2010.

CARIFORUM–EU. 2008. ECONOMIC PARTNERSHIP AGREEMENT between the CARIFORUM States, of the one part, and the European Community and its Member States, of the other part. Available online at: http://ec.europa.eu/trade/wider-agenda/ development/economic-partnerships/index_en.htm; accessed 07/01/2009.

CCD. 2009. "Panorama of the European Union current trade negotiations". Available online at: www.ifccd.com/sites/ifccd.com/files/20090320FicheNegosUE_En.pdf; accessed 12/01/2009.

CCIBN. 2008. "Statement by the CCIBN on the launch of the Cultural Industries Task-force". Available online at: www.tropicalfete.com/fusion_news/fullnews.php?id=1827; accessed 20/01/2009.

CCIN. 2007. "Statement from the Caribbean Cultural Industries Network on the CARIFO-RUM–EU Economic Partnership Agreement". Available online at: www.normangirvan. info/wp-content/uploads/2008/01/statement-from-the-caribbean-cultural-industries-network-on-the-cariforum-final.doc; accessed 20/01/2009.

CEDA. 2008. "EU–CARIFORUM Business Forum Launched". Caribbean Export Development Agency. Available online at: http://carib-export.com/website/index. php?option=com_content&view=article&id=253&catid=23; accessed 02/05/2010.

CEDA. 2009. "Caribbean organisations get US$440,000 under EU–ACP film programme". *Newsletter of the Caribbean Export Development Agency*. September 2009, 2(9): 5.

Chaitoo, R. 2004. "Trade Negotiations and Culture: What's at Stake?" Presentation at the CRNM/TRINNEX Workshop on The Impact of Trade and Technology on Caribbean Creative Industries. 28–29 October 2004, Port of Spain, Trinidad. Notes are available at: www.crnm.org/index.php?option=com_docman&task=cat_view&gid= 166&Itemid=116; accessed 20/01/2009.

Commonwealth Foundation & NCF. 2008. "Culture, cultural policy and identity: the case of Barbados". Consultation held in partnership with the National Cultural Foundation of Barbados, St. James, Barbados, 9 July 2008. Available online at: www.commonwealth-foundation.com/uploads/fckeditor/00000076_Culture,%20cultural%20policy%20 and%20identity%20-%20the%20case%20of%20Barbados.pdf; accessed 20/01/2009.

Council of the European Union, 2008. *Council conclusions on the promotion of cultural diversity and intercultural dialogue in the external relations of the union and its member states*. Brussels: European Union. Available online at: www.consilium.europa.eu/ uedocs/cms_data/docs/pressdata/en/educ/104189.pdf; accessed 13/07/2015.

Creighton, A. 2010. "Cultural Industries". *Stabroek News*. 28 March 2010.

CRNM. 2004. "SUMMARY OF KEY ISSUES AND RECOMMENDATIONS". CRNM/TRINNEX Workshop on the Impact of Trade and Technology on Caribbean Creative Industries. 28–29 October 2004, Port of Spain, Trinidad. Available online at: www.crnm.org/index.php?option=com_docman&task=cat_view&gid=166&Itemid= 116; accessed 20/01/2009.

CRNM. 2007. *Presentation of Study on Cultural Industries*. CRNM Press Release No. 01/2007, 23 January 2007.

CRNM. 2008. *EPA Brief: The Cariforum–EC Economic Partnership Agreement (EPA): Provisions on the Cultural Sector in the EPA*. CRNM Brief# 3200.3/EPA-03 [08].

Daley, D. and N. Foga. 2009. "Jamaica: Tapping into the value of intellectual property". In *IP Value 2009: Building and Enforcing Intellectual Property Value*. Available online at: www.fogadaley.com/articles.html; accessed 05/05/2010.

Deane, S. 2015. "Cultural Industries Development Act to take effect next month". *Barbados Today*. 27 January 2015. Available online at: www.barbadostoday.bb/2015/01/17/cultural-industries-development-act-to-take-effect-next-month/; accessed 02/10/2015.

Directorate-General for the External Policies of the Union. 2009. "The CARIFORUM-EU Economic Partnership Agreement (EPA): The development component". European Parliament, EXPO/B/DEVE/2008/60.

Edmonds, K. 2010. "Empty Promises and Empty Bellies: Bill Clinton's doubletalk on Haitian agriculture". *North American Congress on Latin America*. 17 May 2010. Available online at: https: //nacla.org/node/6576; accessed 20/05/2010.

EU–Korea. 2009. "Protocol on Cultural Cooperation". *Free Trade Agreement Between the EU and Republic of Korea*. Available online at: http://trade.ec.europa.eu/doclib/docs/2009/october/tradoc_145194.pdf; accessed 12/01/2010.

European Coalitions for Cultural Diversity. 2009. Letter addressed to the President of the European Commission, 7 May 2009. Available online at: www.filmdirectors.eu/wp-content/uploads/2009/11/Letter-Eur.-organisations-FTA-EU-Korea-7.5.091.pdf; accessed 18/05/2010.

European Commission. 2008a. Follow-Up Argumentaire: On the Culture Cooperation Protocol in Future Trade Agreements, 13 February 2008. Available online at: http://trade.ec.europa.eu/doclib/docs/2008/february/tradoc_137751.pdf; accessed 4/03/2008.

European Commission. 2008b. *European Competitiveness*. Available online at: http://ec.europa.eu/trade/creating-opportunities/trade-topics/european-competitiveness/; accessed 12/01/2009.

Evans, T. 2007. "Reggae Compassionate Act needs revision: Harsh words from Freddie McGregor". *ttgapers.com*. 30 June 2007. Available online at: www.ttgapers.com/News/2007/6/30/reggae-compassionate-act-needs-revision/; accessed 05/06/2009.

Farrell, T.W. 2010. "Caribbean Identity and the Development of the Creative Audio-Visual Industry: A Proposal". Paper presented to the One Caribbean Media/Caribbean Tales Symposium on The Production and Global Distribution of Caribbean Video and Film, The Best of Caribbean Tales Film Festival, Barbados, February 2010.

FERA. 2008. "EUROPEAN UNION TRADE AGREEMENT NEGOCIATIONS PROTOCOL FOR CULTURAL COOPERATION". Memo, 13 February 2008.

Gallagher, P. 2008. "Understanding developing country resistance to the Doha Round". *Review of International Political Economy*. 15(1): 62–85.

Gilroy, P. 1987. *There Ain't No Black in the Union Jack*. Chicago: University of Chicago Press.

Girvan, N. 2008. "Implications of the CARIFORUM–EC EPA". Caribbean Policy Development Centre. Available online at: www.cpdcngo.org/IMG/pdf/girvanimplicationsepa21jan.pdf; accessed 07/01/2009.

Girvan, N. 2009a. "The Caribbean EPA Affair: Lessons For The Progressive Movement". Paper presented at conference on Remembering the Future: The Legacies of Radical Politics in the Caribbean. University of Pittsburgh, Centre for Latin American and Caribbean Studies, 3–4 April 2009.

Girvan, N. 2009b. "The great visa divide". *Trinidad & Tobago Review*. 2 March 2009.

Girvan, N. 2013. "Technification, Sweetification, Treatyfication: Politics of the Caribbean-EU Economic Partnership Agreement". In Puri, S. (ed.). *The Legacies of Radical Caribbean Politics*. Oxon: Routledge.

Goodison, P. 2007. "EU Trade Policy & the Future of Africa's Trade Relationship with the EU". *African Political Economy*. 34(112): 247–266.

Gordon, C. 2007. "Culture and the European Union in a Global Context". *The Journal of Arts Management, Law and Society*. 37(1).

Guardian. 2007, 14 June. "Beenie Man, Sizzla and Capleton renounce homophobia".

Guardian. 2009, 24 February. "No sex please, we're Jamaican".

Haiti Support Group. 2007. Declaration of the Haitian coalition, "Block the EPA" ("Bare APE" in Creole), in the context of Haiti's participation in the negotiation of Partnership Agreements between the European Union and the ACP countries. Port-au-Prince, 17 October 2007. Available online at: www.haitisupport.gn.apc.org/EPA. html; accessed 14/04/2008.

Hallward, P. 2008. *Damming the Flood: Haiti, Aristide and the Politics of Containment*. London: Verso.

Hendrickson, M., B. Lugay, E. Perez Caldentey, N. Mulder and M. Alvarez. 2012. *Creative industries in the Caribbean: a new road for diversification and export growth*. ECLAC: Port of Spain. Available online at: http://repositorio.cepal.org/bitstream/handle/11362/5049/S2012619_en.pdf?sequence=1; accessed 30/09/2015.

Heron, T. 2006. "An Unravelling Development Strategy? Textile Assembly in the Caribbean Basin After the Multifibre Arrangement". *Bulletin of Latin American Research*. 25(2): 264–281.

Heron, T. 2009. "Understanding the CARIFORUM-EU Economic Partnership Agreement". Paper presented to the British International Studies Association annual conference, University of Leicester, UK, 14–16 December 2009.

Heron, T. 2014. "Trading in development: Norms and institutions in the making/unmaking of European Union-African, Caribbean and Pacific trade and development cooperation". *Contemporary Politics*. 20(1): 10–22.

Hurt, S. 2010. "Understanding EU Development Policy: History, Global Context and Self Interest?" *Third World Quarterly*. 31(1): 159–168.

IFCCD. 2008. "EU Cites UNESCO Convention in Embedding Cultural Cooperation Protocol in Trade Pacts". International Federation of Coalitions for Cultural Diversity. Available online at: www.ifccd.com/content/eu-cites-unesco-convention-embedding-cultural-cooperation-protocol-trade-pacts; accessed 12/12/2009.

IFCCD. 2010. "French Government Paper Argues for Reconsideration of EU Cultural Cooperation Protocol model". International Federation of Coalitions for Cultural Diversity. Available online at: www.ifccd.com/content/french-government-paper-argues-reconsideration-eu-cultural-cooperation-protocol-model; accessed 05/05/2010.

Inter Press Service. 2009, 11 February. "Women cheer ban on sexually degrading song lyrics".

Inter Press Service. 2010a, 13 May. "Verdict still out on trade pact with Europe".

Inter Press Service. 2010b, 8 April. "Caribbean Questions EU Development Pledges".

Isar, Y.R. 2015. "Culture in EU external relations': an idea whose time has come?" *International Journal of Cultural Policy*. 21(4): 494–508.

Jamaica Gleaner. 2009, 9 November. "Strength in numbers – Caribbean music network organisation formed". Available online at: www.jamaica-gleaner.com/gleaner/20091109/ent/ent1.html; accessed 12/12/2009.

Jamaica Information Service. 2009. "PM Calls for Meeting to Address Concerns of Music Industry". Office of the Prime Minister, 10 February 2009. Available online at: www. jis.gov.jm/officePM/html/20090210T100000-0500_18399_JIS_PM_CALLS_FOR_MEETING_TO_ADDRESS_CONCERNS_OF_MUSIC_INDUSTRY.asp; accessed 05/06/2009.

Jamaica Observer. 2007, 8 July. "Golding says 'no' to homosexuality". Available online at: www.jamaicaobserver.com/news/125077_Golding-says-no-to-homosexuality; 05/06/2009.

Jamaica Observer. 2010, 9 April. "Visa woes taint music industry". Available online at: www. jamaicaobserver.com/entertainment/visa-sinks-industry_7524306; accessed 11/05/2010.

Jamaicans. 2007, 14 June. "Reggae stars renounce homophobia – Beenie Man, Sizzla and Capleton sign deal". Available online at: www.jamaicans.com/news/announcements/Reggaestarsrenouncehomophobia062007.shtml; accessed 05/06/2009.

JAMPRO. 1996. *Marketing Plan for Music and Entertainment, 1996/1997.* Kingston: Jamaica Promotions.

Jessop, D. 2008. "Understanding the EPA: Cultural Services". Caribbean Council. Available online at: www.crnm.org/documents/ACP_EU_EPA/epa_agreement/Understanding_the_EPA_Cultural_Services%20_by_David_Jessop.pdf; accessed 12/12/2009.

Jessop, D. 2015. "Time to shake up EPA arrangements". Caribbean Council. Available online at: www.caribbean-council.org/time-shake-epa-arrangements/; accessed 08/10/2015.

Joseph, D. 2009. "Culture and Tourism". *Trinidad and Tobago News.* September 28, 2009. Available online at: www.trinidadandtobagonews.com/selfnews/viewnews.cgi?newsid 1254111424,332,.shtml; accessed 14/05/2010.

Lashley, C. 2009. "Barbados to introduce new cultural industries policy". *Caribbean Net News.* 7 December 2009. Available online at: www.caribdaily.com/article/234049/barbados-to-introduce-new-cultural-industries-policy/; accessed 12/12/2009.

Lemke, T. 2003. "Comment on Nancy Fraser: rereading Foucault in the shadow of globalization". *Constellations.* 10(2): 172–179.

Leonard, J. 2009. "As the EPA Ink Dries". *ICTSD Trade Negotiations Insights.* 8(1). February 2009. Available online at: http://ictsd.org/i/news/tni/39382/; accessed 12/12/2009.

Loisen, J. and F. de Ville. 2011. "The EU-Korea Protocol on Cultural Cooperation: Toward Cultural Diversity or Cultural Deficit?" *International Journal of Communication.* 5(2011): 254–271.

Miller, B. 2006. "EPAs in Danger of Becoming Unfulfilled Promises and Expectations". Speech to the 11th Session of the ACP-EU Joint Parliamentary Assembly on the Negotiations of Economic Partnership Agreements, By The Hon. Dame Billie Miller, Chair of the ACP Ministerial Trade Committee and Minister of Foreign Affairs and Foreign Trade of Barbados, Austria Center, Vienna, 20 June 2006. Available online at: www.foreign.gov.bb; accessed 20/02/2010.

NCF. 2010. "Our Mission" and "Our History". National Cultural Foundation of Barbados. Available online at: www.ncf.bb; accessed 14/05/2010.

NTFCI. 2004. "Policy Paper to Inform the Propelling of Barbados' Creative Economy: Cultural Industries Development Strategy". Prepared by the Barbados National Task Force on Cultural Industries, Barbados, 2004. Available online at: www.barbados.gov.bb/Docs/Taskforceonculturalindustries.pdf; accessed 12/12/2009.

Nunez-Tesheira, K. 2009. "T&T's 2009/2010 Budget Statement: The text of the 2009–2010 Budget Statement as was presented in the House of Representatives on Monday, September 08, 2009, by the Minister of Finance the Honourable Karen

Nunez-Tesheira". Government of the Republic of Trinidad and Tobago. Available online at: www.trinidadandtobagonews.com/articles/070909.html; accessed 11/09/09.

Nurse, K. 2005. "Popular Culture and Cultural Industry: Identity and Commodification in Caribbean Popular Music". In Ho, C.G.T. and K. Nurse (eds) *Globalisation, Diaspora and Caribbean Popular Culture*. Kingston/Miami: Ian Randle Publishers.

Nurse, K. 2008. "The Cultural Industries and Sustainable Development in Small Island Developing States". *Creative Industries Exchange*. Available online at: http://portal.unesco.org/en/files/24726/110805219811CLT3.doc/CLT3.doc; accessed 23/03/2010.

Nurse, K., A. Demas, J. Tull, B. Paddington, W. O'Young, M. Gray, H. Hoagland and M. Reis. 2006. *The Cultural Industries in CARICOM: Trade and Development Challenges*. Report prepared for the Caribbean Regional Negotiating Machinery. Available online at: www.crnm.org; accessed 20/02/2010.

OneCaribbeanLtd. 2010. "Clear deficits in Caribbean culture policies, says UNESCO consultant". *Regional News*, 15 June 2010. Available online at: www.onecaribbeanltd.com/onecaribbeanltd/section.php?IssueID=106&SectionID=4; accessed 20/06/2010.

OPM. 1996. *Jamaican National Industry Policy*. Kingston: Office of the Prime Minister, Government of Jamaica

PACE St. Lucia. 2009. "Caribbean Audio-Visual Network is established". *Professionals in Action for Creative Enterprise*. 17 October 2009. Available online at: http://paceslu.blogspot.com/2009/10/caribbean-audio-visual-network-is.html; accessed 14/05/2010.

Parliament of Barbados. 2013. *The Cultural Industries Development Act*. Available online at: www.barbadosparliament.com/htmlarea/uploaded/File/Bills/2013/Cultural%20Industries%20Development%20Bill%202013.pdf; accessed 15/03/2014.

Patterson, J.P. 2015. Presentation by the most Hon. P.J. Patterson, ON, OCC, PC, QC on leveraging CARICOM's human, cultural and natural assets for the economic development at the community. 26th Inter-Sessional Meeting of the Conference of Heads of Government of the Caribbean Community (CARICOM), Nassau, Bahamas, 26–27 February 2015. Available online at: http://today.caricom.org/wp-content/uploads/Speech-PJ-Patterson-CARICOM-26th-Inter-Sessional-Meeting-Feby-26-27-doc-2.doc; accessed 14/10/2015.

Phillips, N. 2005. "U.S. Power and the Politics of Economic Governance in the Americas". *Latin American Politics and Society*. 47(4): 1–25.

Power, D. and D. Hallencreutz. 2004. "Profiting from creativity? The music industry in Stockholm, Sweden and Kingston, Jamaica". In Power, D. and A.J. Scott (eds) *Cultural Industries and the Production of Culture*. London: Routledge.

Radio Jamaica News. 2008, 28 August. "EPA, worst thing since slavery – NWU". Available online at: www.bilaterals.org/spip.php?article13063; accessed 16/03/2010.

RTFCI. 2009. *The Design and Impact of an Exemptions Regime for the CARICOM Cultural Industries*. Report prepared for the CARICOM Regional Task Force on Cultural Industries. Barbados: CRNM.

Sanders, R. 2010. "Caribbean rum in grave danger". *BBC Caribbean*. 29 March 2010. Available online at: www.bbc.co.uk/caribbean/news/story/2010/03/100327_sanders_caribbean_rum.shtml; accessed 02/04/2010.

SCBD. 2005. Strategic Plan for the Film Industry of Trinidad and Tobago. Final Report 3 January 2005. *The Film Industry Team of the Standing Committee on Business Development*. Available online at: www.tradeind.gov.tt/Business_Dev/Film/FilmFinalReport.pdf; accessed 15/05/2010.

SCBD. 2006. *Strategic Plan for the Entertainment Industry of Trinidad and Tobago. Final Report, 20 January 2006*. The Music and Entertainment Industry Team of The

Standing Committee on Business Development. Available online at: www.tradeind.gov.tt/Business_Dev/MusicEnt/EntertainmentFinalReport06-01-20.pdf; accessed 15/05/2010.

Shamsie, Y. 2009. "Export Processing Zones: The Purported Glimmer in Haiti's Development Murk". *Review of International Political Economy.* 16(4): 649–672.

Singh, R.J., S.P. Silva, P. Hare and K.A. Thompson. 2014. *Monitoring the implementation and results of the CARIFORUM-EU EPA Agreement: Final Report.* EUROPEAID/129783/C/SER/multi. Available online at: http://trade.ec.europa.eu/doclib/docs/2014/october/tradoc_152824.pdf; accessed 26/10/2914.

Souyri-Desrosier, C. 2014. "Chapter 14 – EU protocols on cultural cooperation: An attempt to promote and implement the CDCE within the framework of bilateral trade negotiations". In Richieri Hanania, L. (ed.). *Cultural Diversity in International Law: The Effectiveness of the UNESCO Convention on the Protection and Promotion of the Diversity of Cultural Expressions.* Oxon: Routledge.

Thiec, Y. 2009. "Reaping benefits from EPA: Promotion and partnerships for the Caribbean Services Sector in the EU markets". Presentation at the 1st CARIFORUM-EU Business Forum, 24–25 November 2008, Bridgetown, Barbados.

Trade Updates. 2008. "GOLDING: EPA promises big opportunities for reggae music". The Barbados Private Sector Trade Team. 28 May 2008. Available online at: www.tradeteam.bb/cms/pstt/files/tradeupdates/Golding%20-EPA%20Promises%20Big%20Opportunities%20for%20Reggae%20Music.pdf; accessed 20/01/2009.

Tull, J. 2009. "Counting (on) the Economics of Carnival". *Trinidad & Tobago Review.* May 2009. Available online at: http://sta-uwi.academia.edu/JoanneTull/Papers/113594/-Counting-on-the-Economics-of-Carnival; accessed 15/05/2010,

Tutweiler, A. 2009. "Dancehall reggae music: Controversy about explicit lyrics". *Suite101,* 3 June 2009. Available online at: http://reggae-dub-music.suite101.com/article.cfm/dancehall_reggae_music; accessed 05/06/2009.

UNESCO. 2004c. *Preliminary Draft Convention on the Protection and Promotion of the Diversity of Cultural Contents and Artistic Expressions.* CLT/CPD/2004/CONF.607/6. Paris UNESCO.

UNESCO. 2005. *Convention on the Protection and Promotion of the Diversity of Cultural Expressions.* CLT-2005/CONVENTION DIVERSITE-CULT REV. Paris: UNESCO. Available online at: www.unesco.org/culture/en/diversity/convention; accessed 14/03/2007.

UNESCO. 2009. "INFORMATION DOCUMENT – REFERENCE DOCUMENTS CONCERNING ARTICLE 16 OF THE CONVENTION. INTERGOVERNMENTAL COMMITTEE FOR THE PROTECTION AND PROMOTION OF THE DIVERSITY OF CULTURAL EXPRESSIONS". Circulated at the Second Extraordinary Session of the Intergovernmental Committee for the Convention, 23–25 March 2009. Paris: UNESCO. CE/09/2.EXT.IGC/208/INF.3.

UNESCO. 2010a. *UNESCO Sub-Regional Workshop on the Cultural Diversity Programming Lens.* Saint Georges, Grenada, 8–9 June 2010. Available online at: www.unesco.org/new/en/unesco/events/all-events/showUid/1861/; accessed 11/07/2010.

UNESCO. 2010b. *Strengthening the Creative Industries in Five ACP Countries Through Employment and Trade Expansion.* Paris: UNESCO. Available online at: http://portal.unesco.org/culture/en/ev.php-URL_ID=39091&URL_DO=DO_TOPIC&URL_SECTION=201.html; accessed 18/02/2010.

UNESCO. 2014. *Report prepared for the Eighth Ordinary Session of the Intergovernmental Committee for the Convention on the Protection and Promotion of the Diversity of Cultural Expressions, 9–11 December 2014.* Paris: UNESCO. CE/14/8.IGC/11. Available online at: http://en.unesco.org/creativity/sites/creativity/files/8IGC_11_impact_articles_16_et_21_fr_EN.pdf; accessed 17/08/2015.

United Nations. 2005. *Draft Mauritius Strategy for the further Implementation of the Programme of Action for the Sustainable Development of Small Island Developing States*. A/CONF.207/CRP.7 United Nations, adopted in Port Louis, Mauritius, 13 January 2005. Available online at: www.un.org/smallislands2005/pdf/sids_strategy.pdf; accessed 27/07/2007.

Vlassis, A. and L. Richieri Hanania. 2014. "Effects of the CDCE on trade negotiations". In Richieri Hanania, L. (ed.). 2014. *Cultural Diversity in International Law: The Effectiveness of the UNESCO Convention on the Protection and Promotion of the Diversity of Cultural Expressions*. Oxon: Routledge.

Walcott, I. 2007. "Export orientation and the cultural industries: The case of Barbados". Paper presented at SALISES Conference, Cascadia Hotel, Trinidad, 26–28 March 2007. Available online at: http://sta.uwi.edu/conferences/salises/documents/Walcott%20I.pdf; accessed 06/07/2007.

Walker, A. 2010, 18 May. "Caribbean banana industry decline is no slideshow". *The Guardian*. Available online at: www.theguardian.com/commentisfree/2010/may/18/decline-caribbean-banana-trade-europe; accessed 21/10/2010.

Warner, K.Q. 2005. "Is Globalisation Helping or Harming Caribbean Cinema?" In Ho, C.G.T. and K. Nurse (eds). *Globalisation, Diaspora and Caribbean Popular Culture*. Kingston/Miami: Ian Randle Publishers.

World Development Movement. 2010. "European parliamentary hearing of Europe's new trade commissioner". 18 January 2010. Available online at: www.wdm.org.uk/european-parliamentary-hearing-europe%E2%80%99s-new-trade-commissioner; accessed 20/01/2010.

Yúdice, G. 2003. *The Expediency of Culture: Uses of Culture in the Global Era*. London: Duke University Press.

7   Conclusion

After the attempts of the previous decades to find an international political consensus around a set of principles related to culture and development, the adoption of the UNESCO Convention on cultural diversity in 2005 has marked a breakthrough. The key principle upon which the instrument rests is the recognition of the unique (exceptional) status of the cultural sector and its "dual" economic and socio-political role in promoting sustainable development. This principle of the dual nature of culture has provided a productive formula for renewing North–South cooperation at UNESCO (albeit without the blessings of the US) in a way that has helped to bury some of the major political differences of the NWICO era, as well as marking a breakthrough in long-running efforts to secure a more clearly defined and concrete role for culture in national and international development strategies. UNESCO itself has also recovered some of its relevance in this period as a point of reference in the international debate, emerging from the relative wilderness years of the 1980s and 1990s to position itself at the centre of an impressive task of legal and political "rapprochement" that has accommodated a set of concerns centred on the global trade in cultural products along with the growing currency of the "anthropological" and "democratic" concepts of culture.

As we have also seen, however, the Convention's influence in practice has not matched much of the rhetoric that has surrounded its adoption and entry into force (as a new "Magna Carta" for international cultural policy and as a radical breakthrough in international cultural cooperation). While it may have produced a standard-setting instrument in the field of culture and development, and has helped to drive a number of policy changes and initiatives, the legal and policy impact of the Convention in practice has been limited. Its ability to generate an agenda around sustainable cultural development over the coming decades is also questionable, particularly as much of the governmental and civil society momentum that was generated around the cultural diversity agenda around the turn of the millennium has begun to fade. The campaign to include culture in the post-2015 Sustainable Development Goals (SDGs) has been telling in this regard, since it was hindered by the resistance and reluctance of the majority of Northern governments. The special UN thematic debates on culture and development in the period prior to the elaboration of the SDGs were marked by the absence of representatives from developed countries, including not only the US but also Canada and most of Europe. For Canada, one of the key sponsors of the UNESCO Convention, the inclusion of "a 'broad and abstract thematic' such as culture [in the SDGs] was clearly not part of [its] strategy" according to one high-ranking UN official (cited in Vlassis, 2015: 1656). For France, the other key sponsor of the Convention, the regulation of digital cultural services (in particular on-demand audiovisual media) has taken over as a key policy agenda, making the inclusion of culture in the SDGs a secondary priority and prompting France to shift its strategy in this area towards mobilising support within the OIF behind calls to adapt the UNESCO Convention to the digital era (Vlassis, 2015: 1657). Although an international civil society campaign made a case for the inclusion of a distinct goal for culture in the post-2015 SDGs,[1] this was hampered by the absence of intergovernmental support and also by the resulting decline in authority that UNESCO could now call upon in trying to rally support behind the inclusion of culture in the goals. Ultimately, no such goal for culture was included amongst the 17 SDGs and it was given only a passing mention in four of the 169 SDG targets (although in this respect it did mark an advance on the Millennium Development Goals).[2]

According to Vlassis (2015), UNESCO's bid for the inclusion of culture in the SDGs was driven less by any intergovernmental or civil society mandate than by the Secretariat's concern to advance the organisation's standing in the UN's future normative framework (and also, therefore, its ability to attract new streams of development funding), particularly in light of the holes in the budget left by the loss of US contributions in 2011 and renewed criticism now being directed at management inefficiency. Regardless of the organisation's motivations, the relatively disappointing outcome in the SDGs, as far as culture is concerned, means that UNESCO could be entering another period of relative marginalisation in the global discussion. It also makes it difficult to keep culture high on the agenda at national levels as policies and funding streams are formulated over the coming years.

Besides, it could be argued that many of the key actors that breathed life into the culture and development agenda in the 2000s at UNESCO have already secured their main objective of widening the formal recognition of the validity of the cultural exception and creating a binding treaty that has reasserted the sovereignty of national cultural policy. This core provision in the Convention reinforced "pro-culture" arguments in the context of trade negotiations and has had some impact within WTO jurisprudence relating to disputes affecting the cultural sector (although this impact is fairly limited, as has been shown in the decision on the US-China case in 2009). It has also opened up a new dynamic in trade agreements by the key sponsors of the Convention, notably through the EU's pursuit of Protocols on Cultural Cooperation – although the initial momentum behind these has also since cooled. However, many of the Convention's other provisions related more specifically to international cultural cooperation and development are less well defined and it remains unclear whether they can maintain sufficient international political support to keep them operational.

This outcome is perhaps unsurprising. On one hand, it is a consequence of the way that the negotiations over the drafting of the Convention prioritised the trade–culture issue from the beginning, tending to relegate questions of development to secondary importance. On the other hand, where concessions were extracted from developed countries in exchange for developing country support for the instrument's adoption, the resulting provisions were weak and have foundered due to subsequent lack of support and shifting priorities of governments. This has been evident most notably with the IFCD, which has struggled to attract regular contributions over time – particularly in the context of fiscal retrenchment in the North.

One of the other key development provisions in the Convention, Article 16 (which requests developed countries to offer forms of legally binding market access to developing country cultural exports and practitioners), is expressed in stronger language and, by impacting on questions of economic development and diversification, does go significantly beyond the vaguer commitments of the past to forms of international cultural cooperation. This is a point that has been received positively by Caribbean negotiators in the case of the provisions that were secured in the EU–CARIFORUM EPA. In practice, however, this provision on market access appears to have functioned as a "bargaining chip" in trade negotiations, in a way which has dampened enthusiasm – both in the North and in the South – for its application in other contexts. It is also questionable whether there is the kind of commitment to the cultural development agenda proposed in the Caribbean region that would appear to be necessary if it is to take advantage of some of the opportunities that have been opened up by preferential market access.

In this sense, the EU–CARIFORUM EPA has exposed the relatively narrow basis on which the international consensus on cultural policy in the 2000s has been struck. On one hand, it remains unclear how exactly the strategy of cultural development that has been proposed by the EU, CRNM and others in light of the EPA can benefit the region beyond a handful of countries and relatively well-positioned producers and professionals. On the other hand, the EU's commitments to cooperation and assistance appear to be contingent on its particular priorities: development provisions in the EPA are backed up with little substance and, as European negotiators have come in for criticism from key industry stakeholders in Europe for bringing culture into the sphere of trade negotiations in this way, it has put a brake on the extension of similar Protocols to other countries and regions.

The last decade has undoubtedly seen a growing involvement by much of the South in debates about the cultural and creative economy and the role that it can play within strategies of economic diversification and sustainable development. However, it also needs to be noted that these debates have taken place in very different contexts and had different effects. China has been particularly important in this regard, since it has provided an example of a sustained and relatively productive strategy to shift to a new development model based on reconceptualising culture in policy and harnessing the country's cultural resources.

This has fed into a compelling narrative being taken up across the South, reinforced by the work of agencies such as UNESCO, UNCTAD and the EU. Nevertheless, the Chinese experience is relatively unique in the extent to which it has been able to steer a course through the transformations in the global political economy of the last quarter of a century. Here, the new emphasis on culture has been taken up as part of the country's industrial "upgrading" and its graduation to serious global player, whereas for other regions, such as the Caribbean, the turn to culture as a resource has emerged as an expedient "sweetener" for global and regional elites to sell a process of deepened economic and political dependency to the region (this does not mean that the Chinese strategy is without its own contradictions and differential impacts across the population, as we have also seen).

Another broad theme that has been explored throughout this book, taking its cue in particular from the work of Yúdice (2003), is the contemporary transformation of culture into a resource. The effect of the framework created at UNESCO over the 2000s has not been to challenge the ongoing instrumentalisation of culture under contemporary capitalism (as a number of observers and supporters of the Convention have claimed), but in fact to reinforce some of the processes that Yúdice had observed in the decade prior to 2003. Indeed the Convention as a global reference point for cultural policy has tended to intensify the way that culture is being defined as a resource for industrialisation, trade, development and political recognition in the contemporary context. This has simultaneously loosened the hold of the traditional notion that culture should serve a "higher" purpose as a medium of national civic or ethical formation (along with some of the contradictions and elitist biases that are contained in such a notion).

However, we have also seen how the attempts that emerged over the 2000s to enshrine a new framework of international cultural policy have pinned many of their arguments on principles aimed at creating a new ethical framework of cultural diversity for the era of neoliberal globalisation. This was already evident in the work of the WCCD in the 1990s but took on a more concrete form as the trade–culture debate migrated to UNESCO in the early 2000s. In this period, the task of reinforcing cultural policy's ability to generate cultural enterprises capable of participating and competing in the international order of commercial exchange and expression came to be articulated in terms that are not reducible to the episteme of culture as resource: the assertion of the contemporary value of culture within development has been made possible by referring not only to its contemporary contribution as a resource for capital accumulation, employment, economic growth and so on, but also by invoking the imperative to protect and promote the task of civic formation understood as necessary for the "dignity of humanity", "public morals" and the "heart" and "soul" of peoples. Ironically, perhaps, the latter kind of claims have themselves proven to be an expedient source of protagonism for governments and stakeholders and have been a necessary condition for generating the kind of legitimacy that was needed to approach UNESCO with a proposal for an international treaty in the first place.

One dynamic that has been observed in this contemporary mobilisation of culture as resource is the way in which it can be simultaneously inclusive and exclusive: the contemporary attention to the potential developmental value contained in hitherto neglected cultural forms has opened up some room for the recognition of previously marginal and under-prioritised groups within national and international development strategies as they have become identified by governments, industries and development agencies as potential areas of indus-trialisation, enterprise formation and development assistance. Paralleling the kinds of mechanisms seen at work in the creation of the Convention on Biolog-ical Diversity, this has brought some leverage for those groups and members of the "cultural milieu" that have been able to organise and come forward as bearers of alienable and internationally valuable and marketable cultural expres-sions. This has often unsettled entrenched elitist and colonial biases around the judgement of particular cultural forms. However, we have also seen how the attempt to give recognition to a wider range of "ways of life" in the framework created by the Convention has tended to be delimited by the authoritative modalities and development strategies of states and international development agencies – particularly given that alternative claims to cultural recognition and rights have found relatively little protagonism elsewhere or through alternative frameworks of lower political stature (such as those aimed at recognising the value of cultural identities connected to other claims such as the right to land, tenure and place). The tendency for the discourse of the cultural and creative economy to overlap with the discourse of cultural identity and recognition through the formula of the "dual nature of culture" has tended to naturalise this unequal way in which particular groups and activities have been deemed worthy of "exceptional" attention and preferential treatment.

A connected theme under investigation here has been the claim that has often been made that the kind of reinforcement of national cultural sovereignty contained in the Convention would reinforce the ability of national representa-tives and elites to pursue restrictive, authoritarian and enclavist cultural agendas. As we have seen in a number of examples, this observation appears to be partially true, but should also not detract from the fact that those groups for whom the new framework of cultural development appears most useful are not simply conservative or backward-looking cultural nationalists – they are also those that seek to align cultural policy with the "challenges" and "opportun-ities" of the contemporary global economy and some of the broad themes of neoliberal reform. These groups have been as much concerned with securing mechanisms of national protection as with the promotion of greater domestic and regional liberalisation and market mechanisms while opening new market opportunities overseas and tapping into international flows of expertise, techno-logy and finance.

Finally, we have also seen how many of the problems concerning culture and development as they were formulated in the NWICO era came to be brushed aside and into the dustbin of history as neoliberalism became globally ascendant in the 1980s. The analyses and recommendations put forward in the NWICO period contained many flaws but they had the benefit of situating questions around culture and development within the struggle for a broader transformative political and economic project that could overturn systemic global asymmetries. To the extent that many of the issues that gave rise to the NWICO agenda have not gone away (and continue to remain inadequately recognised in the international agenda), there is still much productive work that could be done over the coming years by exploiting some of the openings and innovations that progressive movements and struggles have created in the recent period of neoliberal globalisation.

Notes

1 See www.culture2015goal.net/.
2 The four SDG targets that make explicit reference to culture are:

> **4.7** By 2030, ensure that all learners acquire the knowledge and skills needed to promote sustainable development, including, among others, through education for sustainable development and sustainable lifestyles, human rights, gender equality, promotion of a culture of peace and non-violence, global citizenship and appreciation of cultural diversity and of culture's contribution to sustainable development.
> **8.9** By 2030, devise and implement policies to promote sustainable tourism that creates jobs and promotes local culture and products.
> **11.4** Strengthen efforts to protect and safeguard the world's cultural and natural heritage.
> **12.b** Develop and implement tools to monitor sustainable development impacts for sustainable tourism that creates jobs and promotes local culture and products.
> (UN, 2015)

Bibliography

UN. 2015. *Transforming our world: the 2030 Agenda for Sustainable Development*. United Nations. Available online at: https://sustainabledevelopment.un.org/post2015/transformingourworld/publication; accessed 02/10/2015.

Vlassis, A. 2015. "Culture in the post-2015 development agenda: the anatomy of an international mobilisation". *Third World Quarterly*. 36(9).

Yúdice, G. 2003. *The Expediency of Culture: Uses of Culture in the Global Era*. London: Duke University Press.

Index

Adorno, Theodor 53–4, 60, 64n13–64n14
African National Congress (ANC) 93
American Association for the
  Advancement of Science 90
American Bar Association 90
American Chemical Society 90
Appiah, K.A. 36, 51, 64n11–64n12
Argentina 45, 148, 171
Arizpe, Lourdes 18, 77, 87
Arnold, Matthew 53–4
Arthur, Owen 200, 217
Asmal, Kader 106
Audiovisual Media Services Directive
  25n3, 63n2, 165, 185n11
Australia 25n1, 45, 156–7
Avatar 131–5, 137–8, 139n7
Ayouch, Nabil 173

Barbados 171, 196, 200, 209, 215–21,
  226n1, 228n18; Cultural Industries
  Development Act 219; National
  Cultural Foundation (NCF) 217–18,
  220; National Task Force on Cultural
  Industries (NTFCI) 217
Bauman, Zygmunt 48, 56
Benhabib, Seyla 49–51, 64n9, 64n10
Bennett, Tony 9–10, 33, 48–9, 53–7, 59,
  75–6, 217
Bernier, Ivan 3, 6, 39, 63n1, 63n3; 63n5,
  105–6, 116, 165, 173
Boas, Franz 49
Boko Haram 51
Bolivia 45–6, 150, 156, 184n4
Brazil 41, 106, 148, 171, 177, 180
Bretton Woods *see* United Nations
Brundtland Commission (World
  Commission on Environment and
  Development) 74–5
Bush, George W. 26n10, 87, 95

Canada 20, 34–5, 40–2, 44–5, 104–6,
  109, 114–18, 120, 122, 147–51,
  156–66, 168–73, 175–7, 180–2, 184n5,
  184n9, 207, 223, 226, 227n12, 237;
  Assembly of First Nations (AFN)
  158–9, 184n6; Department of
  Canadian Heritage 162; Department of
  Foreign Affairs and International Trade
  (DFAIT) 149; Coalition for Cultural
  Diversity (CCD) 162, 170–3, 175–6,
  185n15, 216; Cultural Industries
  Sectoral Advisory Group (SAGIT)
  161–4, 170, 176, 216; International
  Liaison Committee (ILC) 172;
  International Network on Cultural
  Policy (INCP) 162, 170–1, 176
Canadian Radio-Television and
  Telecommunications Commission
  25n3, 63n2
Caribbean 9, 12, 42, 112, 138, 168–9,
  178–9, 182, 193–228, 238–9; Caribbean
  Audiovisual Network (CAN) 203, 221;
  Caribbean Council 202; Caribbean
  Copyright Link (CCL) 221, 228n18;
  Caribbean Creative Industries Business
  Network (CCIBN) 202–3, 221–2;
  Caribbean Music Industry Networking
  Organisation (CaMINO) 203, 221–2;
  Caribbean Regional Negotiating
  Machinery (CRNM) 198–211, 215–16,
  222–3, 226n5, 238; Caribbean Single
  Market and Economy (CSME) 208–9;
  Coalition for Cultural Diversity (CCD)
  203, 221; Creative Industries Exchange
  (CIE) 208; Regional Task Force on
  Cultural Industries (RTFCI) 208–9, 211
CARICOM (Caribbean Community) 197,
  200, 203, 206, 208–9, 215, 221, 227n13,
  228n18

Taylor & Francis eBooks

Helping you to choose the right eBooks for your Library

Add Routledge titles to your library's digital collection today. Taylor and Francis ebooks contains over 50,000 titles in the Humanities, Social Sciences, Behavioural Sciences, Built Environment and Law.

Choose from a range of subject packages or create your own!

Benefits for you

» Free MARC records
» COUNTER-compliant usage statistics
» Flexible purchase and pricing options
» All titles DRM-free.

Benefits for your user

» Off-site, anytime access via Athens or referring URL
» Print or copy pages or chapters
» Full content search
» Bookmark, highlight and annotate text
» Access to thousands of pages of quality research at the click of a button.

REQUEST YOUR **FREE** INSTITUTIONAL TRIAL TODAY

Free Trials Available
We offer free trials to qualifying academic, corporate and government customers.

eCollections – Choose from over 30 subject eCollections, including:

Archaeology	Language Learning
Architecture	Law
Asian Studies	Literature
Business & Management	Media & Communication
Classical Studies	Middle East Studies
Construction	Music
Creative & Media Arts	Philosophy
Criminology & Criminal Justice	Planning
Economics	Politics
Education	Psychology & Mental Health
Energy	Religion
Engineering	Security
English Language & Linguistics	Social Work
Environment & Sustainability	Sociology
Geography	Sport
Health Studies	Theatre & Performance
History	Tourism, Hospitality & Events

For more information, pricing enquiries or to order a free trial, please contact your local sales team: www.tandfebooks.com/page/sales

 Routledge
Taylor & Francis Group

The home of Routledge books

www.tandfebooks.com

For Product Safety Concerns and Information please contact our EU
representative GPSR@taylorandfrancis.com
Taylor & Francis Verlag GmbH, Kaufingerstraße 24, 80331 München, Germany

www.ingramcontent.com/pod-product-compliance
Ingram Content Group UK Ltd.
Pitfield, Milton Keynes, MK11 3LW, UK
UKHW021616240425
457818UK00018B/592